THE MIRROR OF CHRISTIANITY, CULTS, AND THE CATHOLIC CHURCH

RICHARD BENNETT

LifeRich Publishing is a registered trademark of The Reader's Digest Association, Inc.

LifeRich Publishing books may be ordered through booksellers or by contacting:

LifeRich Publishing
1663 Liberty Drive
Bloomington, IN 47403
www.liferichpublishing.com
844-686-9607

ISBN: 978-1-4897-3558-4 (sc)
ISBN: 978-1-4897-3557-7 (hc)
ISBN: 978-1-4897-3559-1 (e)

Library of Congress Control Number: 2021908626

Print information available on the last page.

LifeRich Publishing rev. date: 05/10/2021

Knowledge is the key to understanding.

CONTENTS

INTRODUCTION

I wrote this book a couple of years back and while doing research, I discovered just how sensitive the subject of Christianity can be. Listening to people on social media over the years, it's possible to understand why discussing Christianity and/or politics is hard to do when it should not be. Politics maybe, but not Christianity. I found that the more knowledge I acquired about Christianity and the theology of the various denominations, as well as Catholicism, Mormonism, the Jehovah Witnesses, Christian Science, Prosperity preachers, (you know, those who take our money in exchange for a promise of 50, 60, maybe even as much as 100% return) and a few others, as in the New Apostolic Reformation Movement. A rapidly growing charismatic Christian movement that is considered by many not to be your parent's religion, and has conservative pastors taking issue with it.

Also, I wrote this book to find a way logically to understand, and perhaps overcome, reconcile, and resolve, some of the differences that have existed within the Christian family since the days of John Calvin and George Whitefield who broke with the Wesley brothers, John, and Charles, over "Once Saved Always Saved" theology. It appears that many have looked for a bridge to reconcile the two, just maybe this book will give us a better understanding of both. In addition, it might be interesting to explore the landscape during the fourth century when Catholicism and the Orthodox Church, (especially the Greek Orthodox Church) became prevalent upon the religious scene. We will even touch on the reason for the split between the East and the West.

But the information I found most interesting was how some church leaders harbor beliefs that are most divisive among family members when it defeats the message the family of God is trying to project to the lost, the unsaved, especially since most Christians seem to acknowledge the coming of Christ is not far away. To most, just looking around verifies that bit of information. By applying a small degree of logic, a bit of common sense and help from the Holy Spirit, we should be able to find some solutions to many of the age-old problems, as well as perhaps find some answers to some questions that have plagued Christianity since the days of the apostles.

Always curious about the different church members while respecting their decision regarding what they believe, I usually would ask what brought them to the decision of becoming a Christian, maybe even why they go to such and such church as I was genuinely interested. Most people want to discuss Christianity when they do not feel threatened.[1] The knowledge of knowing what others believe makes us all stronger as Christians, as it opens communication among family members, both church family as well as relatives. Also, with knowledge comes confidence, assurance, conviction, and patience. Patience is important in the learning process.

I believe one will approach this book with a certain degree of trepidation, and that is understandable. It seems as if talking about Christianity can be scary if one is not knowledgeable. As mentioned, we are generally reluctant to discuss religion or politics for fear of repercussion, or perhaps we are shy regarding the knowledge we do possess, or we just pass the buck by simply saying, "our pastor can discuss that with you." Eliminating or limiting a portion of our conversation reduces our creativity of conversation.

---

[1] The answers I received the most when asking about becoming a Christian was that something seemed to be missing from their life. And it was the feeling I had when attending a certain church.

It has been a great journey learning about the many beliefs of the various Christian families and having the opportunity to share some of those beliefs with you. It is my hope you will find the logic used to illuminate the differences quite interesting as well as revealing. Again, that is what this book is about, solving some mysteries as to why some church families believe as they do. And that is done by logic, as you will see. Logic solves mysteries, perhaps mysteries many have not even thought about, and of course, listening to the Holy Spirit does not hurt.

You will encounter nothing threatening, and yet you will acquire a ton of knowledge, as well as an understanding as to why Christians harbor a diversity of beliefs. Understanding those diversities is another reason this book was written. To impart knowledge that many say is needed to instill confidence, as well as establish a position for Christians to be grounded firmly in Scripture, wisdom, and the logic of common sense which we all possess.

I attended many different churches, as I wanted to know as much as possible regarding Christianity and religion. I saw a lot of upside promise in becoming a Christian, while seeing little reward suffering the downside of life. It was from this reference point that I turned my attention to the various religions as presented by the different church families. At the same time, I listened to numerous pastors over the years, acquiring as much knowledge as possible. After all, we are discussing the opportunity to acquire eternal life. When I found out I could obtain eternal life I was all ears. Many people can be satisfied just knowing they are saved and on their way to heaven, with the assurance of living forever, others seek information to fulfill perhaps a deeper yearning in their life. I found myself in the latter group.

For example, the Rapture refers to a taking away of the family of God prior to the Second Coming of Christ. Some believe in this theology, perhaps disagreeing on the timing of the event, while others do not. And does it really matter? Or the Trinity—Father, Son and Holy Spirit—that conversation went in a couple of different direction within a couple of denominations. While understanding the differences, I had a conversation with a friend telling me her thoughts regarding the Trinity. She said the Trinity to her was like water, ice, and steam, one substance yet performing three different functions. It was then that I felt I understood the Trinity. And then there is the baptism of infants performed by the Catholic Church along with the lingering question—why? And is it necessary? This book is not about how much Jesus loves us, or how much we love Him, or how to pray, or anything to do with salvation or the acceptance of Christ, as that is up to the individual. Nor is it judgmental or condemning of others in any way, but only written to share what followers seek, Christians believe, and churches teach.

Donald Miller in his book, *Searching for God Knows What*, tells us that "You've got a bunch of Catholics in Rome who think one way about God and a bunch of Baptists in Texas who think another, and that isn't even the beginning." That is true. Probably within the Christian community, one would be hard-pressed to find a greater schism of religious interpretation than what exists between the Baptists and the Catholics—unless perhaps one considers the differences between the Catholics and the Seventh-day Adventists (both of which we will discuss later). This book discusses many of those differences and, in most cases, has the potential to put us all on the same page. Not by changing anything, but by understanding and respecting what each other believes as our core beliefs are the same.

For the most part, the spirituality that I relate to is the same spirituality that can be found in the various evangelical churches: evangelical as in Baptist, Methodist, Assemblies of God, and even the Seventh-day Adventist and many others that preach the message of faith, as well as the many nondenominational churches who also preach faith. Do they all agree on everything? We know the answer to that question. They all have their little idiosyncrasies, but they also all believe in the message of the Bible and are proud to be considered, a Christian—a born-again, Spirit-filled, genuine follower of Christ. They are followers of the early reformers who had roots grounded in the Apostolic Church as founded by the apostles.

In studying the various religions, I came across the religion of Gnosticism, whose followers are called *Gnostics*. Gnosticism is a religion that is so pragmatic it almost does not believe what it does believe. In other words, Gnostics seem to set out to prove what may be unprovable by conjecture or hearsay. Also, insight into the doctrine of Gnosticism is provided by the discovery of some scrolls near Nag Hammadi, Egypt, in 1945. The Gnostics are an interesting lot, to say the least.

Since Gnosticism has nothing to do with the God evangelical Christians follow, we will not be discussing it, other than to say it has nothing to do with the apostolic faith of the early church. When studying the early Christian church Fathers, one finds they constantly fought against the heresy of Gnosticism, considering those who followed that form of religious beliefs, heretics. Not much can be said about Gnosticism when it comes to discussing Christianity. However, you might find the following as interesting as I have.

Helen Ellerbe wrote a book titled, *The Dark Side of Christian History*, which was endorsed by Alice Walker, who said, "This is simply a book that everyone must sit down and read." Well, I did. Normally, I would have lost interest when I read, "A Gnostic text tells how Eve, the daughter of Sophia who had wished the first heavenly light into the world, gives life to Adam":

> …(Eve) said, "Adam live! Rise up on the earth!" Immediately her word became a deed. For when Adam rose up, immediately he opened his eyes. When he saw her, he said, "You will be called 'the mother of the living' because you are the one who gave me life."

I'm not sure I know where to go with that information as I'm not sure any Christian would, other than to describe how it contradicts the very first book in the Bible where God said, "Adam named his wife Eve, because she would become the mother of all the living." (Genesis. 3:20. NIV). The reason I wanted to understand Gnostic thinking was to see just how close to or how far they were from the gospel of Jesus Christ as brought to us by the apostles and handed down through the Bible. Well, the Gnostic text above answered that question.

We are going to discuss them all including the vilest doctrine of all, the Serpent Seed doctrine—thus, the title, *The Mirror of Christianity, Cults, and the Catholic Church.* A mirror (metaphorically speaking) will be held up to some church families and reflect what they claim to believe. According to the patristic tradition, humankind is a "free mirror." If we look at chaos, we will reflect chaos. If we look at light, we will reflect light.[2] If we look at Christianity through the mirror of Christianity, we will reflect Christianity. We reflect who we are and what we think about most of the time.

It was curiosity that led me to pursue an understanding of the different theologies as presented by the various churches. For example, why do some people think the Seventh-day Adventist church family is a cult? Why do some people think—*OMG, I am going to step on many toes with this one*—Catholicism is a cult? And how about the Church of Christ? When a church denies the inspiration of the Holy Spirit and the gifts of the Holy Spirit, denial that puts them in direct contradiction with the Bible, would they be considered outside of normal Christianity as presented by mainline churches, as in Methodist, Baptist, Assemblies of God, and many others?

It was while attending the various church families, that I found myself not excessively concerned with the differences among them, such as whether there will there be a Rapture, whether it is better to be dunked or sprinkled, whether one speaks in tongues or not,

---

2   Jean-Yves Leloup, *The Gospel of Thomas* (Rochester Vermont: Inner Traditions International, 2005).

who wrote the book of Hebrews, and so on. As a matter of fact, noted theologian Dr. Paul E. Billheimer once said when referring to Christians, "We will never agree theologically. It is my position that if we're born-again, we're members of the same family and that is the basis of fellowship, love, and union rather than agreement on the nonessentials." I believe most evangelical Christians would agree with Pastor Paul.

I can truthfully say I have met and continue to meet a lot of great people along the path of Christianity, and I can say unequivocally that I have never met a minister who did not take the time to answer any question I had, either in person or on the phone. Speaking of ministers, why don't we meet some who have made quite a name for themselves? Also, let us look at a rather new movement, a movement embraced by the new millennials called the New Apostolic Reformation. Regarding the New Apostolic Reformation (NAR) church, this is a church that many consider to be the fastest growing and most controversial church on the planet.

Then it might be interesting to discuss one of the most frequently asked questions found in religious circles, "Can we serve other religions and still find the Christian heaven?" The trip has been interesting, intriguing, and exciting, as well as informative. I hope you find this book as interesting to read as I found in writing it. I am going to say it would probably be right about here that many ministers, as well as my friends might say, "Amen, now let's get started."

CHAPTER I

PREACHERS OF INFLUENCE

Preachers who preach the message of salvation and what it means to be a Christian and then proceed to describe what constitutes a follower of Christ. I believe most would agree with the definition of an evangelical Christian as put forth by a prominent leader in the Baptist Bible Fellowship movement of Springfield, Missouri, by the name of Truman Dollar, who many would say nailed it when he listed the five fundamentals of a Christian's beliefs. They are: (1) the inspiration and inerrancy of Scripture; (2) the deity of Christ; (3) the virgin conception and birth of Christ; (4) the substitutionary, atoning works of Christ on the cross; and (5) the physical resurrection of Christ in the past and personal, bodily return of Christ to earth in the future.

As most Christians would probably say, "There we have it—the five elements of belief that comprise the characteristics of an evangelical Christian." Also, I would like to interject the words of John MacArthur[3] when he defines a Christian. He says there are two gates (only two) available to go through while on this earth. The narrow gate is hard to find and hard to go through because it demands denial of self, denial of self-righteousness, recognition

---

[3] John MacArthur is Senior Pastor of Grace Community Church located at Sun Valley, California, and author of several books.

of sin, full repentance, submission to Christ, and a commitment to obey Him and follow Him no matter the cost. I believe pastor Dollar sets the groundwork for what it takes to have the heart of a Christian, while John MacArthur seems to convey to us the cost of becoming a follower.

It is the understanding of an evangelical Christian that the very word *evangelical* means a belief in salvation being achieved by faith in atonement through Jesus Christ. I believe both explanations as we heard from Pastor Dollar and Pastor MacArthur define a Christian. Then, when one throws in born-again theology as discussed by Christ to Nicodemus in the book of John, I believe you have it all. Of course, the Catholic Church, as well as the Orthodox Churches, would add the Sacraments as a condition, but that is them.

Regarding evangelical Christians, according to author, lecturer, and religious mentor Jack Van Impe,[4] the evangelical movement "is not a Baptist, Nazarene, Pentecostal, Wesleyan, Methodist, Christian and Missionary Alliance, or Evangelical Free Church Body. Rather, it is the one body of Jesus Christ, composed of all born-again believers found in numerous denominations." Or, as 1 Corinthians 12:12–13 (NIV) puts it, "The body is a unit, though it is made up of many parts; and though all its parts are many, they form one body. So, it is with Christ. For we were all baptized by one Spirit into one Body…" "Whether Jews or Greeks, slave or free—we were all given the one Spirit to drink."

Given one Spirit to consume—meaning partaking of the only Spirit of God and that is the Holy Spirit, who, upon request, will lead anyone who asks to eternal life. The views of some pastors may vary as to how they view different subjects in the Bible, but that,

---

4   A well-known and respected lecturer, author, theologian, and T.V. personality who has written numerous books and documented thousands of hours over the years explaining Biblical prophesies as they relate to the current times. Jack is renowned for his prophetic insight and inspiration. He is known as "the walking Bible" because of his ability to quote more than 14,000 Bible verses including virtually the entire New Testament.

"baptized by one Spirit into one Body"—the "Oneness" body of Christ is one constant of truism all Christians should be able to agree upon. It is that agreement that puts us all into one family, and as with all family members, we have various opinions.

As you may have noticed, Jack Van Impe mentioned "all born-again believers" as an apparent condition to find salvation regardless of which church anyone attends. While Jack was emphasizing that evangelical Christians, as we saw, can be found in many denominations, he was also emphasizing the importance of being a "born-again" Christian. *Born-again*—it sounds as if he were talking about an experience that would indicate a second birth. He was—a birth from death into life. To many Christians, Jack was referencing the life-or-death choice as discussed in Deuteronomy 30:19 and by Christ in a discussion had with Nicodemus in the book of John.

And where do born-again evangelical Christians go to church? The Bible refers to the church as the "body of Christ" more than a brick-and-mortar structure—but then, most Christians attend brick-and-mortar structures to worship and praise Christ. So, it appears that the body of Christ consists of all born-again Christians, most of whom are attending the various brick-and-mortar structures with names that identify their theology.

As we know, there have been many Christians, including pastors called of God preaching in those brick-and-mortar structurers who have passed through the annals of earlier Christian history, many dying horrible deaths for their testimony. If there was ever a Christian Hall of Fame, thousands of great pastors would deserve to be there. This includes preachers who have a strong desire to preach the message of Christ when persecution stands at the door, thereby passing their knowledge of the Bible and the secret of acquiring eternal life to those who are seeking answers while offering them an umbrella of protection in the here and now.

The message of Jesus Christ's birth, death, and resurrection, as well as His gift of eternal life and how to receive that gift, is passed from the apostles to those pastors who feel the calling upon their lives to continue spreading that message. These are pastors who inspire us, listen to us, teach us, encourage us, and even help us say goodbye to our loved ones when they depart from us. Too bad there isn't a Hall of Fame for all the great preachers—as well as all the born-again Christians—who have carried the banner of Christianity from the time of Christ until now. And will continue to do so until He comes for His family, His church.

It would probably be safe to say that we all have our favorite preacher(s) and given the opportunity, we would probably include his or her name in this book, but since that is impossible, I would like to mention a few you might identify with and explain why I feel they should be listed in any Hall of Fame. Perhaps in so doing, you will be able to reinforce in your mind's eye your pastor's preaching and teaching, as well as others who have knowledge, experience, wisdom, and a strong desire to lead Christians into a relationship with Christ.

Even though they sometime express various opinions, perhaps even interpretations of theology, they all seem to preach the message of salvation by preaching about the resurrection of Christ and what that means to a Christian. Perhaps the most divisive theology was implemented with a split between two major heavyweights, and that would be John Wesley (1703-1791) and George Whitefield (1714-1770), who were instrumental in bringing forth the Methodist family of Christians. While they may have been good friends, John Wesley differed in the theology embraced and taught by George Whitefield as presented by John Calvin (1509-1564). Theology that was introduced into Christianity by St. Augustine (354-430 A.D.) and the influence of that difference remains with us today. So maybe a good place to start this chapter would be to discuss a couple of preachers who have had a tremendous influence on religion, and what caused them to go their separate ways. And, as we know, that day brought such diversity into the family of God, the differences are still felt within the Christian community.

DIFFERING OPINION

While there are differences among pastors who have our best interest at heart, they each embrace theology that is questioned by others, yet they all preach the same Christology. How the different preachers and denominations preach their understanding of the Bible has come under scrutiny over the centuries and remains so today. We can go back to John Wesley, who had a falling out with George Whitefield over the "once saved, always saved" concept that irradiated the doctrine of the "elect."

Wesley believed humans received salvation by free will, while George Whitefield, teaching from John Calvin's playbook, who himself was playing from St. Augustine's playbook, believed in "predestined salvation," meaning that only a certain number had been chosen by God for eternal life and the rest were discarded as reprobates,[5] (St. Augustine's word not mine) as they were unable to grasp the concept of salvation and therefore were doomed to— doomed to what?

What should I say? Doomed to be separated from God? They were separated from God when they were not one of the predestined when they were born. Since they were born without the opportunity to know God, that does not seem to be much punishment. Do we say doomed to eternal torment? Would anyone think that is fair when they did not ask to be born in the first place, and especially as reprobates? There are those such as the Seventh-day Adventist who think that the "doomed forever" part of an eternal hell is a bit excessive. That seems to be the verdict of those who question the thought of the fires of hell burning forever, yet the Bible does use those very words—for ever and ever—more than once. Another one of those quandaries.

---

[5] Titus 1:16. KJV. They profess that they know God, but in works they deny Him, being abominable and disobedient, and every good work rebate.

Anyway, many might conclude that eternal torment may appear slightly harsh, maybe even cruel, even coldhearted coming from a God who is all about love. Believing that theology might raise some serious questions about the loving, caring, compassionate, nature of God. And yet, before you complete this discussion, I'm betting you will see God's justice for those who have become known as reprobates is quite justified and fair. As a matter of fact, my editor made some comments that justify such punishment.

I wrote, "I believe we can all attest to the fact that there will always be those among us who will never believe in Christ." And I should have stopped there. But I didn't. I continued, "But most Christians believe that once someone realizes how doomed they are, they will want to be saved." I thought that was a fair thing to say, but then, my editor added the following which I found interesting. He said: "While this is true for many, there are many others who are so rebellious against God that they don't want to be saved. They are so rebellious against God that they don't want Him."

Don continues, "I heard a Christian apologist speaker who talks on college campuses note that when he asks people if they would receive Jesus as Savior if they could know for sure that He is who He said He was, a huge majority of them said they would still not want Him. They want to be their own god. People who are only ignorant of Christ can be converted through knowledge of Him; people who are rebellious cannot." And reprobates are rebellious towards God.

Perhaps the thing that Christians have in common is that they can't agree upon some issues and therefore they seem to remain at odds with each other. A problem the world seems to have taken notice of and holds against us. Once I understood some deeper meaning, I found it gratifying that we could be given the opportunity to be on the same page with some understanding without changing anything. A page that John Calvin and John Wesley debated for many hours and reached no satisfactory conclusion. They met, I believe for the last time early in 1741, but could not find common ground to satisfy either one, and, that seems to be where we are today. But through it all, it is important to remember that we are "Christians," evangelical Christians, standing against the same "world" feeling the same "persecution" going to the same place.

Theology such as predestined salvation for the elect as is being discussed, and where an important caveat will be discussed later to perhaps narrow the gap between the two beliefs as the issue is that important. R.C. Sproul, an ordained pastor in the Presbyterian Church, and John MacArthur (an international syndicated Christian pastor-teacher who accepts the once saved always saved theology) along with James White, author of the Potter's Freedom and Dave Hunt, a freewill advocate and author of "What Love is" have debated this subject for hours.

According to St. Augustine, anyone born outside of eternal salvation, those who were not chosen as the "elect" were deemed incapable of understanding the message of salvation. Those who St. Augustine rendered only worthy of suffering an eternity in burning sulfur. (You can probably begin to understand the thinking that introduced purgatory). I wrote, and I think all would agree, that God would appear to be unloving if he sentenced anyone to hell as reprobates prior to them even being born. But then in defense of this theology, God, after all, is all Omniscient and just as with Jacob and Esau, He knew who would follow Him—while they were still in their mother's womb. Romans 9:13: "So it is written Jacob I loved but Esau I hated." Christ refers to them as "antichrist," (they certainly are not "pro-Christ Christians"), but they are not the "Antichrist" either, even though they are a form of antichrist, who possess the spirit of the antichrist.

Many become Christians, born-again followers of Christ, by making Jesus Lord of their life, especially when they realize life offers something better than what is visible to the senses. Based upon that information, the question becomes, is that opportunity of a better life and eternity to enjoy it initiated by their own free will, or was it destined to happen? Then the question becomes, does it matter? Followed by the answer: Not to a Christian who follows Christ and feels very blessed just knowing they are in the family of God. That family Jesus will be coming for when He comes for His family. An event every Christian looks forward to, and it does not matter if we follow Wesley, or Calvin, or become a Baptist, or a Methodist, or perhaps a member of the Church of God, Assemblies of God, or Seventh-day Adventist, if we are born again, if we follow Jesus, proclaiming Him as our Lord and savior, we are going to be included in the taking away of the body of Christ at the Rapture when the time is right.

When it comes to being a Christian, it somehow seems to be a part of a Christian's DNA to be a follower. If for no other reason than the ability to see what others either cannot see, or do not want to see, or will not pay the price to see. Wow! Suddenly, we begin to see how special we are. I'm betting that some followers of Christ upon feeling special, and knowing we have something unique, something exceptional, sometimes might worry about their salvation and wonder if it is possible to, as some say, fall from grace, back slide, perhaps even fearing we might "lose our salvation." That sounds like something that might be interesting to discuss.

Can We Fall from Grace?

The second largest issue dividing Christianity appears to be the question: "Can we lose our salvation?" A question that brings division between families, as some born-again Christians say, "yes" we can lose our salvation, (well not exactly in those words, as we will see) while there are others who say, "no," "never" once we are saved. What a quandary. Some pastors preaching eternal salvation to a new convert, upon repeating the "sinners prayer," include the assurance of knowing he or she is permanently sealed by the blood of Christ by saying, you cannot "lose" your salvation as you are eternally saved. While that is true, they can't lose their salvation, they are never told that they can forfeit it by removing themselves from Christ and His family as perhaps some other pastors might preach.

Why is there such a difference of opinion when everyone is reading from the same Bible? It appears that the use of just one word—a single word—makes all the difference, and that one word does not even have anything to do with salvation, as we are about to see. Perhaps the downfall for those who believe they are already predestined into eternal salvation[6] and nothing they could do would change that situation might be more "liberal" in how they live their lives, especially since they cannot "lose" their salvation. Or, as a pastor I was talking with several years ago said, while they may not lose their salvation, they can forfeit it.

I approached a Methodist minister and asked if he thought we could lose our salvation. Those were the exact words I used: "Once saved, can we lose our salvation?" After what appeared to be an hour, he said, "I don't like the word *lose*. Salvation is not something one can lose. I would rather use the word *forfeit*." Then he proceeded to quote a verse from Colossians that said something along the lines that we can *forfeit* our salvation *if* we turn away from the faith.

Charles Stanley, a pastor I admire and a pastor many people respect, believes in predestined salvation.

The salvation of the "elect" the chosen of God prior to the laying of the earth's foundation. I have listened to Dr. Stanley for several years and have enjoyed his preaching, while at the same time trying to figure out how he arrived at the conclusion regarding the theology of "once saved, always saved." Indicating we will never lose our salvation, not that there is anything wrong with that theology as we will see, but why does Dr. Stanley believe and teach as he does regarding this theology? A question for which my curiosity just had to seek an answer.

There is nothing wrong with John Calvin's perspective on salvation, or the way it is embraced and taught by Charles Stanley,

---

[6]   If the saved are already saved, "and sealed," with eternal salvation from the beginning of creation, and the lost, the reprobates, cannot be saved, then why did Christ have to suffer and die as He did? Especially if we are already born with total salvation secured?

as well as the many others who embrace this theology. And then it finally happened. After all these years, today, May 12, 2019, as I am listening to Pastor Stanley, I believe I understand what that Methodist minister I had talked with years earlier meant when he used the word *forfeit* rather than *lose* regarding our salvation. While listening to Dr. Stanley that morning, it was as if a light went on. I thought, *"There appears to be a disconnect between the words* "lose" *and* "forfeit."

Then on a different occasion while listening to Pastor Stanley, he said something that once again caught my attention: "I want to say to people who believe today that you can be lost next week or next month, as taught by some pastors, is just pure error." The error seems to exist between the use of the words *lost* or *lose* and *forfeit*. I believe, as the pastor said earlier, one cannot *lose* one's salvation, but one can *forfeit* it by returning to the world. Does not the parable of the sower say exactly that? Some call it back sliding which many interpret to mean a conscience decision to leave the family, step away from God, but as many say, they will be back.

That leaving the family happened to Demas, one of the followers of Christ who went on missionary journeys with the disciples from time to time. Slept where they slept, ate with them, learned from them, and went on missionary trips with them. On one such trip he just decided to leave Paul in a lurch and return to the world (2 Timothy 4:10 NIV). "For Demas because he loved this world has deserted me and has gone to Thessalonica." But then the question becomes: Was he really saved in the first place? Was he really one of us? Obviously, he was lacking in his commitment. Those who are among us but are not a part of us are referred to as "Tares" in the Bible. Judas was a tare, a weed among the righteous.

Born-again Christians understand the message of salvation and the wisdom passed to them from those who walked and talked with Jesus, including the 500 who saw Him during the forty days he walked among them following His resurrection. The forty days he talked with them, ate with them, and this was after being crucified, buried, and then brought back to life by His Father, considered the resurrection. This is the cornerstone, the building block, the apex, the very foundation upon which Christianity is built. And a belief in that by faith is the foundation upon which every born-again Christian stands. Upon having that knowledge, what one believes about freewill or predestined salvation is irrelevant as I believe most would agree.

Pastor Stanley as he continues discussing the thought of someone, anyone, losing their salvation asks the question, "How can I have confidence and joy in my heart when I can lose my salvation at any time for sinning?" I am going to say one can't. Every word of what Pastor Stanley said is true. How can we have confidence and joy in our heart if we live in fear of doing something wrong that could cause us to lose our salvation, and along the way, miss the opportunity of eternal life? That is an excellent question that we are in the process of discussing, while keeping in mind, one cannot lose their salvation, but they can forfeit God's gift by either walking away from it or not accepting it in the first place. That is the very definition of freewill. To reject that is to reject the thought that we have freewill. Would that be what God wants? Are we not free to choose whether we want to follow Him or not? Just something to think about.

Regarding those who embrace the "once saved always saved" as well as "freewill" thinking, I believe I figured it out. Even as a chosen of God, there seems to be an implied covenant. "*I must accept the Cross.*" Predestined or not, *one must accept the cross* and become a believer thus becoming "born again." By accepting, but probably just as importantly, understanding the price Christ paid at the cross and why He paid that price, gives us the opportunity of accepting Him as the Son of the one who sent Him and believing by faith that to be true. A Christ, a Messiah who came to the world to save those who would listen from a life of despair, loneliness, and emptiness, complete with the promise of eternal life.

Being the omniscience God as He is, He seems to know who has His Spirit and who doesn't, as well as the name of each. And what separates those who know Christ from those who don't. What I am alluding to is two people visit a church service and as they are leaving, one says that was quite an enjoyable experience, very uplifting and inspiring, while the other says that was a big waste of time. As probably with you, I do not understand it, but it appears born-again Christians are an incredibly special group consisting of incredibly special people who see what many others seem to miss. And because of this, they will be given life eternally.

I like how Pastor David Jeremiah answers the question about losing our salvation. He says, "One cannot lose their salvation, (and as we saw that is true), but they can lose the joy of it." There is not much joy in one's life when they reject Christ, and upon that rejection their salvation comes into question. Many say that the sins after salvation affect our fellowship with God, but not our eternal relationship with Him. They explain it this way: Our relationship with Christ is that of a father with his child and is not affected by misbehaving. This is unconditional love. Probably somewhere along the way, the child would want to apologize and stop misbehaving, just as we would with our heavenly Father, but regardless, he or she remains the child of the father, just as God remains our Father, and He said He will never leave us nor forsake us.

As a matter of fact, many might like how Joel Osteen described his thoughts regarding this very issue. He said, "Nothing we've done will change who we are. No mistake we have made will disqualify us. When we give our life to Christ we are born into God's family. We cannot get unborn. The calling on one's life doesn't go away because we made mistakes, took wrong turns, got off course, we are still His child." Joel, as well as most preachers, predicate everything upon being born again.

Regardless of the belief we follow, Calvin's or Wesley's, Baptist, or Methodist, Seventh-day Adventist, Assemblies of God, Church of God, they all preach "We are justified (brought into righteousness) by faith" just as the Bible instructs, and are heaven bound. But that would come with perhaps a caveat. I would not temp God with disobedience towards Him, or His word, relying on the protection of being one of the chosen, one of the elect, to assure my name will ALWAYS remain in the book of life. Always assuming that our status as a member of the "Elect" will be all that is necessary to preserve our name in God's book.

Those who embrace "once saved always saved" theology teach we can never lose our salvation, same as those who embrace freewill theology—*if*, as we are told in Colossians—if, (and that is a mighty big word used in this context) we continue to follow Him. Because of this acceptance, a foundation of belief is established that removes members of both families from being among the unsaved. That decision of accepting the cross puts all of us in the same family and assures our name is recorded in the book of life. And as the Bible says, once we are in that book and a member of that family, nobody will ever be able to pluck us from that family.

The Book of Life

When would you say our name is entered into the book of life? Some say when we are born, some say when we convert, and others say before the foundations of the earth were poured. They all sound good. And when that event occurs, many say that is an irreversible act. And they may be right. But being capable of being blotted out of God's book for sinning against Him is exactly how many understand Exodus 32:33 NIV when God told Moses, "Whoever has sinned against me I will blot out of my book." He said that when he was angry at the Israelites for being disobedient, but those were His exact words.

I do not believe anyone thinks that God is going to remove a Christian, a born-again Christians name from His book for sinning against him otherwise repentance would not be in the Bible.

13

Christians who recognizing the cross and the price paid at that cross, as well as a belief in the resurrection will undoubtedly reach heaven. The key is in the cross and the blood spilled to buy our soul from eternal damnation. The cross and the life given at the cross is, as many say, the key to salvation, and for God to deny that would go against His very nature. To think that our name may be removed might invoke a spirit of fear and that is not a Spirit from God.

Regarding the blotting out, God used a much broader brush to paint with than just saying, "Whoever has sinned against me I will blot out of my book" when he repeated himself in Revelation 3:5, where he said, "He that overcometh, the same shall be clothed in white raiment; and I will not 'blot his name out of the book of life, but I will confess his name before my father, and before the angels.'" I will not blot his name from the book of life. Many say that indicates a name can be removed, but the name of them who overcome will never be removed and that is a promise from God. And in Psalm 69:28, King David said of his enemies, "May they be blotted out of the book of life and not be listed with the righteous."

I found interesting what Tim LaHaye had to say about our name being blotted out of God's book. He says there are three reasons for this to occur: (1) for sinning against God; (2) for not being an overcomer, which is synonymous with being born again or putting one's trust in Christ Jesus (I John 5:1–4); and (3) for taking away from the words of the prophecy of Revelation 22:19. So true. All three so true. Tim continues: In short, then anyone who has sinned against God has his or her name blotted out of the book of life upon death. Tim is just repeating what God said.

Tim continues; "The book of life contains the names of the living. It is God's book of anticipation. That is, whenever a human being is born, god writes that person's name in his book; if he or she dies without receiving Christ (Rev. 3:5), that name is blotted out of the book so that in eternity the only people whose names remain in the book of life are those who have received Christ by faith while they lived."

There are some as mentioned, who believe in predestined salvation such as Pastor John Piper, and in trying to interpret this blotting out situation he says all names (everyone) was recorded in the "book of life" when the earth was created and is removed when we die. Hal says that when we are born our name is entered into God's book, and during a lifetime, if that person does not receive Christ, then their names are removed.

As one might expect, having this discussion raises objections regarding the possibility of names being removed from God's book for disobedience. The elect say unequivocally that is not possible. And they may be right. I hope their right as that would indicate to those following freewill theology, perhaps without even realizing it, they have automatically become one of the elect with their name recorded in God's book, regardless of which church or denomination they belong to.

Dr. Stanley implied earlier; we are all subject to sin from time to time but the act of sin—being disobedient—will not remove our name from God's book. We are human; therefore, we will probably remain under construction for the duration of our earthly journey, so doing something wrong is a given. Considering we are destined to find ourselves, as Paul when he said he struggled so with the flesh, giving in to our sinful nature might happen. But that does not cause us to lose our salvation. Besides, many feel God would not put us under that kind of bondage of fear.

Logic would dictate that if our name could be blotted out for sinning against God then there would probably not be any names left in His book as God talks about sin enough to know it is a problem. However, knowing we are capable of sinning, he has given us a way to be forgiven. Thus, always being guaranteed our name will remain in His book. Perhaps that is why He included repentance in the Bible. Perhaps a question to ponder would be, "Why would we need repentance if we can never be unsaved?

Everyone, those saved by election and those saved by freewill, must enter heaven by way of the cross. The elect must recognize the cross and accept Christ, just as those who follow freewill theology. That is a step no Christian can ignore. Not even the chosen as defined by St. Augustine. I believe all Christians accept that as being a biblical fact. And when one accepts the cross, and the price paid at that cross, and the suffering of the one who died that day on that cross, if their heart is pierced, as was Peter's, Paul's, and Lydia's, then most would say, they become born again followers and will enter into the same family of Christians that Christ will be coming for at the time of the Rapture as their name will be found in God's book.

We also have God's assurance that the sinful act has been stricken from the records; in other words, the stain of sin is removed, washed from our robe, the robe of righteousness, that was given to us upon our baptism. It was at the time of our baptism that Christ took our dirty robe and gave us a clean one. Again, Satan will try to convince us otherwise, but that would be a lie. We will always retain the robe of righteousness, the question becomes, how dirty does it have to become before we fall from grace? That is a question to be answered when we stand before Christ. Maybe it would depend upon just how dirty our robe becomes. We know upon repentance the stains will be removed, but without repentance...? Only God can answer that question.

Always knowing God will be there, and with faith in the words of Christ, we are released from any fear of losing our salvation and eternal life. That assurance comes from God Himself. Most of us will stumble from time to time, as did the apostle Peter, but unless we reject salvation, and that would come with a rejection of Christ, we will always be saved with a ticket to eternal life. We may drift from time to time, a time many might consider "back sliding" or "falling away," but many feel God will find a way to bring us back into the family. Although, if one listens to Hebrews. 6:6 in the NIV, they hear, "If they fall away, (God didn't reject them, they "fell" away) to be brought back to repentance because to their loss they are crucifying the Son of God all over again and subjecting him to public disgrace." Of them the proverbs are true: "A dog returns to its vomit," and, "A sow that is washed returns to her wallowing in the mud." (2 Peter 2:22 NIV). Wow! Who could God be talking about with such disappointment? In such disapproving vernacular?

Pastors falling from Grace

In listening to a message from Pastor Jeremiah a few years back I remember him saying that he was asked a question that many people seem to be asking. The question was, "Why is it that there are so many people who are in spiritual leadership and have great influence over the family of God and yet, they fall into some sin and their life is ruined and the testimony of their Church is destroyed?" Why is that? Because Satan's number one goal is to snuff out the influence of anyone who is making a difference in the kingdom of God. That is why we are so thankful for those who Satan cannot influence with his propaganda.

Can you imagine pastors such as John Hagee, or David Jeremiah, or Charles Stanley, or perhaps even your own pastor denouncing Christ? Or, being caught in some scandalous newsworthy event, As was Jim Bakker, Jimmy Swagger, and another one I remember Sandy Patty. How much harm and shame that would bring to God if they abandoned their Christian faith? And how much guilt would that bring them? Guilt, that is the big gorilla in the room. They may find any future acceptance by God harder than they might have anticipated, if for no other reason than heavy guilt. God trusted them, and it could appear they let Him down, and they did, but He will forgive and forget, otherwise he would not be true to His word. Although, the lingering doubt may remain at least in the minds of the perpetrator from guilt. I'm not saying it would be impossible to reconcile with God, just difficult.

Like the prodigal son, who Satan tempted into doing something unpleasing, we repent by telling God—our Father, we are sorry and knowing God is a forgiving God, and that, He will forgive us our trespasses, but there may remain a trust issue in our mind. Every Christian goes through this from whatever platform in life they hold, a disobedient moment, that can be overcome with just approaching God and asking Him for forgiveness. Some go to the alter, perhaps depending upon the offence and our level of guilt. Otherwise, most ministers say we can approach God from anywhere at any time and ask forgiveness.

God has forgotten the disobedience as soon as we ask. How do we know that? Because we acknowledge disobedience. Do you think the secular world, those unsaved, would have the same mind set? He also removes it from the book that keeps track of that sort of stuff. That is biblical. But when discussing servants on the level of John Hagee, or David Jeremiah or Charles Stanley, and the myriad of great, born again preachers, the Bible tells us they are held to a higher standard. We do not know the mind of God in this circumstance but in the eyes of the sinner he or she may feel God is asking the question: "How do I know if I can trust you?" And do not think that question is not visited several times a day by many Christians, and until it is answered there will remain a barrier of guilt.

I believe Jimmy Swaggart suffers from this situation a bit. Guilt is a hard task master to carry around. Guilt and the deception that allowed the guilt to take root in the first place. Guilt and deception are two of Satan's mighty weapons, those and pride are perhaps his three mightiest weapons. But to address the question, "how does God know He can trust us?" Only we can answer that question. However, if listening to God regarding that question, we are instructed to tell Him we are sorry, and mean it—remember, God will not be mocked—then trust in Him and His word to remember the infraction no more, and move forward, knowing we have done exactly what He has asked of us.

CHAPTER II

THE RELENTLESSNESS OF PASTORS

Nobody has ever said being a pastor or even a Christian would be easy, and that is a major reason why everyone is not a Christian, a believer, or even a follower. It takes a desire to be a Christian. A desire as we know not everyone has. Sometime back Steve Hill wrote a book titled, *Spiritual Avalanche,* wherein he said that many cannot pay the price of being a follower, a Christian. They will not pay the price to walk from a known life into a life outside of their comfort zone, and many will fall by the wayside. Remember, as Pastor Jeremiah says, "Satan's goal is to devour the influence of God's people."

It takes a lot of faith to stay the course, especially knowing that Satan is a sore loser, and it becomes doubly hard as a pastor. And as we know, the parable of the sower, as found in Matthew chapter 13, addresses those who have accepted Christ and when the winds of adversity begin to blow, they fall, walk, or run from Christ. They are doing exactly the opposite of what should be done.

It appears to be the overcoming of adversities of daily living that life provides additional faith to ease the pain and reduce the drama that many of us probably face more than we would like. Faith that in turn produces the capability of overcoming whatever adversity is put in front of us. It is the responsibility of pastors to teach the importance of working through the adversities of life, with the goal being to achieve the purpose for our life as God had intended. Pastors who also teach and equip us to do the work of ministry. They teach and equip us to do the work of going outside the church building to reach the lost.

Many believe that if we leave the responsibility of reaching the lost all up to the pastors, the Christian church will be lacking in the responsibility of continuously carrying the message to the lost. But in all fairness, the post-Christian age of apathy, along with the spirit of the antichrist, seem to be running freely making the leadership of pastors more difficult by the day. Considering the times that many are referring to as the end times, as discussed in the book of Revelation, what an awesome responsibility for those pastors who are giving lots of thought and consideration to the current times in which we live.

The times many are equating to the times predicted to befall humanity as written in the Bible prior to the return of Christ. Awesome times for all Christians but especially for pastors, as well as perhaps scary times. The Bible conveys that there will come a time when persecution becomes apparent with Christians, but especially with those pastors who wish to gather and preach the word of God. Did we not see this reality during the Coronavirus pandemic? Were some pastors not arrested, fined, or burned at the stake? Oop's, sorry, that was during the days of the Roman Emperors when Christians were being burned alive for their beliefs, now Christians are refused entrance into places of worship without any reason, at least not any justifiable, rational, reason. Some churches were even locked and blocked by the authorities.

That is taking away civil liberties, and in some places going so far as to declare martial law. Even open-air gatherings by Christians who were wearing mask at the time brought arrest. How ludicrous is that? Eventually if the Bible is correct, we will be refused entrance into Walmart unless…Unless what?" Unless we join the club of atheism. A society, with a Godless mentality, a world that shows intolerance of a mindset that includes a God. Many pastors address the biblical eternity of those who reject Christ and choose a path so different from the path that Christians so plainly see?

Atheism and Destiny

Just as the saved have a scripted destiny so do the unsaved. Earlier we discussed the deception of the faith preachers as being a poison to Christianity, now I would like to say a few words about atheist who are also a poison to Christianity. When we think of "life after death" we perhaps think of the saved, but there are those unsaved who will also face "life after death." Atheist authors such as Richard Dawkins and those who champion the atheist movement, including the Michael Newdows of the world (who would remove God from everything if he could) will lack the necessary credentials necessary to receive eternal life.

Some years back he made news by taking offence to his daughter having to say the Pledge of Allegiance and referring to God. Probably not so much the pledge itself, but the word "God" was unacceptable. He took the case to remove God from the Pledge of Allegiance to the United States Supreme Court. The court refused to rule upon the issue as he filed the case in the name of his daughter. Since she was his "step-daughter" and not his real daughter, the Supreme Court apparently dodged the issue by refusing to hear the case on those grounds.

Some call them "atheist" or "evangelistic atheist" from their constant attacks against religion, especially against Christianity and the God of the Christians. Here are some of them and the books they authored: Richard Dawkins, *The God Delusion* (2006); Christopher Hitchens, *God Is Not Great: How Religion Poisons Everything* (2007) and Sam Harris, *The End of Faith: Religion, Terror, and the Future of Reason* (2004) and *Letter to a Christian Nation* (2002). The constant in the books, although somewhat presented in different ways, is the thinking that "traditional religious worldviews have run their course, for science and rational thinking have made a mockery of religion."[7] Of course, every Christian should challenge the atheist's point of view.

The evangelistic atheists preach the message that all religions are delusional and pernicious. I was listening to a sermon by John MacArthur when he said, "Man-centered heathenism mocks Divine Judgment." Then he proceeded to give the definition of an atheist by quoting from the evolutionist Aldous Huxley, grandson of Thomas Huxley (he coined the word agnostic in 1869), when he read from a document called *Confessions of a Professional Atheist*, where Aldous wrote:

> "I had motives for not wanting the world to have meaning. Consequently, assuming it had none, and I was able without any difficulty to find satisfying reasons for this assumption. The philosopher who finds no meaning in the world is not concerned exclusively with a problem in pure metaphysics. He is also concerned to prove that there is no valid reason why he should personally not do just what he wants to do. For myself, as no doubt for most of my contemporaries, the philosophy of meaninglessness was essentially an instrument of liberation. The liberation we desired was simultaneously a liberation from a person, political and economic system, and liberation from a certain system of morality. We objected to the morality because it interfered with our sexual freedom." Wow!

---

7   Charles Kimball. *When Religion Becomes Evil.* Harper Collins: New York: Harper Collins Publisher. 2008.

From time to time, we have the experience of listening to an atheist. Some entertain us, such as Bill Maher and the late George Carlin. Others entertain us with their knowledge of magic, as in Penn Jillette. Still others act as contributing news commentators as in Ron Reagan, and still others are in government, and in the world in general, including Hollywood. But remember, atheists follow their mentors and the atheists mentioned are mentors. Some of these mentors sound openly hostile to, and dismissive of anyone, who might continue to wallow in the ignorance and stupidity with which all religion is hopelessly infected. I remember listening to George Carlin who said while visiting with Bill Maher, "The base of most evils in the world is religion of any kind." How about that. According to them "religions" are evil and are hopelessly infected with a degree of ignorance and stupidity.

Anyway, to join the coming society, one would be expected to embrace a mindset that requires the elimination of worshiping God and eventually forgetting about Him. Otherwise, we are challenging their authority—an authority opposed to God. You do realize, all of this is heading into the times described in the books of Revelation and Daniel. Daniel by way of describing the last of the five kingdoms.

Today's leaders preach the message of Christ at a time when time is short and fewer and fewer people are interested in Christianity. As a matter of fact, I saw the other day where two-thirds of young people are either departing the faith or abandoning Christianity altogether after high school. Wow! That is two-thirds. These times, at best, must be considered disturbing to many Christians. This is the time in the history the churches and the leaders, while facing adversity, know they are doing the best they can for Christ to save as many as possible from the coming times and the second death.

But as the Bible says, the last days will be hard because of the apathy that will be rampant upon the earth. A society that continues to turn away from Christianity and pursuing, even embracing, a world without a God. Christians see this while non-Christians do not. But then, does not the Bible say they cannot see, nor can they hear. A time in which Christianity is producing many pastors like Joel Osteen and Joyce Meyers. Not saying there is anything wrong with either, they just do not happen to preach the crucified Christ. For now, it might be interesting to discuss a couple of pastors who preach the risen Christ and have had an extraordinary impact upon the lives of many.

Experts for our Time

Any list of experts would have to include such preachers as Dr. David Jeremiah. Pastor Jeremiah is such a good pastor, I had some reservations when I began listening to him. Did he believe as do most of the churches who were preaching the gospel? Or was he preaching beliefs more embraced by those who would have a hard time finding their church in the Bible? Until those questions were answered, I watched with caution. Curious caution, but caution, nevertheless.

Since he was discussing the end times and the players who will be present during those times with such authority, one could think he might be painting a picture different from most of the futurists one can hear preaching the same message. Either way, I listened to what he had to say and can honestly say I look forward to listening to him. He is an excellent, well-informed, and interesting preacher. A preacher that anyone listening to would attest to as authentic. And the preludes to his weekly sermons are superb, as well.

David has written several books, and with his sermons coinciding with his writings make his sermons even more interesting. One such book, *Agents of the Apocalypse*, which I have not yet read, but each week as he breaks down a chapter and discusses it, he almost becomes mesmerizing. When it comes to the last days and the times leading up to those days, one would have to look long and hard to find someone better qualified at laying out a better hypothesis. He opened (unsealed) the book of Daniel like few before him. It probably is a safe bet that those who listen to him, and those who are encouraged and enlightened by him, agree that he is a very illuminating pastor. Listeners always seem to come away with useful information that seems to address current times and places in the world, and what the current signs mean in the days to come.

I have only mentioned a couple of topics Pastor Jeremiah has preached about, but it does not seem to matter. David's knowledge of the Bible and his grasp on Christianity is superb, regardless of the subject. And the way he delivers God's word every week is always captivating. David is a cancer survivor and an all-around great pastor, as well as someone I would consider it an honor to spend time with after we move on from this life. We will be hearing more from him regarding some of the ideas he embraces and the theology he preaches as we go through this book.

Charles Stanley and the Baptists

We have discussed so much of the beliefs of Charles Stanley one might begin to feel they know him and can relate to him. One reason for that might be that Charles Stanley is an excellent preacher who touches the lives of millions. A preacher I, along with probably millions, would nominate for any Hall of Fame. While there are many good pastors preaching the word of God, few evoke the feeling that they have lived it as does Pastor Stanley. The reason I like Pastor Stanley is that he has experienced what he preaches and continues to trust in God to lead him to the conclusion of a life dedicated to Christ and His message.

Maybe you have noticed that many pastors preaching God's word spend a lot of time telling Christians what they should be doing, and there is nothing wrong with that. But Pastor Stanley convinces us through his messages that he has lived through the trials and tribulations that most Christians go through once they decide to follow Christ. It is as if Pastor Stanley has put faith to the test during his journey through life and found that it works, and that is the message he puts into his words from week to week.

When walking by faith, sometimes we cannot always see the way forward, but as Charles Stanley says, "*keep walking.*" Perhaps we do not always understand our current situation (maybe even feeling let down by God) and are short on hope, Charles Stanley says, "*keep walking.*" Maybe we feel as if there is no hope, and no promise of anything better, "*keep walking.*" Faith, the Holy Spirit, and a relationship with God will help one endure those times of trouble. Faith has been proven to reduce fear and instill confidence. By overcoming fear with faith, we become stronger in our beliefs. And one of those beliefs is that faith builds, spiritual strength. It is spiritual strength that helps us endure the trials and tribulations of life. While it might be a little rough going through the storms that sometime besiege Christians, most would concur that once on the other side, not only does our faith increase, but we also find our relationship with God is stronger.

I came across a sign the other day in front of a florist shop that had an exceptionally good message, especially for people who feel as if they have reached the end of the line or the end of their rope and are barely holding on. It read, "Hope is being able to see that there is light despite all of the darkness."[8] I believe every Christian could say "amen" to that. Hope combined with faith is a must when it comes to living a Christian life. Another good definition of faith comes from Charles Stanley when he says faith is the "conviction" that God will do what he promises. Sounds good to me. I believe most Christians would say that sounds darn good.

I have learned a lot by listening to Pastor Stanley, as I am sure others have as well. He appears to have followed his convictions, and by so doing, he is, at least in my book, and obviously in the book of a few million more, an exceptionally good preacher. I understood

---

[8]   I'm sorry I do not know who wrote this, but the florist shop was called "Black Tie Roses" in Corpus Christi, TX.

for the first time what it meant to be a Baptist while listening to one of his sermons titled, "The Missing Link." Finally, I was able to reconcile the question, "Does God choose us, or do we choose God?" Although, as we saw earlier, that question does not seem to be as important as the fact that we are saved by the grace of God. I believe most would say: "That is sufficient."

I do like how the Baptists—of which Charles Stanley is a member—declares a belief in eternal salvation by asking, "Does God choose us, or do we choose God?" Regarding God choosing us, they say: "The truth is God does not violate our wills by choosing us and redeeming us." Then what would one call it? If I am chosen or not chosen prior to the foundations of the earth being poured as some teach, that would seem to limit, probably more like take away, perhaps even eliminate my free will, and that would be a violation of my free will. Then they continue: "Rather, He changes our hearts so that our wills choose Him." Very nicely put. That is a line I believe every evangelical Christian could get behind.

It appears we are given the opportunity to be a follower when the Spirit touches our heart, as was the case with Lydia when she heard Paul preach about Christ. Most of us can probably relate to how Lydia found salvation. The Bible says her heart was opened and she received the words Paul was speaking, exactly as the Baptists say. Her heart was changed upon hearing the word, but only after God allowed her to hear the words with her heart. In Lydia's case, she heard the words with her heart, thus, many might say she was born from the darkness of the world into the light of eternal life. She chose the life God talked about in Deuteronomy and she will not, according to God's word, face death at the judgment seat of Christ. The Bible says that even the angels rejoice when that happens. However, for the time being, it appears we will just have to listen to C.H. Spurgeon who addresses this age-old problem of freewill by saying, "whether God choosing man is consistent with the free agency of man or not, just might have to remain a conundrum for the moment."

Those who embrace "once saved always saved" theology accept Christ as their Savior as well as the others who preach as Charles Stanley. They teach we can never lose our salvation, same as those who embrace freewill theology, *if,* as we are told in Colossians, we continue to follow Him. Because of this acceptance, a foundation of belief is established that separates both from being a reprobate, and that decision of accepting the cross puts all Christians into the same family. And as the Bible says, once we are in that family, nobody will ever be able to pluck us from that family.

CHAPTER III

FUTURIST FOR OUR TIME...

...who are considered by many to be modern day prophets. Those preachers who possess the ability to correlate current events with biblical prophecy and predict with a certain degree of accuracy where everything is headed. Preachers and teachers who deserve to be in any Hall of Fame. Great pastors who preach the word of God, as well as give us some insight as to where we might be in biblical history, especially when it comes to explaining the current times in which we are living and comparing those times with the Bible's description of what to expect in the future.

Before we discuss some of the predictions of the modern-day futurists, let me ask a question. What do you think conjures up in the minds of those who are asked their thoughts about the "last days" or the "end times?" There are probably several responses to that question, but there are two major camps of thought. There is the Christian camp, which mainly agrees that we could be either living in or approaching the end times as defined by the Bible. Or there is the second camp, which is more secular in nature, who might respond with: "For as long as I can remember, people have been saying we are living in, or approaching, the last days or the end times." They both sound true to me. Ever since Jesus said, "Repent, for the kingdom of heaven is at hand," people have been preaching that message, and now we are about to discuss a couple of those who carry on that tradition.

Most of the pastors, especially futurist pastors and end-time pastors whom I have listened to, and whose books I have read and acquired knowledge from, seem to have one thread of continuity, and that is how close we may be to the times revealed in the books of Daniel and Revelation. They say time may be running out for this world to continue as it is now. John Hagee and Tim LaHaye believe the times we are living in represent the last generation or the terminal generation—the last generation before the coming of Christ. David Jeremiah gives the impression he thinks the same way, and Jack Van Impe has said he believes the current pope will be the last.

Again, are they right? Who knows, but looking around at the condition of the world, they might not be too far off. Patrick Herron tells us in his book, *Apocalypse Soon,* that perhaps we have reached that time in history where this may be the final warning God is giving us before His judgments begin to fall.[9] Just a note: All those mentioned are theological experts who have for years been proclaiming the return of Christ and how close to reality that might be, as well as the events leading up to that apocalyptic event. These are all fascinating pastors proclaiming the word of God with a degree of accuracy that cannot be ignored.

These are authors, researchers, analyst, who assimilate information from the Bible with the ability to communicate the message of salvation and eternal life, as well as to paint a picture of the future as if they were blessed with divine revelation knowledge directly from God. We have already discussed one of them when we discussed Dr. David Jeremiah, but there are a few others who would make any Hall of Fame proud.

Probably at the top of that list would be Hal Lindsey, John Hagee, and Jack Van Impe. I am going to call that a three-way tie, as they each have written multiple books, many of which I

---

9   Patrick Heron. *Apocalypse Soon.* Published in Gresham, Oregon: Anomalos Publishing. 2007.

have borrowed from, and who have a genuine curiosity about the Bible and the future. It was from the writings of John Hagee that I connected the dots as to just how important it was in Bible prophecy for the Jews to return to the land of Israel and eventually control Jerusalem. It was what John brought to our attention regarding prophecy that I found to be quite interesting. As we know, the event that arranged for the Jews to return to the land of Israel in the early 1900s, took place as the Bible foretold it would almost three thousand years earlier.

Since it was prophesied that the Jews would return home prior to the coming of Christ, they had to return to the land promised to them by God through Abraham, and they had to have control of Jerusalem as well, which happened during the Six-Day War in 1967, when they wrestled control away from the Muslims. The Muslims say they want that real estate back, and nothing short of pushing Israel into the sea will suffice while taking it back.

Biblical scholars have been telling us of the return of the Jews and the reestablishment of a Jewish state for hundreds of years, and it is somewhat interesting to see just what transpired to allow the Jews to begin the pilgrimage of "coming home"—coming home to the land promised by God to Abraham and handed down through the descendants of Abraham beginning with the patriarchs Isaac and Jacob, who brought forth the twelve tribes of Israel.

Now remember, the Jews, for the most part, have been dislodged from this land ever since the Romans made the land of Israel desolate in A.D. 70 for the second time. Nebuchadnezzar was the first in 589 B.C. when he destroyed the temple that had been completed in 957 B.C. by King David's son Solomon. Nebuchadnezzar left the land mostly desecrated and obliterated of any borders and the Jewish people were scattered throughout the land of Babylon where they remained for seventy years as predicted in Jer.25:1-11, especially verse 11. After seventy years, they were granted permission to rebuild the temple. And when they did rebuild with permission of King Cyrus, that temple stood until A.D. 70 before it was destroyed by Emperor Titus.

A few Jews returned over time, but eventually came under the rule of the Turks of the Ottoman Empire, who ruled much of southeastern Europe, western Asia, and North Africa between the 14th and early 20th centuries. (For a good read regarding the condition of the Middle East at that time, acquire Karen Armstrong's book, *A History of God.*) But then again, the question arises as to what transpired to motivate the Jews to return and occupy the land of Canaan in the early 1900s and in 1948 making it a Jewish State? Once again, that is where John Hagee comes in as he tells us of the Balfour Declaration.

In World War I, the British were cut off from their source of cordite gunpowder. First Lord of the Admiralty Winston Churchill went to Chaim Weizmann, a Jewish chemist, and asked him if he would find a way to make several tons of synthetic gunpowder. Without it, bullets could not be fired, artillery was useless, and cannons on ships were mere ornaments. The outcome of the war was at stake.

The Jewish inventor played a major role in the victory of WW1 over Germany by fulfilling Churchill's request. Within weeks Weizmann and his associates discovered how to make this massive amount of synthetic gunpowder. John writes: "After the war, Lord Balfour asked Chaim Weizmann what England could do to honor him. Weizmann asked that his people be given a homeland. Lord Balfour created a historic document known to this day as the 'Balfour Declaration,'" giving—or as many might say, returning to the Jewish people what God had already promised in the book of Genesis—a homeland."

Then John wraps it up by saying, "Though the Balfour Declaration went through several drafts, the final version was issued on November 2, 1917, in a letter from Balfour to Lord Rothschild, president of the British Zionist Federation." This final version guaranteed the Jews the homeland they had been promised centuries earlier. This was Bible prophecy being fulfilled in two areas right before our eyes. God said Jerusalem would be occupied by the nation of Israel when He returns, as it currently is, and it was going to be the nation that He would be coming to protect at His Second Coming. Not at the Rapture but at His Second Coming. And that we will see as we will be coming with Him.

The Jews returning to Israel, to the land of Canaan, the land promised to Abraham after such a long absence speaks volumes about the validity of the Bible and the God who promised to the Jews that He would remain their God forever. We were told of the Jews returning to the land promised them by James Grant, an English Bible scholar, from information furnished in Walter Martin's book, *Kingdom of the Cults*. He wrote in 1866—long before the Jews returned that they would return to the land promised to them by God. And they did. How about that?

The Jews commenced the trek of coming home, back to the land of Canaan, as was prophesied more than two thousand years earlier by Ezekiel (Ezek. 37:21–22 and Jer. 3:18), and in 1948, Israel became a sovereign state, making future prophecy possible to understand. For those who do not believe the Bible, explain that. And while you are at it, explain Jerusalem coming under Jewish control in 1967, putting in place everything necessary for end time events to occur. Nearly everything the Bible conveys about the Jews and the promise God made to Abraham regarding the land of Canaan—now Israel—has been fulfilled, with only the final chapter remaining to be realized.

The Changing Times

I have watched several pastors for perhaps twenty to twenty-five years. I can probably trace my involvement with prophesy to about the time Hal Lindsey released his book, *The Late Great Planet Earth*, in 1970, although I did not realize how interested in the subject

I would become until sometime later, when most of what he had conveyed was unfolding right before my very eyes. These are pastors I have found who take seriously the times in which we are currently living and convey through their writings and teachings many of the circumstances that are already upon us, and how the surrounding circumstances influence our minds to what is coming and why. These experts tell us that some serious judgments are predicted to befall humanity before the return of Christ,

If Christ returns prior to the commencement of tribulation, as embraced by those who are pretribulation believers, then looking around, many might agree that we need to be getting out of here, as it is beginning to get quite ugly. Many remember a time when politics weren't as troubling as they are today and Mother Nature was, well, just Mother Nature. Before hurricane Katrina people were hosting "hurricane parties." Not anymore.

In addition to the weather, we face social disturbances, like the Boston marathon pressure cooker bombing that many witnessed personally, and the random school shootings that continue to jar everyone to their core. Today an event occurred that reminds some of us of those times and ask, how much longer God must we endure. A couple of years ago, we endured 60 people killed and many more hurt during a Los Vegas concert mainly for young people. We endured other happenings like the four Asians who were recently shot and killed just going about the day of living their lives. Heartbreaking news as death removes the memories of what could have been.

Today March 22, 2021, ten people were shot and killed, in a grocery store in Boulder Colorado. Sad, very sad as a 57-year-old-father of seven was killed and memories of what could have been were lost forever. That can happen anywhere at any time, as we know. And according to the Bible it will. Then we have the latest plague, known as coronavirus, that continues to unfold before our very eyes taking the lives of over 200,000 just in the United States alone. This is one in a series of plagues, as we remember SARS,

H1N1, and the swine flu, and do not forget the viral strain that drove the 2014-2016 Ebola outbreak in West Africa, killing up to 90% of the people it infected. But none has affected America and taken down our economy like the latest plague.

There are many, including most of the futurists who are predicting the book of Revelation has been opened and the first four seals releasing the four horsemen of the apocalypse are upon us with each seal, or horseman, designated to remove peace from the world. Each horseman in his own way through wars and rumors of wars, famine, climate change, out-of-control wildfires, and massive floods, responsible for causing people to lose their homes and their life to flooding and to mud slides. Poverty, hunger, inflation, and the various plagues that will be unleashed upon the world are evidence of God's wrath. (The beginning of birth pains). We are told about the times we currently are experiencing and what is to come.

While reading information from past statistics, earthquakes are occurring with ever-increasing frequency, and fires and floods are occurring with greater intensity with each passing year. Whether we go from "normal" weather conditions, bringing about various degrees of change gradually leading up to the Tribulation period, or whether disasters begin to occur suddenly, as if overnight, to unprecedented and spectacularly high degrees of intensity with each leading to the Tribulation period, is open to conjecture.

My editor believes in a pre-Tribulation Rapture, while I believe in a mid-Tribulation one. He said, "We pre-tribulation folks would like to have an easy life before Jesus snatches us away to safety. This could happen." And there is not a Christian that would not like to see that happen. But believing in a mid-Tribulation Rapture, I expect to go through some tribulation, maybe tribulation as we are currently enduring with the coronavirus and the devastation that is being unleashed upon people around the world. Never has a virus caused unprecedented collapse of world economies as the one we are currently experiencing. And never have we come so close to understanding the mark of the beast. Wear a mask or you can't enter a place of business. Get vaccinated, or you can't buy or sale. The time appears to be close where the ability to buy and sell may become jeopardized. Who wants to face that reality?

The world could be headed for some precarious times as the Bible and the futurist are telling us. And without a pretribulation Rapture, Christians may have to face some tribulation. But as Charles Stanley says, "Christians walk through those times of trouble with Jesus by their side as opposed to the non-Christians who go it alone." What a frightening journey that can be, as even now people are frightened just thinking about the future. We seem to have passed up the opportunity of not being frightened long ago when we allowed Madalyn Murray O'Hair, the well-known atheist, to have Bibles banned from public schools. And the assault upon Christianity to remove God from "everywhere" has continued with more determination and intensity now than ever before. And we have been informed every step of the way by those scholars of the Bible, those futurists, who have for many years, been predicting the outcome this removal of Bibles would have on Christianity.

The Time of Desensitizing

To many Christians the desensitization appears to have taken us to the place in our journey where many can begin to relate with the frog sitting in the pot, unaware he is approaching the end of his life. To many it appears that we are living through times where the water is beginning to boil without us perhaps even realizing it. Again, the word desensitized comes to mind. We are beginning to experience serious changes in our planet's environment, and within our social structure as well, which could be a forerunner of even more severe judgment of God upon humanity, which in turn, as the Bible says, will cause men's heart to fail them.

Will we listen to the experts and the futurist? Are we listening? Have we been listening? Sea levels are rising. Dr. Lonnie Thompson of Ohio State University, a well-respected and leading expert on mountain glaciers, said recently (it was 2015 when I came across this information) that within the next few years, the snows of Mt. Kilimanjaro will be gone. I thought then the information I was hearing was not very encouraging.

Dr. Thompson continues: We are destabilizing the massive mound of ice in Greenland, as well as the equally enormous mass of ice propped on top of islands in western Antarctica, threatening a worldwide increase in sea levels of as much as twenty feet. Wow! Glaciers, some say approaching the size of a football field or two, or three, or four, are constantly falling into the ocean with the world's largest coming in at more than 60 miles (96 km) wide at its widest point and about 270 miles long and measured to be 8,200 feet (2,500 meters) deep at its center.

In addition to sea levels rising from these glaciers, huge dead spots have been discovered in our oceans, with rising temperatures threatening many more cataclysmic events, and environmentalists are constantly warning of other great disasters, as well as plagues waiting to occur. Are we listening now? On June 20, 2017, the temperature in Phoenix reached a high of 118 degrees. For the first time ever, I heard planes were grounded because of high temperatures. The all-time high recorded was in 1990 when the temperature reached 122 degrees. As temperatures rise across the globe, the reach of disruption reaches far and wide. For example, when Polar Bears began making trouble in Manitoba Canada, they were, and are, put into holding cages and then released back into the wild sometime later. The Polar Bears rate of disruption has skyrocketed as of late because of poverty in their natural habitat. Global Warming? Climate change? Whatever it is, it is happening.

Have we as humans done something to cause rising temperatures, bringing about changes to the earth's atmosphere, as well as our ozone layer? Most if not all the futurist pastors have been conveying this assault against the planet for some time, and that assault has been under way for many years. As for the question, "Are we listening?" I would say yes, although America is a land divided; but we do care. It is conditions outside of our control, conditions that are in God's control, that will dictate our future—probably brought about by humans being human and doing what humans do.

Leaving this behind for now, let us discuss a new apostolic movement that is sweeping the land. A very controversial movement that seems to be at odds with the more conservative Christianity one might find in the more conservative churches. It is as if a divisive situation is beginning to build within the family of Christianity and many Christians who are finding themselves in the middle are finding it to be uncomfortable. The problem seems to be that many are beginning to turn away from the conservatism of the denominational churches as they seem to be finding more spirituality in other places. That is what the next chapter is about. One of those places many are finding a more prevalent Spirit that is much different, or perhaps even more revealing than in the more conservative churches, and many of those conservative churches are not very happy about the situation, as you will see.

CHAPTER IV

THE NEW APOSTOLIC REFORMATION

What is the New Apostolic Reformed Christian church we are beginning to hear a lot about these days? Being an apostolic (reformed) Christian means that we are the result of a reformation movement that began with Martin Luther several centuries ago. I believe I would define a modern-day Protestant as an earlier family member of the apostolic faith, who some say broke ties with the Catholic Church, while others say they never had ties to the Catholic Church or the Church of England. And from that separation, many variations of Christianity have emerged. The current one that is taking the Christian world by storm is a movement referred to as the New Apostolic Reformation (NAR) movement.

Within the Protestant family right at this moment we seem to have a split occurring between what I would call a conservative Protestant Christian and a charismatic Protestant Christian. Examples of conservative Christians might be John MacArthur, Tom Pennington, and Keith Gibson, the pastor and author at Apologetics Research Center. He says that there are people in this movement (NAR) who deny the Trinity as well as, teach a quite different Christology, teaching things that impact the gospel, and even the way people are saved and what salvation looks like. A question I had to ask myself was, what would cause them to express those feelings?

As the world becomes more liberal with each passing day, one could say, as the liberalism of the world goes, so goes the liberalism that enters Christianity and weakens the whole system. That is what conservatives seem to be fighting against: According to them the NAR leaders are mitigating the principles of the Bible and devaluing the mission of Christ. While that has not been proven that appears to be the struggle right now involving conservative pastors who are fighting to maintain their form of a more puritanical Christianity, rather than a liberal Christianity. This is not to be confused with the conservative Baptist Puritan movement that probably was somewhat responsible for the infamous witch trials that were prevalent during 1692 when ugliness raised its head in Salem, Massachusetts. But more "conservative" in the emotional displays while attending church.

You will probably not see any hands being raised, or someone touched by the Holy Spirit, or the shedding of a tear or two, as opposed to attending some of the more charismatic churches, and it does not even have to be a Pentecostal church. I attended a United Methodist Church in Euless, Texas for about a year, and during that time I was introduced to a Spirit that was undeniably the Holy Spirit, as there is no other spirit in the world that makes one feel like the Spirit of God. A great church.

According to John MacArthur, as well as those pastors previously mentioned, there seems to be a disconnect between them as "conservative" preachers and those who are embracing a more liberal charismatic Christianity. A Christianity that is looked upon by some as containing enough differences to constitute heresy. It has become disturbing enough that Michael Brown, writer and journalist for *Charisma News* and *Charisma Magazine*, who, while not a fan of the new charismatic movement, has penned a piece asking John MacArthur, world-renowned Bible teacher, pastor, and author, to recant his strong stand against the charismatic church (NAR) and reign in the harsh words that he uses to describe their doctrine, dogma, and philosophy.

While John MacArthur may be outspoken against this new movement, he is not the only one denouncing it as demonic, Satanic, and outlandish. He is however the most descriptive in his use of words therefore many follow what he says about the NAR, and to a degree, the Charismatic movement in general. But then one cannot necessarily paint with such a wide brush, as perhaps some critics do. The Pentecostal Charismatic Movement is considered Protestant, a church somewhat like the Assemblies of God.

A prime example of a church that embraces the Holy Spirit during their services, as well as the Pentecostal churches in general, although the Pentecostal churches per se have been labeled as cultic. To understand why I say that, just acquire Hank Hanegraaff's tapes "Christianity in Crisis. But then, many say there are Spirit-filled churches pastored by Spirit-filled preachers who preach born-again theology—as well as the doctrine of the Trinity—and conveys the message it is that theology that many might consider more defines the Pentecostal churches. I personally, have found it not unusual to encounter a man-made spirit as opposed to the real spirit of God in a lot of the Pentecostal churches I have visited.

As discussed, there is a "charismatic movement"—a Pentecostal movement—taking the traditional Christianity of the past by storm. A Spirit-filled movement many conservatives have criticized for some time as perhaps demonic because of their freedom of expression. A charismatic movement that brings back memories of a Christianity many first encountered in the late nineteenth century, described by some as the "holy rollers," where people were supposedly swinging from the chandeliers, rolling around in the aisles, and going into convulsive behavior from time to time. They were literally rolling on the floor in an uncontrolled manner, appearing to be obsessed with spirits some scholars were relating to the spirits of Kundalini (more on this shortly). "Holy roller" is a term describing the Holiness and Pentecostal traditions of the Charismatic movement. The term describes dancing, shaking or other boisterous movements by church attendees who perceive themselves as being under the influence of the Holy Spirit.[10]

The origins of the New Apostolic Reformation movement appear to be associated with, at least spiritually, the Pentecostal movement of the late 1800s and earlier 1900s. A Christian movement that Conservative Christians generally find the actions, perhaps even the way of worship, disturbing. There appears to be a resurgence of this form of spiritual Christianity, a form of Christianity that many say falls under the banner of a Spirit-filled movement that emphasizes the work of the Holy Spirit, along with the Holy Spirit's spiritual gifts, including speaking in tongues, healing, and modern-day miracles as an everyday part of a believer's life. They say they do this by the authority of 1 Corinthians 12:7-11.

Some of the more liberal NAR members might be caught jumping around and waving their arms, appearing to be incredibly happy, while others may be standing, appearing to be in a worshiping trance—a condition that many Pentecostals describe as being "slain in the Spirit," or "drunk in the Spirit." "Slain in the Spirit" seems to be a condition that can be found in some Pentecostal churches even today, but because of some charismatic groups being labeled "extreme" the entire charismatic community of Spirit-filled churches is often painted with a wide brush by some conservative pastors.

Although, regarding some "Pentecostal" churches who claim to be Spirit Filled, Hank Hanegraaff along with many others have questioned the Spirit of the church. And probably justifiable as I found the spirit entirely man induced in the churches I visited, thus causing Hank to declare them a cult. But the question remaining has to do with the motivation behind the NAR movement that so many are berating. Is it motivated by the Spirit of Christ? And how much of Bible scripture do they follow?

There are about five (including the Catholic and Greek Orthodox churches) that believe they are the family of Christians that emerged

---

[10]   Ibid.

as the "Apostolic" Church, or a version of it. The Catholics from the root of the apostle Peter and the Greek Orthodox from the root of the apostle Mark, and Protestants from the root of the message delivered from the Bible, particularly the book of Acts and the teachings of the apostle Paul. After all, the Bible specifically conveys to us that it was Paul who Jesus appointed to teach the gentiles. It appears they all lay claim to the Apostolic Church from the book of Acts. But the book of Acts refers to the Protestant Church, the "Church of the Way," as the apostolic church of the apostles.

One of those who has brought this new form of Christianity to our attention would be someone considered a conservative Christian, John MacArthur, pastor of Grace Community Church,[11] He says, "They have wandered off the charts of Christianity and more into demonic possession." (I may be somewhat paraphrasing, but he said "demonic possession" for sure.) But are they? Well, the convulsions and the slithering around almost on top of each other as witnessed in some of the churches—some that appear to be a holdover from the Holy Roller era, might leave one to wonder about the origins of the spirits they embrace.

The New Apostolic Reformation is a movement which seeks to establish a fifth branch within Christendom, distinct from Catholicism, Protestantism, Oriental Orthodoxy and Eastern Orthodoxy.[12] A more "Spirit" filled movement of Christians who appear to find joy in the Spirit, a Spirit that has become very popular, especially among young millennials who are becoming associated with the movement by visiting megachurches, such as Hillsong church in New York or Bethel Church in Redding, California, a couple of churches associated with the NAR movement.

---

[11] A non-denominational, evangelical megachurch founded in 1956 and located in Sun Valley, a neighborhood in the San Fernando Valley of Los Angeles, California.

[12] https://en.m.wikipedia.org.

Since the Bethel church movement is mentioned in conjunction with Hillsong, I googled Bethel Church in California. They were an Assemblies of God church before withdrawing their affiliation with the organization. They are pastored by a gentleman by the name of Bill Johnson. What I found interesting is that some people believe Bethel Church has gradually adopted New Age ideas, especially since their publication of *The Physics of Heaven* (2012) on *Quantum Mysticism*, (I haven't a clue). And because of this, and other reasons, they believe the Bethel Church movement, a part of the International House of Prayer (IHOP) and the Hillsong movement, which is a part of the New Apostolic Reformation Movement, are all considered to be cultic. But again, one must ask, are they?

Some well-known pastors have weighed in on the subject and have expressed their opinions, I mean some heavy hitters. In addition to John MacArthur, others have expressed their opinion such as, Justin Peters, John Piper and Wretched Radio host Todd Friel. It was to seek information as to why some conservative Christian leaders consider this new movement a cult that I was moved to study them. Trying to understand why they are considered satanic became a quest, especially since they are such a dominating factor exploding upon the Christianity scene. This was a quest that interested me, as it gives us a glimpse into the Christianity that may be embraced by the millennials, those born between 1981-1996 (22-37 years old). A movement that is perhaps defining the future of Christianity is being adopted by the new millennials right before our very eyes.

A Millennial Movement

Many of the modern-day denominational churches, especially the more conservative ones, are attracting fewer and fewer young people. As a matter of fact, I saw a couple of interesting statistics the other day stating only eighteen percent of millennials were following Christianity. And many of the eighteen percent are breaking away from the more traditional churches and accepting the informality of this new movement. It is almost as if they are projecting the message, "This is not your parent's church" as the congregants in LA and NYC mirror Carl Lentz's casual style of wearing jeans, replacing stuffy suits and gentile dresses. Forget your printed Bible? No worries—following along on an iPhone is the norm, and selfies in the bathroom are cool, as well.

And the meet-and-greet in most of the oversize foyers where many are found enjoying a cup of coffee and the comradery of the moment before adjourning to the sanctuary to listen to the message always is a welcoming moment. Nothing threatening, wear what you want and enjoy the moment of being in a comfortable place to praise God. Once inside the sanctuaries of the churches I visited I felt praise, but not necessarily a worshiping spirit (there is a difference).

I know some might find this casual attitude of worship and praise towards Christ more liberal than one might find in a conservative church, but different church goers desire different things. Some say the level of liberalism found in the NAR is somewhat drifting away from conservatism, and to a degree it is, and that difference is what this discussion is about. Some might feel that places of worship should be shown more respect, but is any place to worship God wrong? Does it have anything to do with the message of Christ that might be heard? Or is this the new generation of millennials just being themselves?

Whether one is a conservative Christian or more of a charismatic Christian, there are certain things one just does not do and still retain the honor of being considered a Christian. It would be hard for many, if not all, Christians to condone what Jacob Prash brought to our attention in a podcast titled "The Apostasy of Hillsong— Entertainment for the Millennials." The clip he showed was a production including the Naked Cowboy bouncing around the stage, Spiderman, and the Statue of Liberty, who was being portrayed by a hairy bearded man. A production Hollywood would be proud of but would be considered heresy by most born-again Christians and yet it was a production by "Christians." One might have to think about that for a minute.

A Charismatic Movement

A new resurgence of this movement of charismatic Christians that was originally founded in the 1980s in New South Wales, Australia, by Brian and Bobbie Houston is becoming the new wave of modern-day Christianity. Today there are 100,000 parishioners in Australia attending services each week with locations dotting urban centers all over the world. Places like London, Paris, Moscow, San Francisco, Buenos Aires and Hillsong New York. Hillsong was among the first of the NAR churches established in America with a nickname of the "Hipster Church."

Hillsong is a church pastored by a 36-year-old charismatic leader by the name of Carl Lentz, along with his wife Laura, whom many say connect people with their true feelings. On any given Sunday, it is not unusual to see six services accommodating over 8,000 attendees, mainly young people in their 20s and 30s—the new millennials who seem to find this new movement refreshing and want to be a part of it, thus making it an attractive alternative to their parents' Christianity and as such, the New Age Reformed Church is becoming a fast-growing movement.

We are discussing a fast-sweeping, Spirit-filled movement of young millennials. I would call a church membership of over 850,000 a fast-sweeping movement, including another Hillsong church that opened recently in Los Angeles and already is on track to follow in the footsteps of the first American Hillsong church in New York. But the staggering number is the 10 million estimated followers worldwide. Listening to Wretched Radio host Todd Friel the other day he stated that number could be as many as 369 million people who are a part of or influenced by a non-regulated, non-denominational, tax-free entity that is amassing millions upon millions of dollars. Many of the conservative pastors seem to have a problem with that, as well. John MacArthur estimates their followers worldwide to be somewhere between 750 million to perhaps as many as one billion people.

As far as exploding upon the world scene, they are accomplishing what only a few have done before. Even Europe, a place where Islam is becoming more and more of a threat to Christianity, is beginning to recognize this new movement. I received an issue of Charisma magazine recently (May 2019 edition) and want to quote from an article written by Shawn A. Akers to show just how fast this movement is spreading in Europe, as well as other parts of the world. The article went like this:

> "Another indication of potential revival in Europe in recent years is the emergence of numerous houses of prayer, like the International House of Prayer (IHOP) in Kansas City, Missouri, and others found throughout the U.S. Houses of prayer have spread to most major European cities, including Brussels, Belgium; Wien and Vienna, Austria; Berlin. Munich and Heidelberg, Germany; Edinburg and Glasgow, Scotland; Stockholm, Sweden; and Reykjavik, and Iceland as well. Additional 24/7 houses of prayer (churches that appear to be associated with the Hillsong movement) have even opened in Prague, Czech Republic; Oslo, Norway; and Warsaw, Poland."

The article continued by saying, "Dr. Johannes Hartl founded the International House of Prayer in Augsburg, Germany in 2005. Today, it's the largest House of Prayer in Europe." Hartl says, "the growth is driven by the next generation." The generation of Hillsong Christian millennials. He continues, "The level of prayer is rising. With the House of Prayer movement and ministries like 24/7 prayer, the topic of prayer is much more prevalent than it used to be. Dr. Hartl says the younger generation loves worship and is drawn to real Spirit-filled houses of worship."

This movement has not escaped the eyes of many celebrates, such as Justin Bieber and Oprah Winfrey, along with many others who are apparently fans of the NAR. Oprah is one who shares the New Ager mentality and one who embraces what could be construed as the New Age millennials' understanding of life. And, from her platform as a celebrity, she has said some interesting, if not disturbing things in her lifetime. For example, one might hear her saying, "I'm a Christian who believes there are many more paths to God other than Christianity. I'm a Christian who believes in my way, but I don't believe it is the only way."

It sounds like many of the New Agers, especially if they follow Oprah, are creating their own brand of Christianity, as this contradicts the very words of Christ as written in the Bible. Words that tell us He (Jesus) is the only way to God and that He is the only truth and the only life, and that nobody comes to the Father except through Him. (Perhaps Oprah has God and Jesus mixed up, as we will see in a minute.) I believe most Christians look at things a little differently than Oprah, as they believe in a Trinity concept, and it appears that is how the NAR seems to look at Christianity as well, at least from what I can ascertain.

A Different Belief

Speaking of Oprah, she mentioned being a Christian, but to many she seems to embrace a different kind of Christianity. A belief system that is probably more in line with the New Age Millennials and not necessarily the Christianity of the New Apostolic Reformation. Perhaps some of the "New Agers" who would be attracted to Oprah might also be attracted to the New Apostolic Church; although, one might find the Apostolic Church preaches some reality to Christianity, whereas Oprah does not seem to have a clue. I am not trying to disparage her, it is just that Oprah does not seem to have a grasp of the reality of the Bible, where it explains in detail that

Christ is the only way to God. Oprah seems to embrace a brand of New Age mentality that has nothing to do with Christianity as the following seems to indicate:

- *God is an energy or impersonal force in the universe.*
- *Jesus did not come here to die for our sins, but to show us how to live from "Christ Consciousness."*
- *Jesus is not the only path to God or to heaven.* My response:

  Christians know better but be careful with this one. When someone says that Jesus is not the only way to God, as Oprah just did, and believes in their heart as Oprah does, that's heresy. And embracing that concept, as Oprah has, is almost bordering on the unpardonable sin. When asked to clarify perhaps what Oprah meant, T.D. Jakes and Joel Osteen said there are numerous ways to Jesus (which is true), but only one way to God, which is also true and that dispels the thinking of Oprah.

- *Man is divine (godly, heavenly, godlike, great) by nature* (somewhat a Christian Science view) *and not separated from God through sin.* The entire crux of Christianity is knowing that we are separated from God by sin.
- *There is no text (such as the Bible) that defines one-for-all (one version/rendering fits all) doctrine and theology.* (There are numerous pastors who would love to have that debate with her.) *We can create an understanding of God and spirituality that suits our preferences.* (While many of the modern-day churches are being accused of watering down the gospel, at least they understand God does not conform to our preferences—we must conform to His commands). Oprah also believes in reincarnation. Wow! Not much can be said about one who embraces that kind of understanding regarding the message of Christ. If one thinks as Oprah, then many Christians might perceive that as lacking knowledge,

Christian knowledge, and therefore true Christianity cannot penetrate the hold Satan has upon some individuals who live in the darkness of this world. Nothing personal, but it is the beliefs of some that separate them from the beliefs of others.

Would the Hillsong Church fit into a movement of beliefs as defined by Oprah? I did not find that to be the case, but in the end, we will have to make up our own minds as to how we interpret this new movement, described by Forrest Wilder, an environmental issues writer for *The Texas Observer,* as a form of the Old Apostolic Reformation movement. He notes that it is taking place within the New Apostolic "Pentecostalism," with its emphasis on ecstatic worship and the supernatural and has given it an adrenaline shot. Wilder adds that beliefs of people associated with the movement "can tend toward the bizarre" and that it has "taken biblical literalism to an extreme."[13] Perhaps, but then who is to determine what the boundaries are that "extreme" would have to cross before it was considered extreme and not acceptable Christianity? That seems to be an area many are trying to figure out.

Anyone who has witnessed an NAR service or attended a Bethel Church, can attest that there is a vibrant Spirit present. And it is the vibrancy of the Spirit found in many of the places of worship that has come to the attention of some heavy hitters in the Conservative Christian churches. As mentioned, the movement is not without its critics, such as Todd Friel of Wretched Radio in a TV program titled, "The truth behind the world's hipster church" where he was a very outspoken critic of the Hillsong movement.

Todd Friel is not alone in his condemning of the New Apostolic Movement. As mentioned earlier, such names as David Wilkerson and Paul Washer[14] add their two cents when they say the same

---

13   https://en.m.wikipedia.org.
14   Paul Washer is a Protestant Christian evangelist with a Calvinist theology affiliated with the Southern Baptist Convention.

false spirits, known as Kundalini spirits, are spirits associated with Hinduism and other pagan religions considered doctrines of demons, are, or at least appear to be the driving force behind the New Apostolic Movement. Many signs of Kundalini include loving everybody, and people go into trance-like states of consciousness or have states of convulsions complete with shakes, spasms, and tremors. Again, that is according to David Wilkerson and Paul Washer. But for them to claim that the spirit of the church, the driving force behind the NAR, are spirits that may be demonic may be painting with too wide a brush.

One thing I learned by listening to a short documentary prepared by them, *End Time Church: The Great Falling Away II,* was that they seemed to compare the questionable theology of the prosperity preachers to the NAR movement, perhaps because of the enormous amount of money the leaders seem to be accumulating through this movement. And this is also another area of contention from the more conservative Christians, considering them as the Bible's description of those who come as false prophets, as wolves in sheep's clothing and have begun a Christianity, or perhaps a movement, defined as heretical. A Christianity that puts, at a minimum, a new spin on the very concept of Christianity.

The NAR leaders embrace the gifts of the Spirit and consider themselves a new movement embracing the Christianity of the very first church led by the apostles. In other words, the "Old" Apostolic Church—the church of the Way as described in the book of Acts. The church established by the apostles as given to them by Christ and led by the Holy Spirit—is now reopened with a renewed Spirit, and as Forrest Wilder says—with a hefty shot of adrenalin. Everyone, including NAR leaders, appear to be preaching Christ, it is just the role of the Spirit bringing forth the word that seems to be in question by the main line conservatives.

Christianity According to Hillsong

The NAR supports creationism and intelligent design by embracing the words, "in the beginning God created...." When it comes to intelligent design, think of our planet moving at the rate of 66,700 miles per hour around the sun, while at the same time spinning like a top at the rate of 1,000 miles per hour and we feel nothing. That sounds almost inconceivable. The earth makes a complete revolution every twenty-four hours, giving us both night and day.

That information is confirmed to us by the magazine *Tomorrow's World*, March-April 2019, published by the Living Church of God, when it conveys that many scientists believe that our unique moon plays a significant role in stabilizing the earth's spin on its axis. Relative to our orbit around the sun, the axis of the earth is slightly tilted, about 23.4 degrees from vertical. This tilt causes the cycle of seasons, as energy from the sun strikes the surface of the earth at different angles over the course of the planet's year-long orbit.

That is remarkable when one thinks about it. That is remarkable even if one does not think about it. In one year, we will have traveled 584 million miles from our original starting point.[15] Many ask if this was by design or by accident. Bill Maher, along with fellow atheists, believe that it was by accident. They also think we have evolved from monkeys, who evolved from some form of primitive sea life... and they laugh at us.

NAR believe one's eternal destination of either heaven or hell is determined by one's response to the Lord Jesus Christ. And they believe that Jesus Christ is coming back as He promised. Again, all good beliefs for any church, but is the spirit behind this movement from Satan or from God? Also, again, if they be for us, how then can they be against us? So, this appears to come down to motivation, and

---

[15] Information brought to us by Phil Robertson of Duck Dynasty. Eph. 33, The Glen Beck Podcast. April 20, 2019.

what is the force that drives the movement? The prosperity preachers preach Christ, but much of their motivation is money, power, and ego, with a lot of narcissism thrown in. That does not seem to be the motivation behind this new movement.

I'm not saying the criticism is not justified, especially when witnessing people slithering around the floor practically on top of one another, displaying convulsive behavior which includes, spasms, tremors, shaking, jerking, and jumping, among other various contortions that seem to accompany some who follow this movement. I believe they were used for effect, as one would have to look far and wide to encounter this spirit. Again, emotions that seem to accompany the spirits of kundalini. While several on the outside consider this demonic, most within the movement consider this an overflowing of the Spirit of God.

To many, that behavior might seem quite unorthodox, but then to judge the individual as being evil requires looking at the heart of the individual, and how does one see what is in the heart of another? Even though some of the antics seem to be totally off the wall, such as releasing golden flakes of glitter from the ceiling and claiming it to be the Spirit of God. But then, who can say what their motivation was? Again, if they be for us how can they be against us? A gathering of people seeking God, a place of praise, the knowledge of the Holy Spirit (that's an important one) and music arousing the Spirit of God to praise—what more could be asked for?

Some people consider the NAR a cult, others disagree with that assessment. While some look at the Seventh-day Adventists to be cultic, others defend the church. An individual by the name of Dr. Hoekema, who authored *The Four Major Cults,* has condemned the Seventh-day Adventists as a cult, but then, Walter Martin, who wrote in his book, *Kingdom of the Cults,* said that "anyone who believes as the Adventists do, regardless of some of their teachings, would find it hard to classify them as a cult." I cannot be the only one who might feel the same way about the New Apostolic Reformation movement.

Considering everything that has been discussed, I am grateful to David Wilkerson, John MacArthur, Todd Friel, Paul Washer, and the others who have made us aware of some of the things to look for with the NAR. I found out a lot about the NAR by listening to them, and from where I sit it appears there is a pouring out of a Spirit that seems to be gathering momentum among the new millennials who are saying loudly and clearly that "this is not your parents' Christianity." And many Hall of Fame pastors are telling us to be aware of what could be construed as warning signs, maybe even subliminally, but signs nevertheless that may be a part of this new movement. Perhaps we can say we have been warned.

CHAPTER V

CAN WE SERVE OTHER RELIGIONS…

…And still find salvation as defined by the Bible? Let me answer that by asking a question posed by Neale Donald Walsch in his book, *Conversations with God: Book 2*. The question he asked is a very intriguing one that is probably on the minds of a great many of us. He asked, "Do we really, really, *really* believe that God will not accept us into heaven if we are wonderful people who just happen to have practiced the 'wrong' religion?"

I can seriously say the answer to that question is way beyond my pay grade, but if we are going to rely on the Bible as a foundational source of information, then by the very word of God itself, the answer to the question is unequivocally yes. Would the general populous agree with that answer? Many might reply with a resounding "no." But since it comes from God himself, who many believe created everything (an omniscient, omnipotent, and omnipresent God), then I accept the answer. Will everyone? Probably not. In these last days, deception will prevail within the family of God and we should be aware of that deception.

One day while traveling between Memphis and Dallas, I heard Hank Hanegraaff, President of the Christian Research Institute, on the radio playing a tape he produced called, *"Christianity in Crisis,"* which instantly caught my attention. The tapes were about the prosperity preachers, those who constantly tell us we need to send them money to show God the faith we have. As mentioned in the introduction, in the process of sending them money, we have made many of them extremely wealthy. I mean extremely wealthy. I believe Kenneth Copeland is approaching a billion dollars in net worth. We will be discussing several of the more prominent prosperity preachers later, and when we do, we will find out if Copeland is worth close to a billion dollars.

Being unaware of the deception that existed in religion and was revealed when listening to those tapes, my first thought was to ask just how deep did false teaching and preaching run in the family of God, in the family of Christianity? I found interesting what Tim LaHaye and Ed Hindson had to say in one of their books. They said, "There are 4,200 identifiable religions honoring millions of so-called gods. As a result, our world is now flooded with an abundance of competing spiritual information, regarding who God is, who Jesus is, and what truth is. In addition, many have abandoned the concept of absolute truth altogether, thus helping to plunge our world into further deception as it approaches the close of the current era."[16]

I had heard about false teachings before. As a matter of fact, in listening to Jack Van Impe, he tells us in his book, *Sabotaging the World Church*, that there are 20,780 denominations worldwide, according to a news release in *Christianity Today*. What was interesting about the article was that many of these groups proclaim a strict allegiance to the doctrine of Christ. But, as Jack says, many do not. I thought that was a lot until I listened to a podcast produced by Don Blackwell recently titled, "How many churches exist in the world today?"

He began by asking a question: If I were to ask you exactly how many different churches exist in the world today, what would you

---

[16] Tim Lahaye and Ed Hindson, *Global Warning: Are We on the Brink of World War III?* (New York: Harvest House Publishers, 1988). Pg. 34.

say? Many would probably say "a lot, I guess" and that would be right. According to Don, he stated there are approximately 38,000 different churches currently in the world. Some have been outside of the definition of logic, such as the cults initiated by the infamous cult leader Jim Jones of the Guyana, debacle, or David Koresh of the Waco fiasco, or Marshall Applewhite of the Heavens' Gate cult, but others, perhaps not so blatant but just as dangerous, are preaching among us today, and are considered Christian by some people while being considered a cult by others. A form of Christianity that is not Christian at all.

We will be discussing the cults a little later and find out if we can serve any of them and still be considered a Christian. For now, let's discuss a couple of church families who belong to the family of God but leave some questions as to what they say they believe and the theology they embrace. The two I am referring to include the Seventh-day Adventist and the Church of Christ. Let us begin with the Seventh-day Adventist and then discuss the Church of Christ.

THE SEVENTH-DAY ADVENTISTS

I enjoyed writing this section, unlike the next section that contains some hard theology to understand. I found the Seventh-day Adventists an interesting Christian family that is solidly in the Christian camp. Some people have classified the Seventh-day Adventist organization a cult, as its roots stem from a movement that brought forth the Jehovah's Witnesses—which, as most Christians know is a cult. But as many know, the Seventh-day Adventists are good, solid Christians and the theology they teach regarding salvation, the Trinity, regeneration, (a renewed spirit—born-again) and the infallibility of Scripture appears to be beyond reproach, and that is what places them squarely in the Christian camp. And yet, some of the theology you are about to read may leave you scratching your head. And, as we know, it was not other Christians that eliminated the fourth commandment and divided the tenth commandment into two to retain the integrity of the ten. It was, as we know, the Catholic Church.

Adventists believe that others possibly are not going to heaven, as they are guilty of breaking a commandment, and according to them, and the Bible, break one and you are capable of breaking others. The Church of God also believes the same way. I believe the word "intent" would have to play a major part in this discussion. Is it breaking a commandment by having a different understanding regarding the words "remember the Sabbath and keep it holy?" Or perhaps interpreted as the Adventists seem to do with conditions, such as, "remember the Sabbath and keep it holy—by conducting services on the Sabbath, worshipping God on the Sabbath, therefore, obeying *all* of the Commandments as instructed by God. And since they are the only church obeying His commandments it will be for them that Christ will be coming.

It is unfortunate to think, that by embracing some of their thinking, they somewhat isolate themselves from other Christian families. It is hard to communicate with someone who is taught that others may not be going to heaven because they belong to a different church and worship on a different day. Therefore, the Adventist claim that other members of God's family, His universal church of believers, do not understand the Bible, or the message of Christ as they do. Keeping that in mind for just a second, am I wrong to say that we as Christians worship the same God and we are going to the same place? If that be the case, as it is, there should not be any division of the Spirit of harmony separating us.

I like how the Church of God discusses the working together of spiritual gifts, and probably just the discussing of Christianity in general. They ask, "Have you noticed that people in the church don't all think the same way?" They could be talking about those in the Church of God since each church is independent, (autonomous) but I prefer to think they are talking about the Christian family in general. I like to think the Church of God was saying that: When we become frustrated in our attempts to communicate with a fellow believer, we may begin to wonder whether something is wrong in our own spiritual beliefs. To avoid these feelings, one will sometimes just shut down any conversation, but by continuing, we might find a way to be on the same page. After all, aren't we supposed to be a "United" Body of Christ?[17]

Seventh-day Adventist leaders say that by ignoring the fourth commandment, many Protestants are missing the mark regarding the message of Christ and according to them, they may miss heaven. This teaching completely ignores the fact that someone might be a Christian, a born again, solid believing follower of Christ Christian. Someone who may have the same values and same principles and same beliefs on what makes a Christian a Christian, as they do.

Perhaps a family that observes the holiness of the Sabbath and acknowledges the fourth commandment, but which chooses to worship on the day Christ was raised from the dead. A day of new beginnings. A day that changed the world forever. In other words, adhering to the teachings of the apostle Paul, who seemed to believe any day of worship was a good day. To believe anything else, as the Adventist do, begs the question as to where this thinking came from.

The Millerite Movement

It appears that the Seventh-day Adventists' understanding regarding various doctrinal interpretations, as we have seen, may be somewhat different from that of most mainline Christian churches; but to me, that just makes them an interesting church family. Even though both, the Jehovah's Witnesses, and the Seventh-day Adventists, have roots in the same movement, each have gone their own way, although they do share a couple of similarities. These similarities stem from both having an involvement with a movement called the Millerite Movement.

---

[17] *In Touch* devotional August 2018, Vol. 41 No, 8. Published by Intouch Ministries. P.O. Box 7900, Atlanta, GA. 30357).

This movement originated in the 1840s in upstate New York, with a Baptist preacher named William Miller, who in 1833 was instrumental in perpetuating a movement known as the Great Second Advent Awakening. That movement originated from the findings of Archbishop James Ussher, the author of a 17th-century chronology of the history of the world. He calculated that the twenty-three hundred days referred to in Daniel 8:14 meant twenty-three hundred years. The Bible states that to God a day is like a thousand years (2 Peter 3:8). The Adventists use this logic to change the days to years in this scenario, while maintaining it took seven "actual days" to create the earth. That seems to be the belief of most Christians.

Armed with Archbishop Ussher's information, Miller confidently taught that there were about twenty-five years remaining until Jesus Christ would return to earth. Miller wrote, "I believe the time can be known by all who desire to understand and to be ready for His coming. And I am fully convinced that sometime between March 21, 1843 and March 21, 1844, according to the Jewish method of computation of time, Christ will come and bring all his saints with Him, and then He will reward every man as his works shall be." After much consideration, his associates set October 22, 1844, as the final date when Jesus would return, dispense judgment, and establish his kingdom upon the earth.[18]

Miller's followers waited with eager anticipation for the eventful return of the Lord Jesus Christ on that specific date. Tremendous excitement surrounded His anticipated arrival. Several wealthy landowners sold everything they had in anticipation of the glorious arrival of their Savior. Farmers refused to harvest their crops and refused to let anyone else harvest them, as they felt to store grain, corn, and potatoes for a season that would never arrive would be to tempt Providence.

Unfortunately, their joy and enthusiasm turned to overwhelming disappointment and despair when Christ did not appear as they had hoped. As one witness put it, "The day came. And Christ did not."

---

[18]   Ellen G. White. The Great Controversy...Ended.

This set the stage for October 22, 1844, to go down in Millerite history as the day of the Great Disappointment. (This is a term that to this day is found in the Adventist churches.) Joseph Bates, a close associate of Miller's, wrote a friend on the following day: "You can have no idea of the feeling that seized me.... If the earth could have opened and swallowed me up, it would have been sweetness compared to the distress I felt." Another Millerite follower, Hiram Edson, while reflecting on October 22, wrote: "Our fondest hopes and expectations were blasted, and such a spirit of weeping come over us as I never experienced before. It seemed that the loss of all earthly friends could have been no comparison. We all wept, and wept, until dawn."[19]

The Investigative Stage

What is interesting about this is that to salvage some understanding of what went wrong, they invented the theory that God, instead of coming to earth, entered another part of heaven, where he began what has been termed the "investigative judgment" stage, a unique doctrine of the Adventists. Doctrine that asserts God is preparing or completing the logistics of who is saved and who is not, and then He will return to earth,

The Adventists were encouraged by Hiram Edson (a devout Adventist and follower of Miller's), who concluded that Christ, instead of coming to cleanse the earth and set up His kingdom, passed instead into another realm of heaven to do, once again, what the Adventists call investigative judgment. It is during this investigative judgment phase (being conducted as we speak) that decisions are being made, first with reference to the dead, and second, with reference to the living.

The Adventists say, "It is our understanding that Christ as high priest concludes His intercessory ministry in heaven in a work of

---

[19]   Ibid.

Judgment. He begins his great work of judgment in the investigative phase. At the conclusion of the investigation the sentence of judgment is pronounced. Then as judge, Christ descends to execute or carry out that sentence." This doctrine, along with a dissertation by Edson and the upholding of a dissertation by Mr. Crosier (another devout Millerite), seemed to be enough to save the splintered and frail but determined group of Millerites who eventually became known as Seventh-day Adventists and was formally established in 1863 at Battle Creek, Michigan. Among its founders was Ellen G. White, whose extensive writings are still held in high regard by the church. I have read her book The Great Controversy…Ended, and found it to be an excellent book describing the time of the Catholic churches' expansion and the problems they posed to the Jews and Protestants,

Upon completion of the investigative stage, Jesus will return to earth to render judgment. But not before the world, although it might be more accurate to say, "before the Adventist are ready to receive Him," but for now let's just say until the world has become "ready to receive Him." We are introduced to this theology by Ellen G. White when she says: "Christ is waiting with longing desire for the manifestation of Himself in His church. When the character of Christ shall be perfectly reproduced in His people, then He will come and claim them as His own."

Meaning, when the days of the gentiles is complete, the family that has honored the Ten Commandments, (them) will be the church family Christ will be coming to take to heaven. That just does not sound right. That statement seems to lack the understanding of the purpose of Christ and His offer of salvation to all who will accept it. Again, forget about any Rapture. This is a viewpoint held within Adventism by some who assert, with fearsome certainly, that Jesus' Second Coming is dependent on attainment of "sinless perfection" by people within the Remnant Church in the "Last Generation."[20]

---

[20] Article written by Matthew Quarterly. Published October 15, 2020 as seen in spectrummagaine.org.

Since the investigative stage of Adventist theology belongs to them exclusively—theology that originated from a prediction of date setting that lacked credibility—some interesting theology has emerged within the Seventh-day Adventist teachings as we are witnessing. And again, much of the theology taught in the Adventist church appears to be derived from a group of disbanded Millerites from which other denominations comprising of Millerites were beginning to emerge. As we saw, the two that became most recognizable were the Jehovah's Witnesses and the Seventh-day Adventists. While both were founded on ideology and theology of individuals who, through some divine intervention, thought they could decipher the exact date Christ would return, the Adventists have since abandoned any date sitting thinking.

Due to this history of "date setting," both sects had to adjust their thinking to address their erroneous teachings of Christ returning on a specific date. The Jehovah's Witnesses stood by their erroneous theology when they said that Christ did, indeed, come and has already set up His kingdom on earth, and that the one-thousand-year millennium reign of Christ as spoken of in Revelation has already begun. But Revelation is noticeably clear that the thousand-year reign will only begin after the battle of Armageddon, at which time Satan will be bound and then, after the one-thousand-year reign, he will be set free to come against Jerusalem once again. (Revelation 20:7-10).

The theology of the Seventh-day Adventist believes in the infallibility of Scripture (Solo Scriptura) and teach that salvation comes from grace through faith in Jesus Christ.[21] Sounds like a very inviting church family. And they are. They just have some understanding of the Bible that differs from many others. It is these differences that I found interesting and would like to discuss. Are they salvation determining differences? No! Although some seem to think they are. Would they represent the beliefs of a cult? Not that I can tell. They are just differences.

---

[21]   En.m.wikipedia.org

DIFFERENT INTERPRETATIONS

It is no surprise that the Adventist embrace many differences. One of the differences that we have briefly touched upon is the belief that they are the only Christian family of believers going to heaven. Why would they think that way? What evidence do they possess that would indicate they are the only ones who have it right? Knowing the Church of Christ embraces this thinking, when I had the opportunity, I asked a member if he believed that theology. He said no. He said he thought that it would be presumptuous on anyone's part to believe that way. I have to say, I agree. Again, why do the Adventist believe they are the only church family Christ will be coming for at the exclusion of all others?

After all, didn't God say to remember the Sabbath and keep it holy? Did he not say, "If you love me you will keep my commandments?" Every Christian I have met loves God and wants to be obedient, and whether they are not keeping His commandments is conjecture, therefore chronic admonishment does not warrant the constant diatribe regarding their salvation. I believe an understanding of motive would play a big part in understanding the gulf that separates us as Christians, not from God's family, but as Christians. It appears that many read more into this divisiveness than just a different understanding regarding the commandments as the admonishment leveled towards other Christians is just too intense and not justified.

The Church of God also thinks somewhat along these lines. Why the Church of God believe as they do is somewhat interesting. They strive for the perfection they deem necessary to be saved and push hard to pull as many as possible into the ark of safety before Christ comes to establish his earthly kingdom. And that ark of safety is defined as their church. A church dedicated and determined in preparing for his return. A continuous striving for perfection with the main goal of become as close to God as possible, thus showing others the way to perfection. Remember, as Ellen G. White, one of the initial organizers of the Seventh-day Adventist church has said

"When the character of Christ shall be perfectly reproduced in His people, then He will come and claim them as His own." Remember the Adventist don't believe in a Rapture, yet they say they believe in a post tribulation Rapture. A time when Christ returns to take the Adventist family to heaven.

When thinking about what was just said, it seems to beg for some clarification as it deviates from most Protestant beliefs. The message preached by many members of the family of God is a belief in churches all over the world who are of one mind when it comes to Christ and the message of salvation. The birth, death, and resurrection of Christ, and His physical return—the message of the first Apostolic Church. That is the message of salvation, not that everyone agrees, or must agree, upon everything that many consider irrelevant. For example, when the Rapture may take place, or if we are one of the elect, or we pledge our allegiance to freewill, or if we are sprinkled or dunked, but that Christians have a heart with a true intent to follow Jesus even to the cross. That appears to be the "true" church that Jesus will be coming for, regardless of the name on the front of the Building.

The Universal Church

I mentioned a "universal church" in describing the family of God to a Church member one time and he informed me there was no such thing as "universal church" in the Bible. Of course, he was defending the churches belief that they are the true remnant church at the exclusion of all others. I found the church to be split on accepting this exclusivity. And, yes, he is right, the word "universal" is not in the Bible, however, the overall essence of the Bible and the message of Christ seems to put us all in one church with one common denominator and that is our reverence of Christ. The man of course was right, the word "universal" is not in the Bible but it was the best descriptive word I could think of to describe the family of born-again believers who are following God in every Spirit filled church around the world.

Most of the Christian world I have had the opportunity to visit embrace a "World Universal Evangelical Church" consisting of many denominations who have committed themselves to accepting Christ as the Son of God and follow him with the best of their ability. To believe otherwise might be just too restrictive. It appears to be this universal church (world church of born-again believers) that Christ will be redeeming rather than any one specific denomination, or any one church family, as that thinking appears to be just all too inclusive.

I believe most Christians would agree that any church, regardless of the sign on the front of the building harboring a belief in Christ as the Son of God and an acceptance of Him as Lord and savior is a member of the body of Christ. A church, a family of individual believers who say as the Apostle Thomas said upon realizing the person he was standing in front of was Jesus. The moment he recognized who was standing in front of him, he dropping to his knees proclaiming, "My Lord and my God." Upon that conviction, Christ tells us we will be saved. We now belong to the universal church family of evangelical believers, the family that many reformers gave their life to defend. And, as we know, many early Christians, some we will discuss later, chose to be devoured by lions rather than denouncing their faith, all so that we may know the truth.

Many families have idiosyncrasies with many nuances, some even having enough to warrant a discussion. And one of the church families belonging to the universal church family that qualifies for a serious discussion is the Seventh-day Adventist. They have so many nuances within their beliefs, it may take a minute or two to go through them trying to understand what effect those nuances have on their thinking which may give us a better understanding as to how they view various issues. There appear to be four beliefs that differ from the theology taught by most of the other families. It seems to be these beliefs that add to the widening of the gulf that exists between the various families. Are they salvation-determining beliefs? No. Would they constitute a cult? No. They just have perceived various aspects of the Bible a little differently than others. That seems to be what this is about, some of those different understandings.

They are simply different opinions of certain information that one might find when attending an Adventist church. Two of these four doctrines are particularly interesting, so we will analyze them more closely than the first two. They are: (1) they do not believe in an eternal hell, but then, as we've seen, they are not alone in this belief. A belief referred to as Annihilationism; (2) they do not believe in a Rapture (again, they are not alone regarding this belief); (3) they do not believe the soul can exist apart from the body, for, as they contend, the human is one unit; and (4) they do not believe Christ establishes a literal 1,000 year reign on earth as defined in Revelation Chapter 20. But again, they are not alone in their way of thinking. We will discuss the meaning of post, pre, and amillennialism later in this book and you will see the different understanding of the thousand-year reign embraced by the various families.

THE ADVENTIST AND CONTROVERSY

Of their more controversial beliefs, including the issue of the body and soul remaining in the grave until the return of Christ and how their belief regarding the 1,000-year reign of Christ differs from many other Christians, we are going to discuss other idiosyncrasy of the Adventist that some claim puts them in cult land. The first of the divisions that exist between other families and the Adventists, is the Adventist rejection of humans (spirit, soul, and body) being separated at death. They say the deceased will remain in the grave until the return of Christ and then, the entire body, including the spirit and soul, will be raised to be taken to heaven to spend eternity with Christ. Total abstract to any main line doctrine preached in other Christian churches.

Many church families believe the spirit and soul, (spirit being the spiritual body, and soul being the conscious part of that body) departs the body, leaving the physical body in the grave to return to dust, while the spiritual part ascends into a heavenly realm of heaven, some refer to this heavenly realm as an interim heaven. Some Christians, including Dr. Jeremiah refer to this interim heaven as "Paradise." It will be from Paradise that at the time of the Rapture, (some think otherwise as we will see) we may all, at one time, as the family of overcomers, enter heaven where we will spend the next seven years receiving our rewards and enjoying ourselves. Afterall, did not Christ say when He comes to receive his church, He would be bringing our rewards? (More on this later as it is quite interesting). And to think, all those like Bill Mahar and Ron Reagan, the late George Carlin along with hordes of others will not be in that family but will forever be separated from it and all the fun and excitement that awaits all believers. Such a loss for a moment of a frivolous life.

While the Adventist will be in heaven along with the other Christians, it appears the Adventist, as we have seen, disavow Rapture theology. They seem to get their authority to believe that way based upon 1Thessalonians 4:13-18 NIV. With that in mind it might be interesting to take a moment and discuss those verses. Verse 13. "Brothers and sisters, we do not want you to be uninformed about those who sleep in death, so that you do not grieve like the rest of mankind, who have no hope." It appears what Paul is saying is that for the believers not to worry as do the unbelievers because, as Paul says, "they have no hope." Paul continues, "For we believe that Jesus died and rose again, and so we believe that God will bring with Jesus those who have fallen asleep in him." Who are they that have fallen asleep and will be accompanying Jesus? Those who have died trusting in Christ. They are those who Christ took to heaven at the Rapture. What was just said can only occur at the Second Coming as the Adventist claim. That one verse, verse 14 is the only verse among those verses that pertains to the Second Coming. As for the rest, they apply only to the Rapture.

The "Restrainer" and the Adventist

Another difference between main line Protestants and the Adventist is when the Adventist contend that all people, including themselves, will have to endure the woes of tribulation including, the wrath of the Great Tribulation. Punishment from the wrath of God—vengeful, merciless punishment. Punishment that has been exclusively prepared for those who have rejected the Holy Spirit, thus rejecting Christ as they drool over the spirit of the antichrist. Punishment so severe that most pre-tribers and mid-tribers say we will avoid as we will be Raptured during one of those times.

Remember, a time will come when the "restrainer" considered to be the Holy Spirit will be removed, and when that day occurs, Christians, born again Christians, indwelled with the Spirit of God, as are the Adventist, will be included in the family that is taken to heaven. The criteria for being included in the Rapture is to be born-again by receiving Jesus Christ as the Son of God, and to remain in the family by faith. Two criteria's for being included in the Rapture.

I know the Adventist reject Rapture theology, but they must go, or God is not true to His word. God said He would never leave us nor forsake us and that is exactly what He would be doing by leaving the Adventist behind once the Holy Spirit is removed. I had this discussion with an Adventist pastor one time and his response was quite interesting. I mentioned what I thought about them being included in the Rapture and instantly he started defending against the notion. You would have thought he was ready to pull out some crosses, saying "Be gone, be gone, spirit of deception." His main argument was: "How could some event they didn't believe in be possible?" And I am sure all the ramifications of such theology somewhat confused his mind.

Not believing in a Rapture does not change whether a Rapture occurs prior to the Great Tribulation. And thinking they will not be included is irrelevant. That is man-made theology. Personally, I must believe that most Adventist Christians would be happy to hear it is the logic of the Bible that dictates their status as a Christian. Again, according to the Bible, they must be included in the Rapture and be excluded from the "Great Tribulation," Contrary to what they believe. At least that is the thinking of most born again Christians I have talked with.

Considering the Adventist being left behind as they tend to believe, and with the Holy Spirit, the restrainer removed from the world, that would leave them vulnerable to face some horrific times without the Spirit of God. If that is the situation as they say, then, would that not be leaving them to the sadistic whims of Satan? The "woes of judgments" unleashed upon the world in the form of the bowls/vials as described in the last of the judgments revealed in Revelation.

Does anyone believe that will happen? Does anyone believe God would remove his Spirit, his protection, thus leaving his loved ones to endure the full force of Satan's wrath without the Spirit of God holding him back? Wrath that has been prepared for those unbelievers who have rejected Christ and the God who sent Him. Most Christians would say they have a problem with this thinking as that is hard theology to accept.

The Identify of the Restrainer

There are more areas of theology embraced by the Adventist that many find interesting enough to question, but first, I would like to address who the "restrainer" might be. Having an understanding as to the identity of the "restrainer" I wrote to someone I consider a mentor to find out what they might say. I wrote to Dr. Mark Hitchcock for his understanding as to the identity of the "restrainer" as I had come upon several different possibilities. The response from Mark included the following information that I found interesting. He said that down through the centuries many theories as to the identity of the "restrainer" have emerged. I am grateful he sent a list of them. I found as I was going through the list I was saying yes, no, maybe, etc. See what you think:

- **The Roman Empire.** I cannot see the Roman Empire restraining anything.
- **The Jewish State.** Could be as they are restraining a lot of evil, but nowhere in the Bible does it say the State of Israel will leave the earth. As a matter of fact, it is to Israel that Christ will be coming.
- **The Apostle Paul.** No! It was not his calling.
- **The preaching of the gospel.** In the last days, this will be grounds for persecution and eventually the essence of true Christianity will be silenced if not entirely removed from visibility.
- **Human government.** No! Corrupt will not restrain corrupt.
- **Satan.** No! Evil will not restrain evil.
- **Elijah.** No! It also was not his calling.
- **Some unknown heavenly being.** Could be, but the mystery of the restrainer can be known.
- **Michael the archangel.** Could be. But Michael's absentness from the world would not appear to have the impact as more viable options.
- **The Holy Spirit.** Yes. As we have seen, when the Holy Spirit is taken away, the world will be thrown into total Spiritual darkness.
- **The Church.** Yes and no. The Rapture of the family of God (the body of Christ) will remove the "Church," while the Spirit of the Church will continue to be persecuted, and many withstanding the Great Tribulation will be martyred as they were in the days of the mighty Emperors.

As we continue. In Christian eschatology, there are those who believe in post-tribulation Rapture doctrine, such as the Adventist. A belief in a combined resurrection and Rapture of all believers and comes after the Great Tribulation. To the Adventist, when Christ comes, he comes to take those Christians who have obeyed the Ten Commandments back to heaven, which according to their teaching is them. He does not come to earth to establish His kingdom for the 1,000-year reign as premillennialist teach, but to take the Adventist to heaven where they will receive their rewards for, as they say, being the only "true" church, His family. A family that has obeyed His instructions of obeying His commandments, especially the fourth. Again, does that not sound like the "universal" Church Christ died to bring to the world?

There was mention of a 1,000-year reign of Christ as discussed in Chapter 20 of Revelation. Again, the view in Christian eschatology is that some reject the theology that Jesus Christ will physically reign on the earth for 1,000 years and the Adventist are some who believe that way. The Adventist even continue the conversation by saying the reign of Christ will not be on this earth as that information is not what the Bible imparts. This will be discussed more in coming Chapters. Although, we haven't discussed millennialism yet, if we had to pick one that closely resembles the theology the Adventist embrace, it would have to be postmillennialism with perhaps a little amillennialism to go with it, as we will discuss later. A teaching that holds to the beliefs that there will be no millennial reign of the righteous on earth, and that the 1,000 years as discussed in Revelation is occurring currently as some teach or is just symbolic as taught by others.

Another view the Adventist have that differs from other families has to do with the raging fires of hell and who will be sent there and for how long. They say the fires of hell will eventually burn out, but the Bible uses the word "forever" to describe the fate of Satan, the antichrist, the false prophet, and those who take the mark of the beast. Without changing, deleting, or adding to scripture, the word forever is used. We will discuss this more when we discuss those who are going to be going into those fires, as well as how long they may be there when we discuss "Life after death."

It is obvious from the teachings of the Adventist they seem to have taken a different route to heaven than most which again is obvious by their teachings. They are Christians, born again Christians who believe we are ushered into heaven directly from the grave differing from those who believe Christians will be ushered into heaven from Paradise immediately after the sounding of the trumpets and just prior to the seven years of the Great Tribulation. Or will they? Will they be ushered into heaven then or will they have already been ushered into heaven? This is a subject that will be discussed in depth later as you might find it as interesting as I have.

I am thinking much of the theology embraced by the Adventist is the result of some decisions made in the beginning when they regrouped after the great disappointment. Perhaps it was the theology that emerged from a new beginning in 1844 that produced some very debatable theology that appears too many to be very questionable. But they also emerged as a born-again Christian family, that embrace the principles of salvation as solidly as any other family.

The Sabbath Controversy

Although the Adventists cannot condone the belief of an eternal hell or accept the idea of the soul and body being separated upon death, they are absolutely correct when they say the Sabbath day is Saturday. This is an undisputable biblical truth. Nowhere in the Bible is there any indication that the Sabbath day was ever changed from the Jewish Sabbath of Saturday to Sunday, the day of pagan worship—or put another way, from the Jewish "seventh-day" Sabbath to the Christians' "first day" observance in honor of the resurrection of Christ.

The Adventists hold tight to the conviction that Christianity became tainted when Catholicism took over and changed the day of worship to accommodate pagans. (Changing times and laws). The Adventist may not be far off when they mentioned how the apostolic faith got tainted with bad blood (bad theology) when the secularism of the philosophers began showing up as doctrine and confirmed as truths. Especially confirmed as truths by the Catholic leaders when it was apparent, they were changing the intent of the Bible in some areas. Theological understandings that have become known as dogma. (And not the good dogma). Theology that reflected their understanding of the writings as found in the Bible, and it was from the introduction of these interpretations and understandings that the truths begin to wane from the Apostolic Church to a new movement called Catholicism.

It all originated from the time the Catholic Church said, "By worshipping on Sunday, Protestants are paying homage, in spite of themselves, to the authority of the (Catholic) Church." *Ouch!!!* I cannot be the only Protestant who is saying ouch! Many Protestants might take offense to that statement, just as the Adventists, but that should not elicit the division of separation towards other Christian families as one will hear from time to time when attending an Adventist church, especially when the guests who might be attending are born again Christians just as the leaders within the Adventist church who preach this doctrine.

It is a proven fact among those who follow the Apostolic Church of the first century, Sunday represents a pagan day of worship. By worshiping on that day, the Adventists believe other Christians are honoring the Catholic Church even though we know that is not true. All Christians outside of the Seventh-day Adventist agree with them regarding the holiness of both Saturday and Sunday, the Adventist just place more importance upon the day for showing God how faithful we are to His commandments. The Adventist are a great church family that perhaps just needs to be accepted more by other Christians, but that is a two-way street. The Adventist blame other Christians of forsaken Christ in favor of the Catholic church by worshiping on Sunday rather than Saturday, the day God rested, but that thinking could be considered judgmental. We know some Christians consider it to be a form of legalism.

Fact's About Sunday Worship

As we have seen biblical scholars of all denominations have attested that it was the Catholic Church that made the decision to change the day of worship, rather than this being a mandate from God. For example, Dr. Edward T. Hiscox, author of *The Baptist Manual,* writes, "There was and is a commandment to keep holy the Sabbath day, but that Sabbath day was not Sunday... It will be said however, and with some show of triumph, that the Sabbath was transferred from the seventh to the first day of the week." He continues, "Of course, I quite well know that Sunday did come into use in early Christian history as a religious day, as we learn from the Christian Fathers and other sources. But what a pity that it came branded with the mark of paganism, and christened with the name of the sun god, when adopted and sanctioned by the papal apostasy."

It was during the merging of Christianity and the secularism of paganism that began at the end of the first century that decisions regarding the day of worship began to emerge, along with the evolution of many other beliefs, but this is the one the Adventist seem to have the most problem with. While the final decision to change the day of worship was solidified by the Emperor Constantine, it was converted pagan gentiles, along with organized religious leaders of the papacy, who put in place the necessary paperwork to conduct church services on Sunday, rather than Saturday. Again, changing times and laws to coincide with the worship of the sun god as was being observed by the pagans of the day.

To the leaders of the Catholic Church, they saw it was a way to entice pagans, both Romans and Greeks, to join the church and of those joining, many were responsible for bringing forth the interpreted word of God. Forget about being born from above as says John MacArthur and endorsed theology by most Christians. Forget the spiritual indwelling of the Holy Spirit as the one who reveals God to us as they substitute the Catholic Church and the Sacraments as the way to receive Jesus, reveal God, and receive salvation. It appears to many that the omission of the Spirit during the evolution of Catholicism is one reason so much depravity seems to occur within the Catholic Church. But then Protestants do not exactly have clean hands in this area themselves. Nothing to do with the subject at hand but as I am typing this, I am thinking of how Catholics receive Christ via a wafer because a man, St Augustine, said that is how it is done. Upon hearing that, I just must shake my head as do perhaps most Protestants.

While the Catholic Church was in the process of advancing and promoting their theology, again, at any cost, the Protestant Church was always present, they were underground and staying out of sight because of the persecution, but they were always there and when the time was right God brought forth Martin Luther and the reformers. It was, and is, the beliefs of the Protestant Church that maintains a continuity of the "thread of redemption" that one can find in the Bible beginning with Adam and ending with the birth of Christ. That thread is missing from the Catholic Church as they put deity in the form of the pope and the Sacraments in the way.

While we know the Catholic Church began conducting services on Sunday, other Christians, those associated with the Apostolic Church, continued to meet on Saturday until 336, when they succumbed to this edict and began conducting services on Sunday. Thus, breaking the Jewish tradition of meeting on Saturday. To this day, the Adventists, along with the Church of God, have a problem forgiving those who followed the edict, which was basically an edict put into place by the Catholic Church to acquire more fame, prestige, and membership, which gave them money, which in turn gave them power, position, and prestige. All that was necessary to build a great organization as the Catholic Church has become. Clovis G. Chappell in *Ten Rules for Living* gives us some insight into how and why the transfer of authority came about:

The reason we observe the first day instead of the seventh is based on no positive command. One will search the Scripture in vain for authority for changing from the seventh day to the first.

The early Christians began to worship on the first day of the week because Jesus rose from the dead on that day. By and by, this day of worship was made also a day of rest, a legal holiday. This took place in the year 321. Our Christian Sabbath therefore is not a matter of positive command. It is a gift of the church."

> That sounds strange—a gift of the church. If you are Catholic, that is true. As discussed, it was basically the bishops of the Catholic Church who were responsible for having the day of worship changed from Saturday to Sunday. Peter Geiermann tells us in *The Convert's Catechism of Catholic Doctrine* (1910): "We observe Sunday instead of Saturday because the Catholic Church in the Council of Laodicea in the year 336 AD transferred the solemnity from Saturday to Sunday." It was at this time many followers of the Apostolic Church (the church family of Acts) submitted to this decree. If you want to know about the church, or council of Laodicea, go to the churches in Revelation and see what God thought of that church.

It was the Sabbatical Edict of Emperor Constantine that ordained the earliest recognition of the observance of Sunday as a day of worship in 321 and set the stage for the change. This change was at the persuasion of the Catholic Church, which inspired by ambition and the aspiration for new converts, felt that if Sunday (which up to that time had been a pagan holiday set aside to worship the sun god) were observed as the Sabbath, it would advance the power and glory of the church. So therefore, Saturday, the Sabbath day; and Sunday, the day on which pagans worshipped the sun god, were combined in 336, again the changing of times and laws. A move the Adventist abhor. But it does sit the stage for the next conversation.

Is Sunday Worship Wrong?

Although the Adventists observe Saturday (the Jewish Sabbath) as the day set aside to keep holy and admonish those who don't, those who are, according to the Adventist, breaking a Commandment, are they wrong? Only in terms of the admonishing part—the other is just what they believe. (As mentioned earlier, the church of God also follows this line of reasoning, only without the constant admonishing.) For the rest of us, we are pointed in the direction of the apostle Paul's teachings in the book of Romans where he said, "Who are you to judge someone else's servant? To his own master (God) he stands or falls. And he will stand, for the Lord is able to make him stand" (Rom. 14:4 NIV). That verse goes along with the words of Jesus that should leave no doubt about how He feels regarding the Sabbath—as holy as it is—He said, "The Sabbath was made for man, not man for the Sabbath." (Mark 2:27 NIV). He is Lord on any day and in the mist of all who gather to worship Him. Who would deny that? And He said He will judge what anyone does on that day. Nobody else, including the Adventist has that authority.

Besides, the root of what is called Sabbatarianism, originated among early Adventist by Joseph Bates. Remember him from the Millerite movement? He was the foremost proponent of Sabbath keeping among early Adventists. Bates was introduced to the Sabbath doctrine through a tract written by Millerite preacher Thomas M, Preble, who had been influenced by a young Seventh-day Baptist. This theology of Saturday worship was gradually accepted by the Fathers of the church and has remained a stable of the Adventist thinking ever since.

The Bible seems to tell us to remember the Sabbath and keep it holy. To most Protestants worshipping on either Saturday or Sunday, or both, is a good thing. How can even the Adventist reject that thinking? It is as if Saturday is God's day—the Old Testament embraces Saturday as God's day. The Jews then, as well as now, observe the Sabbath, God's day as did Christ when he was with us. On the other hand, most evangelical Christians understand the holiness of the Sabbath while considering Sunday as Christ's day and considered a day when He can be praised and worshipped just for being Christ and doing what He did to bring us salvation. While remembering God as the one who created everything and made salvation possible through His Son. This is how John MacArthur puts it when he says "Saturday is a day to enjoy the creation. Saturday is a perpetual witness to God as Creator. Sunday on the other hand is a perpetual witness to God as redeemer." That was very well put as most evangelical Christians woul probably agree with that assessment.

Sunday is the day a Protestant worships all that Christ did and the price he paid to bring us the opportunity to have everlasting life. How do you thank someone, anyone, for doing that? Probably from the heart with compassion and empathy. Christians also receive communion, usually on Sunday as a moment to thank Christ for all that He endured to make salvation possible. From being spat upon, beaten to a pulp, joshed around in jest by fools who were without any compassion or empathy and then died in excruciating pain on a wooden cross. And he did all of that, endured all of that, to introduce us to God his Father by reconciling us, through the cross, to the Father—and salvation comes with that knowledge. And Jesus was as much a human as we are with all the feelings that come with being a human.

Regarding Saturday as the right day to observe Christ as opposed to Sunday worship, if one wanted to get technical, they could refer to the time Jesus confronted the Pharisees who were exercising complete control over the Mosaic Law. Jesus used the stranglehold the Pharisees had on observing the Sabbath as an example of legalism. His message regarding the Sabbath said that people could now decide for themselves if what they were doing on that day was good or bad. By so declaring, he took the "judgment" of those who were, or were not, guilty of breaking the law out of the hands of the Pharisees and put it between themselves and God, a move the Pharisees did not like.

Again, the reason the veil in the temple split was to demonstrate that we now have direct access to God without the necessity of putting someone, anyone, between us and God. While the ripping of the veil gave us access to the throne of God the veil splitting had far greater ramifications than just allowing us to have a relationship of a more personal nature with God; it also gave us permission to go directly to Him as the Father, or to Christ his Son, and no one else, to ask forgiveness for wrongdoing. The days of Moses where the Levite Priests (middlemen) made atonement for the sins of Israel were over, and a new era of knowing God with the ability to have a relationship with Him was about to begin, called Christianity.

Without question, the day of worship seems to be an important issue to the Seventh-day Adventist, but to severely admonish other Christians of Christ-based churches as they do, seems to be unjustified, unwarranted, and to a degree, not nice. I do not doubt the holiness of the day, and I do not know any Christian who does. But I do not think God will preclude anyone from eternal life if they are His followers. I even seriously doubt He will take anyone to the woodshed for worshipping him on Sunday, rather than Saturday. If he did, he would have to take the apostle Paul to the same woodshed, as Acts 20:7 reveals that Paul spoke until midnight on the first day of the week, when the disciples came together to break bread and see Paul off on another journey (Act 20:7, NIV). To the apostle Paul it did not seem to matter which day one worshipped, just that they did.

Does not the Bible say where two or more are gathered in my name, I will be there? I am assuming he is talking about two or more coming together to learn, to worship, to praise, and even discuss his word, as those who meet on either day seem to do. Christ and Christ alone would have to be the one telling me I have been excluded from the book of life and thus rejected from eternal life by worshiping on a day other than Saturday. And that seems to be what this discussion is about. If not for conducting services on Sunday, apparently no

Commandment would be broken. But they say one is. And because of that, we are excluded from the book of life.

If that be the case, I, as well as every other born-again believer who is not an Adventist might expect to receive an explanation as to why their name is excluded from God's book, and to their surprise, they hear this explanation; "You worshiped on Sunday therefore you broke one of my commandments for which I am sentencing you to spend eternity in burning sulfur." Since the Adventist do not believe in an eternal hell, they would probably say something like, "You are sentenced to spend eternity separated from God." That is hard teachings to accept. Not the church family of Seventh-day Adventist, just some of their teaching.

The acts of disobediences as one journeys through this life can be removed by approaching God and asking him to remove them and coming from the right heart, He will. But how do I or anyone approach God and apologize for worshiping him on Sunday, the day that some perceive as belonging to the sun god. How can I even begin the conversation of apologizing to him for worshiping him on Sunday rather than Saturday? And if anyone is "breaking" a Commandment, God has the power of convection through the Holy Spirit to rectify that situation.

As a Christian among other Christians, we honor Saturday as a special day, the day God finished creation and rested. A day He blessed and considers a special day and has asked us not to forget that. If one gets separated from God, it will be for reasons other than worshipping on Sunday as opposed to Saturday, or any other day for that matter. I am going to have to disagree with the Adventist as to the day we worship. Another area of differences between a couple of churches and the Seventh-day Adventists would converge around the gifts of the Holy Spirit, namely of the gift of speaking in tongues. Not the gift of tongues per se, but who receives that gift in relation to the other gifts of the Spirit.

THE GIFT OF TONGUES

The gift of speaking in tongues is a spiritual gift. It means speaking with words or in a language one does not know or understand to edify both oneself and others as brought to us by Steve Lenk.[22] Jesus foretold of speaking in tongues: *"and these signs shall follow them that believe; In my name they will drive out demons; they will speak in new tongues"* (Mark 16:17 NIV. Emphasis mine). The first recorded time anybody spoke in tongues was on the day of Pentecost, when the Holy Spirit was poured out on the apostles, as related in Acts 2:1-12. The apostles spoke the gospel to the crowds in Jerusalem, and what they said could be understood by people speaking many different languages: "…When they heard this sound, a crowd came together in bewilderment because each one heard them speaking in his own language. (Acts 2:6 NIV).

Then Acts 2:11 says…*we hear them declaring the wonders of god in their own tongues!"* (Acts 2:11 NIV. Emphasis mine). Then they add, Parthians, Medes, and Elamites; residents of Mesopotamia, Judea and Cappadocia, Pontus, Asia and several more were hearing the word of God in their own language followed by the question, how can that be? The Gideons International Version Bible puts it this way, "Cretes and Arabians, we do hear them speak in our tongues the wonderful works of God." But again, how is this possible? Keep the word "gibberish" in mind as you will hear that word again shortly.

The gift of speaking in tongues was one of many gifts given to believers to aid in the edifying or building up of the body of Christ, which many say is the universal church[23] of believers. Yet, there appears to be a degree of disagreement regarding the understanding of this gift. Not the gift of tongues as the gift of tongues is one of the gifts given by the Holy Spirit as outlined in the book of Acts, and contrary to what the Church of Christ says, they are still applicable

---

22   https://actrivechristianity.org.
23   Ibid

today as they were 2,000 years ago. The confusion seems to be around who receives the different gifts of the Spirit, including the gift of tongues, and for what purpose.

If I may, for a moment, I would like to discuss perhaps the biggest wedge between two evangelical church families over a single issue of understanding: namely, the Assemblies of God and the Seventh-day Adventists. That wedge is the gift of tongues. I have listened to both, the Assemblies of God as well as the Seventh-day Adventist and respect both their views on the subject, and again, this has nothing to do with salvation. The Assemblies of God believe the Holy Spirit is *evidenced* by speaking in "tongues"—as they put it, "a heavenly language." (Same with the Church of God). Now put that in contrast with the Seventh-day Adventists, or more specifically, Doug Batchelor. According to Doug, he conveys the message that speaking in tongues (as one might encounter in some Pentecostal Protestant families) may be a deception of Satan that has infiltrated the body of Christ.

According to Batchelor, speaking in tongues is speaking in a language that is unfamiliar to us, and yet the person for which the message was intended can understand the message with clarity. Doug points to the day of Pentecost as an example of what he means. A day when the apostles spoke in different languages, which they did not understand, but the visiting foreigners who were present understood very well what was being conveyed. They even said amongst themselves; "How can this be?" According to Doug, speaking in "tongues" is not gibberish that one might hear when attending some churches. OMG. "Gibberish." It may be just me, but I think he just stepped on some toes with that one.

Just think about what Doug is saying. If someone would be talking to us in Portuguese and we had never heard Portuguese before, it would probably sound like gibberish. Personally, I do not know which is true; but, once on a trip to Mexico, I attended a small Christian group for a worship session and a young woman spoke in tongues and several of the words I heard her utter were the same as my mother's when she prayed. I do not know who the words might have been intended for, but they were very gratifying to me. Very comforting to hear, so far from home.

While speaking or praying in the language of tongues as evidenced by the infilling or indwelling of the Holy Spirit, I had more than one pastor tell me that is not the same as the gift of tongues, which is only given to some, but is available to all. The gift of tongues is a message from God to a group of Christians, usually in a church setting, and should be interpreted for all to benefit. Praying in tongues, on the other hand, is available to all Christian believers as prayer from us to God, thus considered by many to be a "prayer language." Just keep in mind 1 Corinthians chapter 12, especially verses 1-11, that conveys to us the various gifts of the Spirit are given to individuals to edify the church. And it seems to indicate not everyone is necessarily given the same gift.

The Reemergence of Tongues

Much of the fervor surrounding the gift of tongues was driven by revival meetings held by the Holiness movement where there were occasional reports of people speaking in a strange language. The first relatively modern and widespread use of tongues started at a revival in Topeka, Kansas, in January of 1900. There was an outpouring of the Spirit some have equated with the outpouring of the Holy Spirit on the day of Pentecost. The day the Spirit came down as tongues of fire with the sound of a rushing mighty wind. An obvious outpouring of the Holy Spirit that, to a degree, revolutionized the Pentecostal movement and launched a spiritual awaking of the gifts of the Spirit, especially the gift of tongues.

A band of believers led by Charles Parham[24] who started Bethel Bible School (not the same Bethel church as we discussed earlier)

---

[24] He believed that speaking in tongues was the sign of receiving the baptism in the Holy Spirit.

assembled to worship and from that assembly the gift of tongues was encountered as an outpouring of the Holy Spirit. That moment initiated a Charismatic revolution that began sweeping across the country among Christian groups and speaking in tongues accompanied it.

The outpouring of the Holy Spirit was so great that it quickly spread across the Christian community and became the first Pentecostal movement that conservatism Christianity took notice of. A great revival with a tremendous outpouring of the Spirit that was enhanced by the gift of tongues. Since Parham had roots in the Methodist church, many think the movement that began in Topeka was a Methodist movement, joining with the Pentecostal Church and from this association the Assemblies of God church became a household name. A previous outpouring of the Spirit began with John and Charles Wesley when they encountered the Spirit of God that was so strong it eventually started a movement called "Methodist." The Methodist family of Christians do not seem to embrace the theology that the indwelling of the Holy Spirit is evidenced by speaking in tongues, but they do recognize the gift of tongues.

Then in 1906, there was another spiritual awakening that many might say mirrors the NAR movement—an awakening known as the Azusa Street Revival, founded by William J. Seymour.[25] This awakening was a Spirit-filled movement that according to the *Los Angeles Times* was a bizarre new religious sect started in Los Angles by people "breathing strange utterances and mouthing a creed which it would seem no sane mortal could understand." Furthermore, "Devotees of the weird doctrine practice the most fanatical rites, preach the wildest theories, and work themselves into a state of mad excitement."[26]

---

[25] William J. Seymour was a student of early Pentecostal minister Charles Parham, (1873-1927), considered the godfather of Pentecostalism. Both were instrumental in the Topeka Kansas revival movement. They believed that speaking in tongues was the sign of receiving the baptism in the Holy Spirit.

[26] https//newsag.org.

Some of you I'm sure, have been in churches where you have heard people speak in tongues, (not intrusively) but talking to God and praising Him, maybe even with lifted hands, as if no one else was in the room, worshipping Him in the Spirit, as some would say. I'm describing a United Methodist church I attended for about a year that had a movement of the spirit that is rarely encountered. It was obvious an anointing spirit was present. A rare occurrence, especially in today's times. Then on the flip side of that, there are churches where an outburst of "tongues" would occur without the Spirit of God anywhere in sight and no one present to interpret them. Interpretation of tongues, another gift of the Spirit. Also, I have been in churches where they try to induce the Spirit through music or noise, but it is not the same.

There are three places in the Bible from where church families could justify evidence of speaking in tongues is conclusive prove of receiving the Holy Spirit. And those three are: (1) Acts 2:2-4, "...They were all filled with the Holy Spirit and began to speak in other tongues as the Spirit gave the utterance." (2) Acts 10:44-46, "...because the gift of the Holy Spirit had been poured out even on the Gentiles. For they heard them speaking in tongues and extolling God." (3) Acts 19:6, "...And when Paul had laid his hands upon them the Holy Spirit came on them; and they spoke with tongues and prophesied."

Different Gifts of Edification

One other instance occurred when the apostles went to Samaria and laid their hands on some believers so that they would receive the Holy Spirit, but tongues is not mentioned in that instance. Based upon information directly from the Bible, one could assume there is a connection between speaking in tongues and receiving the Holy Spirit, but then when one studies 1 Corinthians chapter 12, especially verses 7-11, they find different gifts are given to different individuals to edify the church. Or as verse seven says, "Now to each one the manifestation of spirit is given for the common good." And then verses 8-11 concludes by listing the different gifts given to different individuals "for the common good" of the church, as well as to edify the members of the body of Christ.

It appears many conservative church families, especially the Baptist are accepting of the method of distribution of the gifts as stated in Romans 12, especially verses 4-8 as being applicable today to form the one body of Christ. Probably the best description of the body of Christ is described in verses 4-5 which reads as follows, "Just as each of us has one body with many members, and these members do not all have the same function, so in Christ we who are many form one body, and each member belongs to all the others. Then verse six is perhaps the most controversial when it says, "We, (as the one body of Christ) have different gifts, according to the grace given us.

Since the gift of tongues is a more personal gift to edify the person more than the church, it is not mentioned as a gift that edifies the church as some of the others, mentioned in Chapter 12 of Romans, such as the gift of prophesying or the gift of serving or teaching, or preaching and many others. One can hear the gift of tongues in churches from time to time, but the Bible says, there will be someone with the gift of interpretation present when this occurs. Just one more thing regarding the gift of tongues, and that is the importance of the gift as a means of edifying the church. When it comes to the various gifts, 1 Corinthians 12:5 NIV implies the gift of prophesy is greater than the gift of tongues. It is said the gift of tongues is the least of the gift, but does it really matter?

The gift of tongues seems to be evidenced more in the traditional charismatic churches, with some of the more conservative churches at least acknowledging this gift. For example, the Southern Baptists. It is said they generally do not seek the gift of tongues, but then a recent *LifeWay Study* reported that half of SBC pastors believe that

God gives some Christians a private prayer language.[27] Assuming the gift of tongues is evidence of the indwelling of the Holy Spirit, at best, this would be conjecture as no one really knows for sure. Some even denounce this gift, but why would anyone not desire everything God offers, including the gift of tongues?

It seems one will encounter the spiritual gift in the more independent churches as they are more liberal in their worship. Most of the time, they are independent for the freedom of worship. The only exception within the many denominational churches I saw was when I attended that United Methodist Church mentioned earlier. If the Methodist could only capture the essence of that church, we would hear another explosion on the same order as the outpouring of the Holy Spirit during the earlier revivals discussed a minute age. A movement of the Spirit that respected the reverence of worship.

I must tell you, when those lights dimmed, and the music set the mood and people were asked to come forth and knell at the altar, if only to thank God for what he was doing in their lives, or they just feel the need to pray for a moment at the alter while the pastor unobtrusively prayed over prayer request, I tell you the movement upon the people, including me, was overwhelming. I got caught up in the Spirit where I shed tears and raised my hands when I could no longer contain the emotions that overwhelmed me. Many preachers say that is the greatest feeling in the world.

Getting back to the gift of tongues, I just had a thought. If those who think the Holy Spirit dwells only in Christians who speak in tongues, as tongues being an indicator of the Holy Spirit, then that would mean every Christian who has not been given the gift of tongues but perhaps another gift or two would not be going to heaven as they would lack the filling of the Holy Spirit. That is true, just think about that. If only those who speak in tongues have the Holy Spirit, as evidenced by the gift of tongues, then when the Holy Spirit (the restrainer) is removed, then those Christians who

---

[27]   https://www.namb.net

do not have the gift of tongues will be left behind at the time of the Rapture. That was just a flash thought I had and wrote it for consideration more than anything else.

But there is logic in what was just said if one thinks about it. Somewhat on the same order as when the Adventist say those who do not keep the Ten Commandments as evidenced by their theology, will be left behind. Or the Church of Christ that denies the inspirational indwelling of the Holy Spirit, by their very theology, may be left behind. Or the Mormons who say, we must accept Joseph Smith, Jr., as a prophet of the Latter-day Saints or we will, not only be left behind, but we will not even find salvation. But then the Mormons are in a totally different world than the world of Christianity. They are nice people and do admirable things for their communities and it pains me to say that, but that comes from Christ himself through the words in the Bible, so do not get mad at the messenger. Anyway, continuing with an attempt to better understand the Seventh-day Adventist and what they think, you might find the following information interesting, I know I did. It might be somewhat of a recap, but an interesting recap, nevertheless.

INTERESTING FACTS

Published in an *Amazing Facts Study Guide*, a Seventh-day Adventist publication, (Study Guide #7 page 10) is the question, "How does God feel about religious leaders who ignore the Sabbath?" followed by the answer, "In hiding their eyes from God's true Sabbath, religious leaders offend the God of heaven." (It's probably safe to say that it is only man's opinion as to whether God is offended or not.) Also, who is hiding their eyes? Christian leaders have consistently acknowledged Saturday as the Jewish Sabbath.

They continue, "God promises punishment for such false shepherds." Yes, he does. God condemns those who lead people away from Christ with their false teachings. We have already studied some of these false teachers. But then again, one would be hard-pressed to believe all the Baptist, Methodist, and Assemblies of God leaders are false shepherds and are preaching a "wrong" Christianity and, because of this, they are to be punished, as well as their followers who will be denied salvation. As Christians we know there are probably those who are unsaved attending all churches (the Bible refers to them as "tares"). We also know that at the same time there are genuinely great Christians in all the faith-based churches who are born again and on their way to heaven, and I genuinely believe the Adventists acknowledge this as well.

So, visit them if you get the chance, and do not take it personally if the pastor might mention you are not saved, as that comment is aimed at the Catholic Church and ricochets to evangelical Christians, as well. Or believe as they do about the only church going to heaven. As I mentioned earlier, I have found the Southern Baptists, as well as the Church of Christ and, to a degree, the Church of God, also believe this way. And while we are at it, let's throw in one more, the Lutheran Church, Missouri Synod[28] who are very outspoken regarding Protestants, who they say do not understand the "Sacraments" of baptism and communion and therefore are rebelling against God. And to stop rebelling against God, we must be more like those who find "Christianity" in the ways of the Catholic Church and the Church of England. Of course, Protestants know better. I believe one would have to say that intent must play a part in the thinking of any church,

That is what determines a Christian, not necessarily the church they are attending, or the people they know, or the day they worship. So, to say any church has an exclusivity on salvation is teaching, as well as embracing theology that is just flat out wrong, at least in

---

[28] Not to be confused with the Evangelical Lutheran Church in America that is less conservative and considered to be in the Protestant family, while the Missouri Synod would follow more closely the Catholic traditions.

that area. I believe they know it also or they would not be on the fence regarding anyone's salvation. Or defensive as some are about the subject. As touched on earlier, since I know the theology of the Adventist Church and understand where they are coming from, I enjoy visiting them when I get the chance and always find it an enjoyable experience. Their welcome always feels genuine.

Most Christians understand that the frustration and contempt harbored by the Adventists is aimed at the Catholic Church, and it is to them that the Adventists are referring probably more than to their peers (Methodist, Baptist, etc.) when alluding to "false shepherds." The Adventists continue to fight a good fight against the ideological false dogma that has infiltrated the family of God, and that is good, as that is a worthwhile cause. They find their roots grounded in the Apostolic Church but here is a news flash: so, do other Christian families as well.

COME OUT OF HER, MY PEOPLE

The Adventist preach that anyone who believes in Christ and worships in another family should remove themselves immediately from what could be a church of jargon or watered-down theology. They even content that some preachers may be shy about teaching the completeness of the Bible. I know the Adventist are a great family, so my question might be, who needs to "come out of her?" Can we reduce the implication of that statement just a tad as it sounds like everyone who is not an Adventist needs to remove themselves from the church they are currently attending and join them? But as we have seen, what they preach is not what they say.

Let us consider what is said in Walter Martin's book, *Kingdom of the Cults,* regarding some of the Adventists' thinking. Although, we already know what they think about Sunday worship as a contention of disobedience which raises the question; "Does that disobedience of worshiping on Sunday break one of the Ten Commandments?

We have seen how they say it does but let's listen in to one of their conversations:

We (Adventists) hold the firm conviction that millions of devout Christians of all faiths throughout all past centuries, as well as those today who are sincerely trusting in Christ their Savior for salvation and are following Him according to their best light, are unquestionably saved. Sounds good. They continue, And the Adventists acknowledge that: We ourselves cannot do so (worship on Sunday). For we believe that God is calling for a reformation in this matter. But we respect and love those of our fellow Christians who do not interpret Gods' word just as we do.

The Adventists embrace theology that God's people are scattered throughout the land and in every Christian denomination; therefore, they contend that they, as Adventists, are not the only born-again Christians. To quote them: While we believe that Revelation 12:17 points to us as a people of prophecy, it is in no spirit of pride that we thus apply the Scripture. To us it is the logical conclusion of our system of prophetic interpretation. But because we apply this Scripture does not imply in any way that we believe we are the only true Christians in the world, or that we are the only ones who will be saved. Sounds great, and according to them they hold the firm conviction that millions of devout Christians of all faiths throughout all past centuries, as well as those today who are sincerely trusting in Christ their Savior for salvation and are following Him according to their best light, are unquestionably saved.

So, we are "unquestionably saved?" Right? But not so fast with that answer. As we have seen we may not be saved because of breaking a Commandment. Which is it? If they contend Christians, who are followers of Christ, basically believing as described by Pastor Dollar earlier, then they are saved based upon the commonality shared by each, and that is the rejuvenation (the born again) experience. In other words, they believe the same theology as was carried forth by the reformers from the Apostolic Church. If I am saved, based upon our shared theology as an evangelical Christian, then who are they talking about when they talk about those who "need to come out of her" those who could be breaking a commandment, basically unsaved? They are talking about the leaders of the Catholic Church and those who they consider falling under their spell, but that is not necessarily clear when displayed on large billboards for the world to see:

Saturday is the Lord's Day / Sunday Laws = The Mark of the Beast

"Come out of her my people that ye be not partakers of her sins, and that ye receive not of her plagues." (Revelation 18:4 KJV).

The Adventists claim that "they are not inventors of new doctrines but the recoverers of old truths—truths long eclipsed by the infiltration of pagan traditions and superstitions into the Christian church." Again, they are talking about the Catholic Church. It would be safe to say that, as followers of Christ, we are all against paganism and the infiltration of pagan ideology into the Christian family.

Those who know the hearts of the Adventist people understand that the above is directed in essence to the Catholic Church, but deep down they believe it applies to all who belong to any church system that conducts services on Sunday, as this is paying homage to the Catholic Church, as well as breaking the fourth commandment. Again, "Break one and we are capable of breaking them all." That's biblical, although I must believe intent and motivation guiding the actions would play a part in any judgment. Because of how hard they hold to this doctrine; many families consider the Adventists to be harboring a bit of legalism.

One thing I learned by listening to ministers of the Seventh-day Adventist Church, especially Doug Batchelor, is their determination to hold tightly to what they believe, regardless of some logic or perhaps even some facts. It is as if the church knows the word of God, but is unwilling to discuss some prevailing facts, as we have seen. It appears they would rather stay with conflicting theology than revisit some of their theology that has been proven to contradict itself. What happened in 1844 when Christ did not come as the Millerites had anticipated became the day in Adventist history that will go down in infamy as it affected their theology and has led to some questionable teachings. We have held up a mirror and saw what was reflected regarding some of their teachings—nothing more. Hopefully, understanding some of the differences has brought us *closer* as a family of believers—born again believers.

CULT OR CHRISTIANITY?

The Adventists reflect Christianity, of course, but probably the most disappointing aspect of the Adventist leaders is the lack of respect they appear to have for other members of God's family, while saying they recognize members of other Christ-based churches who proclaim Jesus as their personal Savior. They mentally beat them up for not believing exactly as they do. And the only way I know to see things as they do would be to join their church. But what if I don't want to join their church? What if I am happy attending a Baptist, or Methodist, or an Assemblies of God, or Church of God or some other faith-based church? The theology of the Adventists is such that they are members of the family of God, although there are some within the Christian community that consider the Adventists to be a cult. Dr. Hoekema, who is no friend of the Adventists, writes in his book, *The Four Major Cults*:

> It is recognized with gratitude that there are certain soundly scriptural emphases in the teaching of the Seventh-day Adventist, one and probably the most important one is a regenerated spirit placing them

into the family of other born-again believers. We are thankful for the Adventist's affirmation of the infallibility of the Bible, of the Trinity, and of the full deity of Jesus Christ. We gratefully acknowledge their teachings on creation and providence, on the incarnation and resurrection of Christ, on the absolute necessity for regeneration (new birth, "born-again") on sanctification by the Holy Spirit, and on Christ's literal return.

In response to what was just said, probably most, if not all, evangelical Christians would go along with Walter Martin when he writes in his book *Kingdom of the Cults,* "It is puzzling to me, as a student of non-Christian cult systems, how any group can *hold the above doctrines in their biblical context, which Dr. Hoekema admits the Adventists do, and still be a non-Christian cult."* (Emphasis mine). I must go along with Walter Martin on this one. As with Martin, I find it hard to believe that anyone holding to the beliefs as described above, could be considered a cult.

The differences between the various church families appear to be nothing more than questioning questionable interpretation in a couple of areas—and not even dangerous areas. I would like to quote Martin's book once again. He says, "it is my conviction that one cannot be a true Jehovah's Witnesses, Mormon, or Christian Science, etc., and be a Christian in the biblical sense of the term; but it is perfectly possible to be a Seventh-day Adventist and be a true follower of Jesus Christ despite certain heterodox concepts." I personally found the same to be true.

Regarding the Ten Commandments, there is a bit of information I found interesting. In the New Testament when Jesus told a young man to keep the commandments, he mentioned several but did not mention the Sabbath (Matthew 19:17–18). But what he did bring to our attention was the two Commandments He left before departing this earth. He said, upon these two Commandments lies the laws of

Christ. Those two Commandments seem to be: Thou shall love the Lord thy God with all they heart, and with all thy soul, and with all thy mind. This is the first and great Commandment. Matthew 22:37-38 KJV. And Matthew 22:39-40 KJV defines the second and says it is like unto the first, "Thou shalt love thy neighbor as thyself." On these two Commandments hang all the law and the prophets. Also, Mark Chapter 12 verses 28-31 are interesting as we will see.

Now this young man, one of the teachers of the law asked Jesus, "of all the commandments, which is the most important?" (Mark 12:28 NIV). Now I am going to assume as a teacher of the Jewish law he was talking about the ten as was given to Moses on Mt. Sinai, which of these would be considered the most important? Talk about a very direct question followed by a very direct answer; "The most important one is this, (verses 30-31). Love the Lord your God with all your heart and with all your soul and with all your mind and with all your strength. The second is this, Love your neighbor as yourself. There is no commandment greater than these." Yet he did not abolish the original ten. These two new Commandments reflect the New Covenant while the Old Commandments, those found in the Torah, reflect the laws to the Israelites, and yet, according to God, they apply to all Christians.

Again, not to diminish the importance of any of the Commandments, although Christ did say the last two, He left with us, "Love Christ and love our neighbor," (fellow Christians) was now at the top of the list, technically making the list 12 with the two new ones. Unlike most churches, the Adventist seem to place the fourth of the ten Commandments the most important which seems to ground them in Old Testament theology. Therefore, some Christians consider them to be teaching, as pointed out earlier, a form of legalism. Even Tim LaHaye used the Adventist church as an example of legalism when he said that anyone who subscribes to certain theology is prone to be entangled by the "law" as are the Seventh-day Adventists who use legalism to admonish those who don't see things their way regarding the Sabbath. Thanks' Tim. That is exactly what I have been say.

I believe it safe to say that Christians obey the Ten Commandments by having no other Gods other than the God of Abraham, Isaac, and Jacob, as well as having no idols, respecting the name of God, remembering the Sabbath, honoring mothers and fathers, not murdering anyone, not committing adultery, not stealing, not lying, and not lusting after what others have including their wife, or anything that belongs to another. Not only good rules for any society to live by but all good rules that one wants to follow when becoming a Christian.

Based upon that information, and the fact we all serve the same God and believe the same Bible and are going to end up in the same place, I believe I speak for others when I say a constant diatribe against members of God's family because they do not necessarily agree with your assessment on parts of the Bible gets old. Not only old, but it is unfounded, unwarranted, and for the most part, drives a wedge between family members. And that is too bad.

Personally, I just wish the leadership of the Adventist Church would acknowledge we are all members of the same family and open the doors for everyone to come and worship on Saturday as an option to Sunday, where for the most part they will hear the same message. Since that will probably never happen, visit them anyway. The Adventist Church family is a great family. And as I have mentioned, their hospitality is heartfelt.

In these waning days, it doesn't matter if the Adventists believe not in a Rapture prior to the "Great Tribulation" or if they believe that the body and soul are inseparable which means Grandma and Grandpa may not be in heaven right now, or that the abomination of desolation has already occurred, or in the importance of Saturday verses Sunday worship—which drives the largest wedge between them and other church families, and the big one to me is their teachings involving the end times. Even with these differences it does not seem to bother most Christians as it does not seem to matter.

What matters is that every Adventist member I met had a strong desire to follow Christ as their Savior. That is a bond between family members regardless of which church they attend. A bond that sits Christians apart from the world and is a bond that will never be broken. The people who consider themselves Seventh-day Adventist are great as is the food and the comradery after most of the morning services. That time of visiting and sharing was always a pleasure.

The only thing in question is the teachings of the church that leaves some unanswered questions, and since those questions will probably remain unanswered, I believe the only words left to say come from the book of Mark 9:38–40 NIV. When the apostles came to Christ one day, John said to him, "Teacher, we saw a man driving out demons in your name and we told him to stop, because he was not one of us. 'Do not stop him' Jesus said, No one who does a miracle in my name can in the next moment say anything bad about me. For whoever is not against us is for us." And to that, I believe, most Christians would say, "Amen."

Now let us discuss the most controversial church I found among all the churches claiming to belong to the family of God. The next section looks at the teachings of those who many might feel are perhaps not where they should be regarding Christianity, as they do not seem to see eye to eye on many issues. They are known in Christian circles as the Church of Christ. Regardless, whether they see eye to eye on issues or not, the question that I cannot seem to get a handle on is the status of the Church. Are they members of the family of God? Or put another way, can they find their church in the Bible?

To deny the existence of an inspirational and spiritual born-again experience as defined by Jesus to Nicodemus in the book of John and contend that the indwelling of the Holy Spirit (as taught by inspiration throughout the Bible) and the gifts imparted by the Holy Spirit to edify the body of Christ are no longer applicable to Christians, would put them in cult land. And to justify their thinking, they embrace a "New Revised Standard Version Bible," copyrighted in 1989 by the Division of Christian Education of the National Council of the Churches of Christ in the United States of America. Yet, while appearing to be in cult land, they appear to be part of the evangelical family of Christians by preaching and teaching Christ. They believe and teach—He lived, He died, He rose, and He is coming back, thus appearing as "pro-Christ," and this puts them in the family of Christianity. Again, a bit of an enigma if you ask me. See what you think.

THE CHURCH OF CHRIST

The Churches of Christ grew out of the Disciples of Christ movement that began in the early nineteenth century. Thomas Campbell organized the "Christian Association of Washington" (Pennsylvania) in 1809. He hoped to reunite Christian churches by restoring the apostolic practices of the early church. We will be discussing, pre, post and amillennialism later but keep in mind that the Church of Christ subscribes to amillennialism theology.

Churches of Christ believe salvation is the gift of God's grace provided through the atoning work of Jesus Christ. They avoid theories of the atonement claiming they are speculative. Those in the Churches of Christ reject Calvinistic theology. They downplay the effect of original sin. The role of the Holy Spirit in conversion is regarded as either non-essential or minimal. (Two believes of importance to Christianity—original sin and the Holy Spirit). They view faith as a rational decision where the individual accepts the biblical facts about Jesus. The Churches of Christ also teach that Christians can lose salvation by apostatizing. They believe that Christians may sin in such a way that they can lose their salvation. Many members understand faith as an "intellectual" acceptance of the biblical facts about Jesus rather than an "inspirational "born again" experience. To have a born-again experience one must believe in the indwelling of the Holy Spirit, which they do not.

"As believers, we all trust in, belong to, and seek to serve the same Lord Jesus Christ. God holds each of us accountable for how we handle the light we have been given, and for how we respond to new light that breaks forth from his holy word."[29] It is from that reference of mind, along with inspiration from the Holy Spirit that I write this section. It was not an easy one to write as the question regarding the indwelling of God's Spirit comes into play. They, unlike most, if not all Christians who embraces the indwelling of the Holy Spirit, reject that theology, as well as rejecting theology that negates the gifts of the Spirit.

I became interested in the Churches of Christ while I was watching a religious special on CNN regarding evangelical Christians titled, *"The Fight over Faith."* I noticed an interesting development. Steve McCoy of the Faith Chapel Church, a nondenominational church, had instituted and was administering, along with the help of Governor Jeb Bush, a Christ-based program to inmates of a Florida prison in the hopes of educating them toward God and perhaps a better life. Sometimes two or three times a week, he would travel to the prison where he would minister the message of the Bible. This is an act most Christians would applaud, but not Reverent Berry Lynn of the Church of Christ.

Pastor Lynn attacked the works of Steve McCoy by saying, "It is wrong to set up a faith-based prison, just as it would be wrong to set up a faith-based school, or a faith-based housing project, or a faith-based police department." The Christians I spoke with regarding Reverend Lynn's remarks found irony in what he said. It was this irony that I took to the Church of Christ to try and find out why one of their own would have such different views than that of some other mainline churches. I know this area is controversial, but common sense must prevail. I found that there are two branches of the Church of Christ, and while several branches of the Church of Christ supported Lynn's actions, others denounced it. It appears that

---

29   Fudge, Edward William. *The fire that consumes: A Biblical and Historical Study of the Doctrine of Final Punishment* Eugene Orgon: Cascade Books. 2011

most of those who defended Lynn belong to the United Church of Christ, as opposed to the Church of Christ, or put another way, the "non-united" Church of Christ.

An Understanding of Hard Theology

I can honestly say that of all the churches I visited, the theology of the Church of Christ was the hardest to grasp an exact understanding of what they believe. While I found the teachings of the church to be interesting, I also found them to contain some theology that does not line up with any of the faith-based churches I visited. For example, there is no indwelling of the Holy Spirit, or a born-again experience that comes with the indwelling of the Spirit when we accept Christ. They seem to embrace a practical indwelling, somewhat pragmatic, but not a spiritual indwelling. And because of this, as we will see, the Church of Christ is considered an enigma by most who are not members.

Thinking that I may have misunderstood the theology of the Church of Christ regarding the born-again experience and the indwelling of the Holy Spirit of God, and the imparting of the gifts of the Spirit, I spoke with several pastors of both the United Church of Christ as well as the "non-united" Church of Christ. They *all* said that the wisdom imparted to the disciples by Christ and eventually handed down through the Bible is all that is required to understand who Jesus was and be saved. Therefore, according to the Church of Christ, the Bible contains our salvation. And because of this theology, the Bible is all that is needed to understand Christ and apparently is all that is needed to work out our salvation. The reason I emphasized "all" is that every time I tried to discuss some differences with one church or the other, they always said it was the United Church of Christ that believed that way, or it was the other Church of Christ, but in the end they both embraced much of the same theology.

Then there is baptism, and while most Christian family members declare baptism an essential element of the Christian faith, they do not necessarily agree that it is "salvation" within itself, or that it is meant to impart salvation as does the Church of Christ. The Church of Christ places so much importance on baptism that they carry this one step further by saying baptism by anyone other than them may not be a valid baptism, but then so do many Baptist, Southern Baptist and Lutheran (Missouri Synod) churches, as well. Some even say that baptism imparts salvation. Most mainline churches would say salvation comes when we invite Christ into our life and make the commitment to follow Him, and then comes the baptism and the washing away of our sins. Now we are down to what many believe is the true meaning of baptism, the washing away of sin—symbolically, of course.

One might get this baptism information from John the Baptist when he said, "Repent and be baptized every one of you in the name of Jesus Christ for the forgiveness of your sins and you will receive the gift of the Holy Spirit." (Acts 2:38 NIV). The apostle Paul said John's baptism was one of repentance. Even Peter gets in on the action when he tells us to repent and be baptized for the remission of sins, and then we shall receive the gift of the Holy Spirit. (None of them mentioned tongues). This is the Spirit of God to help us in this new life we have chosen to live. That is why the understanding of baptism is so important. Not to impart salvation, but to wash away our sins and start us on a new life journey with a clean slate to write that future.

To most Protestants, baptism symbolizes that we have asked Jesus to come into our life and now we are asking Him to remove our sins. It symbolizes that, as Jesus died and was buried, we also died and was buried with Him to rise victoriously with Him. It is upon this action that our old life died, and our new life will begin as soon as we come up from the water—as many might say a new person, a Christian a follower of Christ. Upon our baptism we are officially members of the family of God. The universal family He will be coming to take home. Baptism is not, as the Catholics contend, to remove "original sin."

Most evangelical churches also teach that baptism by water and baptism by fire are two separate occurrences. Baptism by water is an action representative of a desire. The spiritual baptism, the born-again experience comes with an acknowledgment of—and a commitment to Christ. And as John MacArthur says, that spirit comes from above. It is this commitment of belief that grafts us into the vine—Christ. And it is either Christ or God, (explained later with the word *filioque*) that is given the responsibility of imparting the Holy Spirit to lead us with wisdom once we become a believer. It is this inspirational presence of the Holy Spirit the Church of Christ denies.

Without the inspirational Spirit many ask how does one connects with the spirit of God, especially without having the ability to understand spiritual things? Answer: They say that obedience to the Bible is how one connects and learns, and that seems to be their entire premise. One will find that teaching to be quite different from an evangelical, born again Christian, who contends we connect via the Holy Spirit by recognizing born-again theology. Our obedience to the Bible comes as we learn the Bible and learn what it truly means to be a Christian, someone who wants to follow Christ, but just as importantly, know why they want to follow Him. And that usually comes after our moment of commitment.

The word "epiphany" comes to mind, which means "the manifestation of Christ to the Gentiles as represented by the Magi." (Matthew 2:1-12). The epiphany, or the introduction to Christ, is an experience of a sudden and striking realization. Generally, the term is used to describe scientific breakthroughs of religious or philosophical discoveries, but it can also apply in any situation in which an enlightened realization allows a problem or situation to be understood from a new and deeper perspective.

Epiphanies are relatively rare occurrences and generally follow a process of significant thought about a problem or a disturbance of the mind. Often epiphanies, and there can be many, are all triggered by a new key piece of information usually from a soulful depth of prior seeking. In other words, an accumulation of thoughts regarding a subject matter is normally required to allow the leap of understanding from a non-believer to a believer in Christ. That transformation usually comes from hearing and reading God's word, and that comes after our defining moment.

Once a person has their "epiphany" moment, or moments, which is nothing more than recognizing a problem or a need or an emptiness that brings forth emotions, perhaps even a desire to seek God for answers. Not a quick fix, but for answers. Answers that eventually turns into a lifestyle. Not all salvation comes from epiphany moments, but I am betting all those pastors mentioned earlier, pastors who fulfill a higher calling upon their lives, probably had some sort of defining moment. Peter had his defining moment when his eyes met Jesus' and he went and wept. Thomas had his defining moment when he saw the risen Christ, and upon witnessing his nail scared hands and pierced side he fell upon his knees and declared, "my Lord and my God."

One could say the apostle Paul had his defining moment on his way to Damascus. Unlike Paul, the ultimate defining moment for a Christian is perhaps not as a beam of light and Jesus talking to us but is the realization of a need for a change in our life. After which comes the introduction to Jesus and eventually, He becomes more than Lord and Savior of our life, He also becomes the everything we are. Many have an epiphany about the tenuousness of life compared to the reality of living a stable life under the protection of God.

It appears that all Christians have some sort of epiphany about the reality of God, and that is usually followed by epiphanies regarding sin, heaven, hell, and eternity. A Christian's response to a defining moment in the beginning is to feel the need to repent—which means to have a conversation with God and tell him how sorry we are for not understanding sooner and thanking Him for the opportunity He is giving us now. It is this epiphany moment the Church of Christ seems to deny. They contend through their theology that if you join their church, you are a Christian. A Christian who now, according to the leaders, and laity, belong to the family of God as indicated by one's association with their church.

The laity contend one must belong to their church, the "true" remnant church to be saved. In other words, a pragmatic relationship with the church rather than a spiritual one with Christ. Yet Christ is acknowledged for being Christ. The one who died and lived again to bring us salvation. And once again, we are in enigma land. They acknowledge the Spirit but deny the power of the Spirit, the inspirational power. From the moment one receives the indwelling of the Holy Spirit a spiritual moment is felt as opposed to a pragmatic moment that comes when one is taught their obedience to the Bible is from where salvation comes. And it is the requirement of obedience and being a member of the Church of Christ that one is a Christian.

The Holy Spirit & Spiritual Gifts

The more I studied the theology of this church, the more I understood some of the differences they have with mainline Christianity. As just mentioned, probably the biggest difference is a denial of the indwelling of the Holy Spirit, or the gifts imparted by the Holy Spirit for the edification of God's family. The question they ask is, what does it (the theology of the church of Christ) believe about miraculous gifts? Answer: The nine miraculous gifts of Corinthians 12:1–4 (one could also tie in verses 5–11) ceased at the completion of God's perfect law. End of quote.

Upon examining what 1 Corinthians Chapter 12 says about these gifts and the Holy Spirit, one may come away with a different understanding. It says that different gifts are given to different people, at the discretion of the Holy Spirit. I was shocked to learn that John MacArthur does not believe in the gifts of the Spirit being currently active in today's world. He believes the Spirit of God is received from above, but I question his acceptance of the indwelling of the Holy Spirit that imparts the gifts of the Spirit, as he agrees with the Church of Christ when he says that the gifts of the Spirit are no longer available to the body of Christ, as they were in the early church.

The Church of Christ, along with John MacArthur, say these gifts bestowed by the Holy Spirit have ceased. John refers to this as "cessationism," and says the gifts of the Spirit are no longer working within the body of Christ.[30] And he even adds that that theology has been the historical view of the church through its life. Again, this belief would spawn more of a pragmatic spirituality, rather than the spiritual Christianity found in the more mainline evangelical churches.

Based upon this information, and without God's Spirit, and the gifts imparted by God's Spirit to help us navigate this world and guide us in all truths, perhaps our pragmatic mind would be leaning more toward our own understanding in some areas of religion. Spiritual knowledge, as well as spiritual wisdom and discernment, all come from the Holy Spirit, and are referred to as spiritual gifts in 1 Corinthians, chapter 12.

Without the indwelling of the Holy Spirit, it seems impossible to understand much of the Bible. For example, in Acts 5:32, the apostles tell us they were witnesses to what Christ had done because it was revealed to them by the Holy Spirit. "We are witnesses of these things, and so is the Holy Spirit, whom God has given to those who obey him." (Acts 5:32 NIV). In other words, their eyes were opened the moment they encountered that epiphany. A moment that happened to them on the day of Pentecost—the same Spirit, the Holy Spirit that came to them as "tongues of fire" and filled them with the Spirit of God also comes to us when we ask Christ into our heart. Most of the Christians I talked with believe the Holy Spirit works exactly today as he did in the days of the apostles.

---

30 From a podcast; John MacArthur on Education—Cessation of Spiritual Gifts. (https//m.youtube.com).

Without the Holy Spirit, one might also have trouble understanding Romans 8:6 NIV: "The mind of sinful man is death, but the mind controlled by the Spirit is life and peace." Question: The mind, is it controlled by the Holy Spirit, or is it controlled by obedience without the inspiration of the Spirit? That is the question. Is the mind controlled by the actual indwelling of the Holy Spirit? (Mainline theology). Or by our obedience to his Word? Church of Christ theology. I believe most Christians would probably say both are important to our Christian walk, but both do not bring us a mind of peace, joy, and life.

There is a word that comes to mind when discussing the Church of Christ, and that word is "deism." Deism can be defined as a view which assumes as a fact God's existence as the cause of all things and admits its perfection and the existence of natural law and providence but rejects divine revelation or direct intervention of God in the universe by *miracles*. They also reject *revelation* as a source of religious knowledge and assess that *reasons* and *observation* of the *natural* world are enough to determine the existence of a *single creator* or *absolute principle* of the universe. That is true. Proof of a creator abounds, but there is also the Holy Spirit that confirms the existence of the one who created everything.

The members of the Church of Christ affirm that the Father is God, the Son is God, and the Holy Spirit is God. But they have a much different understanding of the Holy Spirit than other more main line Christians. Remember, to them the Holy Spirit, the Spirit that descended as tongues of fire on the day of Pentecost returned to heaven with the death of the last apostle. And from then on, we have the Bible for our education and inspiration. They hold to the historic Christian understanding of the Trinity; however, many avoid the term "Trinity" because it is not a term the Bible uses and is considered to be doctrinal speculation. Posted by Mark Harris. Student of the Bible, July 3, 2020. As viewed on quora.com.

The main issue I see with theology that denies the spirituality, or indwelling of the Holy Spirit, may surface if there is a Rapture.

This is especially true if only those who have been "born of the Spirit" will be taken away when the "restrainer" is removed from the earth (2 Thessalonians 2:1–8). A time many believe will happen at the Rapture. Of course, this is not a problem to them, as they do not believe in the Rapture, but again, they are not alone in their thinking.

The Church of Christ believe they are the only church bound for heaven: They contend that other church families making up the body of Christ are out of harmony with the nature of the Lord's church, which they contend to be "their church," and as such, other Christians are unsaved. This is a big one. I do not think one could find a greater divider than this within the family of God. But then some of the church's members seem to have a problem with this thinking as well, as they consider it to be arrogant as we saw earlier. They also assert the theory that we are born as Christ was...without sin. You heard right, without sin. We will discuss this shortly.

An Enigma Church

Regarding the Christianity of the Church of Christ, if one asked whether they are pro-Christ or anti-Christ, I believe they all would consider themselves to be pro-Christ. Pro-Christ Christians can be recognized as Christians by their desire to follow Christ. Therefore, Christians, (followers of Christ) regardless of which church they are attending, cannot be unsaved. To be considered unsaved would be a contradiction to the Bible, as well as to the very nature of Christ Himself, as Christ cannot oppose Himself.

Therein lies the enigma with the Church of Christ. They recognize Christ and proceed to be Christianized by their obedience to the Bible. In other words, they appear to be pro-Christ (Christians) and yet denounce the spirituality of born-again theology as it was conveyed to Nicodemus by Christ. This is a bit of important information conveying an essential element to enter the kingdom of heaven which they seem to ignore, along with the gifts given by Christ and administered by the Holy Spirit to edify the church. By not accepting the conversation Christ had with Nicodemus regarding the importance of being born again would place them in cult land, yet we know them as Christians. Again, an enigma. Or as someone I feel I know, Patrick Heron put it in his book, *Apocalypse Soon*, "a conundrum wrapped in an enigma and surrounded by a paradox." And I would probably throw in quandary, as well.

Richard P. Heitzenrater tells us in his book, *Wesley and the People Called Methodist*, "...clear apprehension of spiritual things is made possible by the spiritual senses, which can perceive 'the evidence of things not seen' (Hebrews 11:1 KJV). Until these internal senses are brought alive by regeneration (the new birth), there can be no apprehension of things divine." No apprehension of things divine: that means spiritual things. The spiritual senses illuminate the Bible. There can be no apprehension of things divine without the Spirit of God illuminating them. To justify the doctrine of apprehending things without the Spirit, I was handed a pamphlet while visiting a Church of Christ one day.

United Church of Christ member Jerry Moffitt wrote a booklet titled, *The Indwelling and Influence of the Holy Spirit,* explaining how the Bible and the Spirit are the same. Basically, he is reiterating what has already been said. He believes, as well as the Church of Christ, that the Spirit of God comes not from inspiration but from our obedience to the word of God. Most Christians from various churches might respond, "No matter how obedient we may be to the Bible, if we rely on our obedience to carry the day, then perhaps our relationship with Christ comes through works of a pragmatic nature rather than from faith through grace."

It is at this juncture the word 'quandary' comes to mind and raises a question. Without being drawn into salvation by some sort of an epiphany moment followed by receiving the Spirit of God, how are we even saved? They claim to have His Spirit, but that spirit is not the same Spirit mentioned in 1 Corinthians, chapter 2, especially verse

14. The spirit they acknowledge comes from knowledge of the Bible. This is interesting. Most Christians receive Christ by acknowledging Him as Lord and Savior. That grafts them into Christ, thus becoming grafting into the family of God. Now listen to the Church of Christ imply the same thing only from a different perspective. They say, when you believe as they do and study the word and obey the gospel, you become a Christian. When you become a Christian, you are in Christ. When you are in Christ you are in His body. Thus, we are a member of the body of Christ, and therefore a Christian on our way to heaven and everlasting life, as evidenced by our obedience to the Bible. Doesn't that sound more pragmatic than spiritual?

They also say they are not a sect or denomination, but they are the church one reads about in the New Testament. They say that we should obey the gospel and be added to the church for which Jesus died—and of course, that is their church. This theology differentiates them from the more mainline churches. The word enigma comes to mind once again, and I would probably once again throw in the word "quandary" as the Church of Christ poses a quandary to the more mainline Protestant churches, those who teach the indwelling of the Holy Spirit as the revelator of all truths.

Born Without Sin

Since my eyes are beginning to cross, let us change the subject and talk about something we touched upon a second ago. Let me ask a question: Would you say we are born without sin, born without a sinful nature? Regarding that question, I found the following theology of the Church of Christ interesting. They have one belief that I have never come across before. They contend that sin is introduced into our life by our first act of disobedience. They believe that everyone is born sinless, and that sin enters each person the first time he or she knowingly goes against their conscience and does something wrong.

They are saying we are born free of sin and free of the stain of the "original sin." Sin is the opening of our minds to disobedience and gives one a choice to obey God or not, and it is that choice that separates a believer from a nonbeliever. Both believers and nonbelievers have choices to make regarding whether to sin as that nature was infused into them at the Garden of Eden.

We are not born with sins we have not committed, (since we have not had a chance to make that choice yet) but we are born with a sinful nature that makes knowledge and understanding of sin possible. That sinful nature is passed along through the seed of the man in conception, which is why Jesus had to be fathered by the Holy Spirit. The tugging of sin is constantly present from that sinful nature, the one the apostle Paul said he fought with daily, and it is that sinful nature that Christians, born-again, Spirit filled Christians, struggle with as well. And that sinful nature cannot be removed.

An acceptance of Christ by understanding the good and the evil that exists in the world and deciding to follow the path of good, allows Christians the opportunity to overcome obstacles that would distract from and pull them away from God. Obstacles that give each of us the opportunity to choose if we want to follow God or not. But first, sin had to be introduced into the world for there to be a choice. Now we begin to see the purpose of the tree of good and evil to be planted.

The scene was set, man, woman, a tree of temptation and the spirit of Satan that was looking for a way to have entrance into the world, a way to have access to the human mind. Through Adam's fall, the door of disobedience was swung wide open, thus allowing entrance for all the spirits connected with disobedience to gain entrance into the world. All the ingredients necessary for the implementation of God's plan for man to achieve eternal life were in place. The only thing necessary was patience, as everything leading to God's purpose of why the earth, and even us for that matter, were created was ready to be revealed. And this purpose has been so eloquently displayed to us by Christ and recorded in the Bible for all to see.

When disobedience was introduced into the world, salvation was also introduced. But salvation came at a price and that price was to overcome the evil that had been introduced at the time of the fall. Overcoming the evil that was unleashed in the Garden by that first act of disobedience appears to be what "salvation" is all about. As a matter of fact, each of the seven letters in the book of Revelation contain the word, "*Overcome*," or "*to overcome.*"

The importance of understanding the implications of being born sinless as taught by the Church of Christ might lead one to question other theology embraced by the church. I hope my Church of Christ friends have a clearer understanding of sin and how it is in our blood stream, our DNA. Knowledge when combined with logic conveys the message, "we cannot be born without sin or a sinful nature." Yet they say, sin is an action, and as such, cannot be inherited or passed down from generation to generation.

What they say is somewhat true. Literal sin, the actual act resulting from a sinful nature (such as lying, cheating, and stealing), are not passed down. For the most part, such actions are learned, but its inherent in each of us to learn the consequences of disobedience by way of a sinful nature. Satan, when he convinced our first parents they would be like God if they were willing to disobey him. An action that opened their consciousness, their awareness when they disobeyed. In exchange for this act of disobedience, they would be like God, knowing good from evil. And that certainly proved to be true as every Christian can attest to the evil that exist in the world today.

Question: What does the Church of Christ believe about inheriting sin? Answer: Sin is an action. The actions of others cannot be inherited. Children do not inherit or bear the sins of righteousness of their fathers. (Ezek. 18:20). Personally, I do not understand Ezekiel as they do, but they are right about not inheriting the sins or the righteousness of our parents, However, that does not constitute being born without a sinful nature. But they say since the sin of Adam is not inherited, infants are without sin. Therefore, if they die, they are not lost! Correct. They are not lost, nor do they have to go to purgatory. They are not lost because of their lack of knowledge regarding the consequences of sin, not because they were born without a sinful nature. It is this sinful nature the Catholic Church says is eliminated by infant baptism. Someday, maybe someone will explain how that is accomplished, since baptism does not perform a lobotomy, and sin originates from the mind.

One thing the Church of Christ says that is right: we do not bear the sins or righteousness of our fathers. We stand in grace or fall from grace or do not accept grace by our own personal decisions. That is what Ezekiel 18 is all about. Again, all the pastors I spoke with inform us of a sinful nature that has passed through each generation from Adam and Eve until now. And that sinful nature will remain with us until Christ comes to put Satan away and put an end to it. Then, and only then, will our sinful nature be eradicated.

But without that battle, the battle brought about by overcoming the evil that was introduced into the world, we probably would not recognize growth steps which come from the knowledge of always having choices, some good some not so good, some easy some not so easy, some wise others not so wise, but we wouldn't know that without spiritual wisdom. I came across the following on Facebook the other day: "Be thankful for the bad things in life, (those obstacles allowed into our life by Christ for our growth) for they open our eyes to the good things we weren't paying attention to before." Nicely said.

Musical Instruments

Another characteristic of the Church of Christ that you will not find in other churches is their abandonment of instrumental music during their services. Although while they admit that no New

Testament writer ever condoned it, there is also no place where it was condemned in the Old Testament, either. So, what is the problem with having musical instruments in services? Regarding this issue, most Christians feel this is just how members of the Church of Christ desire to conduct their service. No harm, no foul.

Glenn McCoy wrote an eighteen-page flyer explaining "Why Doesn't the Church of Christ Use Instrumental Music in Worship?" First, let me say that the eighteen pages I read are eighteen pages of legalism., I would like to quote one thing from the flyer: "As we approach the study of church music, it is important to determine in advance that the conclusions we reach will not be based on what we enjoy or what is pleasing to us, but rather what is pleasing and acceptable to God."

What is pleasing and acceptable to God seems to be the question. I personally do not believe God is offended when voices are lifted in praise, and those voices are being accompanied by musical instruments being played by individuals who are lending talent— God given talent—to give him praise, glory and honor. There is music throughout the Bible, harps playing and people singing. So, what is the problem? I do not believe anyone has a problem with playing music, or not playing music in church, as that seems to just be a personal preference. If they condemned other Christians or admonished them as do the Adventist, then we might be having a different discussion.

Many might say the Church of Christ (as with the Adventists) may be justified in finding fault with the Catholic Church regarding prayers to saints and images, and conducting Mass for the laypeople to receive Christ, or repeat the Rosary which they believe is a remedy against severe trials and temptations and the hardships of life, rather than just approaching God and talking to Him. Again, that is the reason the vail in the temple was split, to give us access to God. I believe that is something we can all agree upon.

Anyway, not having musical instruments during services is just the way the Church of Christ rolls. And contrary to what some

Church of Christ members may think, music does not seduce the senses, and therefore cannot turn into a form of idolatry. While agreeing with that statement, I wrote it before studying the New Apostolic Reformation movement. It is the music of Hillsong and Bethel that many conservative pastors are having trouble with, as they seem to think their music does seduce the senses.

The Church of Oneness

I have found that members of the Church of Christ have feelings toward the Lord as other Christians and have a strong desire to be good and faithful followers, as do all members of the universal church family. They have their interpretation of theology, which may preclude us from ever coming together as a complete family during our time here on earth. Mainly, because of their theology that embraces rejection of the inspirational Holy Spirit of God. The Spirit they contend was removed from the world when the apostles were through with their work.

Instead of the Holy Spirit, the Church of Christ, as has been mentioned, believes the Bible, the words that Christ left with us, gives us the power of the Spirit, therefore, they say the Holy Spirit that was present at Pentecost is no longer needed as we now receive our inspiration and instructions of how to be saved, how to find salvation, how to live a good, decent, and moral life, are contained in the words Christ taught, words that eventually found their way into the book many call the Bible. As most Christians know, born again followers believe they receive their power from being born again. Did not Jesus himself say one must be born of the Spirit? Without that birth, the birth from above, we never escape the second death,

To resolve the issues that separate the Church of Christ from other Christian families a bridge would have to be built to resolve the Holy Spirit issue, and that alone will probably never occur, even if the Church of Christ leaders say, if only we could build that bridge.

And building that bridge is what most family members might say would be great. Every family has differences of opinions, but they are still family. And by family, I mean Christians—those separated from the world's family of unbelievers.

Like so many other churches, the Church of Christ advocates the need to set aside party names, creeds, and ties, and become "Christians only." And as mentioned that would be a worthwhile goal every Christian would like to see accomplished prior to the return of Christ. For centuries, the accomplishment of oneness within the family of God has been a goal that most churches have strived to achieve, probably from the first split. And without the appearance of any semblance to a church of oneness there appears to be present a church family of oneness called the universal evangelical family of God, or body of Christ.

And as many know the Church of Christ leaders would like for us to believe it is only their church which holds the keys to heaven, and only by joining them will one see heaven, but many might consider that to be unbiblical as it does not follow scripture, or even the intent of the scriptures. Again, not any "one" church holds the keys to heaven. Perhaps it is time for the Church of Christ to reconsider some of their theology, or, according to many, they may just be left behind when the Rapture occurs. Just because they contend a Rapture is not scriptural does not change the fact that the church of believers will be "caught up" to meet Jesus when He comes for his family and we will forever be with Him.

If the Church of Christ really wants to move in the direction of reconciliation, they might acknowledge the teachings on creation and providence, on the incarnation and resurrection of Christ, on the absolute necessity of a spiritual regeneration (new birth, "born-again"), on sanctification by the Holy Spirit, and on Christ's literal return. If the Church of Christ can say they agree with these absolutes of Christianity, as do other church families, (including the Seventh-day Adventist), then there should not be anything separating us from coming together to belong to the universal family of God.

Christians belonging to this universal family of God or body of Christ cross all denominational lines, circumventing all church names from all countries. Do they see eye-to-eye on everything? We all know the answer to that. But then again, if we believe in our heart that Jesus Christ is the Son of God and that he came into this world to save us from death into life with a new birth, then according to the churches I visited, we are that family or church of oneness that stands alone against the world of increasing humanism, secularism, and new ageism.

Regarding humanism and secularism, the following are probably the best definitions of each. Karen Armstrong gives us a good description of a Christian's view relating to humanism in her book, *The History of God*. She says, "Humanism is a religion without God." Straight to the point. An Amazing Facts, Inc. pamphlet put it this way. "The age in which we live has normalized this false religion of self-worship. We even have a name for it—humanism." That is based upon the belief that man's reason (intellect) is sufficient to answer life's most profound questions and needs, and that there is no God or moral absolutes. That is the belief that forms the axis of humanism. Many humanists define humanism as a religious movement in its own right—a religious movement void of any revelation of the existence of a Superior Creator, more of a "mind science" with the focus on intellect.

A secularist, as described by Bill O'Reilly, is someone who "believes there is no room for spirituality in the public arena, in the public debate policy arena. He or she rejects that this country was founded on Judeo-Christian philosophy and that this philosophy permeated our constitution. They reject that entirely, they say 'no, it's entirely man made, we don't base it on any philosophy other than what we feel is right for the occasion at the time.'"

The Church of Christ may have some theology that is quite different from main line churches, but at least the Church of Christ members acknowledge that Christ is the Son of God. There are those who deny a Christian fact, and that fact is—Christ is the Son of God. What a shame to live in a world that denies the fact that Christ is the Son of God, as do Muslims, Hindus, and those who follow Buddha and others who have their own god as do the atheist. And as we saw earlier that god is the "angel of light."

Again, that is a shame. I believe most Christians would probably go along with the apostle Paul when he said that if only for this world, we have hope, then we are to be pitied more than anyone. Also, the words of Martin Luther ring true the day before standing in front of those who wished him dead, when he said: "If it is only in the strength of this world that I must put my trust, all is over..." And to that, I believe most if not all evangelical Christians can say, Amen!

Well, there you have it. And as all evangelical Christians know, the universal Christian family of God, which consists of members from all walks of life attending Christ-based churches, have been built on biblical principles of understanding. In addition to understanding, we all believe beyond any doubt that Christ suffered tremendous pain and humiliation before he went to the cross and paid the ultimate price for each one of us, thus affording us the opportunity to have knowledge regarding life now and have the gift of eternal life later. Jesus stood up for us when He knew He was going to be butchered by the Romans, but He did it anyway.

I would like to ask a question: Would anyone other than the Son of God go that far to reveal to us the truths that had been written thousands of years earlier by the prophets? This and this alone (especially when you throw in the resurrection), is enough to convince Christians of the reality of Christ. That is a bond we all share, a bond that the non-Christian world with its worldly mentality, secularist views, and humanist wisdom does not seem to understand or comprehend. Sometimes even Christians have trouble when pursuing the answers to life. The searching for understanding has led some individuals, as well as pastors, to deviate from the straight path. And combined with the lack of understanding, as revealed by the Holy Spirit has led to what many consider to be "cults" and that will be the next chapter.

CHAPTER VI

CULTS: HOW TO RECOGNIZE THEM

Let us begin this chapter by examining three of the most notorious cults that for the most part consider themselves Christians yet follow what many consider to be false doctrine created by humans, rather than God as defined by Christ, and brought to us by the Bible. A cult according to the recently passed Ravi Zacharias, for whom many had the greatest love and admiration, defines cults as they pertain to religious organizations who have wondered off the true path to Christ for a false one, especially Mormonism.

I say Mormonism as opposed to the others we are going to discuss only because Mormons are good people just involved with the wrong religion. Ravi defines a cult as "that which claims to be rooted in historical Christianity but has deviated from or abandoned the finish work of Christ or compromised on His person." All cults follow an illusion, a deceptive theology, a house of cards built upon sand. And if that be the case as most Christian denominations preach, then how can it be brought forth by the Spirit of God? Would God not be going against himself?

The three primary "religions" considered to be cults by most, if not all Christians, would include the Mormons, Jehovah's Witnesses, and the church of Christian Science. While the Mormons and the

Jehovah's Witnesses were concocted by men Christian Science was conceived by a woman. Most Christian organizations consider all three to have been brought into existence by the "angel of light" to deceive millions—the same "angel of light" who is deceiving billions of Muslims, among others as in Hinduism, Buddhism, and, as we know many more.

As pointed out, across the major denominations of religion and the various nondenominational churches where Christ reigns supreme, there are only three major allegedly Christian players who have missed the mark entirely, only three that completely missed the message of Christianity, salvation, and even Christ for that matter. Again, that would be the Mormons, Jehovah's Witnesses, and the Christian Science. All generally consisting of great people who have chosen to follow a different religion than the one brought forth by the early church Fathers of the Apostolic Church. Is anyone happy about that? No, of course not. The consequences for being wrong is to be left behind and perhaps permanently separated from God. None of these three entities appear to follow the God of the Bible as brought to us by the teachings from Christ and passed along to us by the apostles and recorded in the Bible, and not in the book of Mormon, for all generations to read and to learn the way to salvation and eternal life.

For Christians, the concern for people in cults is that those who are in a cult appear not to recognize that as a fact. If they were ever able to realize they are in a cult, it may become a situation that might be almost impossible to back away from. Perhaps the person comes from a family where association with a cult has been a tradition for one or two generations, maybe even more. It would only be right to assume that many probably have strong relationships with family, friends, and relatives who embrace the theology as presented by the "church" to which they belong. It may be for social reasons, personal reasons, monetary reasons, and so on, that leaving would impose such a difficult and complicated outcome, that to many it might not be worth the effort.

I am reminded of an exception, Leah Remini, and her activism against Scientology. To understand the dangers of Scientology is to realize that they are not a Christian organization. The first clue regarding Scientology would be the understanding that Jesus Christ is a foreign entity to them, and the second clue is the craziness that brought Scientology into existence in the first place.

Whatever the reason for continuing to remain in a cult—family, friends, money, or position—if the religion served is proven to be a cult and not Christianity (in other words, they cannot find their church in the Bible), then every member has a decision to make. If any religious organization is proven to be teaching theology that is different from that found in the Bible, theology that is more from the "angel of light" rather than the religion that Christ brought into the world, then even the apostle Paul says, "Run!"

Speaking of Mormonism, a friend texted me the other day and asked the question, "In a nutshell, what makes Mormons a cult?" In a nutshell, I texted back, "they don't believe in the virgin birth of Christ. They believe Christ being conceived by the Holy Spirit is a perverted concept." I also texted, "They are a polytheist religion believing in many gods. I could go on, but you get the point." She texted back, "Got it."

My journey began when I heard a pastor preaching a sermon that included a title I found remarkably interesting, "Can you find your church in the Bible?" That was the title of his sermon, and those words have never left my mind. I was having a discussion one day with some Mormons when I asked that question, and to my surprise they said yes, they could find their church in the Bible and then proceeded to explain to me why, and then concluded by saying they were the only true church of the Bible. They said it is right there in our name: "The Church of Jesus Christ of Latter-day Saints." I was not expecting that answer. As most Christians would predict Mormons might have problems finding their church in the Bible. Mormonism is an interesting and extremely wealthy organization, as we will see later.

Why don't we begin by examining some of their beliefs and find out why they are not accepted as Christians as defined by most Christian Organizations and by the Word of God? Hank Hanegraaff reveals that answer to us in Walter Martin's book, *Kingdom of the Cults,* when he wrote, "As man is, God once was; as God is, man may become." The next time a Mormon comes to your door, read this to him or her and ask them how they would interpret what was just said. You might find the answer interesting.

When discussing cults, it is important to keep in mind one of the most confusing aspects of cults is in the realm of language. They use much of the same vocabulary, but with a vastly different dictionary. As we will see, this is a proven fact and a fact that is perhaps more prevalent and better demonstrated within the theology of Mormonism than any other "religious institution." Having said that, why don't we proceed through cult land beginning with the Mormons?

MORMONS: IDEOLOGY/THEOLOGY

"There is no salvation without accepting Joseph Smith, Jr., the founder of Mormonism, and the author of the book of Mormon as a prophet of God." Doctrines of Salvation vol 1 pg. 188. As a prophet of God, Joseph Smith has failed many times in his predictions that he made in the name of the Lord. In 1835 he prophesied that the coming of the Lord was near and that fifty-six years should his prophecy be fulfilled. Well, it wasn't. To most Christians that thinking might seem somewhat date-sitting, and the part about accepting Joseph Smith, Jr., as a prophet could be considered breaking the first Commandment of putting someone, anyone, or anything between them and God except Jesus Christ? Welcome to the introduction of the Mormon Church.

The Church of Jesus Christ of Latter-day Saints, as they prefer to be called, are for the most part recognized as Mormons. Although technically, there is no such thing as a "Mormon," as this is merely a nickname for a member of the Church of Jesus Christ of Latter-day Saints. There are Mormons of the Church of Jesus Christ of Latter-day Saints headquartered in Salt Lake City, Utah (the group most recognized as Mormons), as opposed to the one headquartered in Missouri, commonly known as the "Reorganized Church of Jesus Christ of Latter-day Saints."

The Church of Jesus Christ of Latter-day Saints headquartered in Salt Lake City, Utah, was led by an individual known as Thomas S. Monson, commonly referred to as the President until his death in January of 2018. Regardless of who will be the new leader of the church it will be an individual whom Mormons believe to be a living prophet. What an organization he will lead! While Mormons make up only 1.4 percent of the US population, their holdings are vast. In the religious world, they are probably only equaled to or surpassed by the Catholic Church in wealth. We are talking billions upon billions of dollars.

I say that based upon information brought to our attention by Caroline Winter, who wrote a remarkably interesting article for *Bloomberg Businessweek* in July of 2012. Based upon that article, if we listen closely enough to what Caroline has brought to our attention, we might be able to hear Joe Jr., preaching from the grave:

> Hallelujah…and thou shalt build a shopping mall, own stock in Burger King, and open a Polynesian theme park in Hawaii that shall be largely exempt from the frustrations of tax…Own thousands of acres of land and commercial properties around the world and have people giving thanks to me. Praise be to me. Yes sir, praise be to me. Look what I started. Not Peter or Paul or even Jesus accomplished what I have. Everyone ran away from Jesus, but the Latter-Day Saints never ran away from me. Hallelujah, Hallelujah, Hallelujah. He actually said that about Peter, Paul, and Jesus.

In this excellent article, titled "How the Mormon Church Makes its Billions," it's interesting to learn about some of the vast holdings of the church revealed by that article—holdings that include a newspaper, eleven radio stations, a TV station, a publishing and distribution company, a digital media company, a hospitality business, and an insurance business with assets worth $3.3 billion.

An umbrella company along with other church-run agricultural affiliates that reportedly owns about one million acres in the continental United States on which the church has farms, hunting preserves, orchards, and ranches. These include the $1 billion, 290,000-acre Deseret Ranches in Florida, which in addition to housing forty-four thousand cows and thirteen hundred bulls, also has citrus, sod, and timber operations. Outside of the United States, a subsidiary known as AgReserves operates in Britain, Canada, Australia, Mexico, Argentina, and Brazil. In Australia alone, this subsidiary controls property that in 1997 was valued at $278 million with estimated annual sales of $61 million according to Dun and Bradstreet. That was in 1997.

The church also runs several for-profit real estate arms that own, develop, and manage malls, parking lots, office parks, residential buildings, and more. Hawaii Reserve, for example, owns or manages more than seven thousand acres on Oahu, where it maintains commercial and residential buildings, parks, water, and sewage infrastructure, and two cemeteries. Utah Property Management Associates, a real estate arm of the church, manages portions of City Creek Center where a new mall is being built. According to Spencer P. Eccles from the Utah Governor's Office of Economic Development, the mall cost the church an estimated $2 billion. It appears the mall is only one part of a $5 billion church-funded revamping of downtown Salt Lake City, according to the Mormon-owned news site KSL. It would be hard to dispute the success of the Mormon empire. And what has been mentioned here only scratches the surface.

For example, the church owns several nonprofit organizations, some of which appear to be extremely lucrative. Take, for example, the Polynesian Cultural Center (PCC), a forty-two-acre tropical theme park on Oahu's north shore that hosts luaus, canoe rides, and tours through seven simulated Polynesian villages. General admission adult tickets cost $49.95, and VIP tickets cost up to $228.95. In 2010 the PCC had net assets worth $70 million and collected $23 million in ticket sales, as well as $36 million in tax-free donations. And that was in 2010. Amazing! Simply amazing! I believe many would like to thank Caroline Winter for the countless hours of research and dedication she spent to bring us this information. And a big thanks to *Businessweek* for publishing the information.

This was recently but let us go back a few years prior to 1991. According to the Arizona Republic newspaper and conveyed to us by Walter Martin, the Mormon Church conservatively "collects about $4.3 billion from its members a year. And, I am going to assume, tax free. Wow! And that was in 1991, plus $400 million from its many other enterprises. The article maintained that the church's investment portfolio "easily exceeds $5 billion, including $1 billion in stocks and bonds and another $1 billion in real estate. And again, that was in 1991.

The holdings of the Mormon organization are probably equaled only by the holdings of the Catholic Church. However, material success is not the issue when it comes to Christianity. Notwithstanding their material success, the question on the table remains: Is the Mormon organization preaching and teaching the Christianity handed down by the apostles and carried forth by the living word of God...the Bible? The Bible as defined by Ellen G. White earlier.

Although we already know the answer, a question to ask might be do the Mormon leaders teach and preach the same gospel as one would find in, say, a Baptist church, or a Methodist church, or an Assemblies of God church—and all the rest who teach the Risen Lord, the Lord of the Bible and the God He represents? If not, then they are teaching a different "Christianity" than the one found in the entire universal church of believers and regarding a different kind of Christianity, remember what the apostle Paul said: "Run!" Run like the wind. If you cannot find the Christianity as defined by the Bible, then perhaps the "religion" found could be classified as a cult—a cult using religion to ensnare an uninformed public into an undeserving trap. If this is the case, then the religion they have built is considered by many to be built upon false teachings designed to mislead an unsuspecting public.

When it comes to the Mormon religion, in addition to most Christians considering them a cult, most Christians would probably consider them also to be an enigma. Intelligent people, presented with facts of truth, should have wisdom enough to discern the truth—to differentiate fact from fiction and recognize the difference. Yet intelligent people such as Glenn Beck, George Romney, a former Michigan governor, and his son Mitt Romney, who recently ran for president (along with Jon Huntsman) all come from the ranks of the Mormon Church. All come from the ranks of a religion considered to be a cult by almost all mainstream Christian organizations. Other dignitaries include Harry Reid, Orrin Hatch, former Secretary of Agriculture Ezra Taft Benson, former Treasury Secretary David M. Kennedy, and former Education Secretary Terrell H. Bell.

In addition to these distinguished and respected dignitaries, there have been numerous US senators, representatives, and even entertainers, such as Donny and Marie Osmond, Katherine Heigl, Julianne Hough, Christina Aguilera, and Ricky Schroder, who have come from the Mormon Church. So, for the most part, Mormons are honest, intelligent, industrious, thrifty, and zealous people, and the proclamation and promulgation of their faith is beyond question. But if that faith is built upon a false belief system, a belief system that believes "As man is, God once was; as God is, man may become," then why would they not be able to see God was not once a man and man will not become a God? There is absolutely nothing biblical to support this theology. Thus, the enigma.

The Positivity of Mormonism

On the positive side of Mormonism, the Mormon Church expounds some attributes that mainstream Christian churches would probably wish more of their members would follow. For example, the Mormon organization strongly requests and teaches its members to follow biblical principles by committing one-tenth of their gross income to the church. Usually, if this requirement is ignored, then heavy moral persuasion is utilized, up to and including excommunication from the church as the ultimate price.

Mormons also encourage what is termed "fast offerings," which involves the practice of giving up two meals on the first Sunday of each month, the price of which is donated to the church as a voluntary contribution to support and feed the needy. They are encouraged to store from six months to a year of food so they will be prepared in case of an emergency. And here is a little-known fact: during the Depression of the early 1930s, the Mormons looked after their own. None of their members went hungry or homeless.

Mormons emphasize education as well as strongly supporting programs designed especially for the younger generations, such as sports, hobbies, dramatics, music, dances, and festivals. They do everything possible to make visiting and joining them as cozy as possible. Martin writes in his book, Kingdom of the Cults on page 181, "Mormonism does all that is humanly possible to make its Church organization a home away from home for Mormon children and young people, and its low level of juvenile delinquency is in a marked proportion among Mormons, testifying to the success of the church-centered program." I do not believe anyone can argue with the way they go out of their way to take care of their own. Also, I bet one would be hard pressed to find one Mormon young person involved in the riots and destructiveness that took place during the Coronavirus outbreak, and the Black Lives Matter" movement.

These are great teachings as well as great attributes, but the one in which they can be the proudest is their ability to recruit new members. Mormons have been blessed with an admirable missionary spirit, which when combined with the spirit of zeal, makes them virtually an unstoppable recruiting machine. As a matter of fact, they are said to be recruiting more new members than Protestants and Catholics combined.

When it comes to new recruits, be assured that Mormons are not out recruiting people to attend a Baptist or Methodist church, or an Assemblies of God convention, or lining people up for a Billy Graham, (when he was with us) crusade or a Franklin Graham crusade, as would most Christians. No! They are recruiting to teach the new recruits about their religion, to make them a part of their group, and to make them part of the Mormon organization—and as we have been discussing, this is not a bad-appearing organization.

It is no secret the Mormons expound many admirable attributes, yet the question remains…are the Mormons Christians as defined by Christ, promulgated by the apostles, and brought to us by the teachings of the King James Bible? Or are they a man-made religious organization designed to suck the unsuspecting into a web of deception concocted by a man with the sole intent of making the new recruits one of them…*to make them Mormons?* Not Christians as defined by the Bible, nor the Christianity for which Christ gave his life, but to make them "Mormons" and retain them as Mormons for generations to come. You be the judge. After considering the facts as written here and elsewhere, you decide if Mormons are evangelical Christians or whether they are a cult.

The Logic of Adam as God

Brigham Young, the second Mormon prophet following the leadership of Joseph Smith Jr., wrote in the Journal of Discourses, as revealed to us by Wayne Martin's book, *Kingdom of the Cults:* When our father Adam came into the Garden of Eden, he came into it with a celestial body, and brought Eve, one of his wives with him.

He helped to make and organized this world. He is MICHAEL, the Archangel, the ANCIENT OF DAYS! About whom holy men have written and spoken—HE is our FATHER and GOD, and the only God with whom we have to do.

A couple of observations come to mind regarding the information Brigham Young just shared with us When our father Adam came into the Garden of Eden, he brought one of his wives. So, Adam is their father and their god. But then Adam appears to be the archangel Michael, and they say he is "their Father and God." Confusing. Brigham also said, "He (Adam) helped to 'make and organize' this world." Interesting. It's interesting because Mormonism begins distorting the Bible from the very beginning. The Bible tells us God created this world and why he created it.

The one thing we need to acknowledge is that the teachings of Mormonism will always line up with their doctrine regardless of whether it lines up with the Bible. The same can be said regarding the doctrine from the imagination of another illusionist, L. Ron Hubbard (the founder of Scientology), As both seem to share many of the same distortions. That is why Mormonism is such an enigma. It can be proven that it is not the Christianity as brought forth by the Bible (the King James, the New International Version, and the New American Standard), yet millions are drawn to it.

As we have seen, there is a lot of distortion within the Mormon belief system. In addition to Adam being the god of this world, there is another example of distorted teachings, and this is a big one, as it has to do with the virgin conception of Christ—a crux, even the apex if you will, upon which *all* Christians stand. When describing the virgin conception of Christ by the Holy Spirit (which was told to Mary by the angel Gabriel), the Mormons teach that the concept of Christ being conceived by the Holy Spirit of God is a perverted concept (meaning distorted, tainted, and misrepresented). Can you believe that? Through their teachings, they accuse the Bible of conveying a perverted and distorted concept regarding the message from God himself delivered to Mary by the angel Gabriel, who, as we know was sent by God.

Probably without realizing it they seem to indicate the Bible is wrong. But then, maybe they do realize that fact, but the die has been cast, and they will live or die by that belief. That was what surprised me when I asked if they could find their church in the Bible and they said yes. Don't they realize the contradictions between them and "all" the evangelical churches? With the big one being the denial of the virgin conception of Christ by the Holy Spirit.

To back up the Mormon perversion of Christ being conceived by the Holy Spirit, we once again turn to the *Journal of Discourses*, 1:50–51, where Brigham Young wrote, "When the Virgin Mary conceived the child Jesus, the Father had begotten him in his own likeness. He was *not* begotten by the Holy Ghost." Wow! Since the Bible says He was, whom do we believe? Mr. Young continues: "Jesus, our elder brother, was begotten in the flesh (not by Spirit) by the same character that was in the Garden of Eden and who is our Father in Heaven." According to them, that would be Adam, the man who had reached godhead status and apparently the man who became Michael the archangel. So, Christ was conceived by either Adam (the Mormon god) or Michael the archangel who became the Mormon god? Not by the Holy Spirit of God. Again…interesting. Confusing, but somewhat interesting.

What is confusing about Adam being god, or Adam being Michael being the god of this world, is the logic that gets in the way. With the logic of Adam being the god of this world, then the God of the Bible and his Son would be relegated to mythology. It is only logical to assume that both teachings cannot be right. Just some of the confusion that reigns from this premise would include the time God ordered Adam and Eve out of the Garden of Eden because of their disobedience. Question: Was it Adam, or even Michael as the god of this world, ordering himself out? (No logic.)

Christian and Mormon Salvation

As mystified as I am about Mormonism, there is one thing that stands above the rest. When I bring it to their attention, they look like a deer caught in headlights. Then, as they bump it up their leadership chain, they cannot come up with any rational explanation. Maybe Joseph Smith Jr., and Brigham Young did not think this one all the way through.

When asked what happens to non-Mormons upon death, the Mormons say they go to a "spirit world" where they learn about Mormonism. Once they understand Mormonism, if they accept it as the "true" saving dispensation period of the time, then they are spared from the burning fires of hell. I ask, who in their right mind would refuse that offer? If this be the case, then it would be impossible to deny that Mormons had it right all along—-that God, as Mormons point out, did agree that he had failed with Jesus and started over with Joseph Smith, Jr. Personally, I don't think any born-again Christian would accept that as gospel, but Mormons do.

As you will see, according to the above logic, a Christian has it made. Now think about this for a moment. If people are saved by the grace of God as explained to them by the Bible, they go to heaven. If they are wrong and the Mormons are right, then, we as "non-Mormons" go to a place (the spirit world) where Mormonism is shown to be the right way and that Joseph Smith Jr., was in fact a prophet chosen of God to change Christianity as we know it and reunite a "wayward" people back to God through some golden plates that were visible only to him. If this can be proven, then sign me up right now and call me a Mormon.

As speechless as the above has left me, the following information found within Walter Martin's book on page 182 leaves me dumbfounded. What is one to think about Joseph Smith Jr., when he says, "I have more to boast of than ever any man had. I am the only man that has ever been able to keep a whole church together since the days of Adam"? (Used in this context, I'm assuming he means the Adam of the Bible and not the Adam-Michael god.)

Smith continues, "A large majority of the whole have stood by me. Neither Paul, Peter, nor Jesus ever did it. I boast that no man ever did such a work as I. The followers of Jesus ran away from him; but the Latter-day Saints never ran away from me yet." Wow! We heard those words earlier and I still must ask, where do we go with that information? Where does anyone go with that narcissism?

Now, I believe that most, if not all, Christians would concur that for him to say he accomplished more than Peter or Paul is the ultimate of egomania and arrogance (with plenty of narcissism thrown in), but for him to claim that he accomplished more than Jesus would probably be considered outrageous by most. And do not forget, this is the man who began the religion of Mormonism.

The Language Barrier

One of the most confusing aspects of Mormonism that I have found, as well as Walter Martin and others, is how biblical terms and words are interpreted. I cannot stress enough the importance of the interpretation of words being the "most confusing aspects of Mormonism..." Again, as Walter says in his book, "When having conversations with cult members, it's almost as though we're not talking the same language, and yet we feel we are."

Any student of cults must be prepared to scale the language barrier of terminology. First, he must recognize that it exists. Second, he must acknowledge the very real fact that unless terms are defined when one is either speaking or reading cult theology, the semantic jungle the cults have created will envelop him or her, making it difficult, if not impossible, to have an informative exchange of information. Christians must realize that for every biblical or doctrinal term they mention, a redefined light flashes on in the mind of the cultist.[31] Cults use the same vocabulary as Christians, but with a vastly different dictionary.

---

[31] Walter Martin, *Kingdom of the Cults* (Minneapolis, Minnesota: Bethany House, 1997).

Take, for example, a Christian's understanding of the words "Father, Son, and Holy Spirit" and compare the meaning of these three entities in the Mormon religion. To a Christian, the word Father conjures up an image of a heavenly Father, creator of both heaven and earth, and the word Son, as in Son of God conjures up the image of his actual Son who was born of a virgin. And they accept the Holy Spirit as the Spirit of God. So when Christians hear something such as, "I baptize you in the name of the Father, Son, and the Holy Spirit," they don't conjure up in their mind a God from another planet named Adam as the "god" being spoken of, or Christ as the younger brother of Satan, or the Holy Spirit as just another one of their gods, "a personage of spirit," an important person—but still a god that belongs to the Mormon pantheon of gods…that is, according to writings found in the doctrine and covenants of the church, as brought to our attention by Hank Hanegraaff.

The following is a part of Mormon theology that brings chuckles to most Christians. The Mormons believe that Satan, as the elder brother of Jesus, got upset when the gods appointed Jesus to become the redeemer of the race that would *fall because of Adam's sins.* Now, correct me if I am wrong, but didn't we just read that Adam was the "god" of this world? That other gods got together and created this world for him because he had reached godhead status?

If that is true, as they say it is, then how can a race fall from the results of the main god's sins? That is like saying Christ was appointed to become the redeemer of a race of people that would fall as the results of His sins so that he could become their redeemer. What? That just does not make any sense. The logic put forth here negates pretty much everything the Bible has to say about who Christ was and God's plan of salvation. Again, the religion of Mormonism is totally disjointed, as it makes no sense when one compares the theology of Mormonism and the Book of Mormon to Christianity and the Bible. I believe when the Seventh-day Adventist say of the Catholics to "come out of her my people," that could also apply to Mormons.

JOSEPH SMITH JR., FOUNDER

The history of Mormonism can be traced back in time to a man known as Joseph Smith, Jr., or Joe Smith, as the locals called him. Joe Smith was born in Sharon, Vermont, on December 23, 1805, the fourth child of Lucy and Joseph Smith. His family was not what one would consider spiritual in the Christian aspect of the word. His father subscribed to some occult practices, including visits to fortune tellers, and introduced young Joe Jr. to the practices of using mystic powers, such as seer stones and divining rods, to locate buried treasure. The environment in which Joe Jr. grew up was just average—in other words, nothing indicating a higher calling of God to change the church system that had been established by the apostles with the guidance of the Holy Spirit.

Christians believe in an apostolic system that taught the way to salvation was through Jesus Christ and his teachings as recorded in the Bible and handed down through his followers for the past two thousand years. It was this structure of beliefs and traditions that Joseph Smith, Jr., claims God told him to rewrite as He (God) was not satisfied with the way humanity had ended up. If this is true, it would negate the omniscience (he knows how everything is going to turn out) of God. The calling of Joe Jr. to write another religion because God wasn't pleased with how humanity turned out following the death of his Son would indicate that God said "oops" with what he initiated through his Son and started over with Joe Jr., as his elect to pass on a new order—even a new "Christianity."

How would a new religion, a new Christianity, come about? Many might be surprised to learn that according to Mormons the seed to establish a Mormon God was planted shortly after Adam and Eve were removed from the Garden of Eden. Some might be surprised to learn that Adam, according to Mormons, official became the god of this world, and the God they follow, just exactly as they say, because of the fall of humanity and providence. According to the Later-day Saints an angel appeared to Adam and Eve soon after they were driven out of the Garden of Eden. A spiritual entity who taught them the gospel and gave Adam priesthood authority which was passed down to his children (see Moses 5:5-9, Moses 6:64-65). As we will see later, it was from this "visitation" by another spiritual entity many consider to be the "angel of light" that the Mormon seed was planted for Adam to become the God of this world.

After the fall of Adam and Eve Mormons contend they, "Began from that time forth to be carnal, sensual, and devilish" (see Moses 5:12-13) and the priesthood was lost thus leaving the roots of future Christianity in complete apostasy and finally, after the death of the apostles, according to Mormon literature, they stepped in with the calling of Joseph Smith, Jr., and became the Church consisting of "committed" people that God chose as his family. A strong contention of Mormons has always been that God was not pleased with how humanity turned out following the death of his Son. Mormon leaders have consistently taught that after the death of the apostles, true Christianity fell into complete apostasy and disarray, making it necessary for a "restoration" which opened the door for Mormonism. In Mormon doctrine, it is written that "Mormonism is Christianity, and Christianity is Mormonism."[32]

The Beginning of Mormonism

Mormonism started one morning when young Joe Jr. retired to pray in a wooden grove near Palmyra in western New York where the family farm was located. What he allegedly saw and experienced is recorded in a widely published pamphlet titled, "The Testimony of the Prophet Joseph Smith." The alleged sighting included the appearance of "two Personages" whose brightness and glory defy all description. According to Smith, "One of them spake unto me...and said, pointing to the other— 'This is my Beloved Son, Hear Him!'"

---

[32] Martin, *Kingdom of the Cults.*

Since we know by the Mormon's own teachings this is not the God of the Bible who appeared to him, then one might ask just who were the two personages? I will let you decide who you think it might be after reading the following paragraph.

The two "personages" conveyed to young Joe Jr., that they took a rather dim view of Christianity, the Christian church, and for that matter, the world in general. Therefore, it was the "great commission" of Joseph Smith Jr., the prophet—according to Mormon literature—to announce the restoration of "true Christianity" and restore the church as God had intended. I am not sure I know what to do with that information but one question I have would be—which God? The question of which God is a valid question since Mormonism is a polytheistic religion. And because of that, it is hard to understand just who the main god of the many gods might be who leads them. Who offers them salvation? Who offers them eternal life? —especially since they contend, "As man is, God once was; as God is, man may become." Where does this thinking have anything to do with Christianity? They preach the same God as Christians but follow a distorted concept in describing that God and His message.

The same deceptive spirit that Mormons claim visited Adam after he was removed from the Garden of Eden is the same deceiving spirit that is leading billions of Muslims to destruction. Muslims, Buddhist, atheist, and others. God's plan of salvation was, and is, and always will be, perfect. No one will stand in place of Christ. And to an evangelical Christian that is the end of the story. Period! It is interesting to note how both Muhammad and Joseph Smith, Jr., had supernatural visitations. The Jehovah's Witnesses apparently (as we will see shortly) did not need any mystical spirits; they just flat out wrote a religion of deception.

Since Mormonism is so far from mainstream Christianity or the Christianity pursued by evangelical Christians, a question asked by many might be, how did the Mormons accomplish the genesis of a new religion? How would a new "religious order" be brought about? A religion that many understand to be Christianity, and yet is so different from the beliefs of Protestants. Interesting questions, indeed.

The Foundation of Mormonism

Now enters the Book of Mormon. Where Christians look to the Bible as their foundation, the Mormons look to the Book of Mormon, a book that was put together with thoughts and teachings from some golden plates that Joe Jr., allegedly found one day while digging for buried treasure. These plates were only discernible by Smith and could only be read by him when he was wearing a pair of supernatural "golden spectacles." Nobody was ever allowed to see the evidence that produced the foundation of Mormonism before this evidence was, according to Joe, "returned to heaven." Considering the foundation of Mormonism, the entire religion is based upon the imagination, writings, and teachings of a man named, Joseph Smith, Jr. A man many put their faith and trust in to lead them to the promised land. Perhaps they did find that promise land in Utah, but they may have missed heaven during the journey.

It was from these discovered golden plates where either Mormon or his son Moroni (who had been visited by Christ when Christ visited the Americas—that is, according to the Book of Mormon) had buried them before being killed by evil people that a religion was born. From these alleged plates and reformed Egyptian hieroglyphics and the interpretation of these hieroglyphics (which has been proven in court that Smith did not have the ability to interpret), the religion of Mormonism was born.

Amazing. Simply amazing. Are you beginning to understand why many people consider Mormonism an enigma? Again, intelligent people presented with facts should be able to understand that Mormonism has nothing to do with Christianity. Yet there are millions of people who have put their very eternity into the hands of a man, who along with his brother Hyrum, was killed by an angry mob in 1844 when they were taken from a jail in Carthage, Illinois, where they were awaiting trial for apparently being responsible for the destruction of a newspaper office that had been printing anti-Mormonism literature. This "persecution" established Joseph Smith, Jr., as the church's first martyr. I ask you, does this sound like someone who has the answers for our very existence, our salvation, even our eternity? As we know, there are a lot of people who have answered yes to that question. What do you think: cult or Christianity?

The crux of Mormonism

The basis of Mormonism, the very foundation upon which Mormons place their eternal future, the very logic, the very ideology of Mormonism, just does not make any sense, especially if one tries to reconcile the religion of Mormonism with the Christianity of the Bible. Mormonism is so disjointed, and most of the disjointedness comes from the beliefs promulgated by their teachings. Teachings that sometime even defy logic.

For example, who is the God of this world? Remember earlier, when it was said: "As man is, God once was; as God is, man may become"? To Mormons, Adam (of Adam and Eve) is the god of this world. They say Adam was a created man who lived on a planet such as earth and reached "godhead" status. As a reward, other gods (again, Mormonism is a polytheistic religion) who had also reached "godhead" status came together and built this world for him, and one of his wives whose name just happened to be Eve.

Based upon the information just presented, it is Adam who is the god the Mormons say they want to emulate so they can become a god and the other gods will come together and build a world for them. Many Mormons may not realize that reaching "godhead" status is the concept the church has been built upon. Preach what they want, teach what they want, believe what they want, but with the understanding of, "As man is, God once was; as God is, man may become," being the foundation upon which their teachings and their literature portrays is a questionable "Christianity." No! It is a cultic Christianity. What was just said sounds more like Scientology

138

than Christianity, especially when we throw in other "gods" who are currently living on other planets that were built for them just as this one was built for a Mormon god named Adam. When you start going in that direction you start leaning towards Scientology.

To Be or Not to Be...a Mormon

That is a question every individual might be asked as everyone is given the opportunity to join the church of Mormonism. Weigh the facts presented here and elsewhere and decide for yourself. Do you believe Joseph Smith, Jr., was called of God to write a new "Bible"—the Book of Mormon, another gospel of Jesus Christ? A gospel written by man with the intent of reconciling humanity back to God. I bet there is not a Christian on this planet who would accept the thought of God making a mistake where He would have to "anoint" Joseph Smith, Jr., or anyone for that matter, to take the place of Jesus.

If you believe and trust your salvation and your very eternity to Joseph Smith, Jr., and Brigham Young and those who followed in their footsteps rather than Christ and the apostles, then perhaps Mormonism is your religion. Even though Mormonism might work on earth and bring a certain amount of stability into the family unit by following Christian values and Christian principles, that does not make them Christians, it makes them nice people.

If you believe in the Christianity that includes the virgin birth by the Holy Spirit, then Mormonism is not for you. Remember, Mormons think that is a perverted concept. If you believe god was once a man who became a god, then you can also evolve to becoming a god and join with other gods to someday build a world of your own then Mormonism may be your religion. It was being aware of that information that rendered me somewhat lost for words when I asked one day if they could find their church in the Bible and they answered in the affirmative—but they could never show it to me.

The important thing about any decision is that someday we will all stand before Christ and be given the opportunity to explain our decisions.

JEHOVAH'S WITNESSES: IDEOLOGY/THEOLOGY

As we saw earlier, the Jehovah's Witnesses is an organization that originated as the result of a movement called the Millerite Movement—a movement predicting that the coming of Christ would occur on October 22, 1844 (the same year Joseph Smith was hanged). When Christ did not appear to establish His kingdom, the members of the movement disbanded amid great sorrow and anguish. The Seventh-day Adventist family emerged from this group of Millerites as did the Jehovah Witnesses. It was from a group of disbanded Millerites that the religion of the Jehovah's Witnesses began, just as we saw earlier when discussing the Seventh-day Adventists.

It appears both groups, Jehovah Witnesses, and the Seventh-day Adventists, adhered to the idea of a movement that was predicting the coming of Christ to establish His kingdom upon the earth on a specific date. The Adventists, under the leadership of Ellen G. White (a name widely recognized within the Adventist church), who, as a former follower of Miller's, and belonging to a very distraught group of Millerites, eschewed this practice; thus, eliminating any future date setting.

The Seventh-day Adventists appear to adhere to some of the teachings of Miller, and yet they evolved as a Christian family that promotes the concept of the virgin birth, born-again theology, and the Trinity. The Jehovah's Witnesses, on the other hand, became a religious cult consisting of approximately nine million people worldwide. The Jehovah Witnesses evolved into a religious system devoted to the worship of a religion (an "organization") concocted by an individual who appears to have been driven more by ambition and ego rather than the Christianity Christ died bringing into the world.

Just as the Mormons, the Jehovah's Witnesses are classified as a religious cult because they use religion (Christ and the Bible) to lure unsuspecting converts into their web of deception with the intent of converting them to *their* religion—not the Christianity of the Baptist or the Christianity of the Methodist, not even the Christianity of the Bible, but to "their" manmade religion concocted from the imagination of an individual named Charles Taze Russell.

Think about this for a minute. We can go to a Baptist church, an Assemblies of God church, or a Methodist church, along with many others, and find the conformity and harmony of the message of Christ leading people to salvation and the road to eternal life and confirmed by the Bible. On the other hand, would one hear the same attending a Jehovah's Witness meeting?

To Charles Russell and to the Jehovah's Witnesses, the understanding of the character of Christ did not come in the miracle of his resurrection (which is the very foundation upon which every Christian believes) but in the ability of an organization known as "the Watchtower Organization" to logically reason out the character of God by a process of human rationality. Error upon error developed from this rationality. For example, the Jehovah's Witnesses say that "the birth of Christ was not an incarnation"— *the embodiment of God in human form as Christ.* Not only does the Bible dispute their thinking, but even *Webster's Dictionary* defines incarnation as "the union of divinity with humanity in Jesus Christ."

Another strange belief of the Witnesses is their belief that Christ has, in fact, come to earth and has set up His kingdom and the one-thousand-year reign as described in Revelation has begun. This occurred in 1914. It appears the Jehovah's Witnesses did not back away from date setting as the Seventh-day Adventists had done earlier. The Jehovah's Witnesses say Christ is currently directing His activities through his theocratic organization in Brooklyn, New York, and has been since 1914.

Miller points this fact out as written by Walter in his book *Kingdom of the Cults* when he says, "Christ is not coming; He is here! (A.D. 1914)—only invisible—and directing His activities through His theocratic organization in Brooklyn, New York." But then this belief is followed by the erroneous belief that the battle of Armageddon will take place prior to the demise of the last Jehovah's Witness who was alive in 1914. All of this is nothing more than the figment of someone's imagination—although it would have been ironic if the world as we know it had come to an end in 2012 as conveyed by the Mayans and the Mayan calendar, especially, if a Jehovah's Witness over one hundred years old came forth.

It is through the Watchtower Bible and Tract Society that Jehovah's Witness literature is published, from which many erroneous beliefs are promulgated upon an unsuspecting public. The writings of Charles Taze Russell came forth through this propaganda machine and continues to do so to this day. From early on, it was concluded that it would be better to leave the scriptures of the Bible unread and read the literature of the Jehovah's Witnesses to learn about the here, the now, and the later. They teach that the Watchtower Organization will reveal all that will ever be required to know and understand about the subject of religion and Christianity. I am reminded of the blind leading the blind; Jesus said that they would both fall into a ditch.

Although the Jehovah's Witnesses are not as rich as the Mormons, they have done all right for themselves. Over the last hundred years, they have purchased large tracts of property in Columbia Heights, New York, which today is valued in the tens if not hundreds of millions of dollars. They also own large printing presses with the capability of printing billions of pamphlets and literature for distribution to anyone who will listen. In addition, they have the ability through these large printing plants to receive millions from commercial use.

The Jehovah Witnesses own a Bible school (where they teach from their own Bible, the New World Translation of the Holy Scriptures) along with many other business ventures, modern apartment buildings, office buildings, and even a farm (referred to as the "Kingdom Farm") from which food and wood for making furniture are supplied to a factory where workers are paid only a few dollars a month for spending money. But they get free room and board.[33] And it is all thanks to Charles Taze Russell and the leaders who have followed.

Charles Taze Russell, Founder

Just who was Charles Taze Russell anyway, the man who devised a religion that over time has deceived millions? Born on February 16, 1852, Russell spent most of his early years in Pittsburgh and Allegheny, Pennsylvania. Scholastically, he only attended school for seven years, which at the time was not unusual. He was a zealous, charismatic, shrewd, and manipulative individual who seemed to delight in attacking Protestants at every turn because of their rejection of his religious beliefs.

Even to this day, it is speculated that some of the sentiments of Mr. Russell toward Christians and Christian clergy (referring to them as "dumb dogs") still prevail in the organization. According to them, every person who is not a member of their organization (such as evangelical Christians) are "false prophets" to be avoided at all costs. Why is that? Because, according to them, Christianity has been built upon lies—thus, the "false prophets." A Christian is a false prophet and what he or she says consists of lies, so why clutter up one's mind with deception? To know the truth is to be a Jehovah's Witness, according to them.

Most would give Mr. Russell credit for being a shrewd businessman, and as we just saw, an exceptionally good manipulator, but a theologian he was not. For example, all Christians would consider hate, if not a sin, at least a moral decadent. But here is

---

[33] Martin, *Kingdom of the Cults.*

what Mr. Russell had to say regarding hate: "Haters of God and His people are to be hated." (He is talking about Christians—the false prophets of the world.) Mr. Russell continues: But this does not mean that we will take any opportunity of bringing physical hurt to them in the spirit of malice or spite, for both malice and spite belong to the devil, whereas pure hatred does not."[34] What? Are you kidding me? Malice and spite breed hate! How smart does one have to be to understand that logic? Again, the manipulator.

Russell has also been quoted as saying, "In the year 1918, when God destroys the churches wholesale and the church members by millions, it shall be that any that escape shall come to the works of Pastor Russell to learn the meaning of the downfall of 'Christianity.'" Since this prophecy did not occur, one could look upon it as false, thus making the prophesier a false prophet. It is ironic that while the theology of the Jehovah's Witnesses has been proven to be false, it is probably safe to say that they are afraid of the very thing to which they are attracted. Like a moth to a flame.

Wayne Martin writes, "One of the most distressing traits manifested in the literature and teachings of the Jehovah's Witnesses is their seemingly complete disregard for historical facts and dependable literary consistence (including the Bible). While at the same time, they condemn all religious opponents as 'enemies of God' and perpetrators of what they term 'a racket.'" Walter continues, "The Witnesses contend that just as William Tyndale (he wrote the first English version of the Bible) was used to bring an understanding of the Bible to the attention of the people, particularly of those truths that had been taken away by the machinations of the devil and his agencies, Charles Taze Russell was also used."

Really, they want to go there? First, William Tyndale's desire was to put into the hands of people the handed-down Word of God, which led to an understanding of the mission of Christ and an awareness of God in language laymen could understand—an act

---

34   Martin, *Kingdom of the Cults*, page 42.

for which he (Tyndale) was martyred. In contrast, it appears Charles Taze Russell desired to write a new religion that negated the mission of Christ, a religion that leads people away from Christ rather than to Him and steers them toward an "organization." An organization from which all truths are believed to flow.

The Watchtower Organization

To the Jehovah's Witnesses, the Watchtower Organization teaches members to walk in the light of truth and not be misled by false prophets, such as any member of the Methodist or Baptist churches along with the ministers. I guess that would include the late Billy Graham and his son Franklin, David Jeremiah and even Charles Stanley, if not all evangelical Christians as well as all Protestant ministers, just to name a few of their false prophets. The Jehovah's Witnesses teach that one must turn from such people and that, "to receive everlasting life in the earthly Paradise we must identify with that organization and serve God as part of it."

In other words, to receive eternal life we must be one of them—a Jehovah's Witness Christian, as defined by the Jehovah Witnesses theology and brought to us by the Jehovah Witnesses literature and doctrine. They teach that the "organization" is the "mother," a mother who apparently teaches all truths and it is from this organization that all truths flow. Members are to fight against independent thinking.[35] They cannot be serious. I must repeat that: *They cannot be serious.* And people follow this organization?

They say, "Do not take the word of some religious clergyman for it but search the inspired written record for yourself." Ministers of all denominations—Protestants as well as Catholics—are said to distort the Bible by making it fit their traditional ideas.[36] Look

---

[35] Ibid.

[36] Gordon R. Lewis, *Confronting the Cults* (New Jersey: Presbyterian and Reformed Publishing, 1966).

who is distorting the Bible. Wow! Speaking of distortion, one of the biggest distortions in Christendom is the Witnesses' distortion of the Trinity. They say, "Sincere persons who want to know the true God and serve Him find it a bit difficult to love and worship a complicated, freakish-looking, three headed God." I am sure most Christians might say they completely missed the boat on that one.

Based upon the teachings of the Jehovah's Witnesses, instead of Christ as the foundation of truths, the Witnesses have made the teachings of Charles Taze Russell and Judge J.F. Rutherford (who succeeded Russell as leader) the anchor of their eternal soul, and the Watchtower Organization the infallible guide of their very existence. Under Rutherford's leadership, the "Society" of Jehovah Witnesses became known as the Watchtower Bible and Tract Society with its international office in Brooklyn, New York. An organization as we have seen referred to as "the organization" of which Jesus is the "head."

Again, I am not making any of this up. As we saw earlier, they claim that from the year 1914 onward, the times of the Gentiles ended and the "second presence" (the one-thousand-year millennium) of Christ began upon the earth. I believe most Christians find from studying Revelation, Chapter 20 this not to be true. Another distortion would be their assertion that Christ is the created Son of God whom God adopted, rather than the Christ who eternally existed and was conceived as a man by the Holy Spirit.

They believe the Archangel Michael was the first created being, and that it was Michael who came to earth as the chief representative of God, not Christ. [37] Michael was asked to exchange his spiritual existence for a human one, live a perfect life, and die to ransom the guilty.[38] The problem with this theology is that Michael, the only archangel was, and still is, an archangel of God. Most Christians believe Christ, the only one conceived by the Holy Spirit, to be the

---

[37] Ibid.

[38] Gordon R. Lewis, *"The Bible, the Christian, and Jehovah's Witnesses"* (Pamphlet) (New Jersey: Presbyterian and Reformed Publishing, 1966).

"chief representative of God" and the Savior of the world, rather than teachings from "an organization." An organization created by man. I feel as if I am back discussing Mormonism, where God was Adam, who became Michael.

It appears the Jehovah Witnesses have written their own interpretation of religion and in the process, they have questioned the deity of Christ to the point of rejecting it. While they may have some strange idiosyncrasies (such as the belief in a satanic nature of all governments, the idolatry of saluting flags, the evil of military service for a human government, and so on), none of this has anything to do with Christianity. But to denounce the Trinity and proclaim Christ as a created being, thus denying the virgin birth, as well as denying the incarnated nature of Christ, are all dangerous interpretations of theology. It is from these erroneous interpretations that mainstream Christians consider the Jehovah Witnesses to be a cult. Of course, they would adamantly deny that and contend they will be the family of believers who will spend eternity with other Jehovah's Witnesses in heavenly Paradise.

Hell: The Final Destination

While this is not about hell or anyone's destination, it does however bring to the table an interesting perspective on the Jehovah's Witnesses' theology regarding hell. As we know, some church families say that those whose names are not found in the book of life will eventually be cast into the lake of fire, consisting of burning sulfur where they will be tormented forever, along with the Antichrist, false prophet, Satan, and all who follow them. Tim LaHaye says that the second death is that state when people who have died in unbelief are resurrected and cast alive into an eternal state of separation from God in the place called "the lake of fire," which is the second death (Revelation 20:14). If you notice, Tim said a "state of separation" not a "state of torment," as some do.

The Jehovah's Witnesses (along with the Seventh-day Adventists) dispute the theory of an eternal tormenting hell. The Jehovah's Witnesses go so far as to say, "Those who have been taught by Christendom believe the God dishonoring doctrine of a fiery hell for tormenting conscious human souls eternally. It is so plain that the Bible hell is mankind's common grave that even an honest little child can understand it, but not the religious theologians." They continue, "The doctrine of a burning hell where the wicked are tortured eternally after death cannot be true, mainly for four reasons":

- It is wholly unscriptural.
- It is unreasonable.
- It is contrary to God's love.
- It is repugnant to justice.

The above information can be found in the Watchtower and Tract Society Publication *Awake Magazine,* as pointed out on page 105 in Martin's book, *Kingdom of the Cults.* Incidentally, some liberal Baptists also find it difficult to reconcile the fact of an all-merciful and loving God with endless punishment for sins committed within the short span of a lifetime. Many people seem to feel this way. Not the separation from God just the eternal tormenting part.

According to most Christians, where we spend eternity depends upon the decisions we make as we journey through this life. During our time on this earth, we have the opportunity of grabbing the golden ring that offers us eternal life or finding that field of golden nuggets as mentioned in the Bible. We have the opportunity of a life that many only dream about while perhaps missing the great opportunity that is given to them, the opportunity that delivers us from death and punishment of some sort into a life of fulfillment. Salvation is an event at a point in time where we decide by faith (faith is the key word) to receive Jesus as Lord and Savior for the forgiveness of our sins and for a better life—if for no other reason than now we have a foundation upon which to live and to build that better life. Perhaps stumbling from time to time but always heading towards the mark.

God's plan from the very beginning, commencing with the disobedience of Adam and Eve, articulates the plan of salvation through Jesus Christ as brought to us by the teachings and writings of the apostles, especially the New Testament writings of Paul. But again, we would not be having any of these discussions if it were not for the resurrection. Without the resurrection all anyone would be saying is that Jesus appeared to be a good guy, a little crazy, even eccentric but a good man. Somewhat on the order as the Christian Science believe.

Unfortunately, the Jehovah's Witnesses are unable to see the truth, as the "organization, the Mother from which all truths seem to flow" is in the way…and will probably remain in the way as long as the "deceived remain deceived" and "falsities are perceived as truths." Again, like a moth to a flame. Well, there you have it. Now it is up to you. What do you think? Cult or Christianity? To many the Jehovah's Witness are comprised of an organization claiming Christianity, and yet, their form of Christianity will cause them to miss the Rapture.

To Be or Not to Be…a Jehovah's Witness

To be a member of the Jehovah's Witnesses, requires you to put your eternity in the hands of those who are guilty of bringing forth distorted teachings and subjecting their followers to explain at the judgment seat of Christ why they taught their followers a different Christianity than the one outlined in the Bible. And for those listening they will be asked why they denied the existence of Christ being the very embodiment of God. That denial alone places the Jehovah's Witnesses into a religion that has nothing to do with the Christianity passed down by the apostles.

Also, if you believe that Jesus was a created being just as the angels and not a part of the Holy Trinity, then the Jehovah's Witnesses may be for you. And if you believe Satan is the originator of the Holy Trinity, and that Jesus is the younger brother of Satan then again, perhaps the Jehovah's Witness organization is the religion for you. But keep the following in mind when making that decision. The Jehovah Witnesses have the truth available to them, but they are blinded by an "organization" from which *all* truths are believed to flow. But in the end, the final decision is ours. We either follow the teachings of Christ and the apostles or the teachings of Charles Taze Russell and the Jehovah's Witnesses. The Bible tells us that it will be upon this decision that one will stand accountable before Christ.

CHRISTIAN SCIENCE: IDEOLOGY/THEOLOGY

The Christian Science is a set of beliefs and practices belonging to the metaphysical, (hypothetical, conjecture, speculative) family of New religious movements. It was developed in 19th century New England by Mary Baker Eddy, who argued in her 1875 book Science and Health that sickness is an illusion that can be corrected by prayer alone. (en.m.wikipedia.org). That is the crux of the family of Christian Science but from a Christians standpoint there is a lot more to it than just a denial of sickness.

The Christian Science organization teaches through its writings that "Jesus was not Christ, the anointed one." They say there is no atonement for sin because Jesus was only a "Galilean prophet." They say, "The material blood of Jesus was no more efficacious to cleanse from sin when it was shed upon 'the accursed tree' than when it was flowing in His veins." Information from the book, *Kingdom of the Cults*.

They also say that the dying of one man could not possibly atone for humanity. Therefore, they hold to the logic that, "One sacrifice, however great, is insufficient to pay the debt of sin." Mary Baker Eddy would have us believe Christ was a great man—as cited, a "prophet," but one who never really died for our sins—in other words, denying the sacrificial Blood of Christ as payment for our sins. As Mary Baker Eddy said, "the dying of one man could not possible atone for humanity." Sin is somewhat foreign to the Christian Science as their heaven and hell seems to be of our own making while here on earth, not in some after life. Information also, from the book, Kingdom of the Cults.[39] I only mention that again, as there has been some contradiction from the Christian Science as we will see shortly.

For now, regarding the claim there is no sin in the world, the following clarifies their position on the subject. According to A.M.W. from the July 1888 issue of The Christian Science Journal the question arises; Is there sin? And what is sin? Followed by a response from A.M.W. who appears to be a Christian Science scholar. "These questions are of great importance, because it grows clearer to me daily that, if there were no sin, there would be no sickness or death." The writer continued, "I say emphatically, there is no sin. If there is no sin, there is no need for the second question. What is sin? If my assertion (as with Mary Baker Eddy) is true, that there is no sin, then the world is making a great ado about nothing."

That is hard teaching for an evangelical Christian to accept as it contradicts the Bible. To confirm what was just said about having no sin, the Christian Science say that man being made in the image of God cannot sin, as they say, "then man, of necessity, must be like God, and like Him only; and if God is without sin, then man must be without sin also." While an interesting conjecture we know that is not true, but it does sit-up an interesting hypothesis for those who want to go down that rabbit hole.

Where on earth did their theology come from that teaches there is no sin and denies the deity of Christ? By denying the deity (divinity, godliness, holiness) of Christ, how can one even call themselves

---

[39] Just a note: Much of the information regarding cults came from personal research and from information furnished by Hank Hanegraaff (president of the Christian Research Institute International), as well as from Walter Martin's book, *Kingdom of the Cults,* as edited by Hank Hanegraaff. I will forever be grateful to them.

a Christian, or for that matter, even a Christian organization? Personally, I don't think they do, but much of their literature leads one to believe they are. What they say departs from traditional Christianity in rejecting the deity, while at the same time saying they accept the divinity of Jesus. That seems to relate to denying a Father and Son relationship between God and Jesus, but accepting the authority of Christ, especially over healing, sickness, and death. They find authority in the works of Christ as demonstrated by the one Mary Baker Eddy called, a good man, "the Galilean Prophet."

As you have probably surmised by now, the Christian Science is an interesting group but are outside of the guidelines of the Bible to be considered a member of the family of God. And yet, an organization with the word "Christian" in the name. An organization concocted by a single person with a very vivid imagination that perhaps leads some to follow an organization like the others that have been mentioned as some of those who will be left behind at the time of the Rapture. And for those who don't accept Rapture theology, then at His Second Coming.

The origin of the Christian Science appears to be from the writings and imagination of a woman born in 1821 in Bow, New Hampshire, by the name of Mary Baker Eddy. Mrs. Eddy's teachings have been proven beyond doubt that they are not grounded whatsoever in the word of God or Christianity. What I found ironic about the Christian Science was the variance between what Mrs. Eddy has written and what has been written about what she has portrayed as truth.

For example, the crux of a Christians belief is to understand the importance of the *death and resurrection of Christ*. The Christian Science, through their writings, as exposed by Walter Martin, teach that Christ never died as declared by the Bible, but was only hidden in the sepulcher, where he later emerged. (He was probably going to France with Mary Magdalene, where Dan Brown discovered their descendants. Fiction, only fiction.) They do, however, acknowledge that the crucifixion of Jesus and His resurrection served to uplift faith to understand eternal life. Not the same understanding of eternal life as a Christian might have as we will see later.

As we saw earlier, Mrs. Eddy contends that *Christ was a good man, but he never "died" for our sins.* They just "totally" lost me as well as perhaps every evangelical Christian who follows Christ. But for the sake of a better understanding of the Christian Science organization, let us continue. When viewing the Christian Science from those who do editorials from time to time, one finds the writing to lean more towards Christian beliefs, maybe even excluding some actual beliefs of Mrs. Eddy. One example was when I Googled, "Does the Christian Science believe in a resurrection?" I found the following information, "They accept the biblical account of Jesus' life as literally true, including the virgin birth, the miracles performed and his crucifixion and resurrection from the grave; and see his place in history as unique." We just saw a moment ago where Mrs. Eddy did not believe in the resurrection.

They believe in an omnipotent purposeful God, accepts the authority (though not the inerrancy—not without error or fault) of the Bible, and they hold, as stated, the Crucifixion and the Resurrection of Jesus Christ to be indispensable to the redemption of mankind. Again, Mrs. Baker said He wasn't resurrected, she said he lived to see another day. I wish someone would make up their mind. It appears to be a, he said she said situation, but by a stroke of luck my final editor was a Christian Science member for several years and he seemed to concur with the information as presented with little change. I am very appreciative of his input.

The Creation of a Different Religion

Just as Charles Taze Russell of the Jehovah's Witnesses, and Joseph Smith Jr., of the Mormons, Mrs. Eddy felt she had a higher calling from God and an understanding of spiritual matters that were beyond the grasp of average people. To understand the depth of what most would consider narcissism displayed by Mary Baker Eddy, narcissism that must have been misunderstood as "a higher calling," we turn to Dr. Lehman Strauss and the book he wrote titled, *The Book of the Revelation.*

In his book, he says Revelation, chapter 12, reveals to us a woman clothed with the sun, with the moon under her feet and a crown of twelve stars on her head. Much speculation surrounds just who this woman is, but none even comes close to the crazy theory revealed by Dr. Lehman's book, as he says, "Then there is the blasphemous teaching of Mary Baker Glover Patterson Eddy, who was conceited enough to claim that this woman of Revelation 12 represented herself."

Mrs. Eddy has even gone so far as to aspire to be considered equal with Christ. In the *Christian Science Journal* of April 1889, she allowed the claim to be made in her behalf to the effect that she was equal, as chosen successor, to Christ.[40] I'm not sure where to go with that kind of thinking. I am not sure any evangelical Christian does. Her writings, as well as the writings of those who are devout followers, can be found in several publications, such as the *Christian Science Monitor, Retrospection and Introspection,* and *Science and Health.* These are all available in the Christian Science reading rooms that can be found in local neighborhoods or in locations where Christian Science members meet.

Regarding the Christian Science Monitor, its original print edition was established in 1908 (two years prior to the demise of Mrs. Eddy) at the urging of Mrs. Eddy as a protest against the sensationalism of the popular press. The Monitor became famous for its thoughtful treatment of the news and for the quality of its long range, comprehensive assessments of political, social, and economic developments. A publication that to this day is held in high esteem.[41]

Perhaps, of all publications except for the *Christian Science Monitor,* the most recognizable would be from the writings of Eddy's book *Science and Health with Key to the Scriptures,* a book that has

---

[40]   Martin, *Kingdom of the Cults.*
[41]   Encyclopediabritannica.com

been a best seller for decades and was selected as one of the "75 Books by Women whose words have changed the World." One can get the impression from reading Christian Science literature that the Christian Science organization has possession of the keys necessary to unlock the scriptures in the Bible, the same keys the Catholics claim to have possession of. Mrs. Eddy, in fact, claims in her book that her writings are "uncontaminated by human hypotheses"—a bold claim, indeed.

Since the mid-1980s, the Christian Science organization has solidified its public image as a benign Christian denomination of thoughtful, spiritually mature people who enjoy a rather intellectual, quiet faith that gives them peace without recognizing the omniscience of Christ through God. Also, they wander through this world without any of the characteristics of traditional Christianity, such as the existence of hell, the doctrine of the Trinity, or the incarnation, resurrection, or atonement of Jesus Christ. (Again, according to Mrs. Eddy). All of which are cornerstones of the Christian faith. Their view regarding the Trinity or perhaps nontrinitarian would fit better, as they view the Trinity as polytheism. (Same as the Muslims).

In addition to disclaiming the Trinity, Christian Science members reject born-again theology. It appears that most of their theology is centered around the idea that man, as God's idea, is born perfect and already saved with an everlasting salvation, therefore there is no need of any second birth, thus eliminating any born-again theology as discussed in the book of John. They seem to claim that man as God's idea is perfect and therefore there is no need for a second birth. This belief completely misses the point of Christ, salvation, and the redemption power of the cross. They also feel immune to personal guilt because of sin. Remember, as they say, there is none. (Antinomian theology—more on this later.) Guilt implies the threat of judgment, and Christian Science members do not believe in this judgment (again, antinomian theology).

Be that as it may, to a Christian it is this judgment that is the very basis of God's law. This is fact and facts do not change regardless of what someone thinks. To a Christian, the very act of disobedience toward God implies judgment. But the good news from the Bible is that a repenting heart will have the disobedience toward God blotted from His memory, as well as a book many would describe as "the book of Deeds" and not be counted against us. This is one of the very reasons God sent His Son into the world. This is the very message of salvation. A message the Christian Science organization seems to be missing.

Repeatedly, Mary Baker Eddy asserts that Jesus is not the Christ, that he did not die for our sins, that he did not rise from the dead, and He is not truly God, completely contradicting every basic doctrine of the Christian faith. She affirms Him only as the Way-shower, (identifying with his spiritual identify for healing powers) but she perverts the message that he conveyed and bends it to confirm with her demonic doctrines. As I John 2:22 states, "Who is the liar, if not the one who denies that Jesus is the Messiah? This one is the antichrist who denies the Father and the Son" as does Mary Baker Eddy. Note: Not "the" antichrist who is to come later but anyone who denies Christ as having come in the flesh as does Mary Baker Eddie is an antichrist. A liar and an antichrist.[42]

Personally, I do not see any reason to continue as I would say, "Christian Science members meet the New Age generation members as you both have a lot in common," but they still bring more heresy to the table to discuss. Christian Science members believe that evil is only an illusion, unreal, a fabrication that has no basis. (On what planet are they living?) And hell is not regarded as a physical place but more as "states of thought" expressed in varying degrees as we travel through this life. They say the thoughts of an individual dictate the current "state" of a person rather than any future dwelling place. They feel humans bear responsibility for all situations in their lives, as well as in the way they act towards one another They say reward, punishment, happiness, and grief all depend on how a

---

[42]   Most of this paragraph was added by the final editor.

person lives their life. Probably on the principle of what goes around comes around, with lots of karma thrown in.

To the layperson probably the most recognizable beliefs of the Christian Science would be around sickness and healing, as that is what the organization has been built upon, rather than the blood of Christ. Regarding sickness, they apparently interpret somewhere in the Bible that the sick are not healed by verbally proclaiming there is no sickness but by having a mind of "knowing there is no sickness." It is from this denial that the Christian Science members have been sued and have had to somewhat back away from this theology. There are many documented cases where Christian Science members have let their own children die when perhaps a simple appendectomy would have saved the child.

Probably the best example of someone holding on tightly to the teachings of the Christian Science theology, perhaps to their own detriment, would be the actor Val Kilmer (remember *Top Gun* and *Tombstone?*). Val is a great actor and a devout Christian Science member, and by his devotion he may lose his life. Only he can make those decisions. I only use this bit of information as an example of someone who embraces Christian Science doctrine. He has been diagnosed with a throat tumor that may take his life but because of his faith in Christian Science beliefs, he refuses to seek life-saving treatment. It seems Val may be in denial when he refuses to acknowledge the severity of his condition, as he has been quoted as saying, "No tumor, no surgery—will stay close to my doctors advising, my family, and Christian Science practitioner when the facts are in."[43] Val Kilmer figures prominently into the church headquartered in Boston and has for several years.

By following the theology of what was just said, the leper whom Jesus cured would have been told, "You have no disease; it cannot exist." In contrast, Jesus acknowledged the disease and took steps to heal the person. Jesus affirmed the disease and glorified God for

---

[43]   *National Enquirer*, Writer unknown. (February 23, 2015).

curing the leper. If Mrs. Eddy were right in her theology of "Mind Science of Healing," we would probably be paying homage to her instead of Jesus.

A Philosophical Hoax

Probably all evangelical Christians would agree with Walter Martin when he says that the Christian Science organization is a huge philosophical hoax, a sorry foundation for faith, and an almost unbelievable imposition upon the principles of sound logic. The Christian Science organization, just as the Mormons and Jehovah's Witnesses, teaches that you must be a member of their organization, be faithful to that organization, and trust in the leaders to be teaching the true words of Christ.

In an evangelical church, you may hear that Christ was born of a virgin. He was physically born and walked upon this earth. After two thousand years, his message still resonates with people. These are facts that even secularists have trouble denying. Jesus fulfilled to the letter the facts that are presented in the Bible regarding his birth, death, and resurrection (and his soon coming). These are facts that are vehemently denied by Christian Science. Rather than consider the physical Jesus as a fact, they consider the "spiritual idea of God" as a fact and this thought process became God and was named Jesus. Does that sound confusing? It is. But then the whole religion of Christian Science is confusing. However, regarding this point, God was not a "spiritual idea" that was brought about by a thought process, thus becoming God, and named Jesus.

Gordon R. Lewis wrote a book some time back titled, *Confronting the Cults,* wherein he wrote, "Christian denominations, in spite of their intramural debates on theological and ecclesiastical matters, give preeminence to the gospel of Christ." Well stated. It is no secret evangelical Christians may have some differences, but those differences are not cultic. Lewis continues, "Cults, on the other hand, while claiming to be Christian, alter or minimize the core of Christian faith—the gospel." Absolutely true. Cults sell an illusion, and the Christian Science are at the top of that illusion. Unfortunately, many unsuspecting people are sucked into that illusion believing it to be associated with "Christianity." Just a few more who will be here after the Rapture.

To Be or Not to Be...a Christian Science Member

Most Christians use the word deism to describe the theology of the Christian Science organization. *Webster's Dictionary* defines deism as a belief in the existence of God without accepting revelation as revealed by the Holy Spirit. The Christian Science and the Unitarian Universal church are both totally into "deism." There has been enough said that we need not elaborate further as we have seen beyond a doubt, the Christian Science do not belong to the family of born-again Christians.

With that in mind, if I had but one thing to say to a Christian Science member (and the Unitarian Church), it would be the words of the late Kenny Rogers when he said, "You've got to know when to hold 'em, know when to fold 'em, know when to walk away, know when to run." I suggest that perhaps this is the time to fold and run. But then this is me. How about you: cult or Christianity? How we answer that question may determine where we will spend eternity.

To many, discerning false Christianity would have to be considered a matter of looking at the facts and following the guidance of the Holy Spirit as confirmed by the Bible. I do not believe many Christians would deny that most cults, as we have seen, are far enough removed from the true message of Christianity to know they are cults, whereas others may not be as easily discernible. I am talking about the above cults we have been discussing as opposed to the "Christianity" discussed in the next chapter.

The following chapter, "The Poison of Christianity," has been defined as perhaps the most provocative chapter included in this book, as it examines those individuals who preach God's Word with authority, but underneath seem not to believe in the core principles of Christ and his mission... yet they appear as if they do. You will have to decide for yourself, cult, or Christianity? Cultic dogma or biblical facts? Cultic teachers or evangelical Christian preachers? I will leave that decision up to you.

CHAPTER VII

A CHRISTIAN CULT: THE POISON OF CHRISTIANITY...

...or as some may say, "the religion inside of Christianity." For the most part, the cults that have been exposed up to now are far enough removed from the true intent of Christ and the teachings of the Bible that they are easily recognized as cults. I do not believe any born-again Christian would deny that. This chapter defines individuals who deliver deceptive information within the Christian community and may not be as recognizable as the cults that have been discussed.

How dangerous are they to the body of Christ? Several dedicated pastors including Hank Hanegraaff, the late Walter Martin, John MacArthur, John Piper, and every born-again spiritual leader I have listened to have been sending warnings to the church for at least the last thirty years emphasizing the dangers posed by the faith/prosperity preachers and those warnings echo through the chambers of Christianity today as they did then. You know someone who doesn't warn against the prosperity preachers? Joel Osteen. Perhaps that is because many claim his father, John Osteen was a prosperity preacher.

There are Christian cults among Christianity that have been built upon followers who look up to, and show a great deal of respect for, the preaching that has been proven to be cultic in nature and delivered to them by preachers many respect and admire. These are leaders within the Christian community who are revered as reputable teachers of the word when in fact they are viewed by many to be "wolves in sheep's clothing." The words we hear them speak may sound correct, and for the most part they are, but it is the motives behind the words that are questionable, and the core beliefs of many of the prosperity preachers may astound you as they seem to deny the sacrificial blood of Christ.

I have a couple of Christian friends who read some of this book as it was coming together, and they shared with me some of their thoughts regarding the information contained in this chapter. They thought that the discussion of the individuals who have been mentioned, those whom many Christians consider "faith/prosperity preachers," may have been a little insensitive. I have given that some thought and want to thank them for the opportunity to address a couple of their concerns, as I feel others may have the same concerns as well.

They said that I might have been a little too harsh, and perhaps a little too disrespectful when writing about the religion of the prosperity preachers, seeing as how popular they are among many. They are quite popular, nobody denies that. Perhaps that is because they sound like Christians. If we did not perceive them to be Christians, we probably would not consider what they say to be gospel, therefore we would probably not listen to them. For the most part they know the words and present them well, but it appears to be the motives behind the gospel that many questions arise. As far as the words, we can ask, "If they be for us how can they be against us?" This is followed by the answer—they are against us because they distort the Bible for personal gain. They only appear to be for us. And this deception is poison within the community of Christians.

Most would probably agree that, for the most part, what they preach is right; otherwise, we would know it is inconsistent with the Bible. Justin Peters addresses this in one of his sermons when he refers to their teaching as "cultic doctrine that has been wrapped in some Christian theology." Right up front, this is not about the knowledge one must have to spout religion but about motives—that is what is being discussed, *motives*. Nothing more than motives, but that is enough to determine if they represent a cultic religion. If so, then they are truly a poison within the Christian family.

I also considered that "Sometimes it's better not to say anything than to call someone out." When I found out how dangerous prosperity preachers are to the body of Christ, information that came from tapes of Hank Hanegraaff called, "Christianity in Crises I wanted to write about them and let people decide for themselves what they consider to be the Christianity passed on by the Apostolic Church. After all, the prosperity preachers do preach God, Christ, and the Holy Spirit, at least for a moment or two before diving into what may seem like a diatribe of reasons to send them money. It is this exposure to being "sucked in" by these people that I want to discuss. Nothing more. The time they spend conveying the message of Christ is great, but it is only when their motives are switched to requesting money that questions arise. And it is in the hopes of understanding those motives and answering some of the questions that this chapter was written.

Also, to address some who might find the words in the Bible, "judge not lest ye be judged" justification for not writing this chapter, I must once again go along with Justin Peters who addresses those who think this way. He says, "we shouldn't call anyone out by name unless we can back up what is being said." I am okay with that as I stand by my writing. I also agree when he says, "if we weren't being advised how would we know not to be a Jehovah's Witness or a Mormon?" Or for that matter, a follower of the prosperity preachers?

Follow the Truth

I found interesting what Michael Novak had to say in his latest book, *No One Sees God*, regarding our motives for asking God for something. He said, "Some seem to think that the point of prayer is to be given everything one asks—or at least the important things.

Such an expectation would turn God into a servant of their will." I never thought of it quite like that before, but that is true. This is something to ponder the next time you hear a prosperity preacher asking you to send him or her money so that you may receive and, in the end, guess who is receiving that "increase in wealth" and it ain't the one sending the money.

In the pursuit of answering some questions I have ascertained the following: The Bible tells us we should follow the truth and turn away from deception. Question: How can we do that if we do not acquire information and knowledge from which wise decisions come? It is from information and knowledge, and the wisdom of the Holy Spirit, that we make up our own mind as to whether something is deceptive or not. I have given the concerns of my friends some considerable thought and decided to leave what has been written exactly as it is.

I know what has been said will probably cause concern among some readers, and for that I am truly sorry, but with the end times coming sooner than most want to believe, false teachers will arise among the Christian community as many are calling to our attention. And with the lure of money that religion brings to the table, many have found a way to exploit the public and make money, lots of it, from deceiving those looking for help.

There are many good people who have trouble accepting the fact that sending money to someone who assures them they can have their prayers answered by the simple act of sending money is considered by many to be erroneous theology that fosters erroneous teachings. Of course, there have been coincidences, and some swear by the prosperity preachers. I have met many nice people attending the Pentecostal churches, and a few Assemblies of God churches as well who would support them.

For others, as I would probably consider myself, have listened to the prosperity preachers contending that it is the very action of sending money that supposedly releases (or displays) the necessary faith to bring forth whatever is requested. Sometimes when sending money appears not to be working, in other words, whatever is requested does not materialize, we are asked to send more money because it is obvious the faith we had was insufficient.

Now the fleecing begins as they say more money is required to show that we do have the faith. Because of the lack of faith, the first time we sent money expecting a miracle and it did not materialize we are asked to send more as the second time would positively show the faith necessary for God to answer our prayer. Are you still lacking faith? You will be almost guaranteed an answer to your prayer the second time around, or the third time, or the fourth, and so on.

Prosperity theology has been criticized by leaders from various Christian denominations, even including some within the Pentecostal and Charismatic movements, where most of the prosperity preachers call home. Leaders within the evangelical church family maintain that the message being preached is irresponsible, promotes idolatry, and is contrary to scripture. Unlike most messages delivered by mainline pastors who preach Christ, the message delivered by the prosperity preachers distorts the message Christ came to deliver.

A few of the earlier prosperity preachers, some who have since passed away and some still with us, would include Kenneth Hagen (1917–2003), pastor of Rhema Bible Church and founder of Rhema Bible Training Center, and considered father of the modern-day word of faith movement; Robert Tilton; John Avanzini; T. L. Osborn; Jerry Savelle; Morris Cerullo; Dwight Thompson; Reverend Ike; Rod Parsley and Oral and Richard Roberts.[44]

THE WORLD OF THE PROSPERITY PREACHERS

After meditating upon information here and elsewhere, one may come away with the sense that some individuals are more concerned about being paid well for what they do, and what they do, they do

---

[44]   Ibid.

well. Most deliver a good message before the true intention of their message is realized— and that is to motivate us into sending money, and they use Christianity to accomplish just that. It appears as if the prosperity preachers have found that Christianity affords them an easy way to have trust-fund wealth as well as the many amenities that go along with that wealth.

The apostle Paul instructed Christians to "Test all things, hold fast what is good." Knowledge is important. It is information and spiritual knowledge that keeps a Christian from becoming a Mormon, or a Jehovah's Witness, or a member of the Christian Science organization. Or perhaps a member of the 20,780 denominations worldwide as Jack Van Impe tells us about in his book, *Sabotaging the World Church*. What was interesting about Jack's observation was that many of these groups proclaim a strict allegiance to the doctrine of Christ, but as Jack says, many do not.

The Bible emphasizes that we should seek knowledge, from which we gain wisdom. What has been written is nothing more than what those who promulgate a questionable religion impart to us as gospel, and what appears to be their motivation. And as we will see, they apparently do not like to have their teachings scrutinized for truth, as some have gotten extremely upset and have expressed those emotions.

For example, Benny Hinn wished a curse upon Hank Hanegraaff, president of the Christian Research Institute, for revealing some of their beliefs in his tapes, *Christianity in Crisis*. I suppose they will curse me as they have Hank, and that is even down to my children. It appears that when the mirror is held before them, it reveals information the prosperity preachers would rather have us forget.

I'm sure Kenneth Copeland would like for people to stop reminding him that he described God as the "biggest failure in the Bible" and referring to the Spirit of Christ as an "emaciated, poured-out, wormy little spirit." I am sure William Branham, prior to his demise, would have liked for people to stop reminding him of the time he said that the doctrine of the Trinity was from Satan himself.

(More on this in a minute.) It seems as if exposure to the light of knowledge is the biggest irritant the prosperity preachers have.

Be that as it may, I was motivated to write this portion of the book when I heard the above tapes produced by Hank Hanegraaff, tapes that I later discovered were awarded the Gold Medallion by the evangelical Christian Publishers Association. For those who may be curious, yeah, they really are that good. As I was listening to the tapes, I could not believe what I was hearing, and yet there it was, highly regarded preachers who, over the years, have preached to millions saying things that were so blatantly untrue, wrong, and distorted that they perverted the truth of the Bible as taught by Christ and carried forth by the apostles.

After ordering the tapes, I found I could not stop listening to them. The more I became aware of what was being said, the more I became interested in knowing just how deep false teachings and false doctrine went, lurking under the banner of Christianity. The deeper I probed, the more the question crossed my mind: Are these people really Christians? I could not believe anyone saying the things I was listening to could be grounded in the word of God with a thorough understanding of the mission of Christ.

Dr. John MacArthur who has been mentioned a time or two is a minister, writer, broadcaster, and college President, as well as a friend of Hank Hanegraaff, a golf playing buddy, and yet, when Hank converted to Greek Orthodoxy after being an evangelical Christian for most of his life, John was very outspoken regarding this switch and was very, for lack of a better word "judgmental" of the move. So, he is not opposed to speaking his mind, and when it comes to the prosperity preachers, he has been known to impart his thoughts. In December of 2009 John published several articles that were extremely critical of some televangelists:

"Someone needs to say this plainly: The faith healers and health-and-wealth preachers who dominate religious television are shameless frauds. Their message is not the true gospel of Jesus Christ. There is nothing spiritual or miraculous about their on-stage chicanery. It is all a devious ruse designed to take advantage of desperate people. They are not godly ministers but greedy impostors who corrupt the word of God for money's sake. They are not real pastors who shepherd the flock of God but hirelings whose only design is to fleece the sheep. Their love of money is glaringly obvious in what they say as well as how they live. They claim to possess great spiritual power, but they are rank materialists and enemies of everything holy." Wow! I thought I was outspoken when I called them charlatans.

Who Are These People?

That is what I wanted to find out. This is what I learned. They are considered "faith/prosperity preachers," or members of the "word faith" movement. They inspire millions preaching Christ, motivating them to donate money for whatever happens to be the need of the pastor at that moment. Perhaps another $65 million dollar plane, more million-dollar mansions and expensive automobiles. Many surrounded by opulence wealth that most can only dream of acquiring.

Prosperity theology has been criticized by leaders from various Christian denominations, even including some within the Pentecostal and Charismatic movements, where most of the prosperity preachers call home. Leaders within the evangelical church family maintain that the message being preached is irresponsible, promotes idolatry, and is contrary to scripture. Unlike most messages delivered by mainline pastors who preach Christ, the message delivered by the prosperity preachers distorts the message Christ came to deliver.

In addition to those prosperity preaches already mentioned, there are other televangelists who have joined the ranks of the faith preachers and are preaching the prosperity message of sending money to them as a requirement to "activate our faith." The following is just a sampling of what is being preached by some of the prosperity preachers beginning with Jesse Duplantis, followed by Todd Coontz,

Mike Murdock, James Payne, Marylyn Hickey and Gloria Copeland, Paula White and Creflo Dollar, and Benny Hinn. Then we will discuss some of theology of a couple faith preachers that you might find hard to believe. Let's delve into some preachers who have done quite well for themselves.

Jesse Duplantis

One of those who preaches theology that many born again Christians have problems with would be Jesse Duplantis. Jesse has a great personality and is quite believable. It is easy to see why people are attracted to his style of preaching. A prosperity preacher who can be seen begging for money while residing in a 35,000 square-foot-home (parsonage) that is paid for by donations. He also recently asked his followers to donate money so that he could buy a new $54 million private jet, the Dassault Falcon 7X.

In 2016 Duplantis and fellow televangelist Kenneth Copeland defended their use of private jets because of their assertion that commercial planes were full of "demons" that would bog down their schedules with requests for prayers. Demons asking for prayer? Copeland spewed anger at Lisa Guerrero an award-winning reporter from inside Edition who asked him about that, as he has vehemently denied saying it. He was evasive and kept avoiding the question, but they had this conversation. Again, demons asking for prayer? Come on Jesse—you can do better than that. Later they both denied saying demons are on planes, probably realizing planes are full of people. Besides Jesse said he would have problems standing up to pray, and Copeland agreed.

Both Copeland and Jesse have amassed a fortune as we have seen. The net worth of Jesse Duplantis has been estimated to be $40 million. And the lavish lifestyle that comes with that fortune has brought him harsh criticism from those who consider him to be motivated by money rather than the Christianity of an evangelical, born-again, Spirit-filled Christian. Money that we saw allowing him to continue this journey in the luxury that he believes God intends for him. Obviously, he is considered by many to be an exceptionally talented and gifted individual or people would not continue sending him money.

Todd Coontz

Probably the epitome, at least the most blatant, of prosperity preachers would have to be Todd Coontz, as watched by millions on a television program called "Campmeeting" Inspiration Ministries. In 2017 Coontz, 50, is described on his website as a pastor, evangelist, television host, author, humanitarian, philanthropist, and businessman, yet he has problems managing money. According to Merrit Kennedy, as conveyed to NPR,[45] "North Carolina Televangelist Indicted On Charges Of Tax Crimes." Merrit continues, "North Carolina televangelist Todd Coontz—author of numerous books on faith and finances—has been indicted on charges of tax fraud spanning more than a decade."

The televangelist "promised financial miracles for people who sent money to his ministry," according to Channel 9 WSOC TV of Charlotte, N.C. The news station recounts some examples of his claims:

> "'You need to plant a $273 recovery seed. I'm only going to give you two to three minutes to respond,' Coontz once told his viewers.

> "'Coontz posted videos on Twitter as recently as Wednesday, promising financial blessing to the faithful.

---

[45]   https://www.npr.org

"'Suddenly miracles are happening. I want to work with your faith for quick things, swift things,' Coontz said in the video."

It appears that every word spoken by Coontz relates to money but let us return to that $273 recovery seed for a moment. I never paid much attention to how the prosperity preachers adapted their message for money until one day while watching Todd preaching about the message of "expectation," which was a rather good message, I was interested in how he was going to finish, which I knew was going to be directed towards asking for money.

This is how he finished: expect your expectation, health, wealth, and happiness through your faith. And this is what he said about faith: he emphasized the number 273 had been heavily laid upon his spirit over several days by the Holy Spirit. He was unable to understand what it meant until just before the program, when God revealed the meaning to him. He said God showed him there were three thousand individuals watching the program whom God has asked to have the faith to send in $273. (Today most of them ask for $1,000.) For this action, they would be blessed with all the health, wealth, and happiness that God can bestow.

Think about that. Since this program airs in over 160 countries, let us do some math. If only three thousand of the millions watching sent in $273 that would equal $819,000 (tax-free American dollars). Not a bad payday. Maybe that's why Kenneth Copeland said he was glad he got off the denomination line (I take that as meaning the evangelical line) and got on God's line (the prosperity line) before he starved himself and his whole family to death. If he had stayed on God's line, perhaps he would not have been able to amass an estimated $760 million dollar fortune, which places him number one on the money list of world's richest preachers. I believe I read somewhere it does not profit a man no matter how much wealth he accumulates, if he loses his only soul. I'm going to take that as meaning "giving up eternal life for money".

Richard Bennett

Mike Murdock

Today, most of the prosperity preachers like Mike Murdock ask for $1,000-dollar donations and to induce one to send money, they may say something like; there are 1,189 individuals—the number of chapters in the Bible—that have been touched by God to send in a seed offering of $1,000. He says you must trust it will grow and return to you a hundred times more than what you planted. Ten dollars will come back to you as $1,000. One thousand will become $100,000 and so on. One he likes to use is fifty-eight dollars, a popular sum based on Murdock's 58 blessings. Send in fifty-eight dollars and expect to receive back $5,800. If you have not received your prayer request then send in another fifty-eight dollars to increase your faith, or at least to show God how faithful you are.

If one continues listening to Mike, they just might end up giving their last $100, because, according to Murdock, "God has never responded to pain," "He only responds to faith." So, send in that $100, as difficult and painful as that may be. Then watch God return a $1,000 blessing. As Hank Hanegraaff says, "many people who send money seek what is on the Master's table, rather than the Master." Do not be deceived, this is not the God of the early church, not the God of the apostles, and this certainly—as every born-again Christian knows, is not even the God of the Bible.

This request for money to enrich someone has nothing to do with Christianity. Somewhere along the way someone decided they could make money using religion to lure unsuspecting prey into the net of deceit with promises of health, wealth, and happiness, and as they say, the rest is history. Sadly, this has been occurring since the early days of the Christian church. In 1 Timothy 6:5-6, it references "constant friction between men of depraved and deprived minds who are devoid of the truth. Men who imagine that godliness is the way to material gain." Of course, godliness with contentment *is* great gain, as that chapter also points out. And contentment comes, as we know, with having a relationship with God and His Son.

James Payne

I found it thought-provoking what James Payne had to say about sowing seed (sending money) to have a harvest. He used the parable of the sower by saying some seeds fell by the wayside where birds came and devoured them. The same sower sowed in stony ground, where the seeds sprung up and died. The third time he sowed he sowed among thorns that sprung up and choked the plants, but they kept sowing, and so should you, all the while having faith. In other words, plant a seed so we can get a hundred-fold, and then plant another seed so we can get another hundred-fold, and so on.

James Payne, one who was blessed with a great voice. One of the best I have heard. I believe I could listen to him sing for hours. I recently learned that James is a Grammy nominated songwriter as well as a good singer. James was tutored by John Avanzini, one of the heavy hitters of the prosperity preachers, as revealed by Walter Martin in his book *Kingdom of the Cults*, which does not bode well for him. He mostly asks for money to pay off churches that have debt. James is not your average prosperity preacher, although once when watching a discussion between him and Benny Henn, he preached the importance of sowing seeds to receive a harvest. It appears he is on the prosperity line of Christianity yet doesn't seem to share their same greedy spirit. However, he does like for us to plant a $1,000 seed donation.

While I was unable to ascertain his exact worth it is estimated to be in the millions. Although, compared to the "real" prosperity preachers, he doesn't have an overly abundance of wealth, even though, as mentioned, he does implore their techniques. Having said that, I was unable to find out how much of that $1,000 goes for personal use as opposed to what we are told and by listening to what James tells us. He says of that $1,000 donation the ministry supports missionary work in Africa, India, and several other parts of the world. The ministry also supports inner city ministries in some of America's major cities. And they do this from offerings.

That is admirable as any Christian would agree, but here is the problem. Prosperity preachers, including James, preach an expectation of something in return for a donation. And therein lies the problem with the message of James Payne. Is James a prosperity preacher? Is he crusading for an accomplish of wealth? It appears he isn't. While he adopts many of their methods to raise money, according to him, it is used as was mentioned, and to help pastors pay off their church debt.

Marilyn Hickey and Gloria Copeland

According to the Dallas Observer.com Gloria Copeland is a witch. "She uses incantations to bring about magical results. Of course, I don't believe she ever gets any results because I don't believe in magic. But I know from watching TV that she wants her followers to believe that her incantations get results, and that makes her a witch. You don't have to bring back the dead to be a witch. You just have to make people believe you can bring back the dead. And then, of course, if you charge money for it, that will lock up the case. You're a witch, big time." The above just gives you a sampling of what some people think of Gloria's character. Both Kenneth and Gloria Copeland preach the message of healing. And to be healed it takes faith and to have faith we need to send them money. And Gloria, as well as Marilyn are just as masterful as anyone when it comes to asking for money.

Hank Hanegraaff points out in his previously mentioned tapes that Gloria Copeland and Marilyn Hickey preach the message of perceived money. They preach that all one must do to create money is to start speaking it into your billfold saying, "You big thick billfold full of money, speak to your checkbook, say to your checkbook, you have never been so prosperous since I've owned you, you're jammed full of money." Then they might continue, " *for my beloved friends who have been blessed with a billfold or checkbook that has $150, I feel* *in my spirit that God would have you send it to this ministry as a show of faith so that you may receive. Many need a touch from God. Plant those seeds and watch God work in your life. Hallelujah and Amen. Again, that number is…"*

Apparently, we are to take from our wallet or check book what God had put there, or a designated amount, and send to him or her who had been inspired by God to bring us the message of how to have and increase our faith by allowing us the privilege of sending money to a servant of his—as all prosperity preachers consider themselves. Does not the Bible tell us to give to God that which is his? Many messages of the prosperity preachers include some form of guilt. Guilt is one of the big weapons of Satan and one of the emotions they use to separate us from our money. That takes many back to the good old days of tent revival meetings like those during the days of Oral Roberts, Jack Coe (one of the first faith healers in the united states), and someone we are going to discuss later, A.A. Allen.

Paula White and Creflo Dollar

Sometime back there was a Senate investigation launched to expose many prosperity preachers, in which Creflo Dollar and Paula White were named, along with other televangelists who have made millions of dollars through the prosperity gospel. Paula White was the subject of an inconclusive 2007-2011 Senate investigation, but she also refused to co-operate which gave thought to several questions.

They possess the same qualities of deception that Benny Henn and Kenneth Copeland have but display them slightly differently. Personally, I have not heard either solicit money as blatantly as many others, but they seem to have the same spirit of Greed as the rest. And just like the others, Paula has no problem claiming July is "Prophetically Designated for Victory Over Enemies," and suggesting a $229 "Breakthrough Seed" donation. Probably a request that has led to her amassing almost $5 million in assets. But that is just a paltry sum compared to another televangelist that comes to mind, and that is T.D. Jakes. Someone who has amassed a $150 million fortune. Although not a prosperity preacher per se, he does however, seem to accumulate wealth for his own consumption, as a $150 million fortune might indicate.

Southern Baptist theologian and ethicist Russell D. Moore said that "Paula White (and after listening to Creflo Dollar I would include him) is a charlatan and recognized as a heretic by every orthodox Christian, of whatever tribe." When listening to and reading what Paula has said from time to time one gets the unmistakable impression that she has denied some serious theology. For example, denying the Trinity, as well as stating, "Anyone who tells you to deny yourself is from Satan." Think about that the next time you hear the words uttered by Christ in the Gospel of Matthew: "If anyone would come after me, he must deny himself and take up his cross and follow me." (Matt. 16:24 NIV).

All Christians know they must put God first by denying self. Whoever wants to be a disciple of Christ must *deny themselves* and take up their cross and follow him. Probably the big one that many might consider simply wrong coming from Paula is that she agreed with Larry Huch who said Christ is not the only begotten Son of God. That is so wrong it borders on blasphemy. I would place that right up there with what Oprah implied when she said, "there are more ways to God than just through Jesus."

When one thinks of Creflo, they may wonder how he has been able to amass a fortune of $27 million, which places him number eight on the richest pastors list. Both his prosperity gospel style of teaching and his lavish lifestyle have been criticized—but then, that is possibly because of his two Rolls-Royces, a private jet, and three multi-million-dollar homes. And then he recently asked his parishioners to cover the cost of a new $65 million-dollar jet. Unbelievable. As with other prosperity preachers who preach the power of God, they come across believable, it is just their motivation that is questioned along with their sometimes unbiblical theology.

Benny Hinn

Then there is Benny Hinn, who has been estimated to be equipped with a worth a paltry $42 million. He is best known for hosting "Miracle Crusades"—faith healing summits which are later televised on Trinity Broadcasting Network. (TBN). Hinn has been scrutinized for personal use of church funds to provide a lifestyle most would envy. His nephew, Costi Henn, used to travel with Benny until his eyes were opened, and recently revealed his uncle spent as much as $25,000-$35,000 a night for luxury suites when visiting Dubai. Of course, this is probably after flying there in Benny's private Gulfstream G4SP jet he uses for personal vacations and funded by tax-free donations—and that is probably after he is driven to the airport in his Mercedes-Benz.

While not a tent revivalist, although he would have made a good one, he considers himself a minister of the people, who, in addition to being a prosperity preacher, spews doctrine creating a show that produces an over-abundance of enthusiasm drenched with emotion that appears to be what some refer to as the working of the Holy Ghost. Benny Hinn and the show he produces, the show that provided him with millions of dollars, is someone the Bible describes as one who would lose his soul for the riches of the world.

Where he loses credibility with most Christians is a result of some of the things he has said. Primarily, when he retracts "revelation knowledge" that he claims was given to him by God. Think about that for a second. Retracting "revelation" knowledge, knowledge he said was from God. Would that not indicate the "revelation" knowledge was either a mistake of God, as perhaps revealed to Benny in another "revelation," or a mistake on the part of Benny Henn? And a retraction might warrant questioning the spirit he listens to.

One must question someone, anyone, who retracts information supposedly revealed to them by the Holy Spirit as "revelation knowledge." A couple of questions would be whether that person is preaching truths from the Bible as led by the Holy Spirit, and then how much can the words be he preached be trusted. An example of one of those times of retracting "revelation knowledge" comes by way of Benny Hinn as we are about to see.

On more than one occasion, Kenneth Copeland, a friend of Benny Hinn, and a couple others have stated that they believe we are gods, not big gods as said by Paul Crouch in a conversation with Benny Hinn but little gods. Benny Hinn defended the beliefs of the faith preachers being "gods" when he said: "Kenneth Hagin, (prior to his passing in 2003), has a teaching that a lot of people have trouble with, yet it is absolute truth. Kenneth Copeland has a teaching many Christians have put holes in, but it's divine truth. Hagen and Copeland say…you are god."

Did you get that? Absolute truth! Divine truth! They probably interpret Ps. 82:6 where it conveys the message, "I said, you are gods, sons of the Most High, all of you" As meaning we are "gods." Of course, not "the" God, but a smaller version. Perhaps to them their assumption is supported by Ps. 82:1 where it says "He judges among the gods" to mean a reference to all gods to some degree.

When it comes to an explanation regarding us being gods, some Christians say that is referring to the nation of Israel during the time they were at Mt. Sinai where Moses received the Torah. Jesus alluded directly to psalm 82, where the Elohim[46] (A word that occurs more than 2500 times in the Hebrew Bible) meaning ranging from "gods" in a general sense (as in Exodus 12:12 where it describes "the gods of Egypt"), to specific gods, (e.g., 1 Kings 11:33 where it describes Chemosh "the god of Moab" or the frequent references to Yahweh as the "Elohim" of the Hebrew Bible.[47] Interesting.

Now the retraction. Benny Hinn later said that if anyone tries to sell you this bill of goods, they are, "No different than the snake that

---

[46] The God of Israel in the Old Testament. Elohim is a grammatically plural noun for "gods" or "deities" or various other words in biblical Hebrew.

[47] https://en.m.wikipedia.org.

tempted Eve in the Garden of Eden." So, it was not "divine truth?" Not "revelation knowledge?" Now think about this for a moment, since Hagin prior to his demise, and Copeland, who, still embraces this theology, were and are still friends one must ask how is that possible Especially since Benny just said Copeland and Hagin, prior to his death, were no different than the snake who tempted Eve in the Garden of Eden. Wow! Sometimes it just gets one to wonder. Based upon this retraction, it behooves all Christians to listen to what is being preached and to trust in the Holy Spirit to reveal the truth, regardless of who is delivering the message.

Individual Beliefs of Kenneth Copeland

Kenneth Copeland seems to be the leader of the faith/prosperity preachers and a student of Kenneth Hagin, the granddaddy of the faith preachers, as they appear to follow and promulgate his teachings. I have often thought about Copeland based upon his wealth, his opulent lifestyle, and his obvious disregard for the message of judgment that awaits those who prosper by deception, as well as the price one must eventually pay for that deception. I have often wondered if Copeland's desire for wealth is brought on by a desire to be the first pastor to reach a billion dollars of net financial worth—which to him would equate to Joseph Smith, Jr., saying "Look what I have done. No other has received so much." Of course, he is talking about the money and opulent lifestyle rather than being a disciple of Christ.

A life many would say that has been built, and lived, on the back of those who trusted him. Many never really knowing the "true" Copeland or the fact that he has accumulated his wealth from questionable teachings, or as most of the born-again Christian community might say, from deceptive preaching as his core philosophies do not represent true Christianity. But regardless, his followers will construe this affluent lifestyle all "blessings" that he is receiving from God, and he will gladly accept them as "blessings" from God, thus giving him, as well as most prosperity preachers an entitled mind.

As I mentioned earlier, this is not about the money, or the outlandish things prosperity preachers say from time to time, but about the Christian thing and how they discuss it as contrasted with what most of the evangelical Christians might say. Those who might be attending a Baptist, or a Methodist or an Assemblies of God, and all the other Bible-based churches preaching and teaching the word, as well as the essence of the Bible. The prosperity preachers know the words the people want to hear and then some. I have a couple of questions regarding the "then some." I would like to ask any Christian if he or she would agree with Copeland when he says that God is the biggest failure in the Bible. His exact words as spelled out, once again from the tapes of Hank Hanegraaff, were:

> I was shocked when I found out who the biggest failure in the Bible actually is. Now, when you ask anyone who is the biggest failure they say, Judas, or others might say, I believe it's Adam, well, how about the Devil, now he's the most consistent but he's not the biggest in terms of material failure and so forth. No, the biggest failure is God. He lost his top ranking, most anointed angel, the first man He ever created, the first woman He created, the whole earth and all the fullness therein, and a third of the angels, at least. That is a big loss.

Yes, it is. Copeland is right in everything he said. Perhaps the word "lost" is a bit strong to describe the fall of Adam and the implementation of God's plan of salvation. The Bible tells us that in God's plan for the world, these events were preordained to happen. Just as Judas was destined to do what he did, others were called on by God and destined to complete God's work in their lives.

This includes individuals such as Noah, Moses, Abraham, Peter, Mary, Paul, and yes, even Adam, as well as many others who have been called throughout the centuries. Let us not confuse "loss" and "failure" with the workings of God. All of God's plans will ultimately succeed a with magnificent and eternal epic story ending, including, at last, the rule and reign of Jesus Christ over a previously fallen and lost world.

There is another thing Copeland has said that has amazed me. I have often wondered what he meant when he said he was glad he gave up the denominational lines and got on God's line. Is he saying that all clergy who are in the Christ-based churches preaching the gospel are not on God's line? His exact words were, "I was glad that I gave up the denominational line and got on God's line before I starved me and all my family to death." It sounds as if he just said, "I didn't trust in God to provide for me and my family, so I took matters into my own hands." Or "the money just wasn't right on the denominational lines." There is a particularly good chance he would not have amassed perhaps a $760 million-dollar fortune by staying on the denominational line.

I am reminded of the verse wherein it says, "What good is it for a man to gain the whole world, and yet lose or forfeit their very self?" (Luke 9:25, NIV). I like the New Living Translation slightly better, yet they say the same thing; "And what do you benefit if you gain the whole world but are yourself lost or destroyed?" One more, the Berean Bible, "For what is a man profited, having gained the whole world, and having destroyed or having suffered the loss of himself?" As I was typing that I got to thinking, I wonder how many pastors began the good fight with right motives but became distracted, and then seduced, by the love of money?

Copeland has made it clear from the beginning he saw the opportunity religion afforded him and as they say, the rest is history. Expensive planes, a luxurious $6 million dollar lakefront mansion with a personal air strip and hanger for his $17.5 million jet (one of several) sitting on fifteen hundred acres of breathtaking land equipped with a church overlooking a beautiful lake, along with cars and expensive furnishings near Fort Worth, Texas. A campus equipped with a church and a hanger for his $17,5 million jet. Lavish furnishing throughout, much on the same order as Joyce Meyer. Who knows, he might just have $5.7 million worth of furniture, including a $30,000 malachite round table, a $23,000 antique marble-topped commode, and a $14,000 custom office bookcase. I bet God is impressed at how they are using the money from the talent given to each of them.

Since I am not God, I do not know what will happen to any of them, only God knows their heart and He will judge that. I will say that unlike most evangelical Christians, few, if any, of the faith/prosperity preachers appear to have any fear of God's judgment. If they did, they would not be able to distort the essence of the Bible as they do for what appears to be selfish gains motivated by greed. Greed is an exceptionally large gorilla in the room and when combined with distortion, this gorilla can become most dangerous to the body of Christ. Once again, that is why this chapter is titled, "The Poison of Christianity."

Individual Beliefs of Robert Tilton

For the many followers of the prosperity preachers, it may not appear to them that the prosperity preachers are peddling a cultic Christianity, but then it is important for the prosperity preachers to convince us that what they are saying is gospel—and for the most part, it is. There must be some semblance of reality in what they preach, or we would not mistake it for gospel. But in the end, they are almost all selling the same thing as Robert Tilton. I believe most would place Tilton very high on the deception meter, if not number one.

Robert Tilton (the former pastor of the Word of Faith Church in Carrollton, Texas, a suburb of Dallas) was and is still selling the prosperity message as masterfully as any. From what I have heard, he is preaching from Tulsa, Oklahoma, although the last I heard he was in Florida. When he was in Carrollton, his television program generated thousands upon thousands of weekly letters, most of which included money but also included prayer requests that he promised to pray over, and upon prayer, he would almost guarantee the request would be answered.

To entice people to write to him, he would offer a prayer for them or a family member and promise to send them something, usually a book or pamphlet explaining how to get rich. When they responded, they would be put on a "solicitation list" and contacted from time to time asking for more money. He claimed he would use his special connection to God to personally pray over the requests. Usually, the sender would include an amount of money along with the request as a way of saying thanks, or perhaps to increase the chance of the prayer being answered, or perhaps money was included to increase personal wealth as the prosperity preach said would happen—sometimes a return of 100 times is even possible.

Donald Miller tells us in his book, *Searching for God Knows What,* that Tilton built a complicated direct mail system, capturing the names and addresses of those who called in for prayer. He then contacted them by mail and asked them to return a "widow's step of faith," and if they did, God would reward them. When the thousands, if not hundreds of thousands of letters arrived, they went through a clearinghouse established by Tilton, where the money was extracted, and the letters were then thrown unread into the dumpster awaiting the city dump, along with pictures of many who had requested prayer. Diane Sawyer of ABC's Dateline, in an interview some time back, confirmed what Donald Miller said. "Tilton's money and marketing skills are second to none. Tilton's money-making ministry is state-of-the-art for taking donations."

It was during an exposé of the faith preachers that Tilton, along with others, were exposed for using religion to substantially improve their lifestyles. Following the investigations by ABC's Prime Time

Live, called "The Apple of God's eye," it showed, among other things, how the prayer requests were simple being thrown in the trash—minus the money, of course, and forget about any pray as Tilton never saw them. Many of Tilton's followers departed his ministry once they were brought face-to-face with the reality of the deception that was prevalent.

After the exposure of Tilton's moneymaking machine, the pressure apparently got so bad for him that he left Dallas the year following the scandal. His first ex-wife confessed in divorce proceedings that the televangelist had to carry a disguise kit with him everywhere he went and spent at least 50 percent of his time wearing a fake mustache or a wig.[48] With that exposure, it is hard to conceive Mr. Tilton is once again blatantly preaching the same message of "send money" from Tulsa Oklahoma, or Florida, or somewhere. For him to continue, there must be plenty of innocent, unsuspecting people sending him their hard-earned money. Incredible! But again, most people sending money don't recognize the prosperity preachers for who they really are.

Ron White, a stand-up comedian, epitomizes the essence of Tilton's message when he says, "I was sitting in a bean bag chair in my underwear eating Cheetos flipping channels when I came across Tilton staring at me. He (Tilton) said, 'Are you lonely?' I said, 'Yeah.' He said, 'Have you wasted half your life in bars pursuing sins of the flesh?' I said, 'Yeah.' He said, 'Are you sitting in a bean bag chair in your underwear eating Cheetos right now?' I said, 'Uh-huh, yeah— oh, this guy's good.' He said, 'Do you feel the urge to get up and send me a thousand-dollar check?' Ron said, 'There for a minute I thought he was talking about me.'"

Many Christians question whether the prosperity preachers are working for the accumulation of wealth for self-serving fulfillment or working to proliferate the true meaning of God's purpose and just

---

48 Donald Miller, *Searching for God Knows What* (New York: Thomas Nelson Publishers, 2004).

accumulating wealth along the way. As far as wealth and Christianity, there is nothing wrong with either. God prospered many in the Old Testament. Only when we are motivated by wealth and let wealth become our God do we have a problem. Money is not the "root of all evil," as some believe; rather the love of money is the root of evil as we are told in, 1 Timothy 6:10: "For the love of money is the root of all kinds of evil; which while some coveted after, they have erred from the faith, and pierced themselves through with many sorrows. Some people, eager for money, have wandered from the faith and pierced themselves with many griefs."

Eventually, his television show was dropped, and he was taken off the air shortly after the exposure. Also, Tilton was sued for fraud by some who had sent in prayer requests in the genuine belief that he would be able to help. Though he still pleads for money through his ministry, it will probably never come close to reaching the heights it achieved when his show, Success-N-Life, was beamed into homes throughout the nation and earned the pastor's church millions per year during the late 1980s and early 1990s.

THEN THERE WERE OTHERS

It appears to many that some faith preachers place more importance upon raising money than preaching the word of God. Another example would be Peter Popoff, who, upon receiving donated money, promises *"miracle spring water"* (now in an even "larger size") that offers healing powers. And, like Robert Tilton, to get you on the mailing list, Peter will send you his booklet "Prosperity Thinking" (Tilton's booklet is "How to Have Everything You Ever Wanted"). Both will tell us how we can become rich, which usually is accomplished by planting a seed or priming the pump. God does not operate this way. As most Christians know, this "sending money" theology has nothing to do with true Christianity or the word of God.

Peter Popoff was a big name in faith healing circles in the 1980s with his nationally broadcasted program, and his connection with God, (so it was perceived), to decipher what ailments attendees suffered before laying hands on them and providing a cure. Attendees of Popoff's shows were asked to write down what ailed them the most before the show. The request then went to his wife who used an earpiece to communicate that information to her husband who would call the afflicted onto the stage, feign guessing the issue they were suffering, and proceed to pray for healing. When the deception was discovered, Peter's ministry went broke and he declared bankruptcy. Today he is preaching the message of prosperity and will send a bottle of "miracle spring water" that offers miracles—for a slight "donation," of course. Am I the only one who sees the irony in this?

Someone else who appears to be placing considerable importance upon money is a televangelist pastor by the name of Don Stewart. Who many say was the successor to A.A. Allen. Interesting story. Allen died at the Jack Tar Hotel in San Francisco on June 11, 1970 at the age of 59 after a heavy drinking binge that many suspects was with Don Stewart. It has been recorded that Don was accused of attempting to clean up evidence of his alcoholic binge before the police arrived.

When sending money, to Don do not forget to ask for his *"miracle prosperity handkerchief,"* which is supposed to bring health, wealth (especially wealth), and happiness. Don's message, as with that of Gloria Copeland and Marilyn Hickey, is one of "send money and you will receive as much as 10, 20, and sometimes even 100 times return on your 'investment.'" He almost guarantees it. Unfortunately, the faith preachers who are preaching the message of prosperity and wealth— "prime the pump" or "plant the seed"—are the only ones who seem to be getting blessed.

Christians are told that in the last days the truth will be distorted, if not taken from the world, from within the very heart of Christianity itself. As to the truth being taken from the heart of Christianity, we are perhaps witnessing exactly that. In fact,

2 Corinthians 11:13–15 (NIV) may reinforce what has been said regarding anyone who teaches false doctrine: "For such men are false apostles, deceitful workmen, masquerading as apostles of Christ. And no wonder, for Satan himself masquerades as an angel of light. It is not surprising then, if his servants masquerade as servants of righteousness." Think about that. The apostle Paul commands, under the inspiration of God: "from such people turn away and run."

And Then There Were Two

Perhaps two of the most controversial pastors that one finds on today's world stage, as most would probably agree, would have to be Joel Osteen and Joyce Meyer. I have found Joel Osteen and Joyce Meyer, along with many others, to be great positive connection preachers, but these two appear to be among the best when combining motivation and scripture. You will not hear about the end times or the Islamic threat to America, or how Christ died for our sins or even preaching on the message of salvation. but you will be inspired.

One will not hear much about Christ dying for our sins, or much about his mission as the Son of God sent to reconcile man back to His Father, and so on, but you will hear how God wants his people to step up and become successful, becoming the person they were intended to be. Preaching the message of always moving towards their goal, never giving up and know that the one "greater than you" is there to help you achieve that goal. Then Joel will use examples from the Bible to drive home the points he is making about success and being obedient to God, saying always to following that inner voice, being careful not to miss the opportunities that God is putting in your life. He uses himself and his success as examples of what can be accomplished by stepping out on faith and trusting in God to deliver on His promises.

He was fortunate enough to have the God given talent that we mentioned a couple of times to become as successful as he has, Joyce has that same talent. And from that talent, that God given talent, they have both accumulated vast amounts of money. Do they give God credit for the talent that earns them the money? Probably not as much as some would like, but that is not our call. Do they spend the money from their talents as some would think a Christian should? Again, not our call. Although my Editor did point out the Joyce has contributed much to many organizations and after doing some research, I found that to be true.

They cannot do anything about the talent as that is God given to them, so let us discuss the money, or more precisely, what they do with the money. Some think they should do as Jesus did and help the poor, giving to the needy, and so on. In other words, spend the money as Jesus would. Or at least how they perceive he would. I believe Joyce does spend a vastly sum of money for good causes, at least it appears to be that way. And that got me to thinking, maybe the problem is they just accumulate too much money. What a problem to have.

Others say it is not about the money as much as it is about deceptive teachings or perhaps convections that are questionable that in the end placate more than help. For example, when Joel was asked if he thought Mormons were Christians, he said yes. He said yes. Once again, he said yes, he thought Mormons were Christians. A religion, a Christianity to them, that embraces the teaching that says, "God was once a man and point to Adam who became a God" and as such, belongs to their pantheon of gods, just as Jesus, an important guy, but just another one of their gods. We know this and much more from discussing Mormonism earlier. And this is the organization he said he thought was a Christian organization.

We know Joel was wrong when he answered as he did. And sometimes that pandering is troublesome to the Christian community. Osteen may duck, dodge, weave, bob, and maneuver, but I do not know about distorting the Bible. I realize he comes remarkably close to the edge in defining how he looks at things, especially when it comes to his beliefs regarding homosexuality, abortion, and the big one—how he spends his money, but outright distortion?

Probably most would say they, especially Joel, preaches more motivational and inspirational than the message of salvation, as we know he does, and that message of motivation is a good one, especially when Joel adds examples from the Bible to emphasize a point. For example, the story of Joseph. Joseph was abandoned by his envious brothers and ended up some years later in a prison in Egypt. The story of Joseph is quite interesting, and Joel uses this story to tell how Joseph ended up in Egypt, what he did to get thrown into prison, what caused his release, and how God used him to save his family. A great story of inspiration, as well as a great story to see the awesome hand of God's in arranging events that lead to some awesome endings.

That is the God that Joel preaches rather than Christ dying on the Cross for our sins. If one listens to him, they will find him to say he does not preach the crucified Christ. Many believe both Joel and Joyce should preach the message of salvation, the cross, and the resurrection, especially the resurrection, but as Joel said, that is not his message. I do not remember Joel ever mentioning the resurrection in any of his sermons, or how important the resurrection is to a Christian. Or for that matter, I do not remember him ever discussing what it means to become a born-again Christian as deemed necessary to complete the transformation of becoming a follower of Christ, especially since born again theology is the bedrock of a Christians belief. Again, one will not hear that "salvation message" preaching from Joel, but he does preach the Father of Jesus and how His Father will help us accomplish our dreams and achieve our goals.

Just one more thing before we begin the journey of discussing the money issue. I will give them a pass on the claims of "distorting the Bible" as that I have not personally witnessed. Although, I am convinced someone will be able to show me where they have. As discussed earlier, if what a listener is receiving is received with the spirit of a Christian, then that might make both, Meyers, and Osteen one of us, and if so, how can they be against us? Again, not my call.

I believe most would give prop's where props are due, and Joel probably satisfies some Christians when he finishes every sermon by inviting the people to repent by repeating the "sinners" prayer, thus becoming a born again, (maybe, only God sees their heart) member of the family of Christians, the family of God. He says, if you meant it, (the sinner's prayer) you became a born-again person. Then he says, find a good faith-based church and get involved.

The opulence of wealth

They are pastors who many would consider worthy to be in any Hall of Fame, perhaps with a caveat because of their apparent love of money. If they put money before God, then we, as born-again Christians know, that is wrong, but without knowing their heart, that call is hard to make. And that endorsement comes with another caveat, as both are not without critics, as each has conveyed some very problematic theology. Regarding the fortune of $40 million dollars amassed by Joel Osteen, I came across an article posted on the Babylon Bee by someone who does not seem to respect Joel very much, as the article begins with this headline: *Joel Osteen Sees Own Shadow, Predicts Another Year of Taking Bible Out of Context—* Houston, Texas.

> "Taking his luxury golf cart from the front door of his Houston mansion down to his mailbox to fetch the paper Friday morning, prosperity preacher Joel Osteen reportedly looked down to see his shadow, a traditional sign indicating that he will be preaching the Bible out of context for yet another year."

While his father was considered a prosperity preacher, Joel does not preach the same message, although they associate with some of the same people. Neither Joyce Meyer nor Joel seems to ask for money to "activate our faith" which is the core message of the prosperity preachers. They seem to accumulate wealth by their message of inspiration and motivation and publishing several books. If wealth comes to either Joel or Joyce resulting from having extreme talent then, so be it. How they spend it is between them and God, and as the Bible says, who are we to judge the works of another.

Both Joel and Joyce are not without their detractors, and sometimes their teachings are characterized as prosperity gospel. Speaking of Joyce, she has been criticized by some of her peers for living an excessive lifestyle herself on her way to accumulating a fortune of $25 million. In 2003, the St. Louis Post-Dispatch published a four-part special report revealing information regarding her Massive amount of wealth that includes Meyer's $10 million corporate jet, her husband's $107,000 silver-gray Mercedes sedan, her $2 million home and other houses worth millions more located within her own private compound built for her children and her. All built from tax-free millions collected from her ministry.

Must we continue? We must, we must. A $20 million headquarters outfitted with $5.7 million worth of furniture including a $30,000 malachite round table, a $23,000 antique marble-topped commode, a $14,000 custom office bookcase and much, much, more that many have considered excessive for someone preaching the gospel of Christ and supposedly living according to the word of God. Is it just me or is that the epitome of having the kind of wealth that could land one a spot among the "Rich and Famous?" Remember that production, "Lifestyles of the Rich and Famous" hosted by Robin Leach?

It appears both Joel and Joyce have amassed trust fund wealth talking about Christianity, and yet the true message of Christ somehow gets lost from the opulent wealth they both seem to enjoy. I saved this one for the last of Joyce Meyers frivolous spending. A $23,000 antique marble-topped commode. I would like to be there when she explains that to Jesus. But then, how can either genuinely believe in Jesus or His message, which includes judgment, and feel justified in spending $23,000 on an antique marble-topped commode? Just asking.

We are told to test the spirits and shy away from the ones that are deceptive. Again, I'm not saying they possess deceptive spirits, just passing along what some other fellow Christians have said and why. And it is easy to come to that conclusion. When it comes to the prosperity preachers the line between truth and deception is very much obscured. If wealth comes to Joel or Joyce because they preach a message that resonates with others, as it seems to do, then maybe, just maybe, they are one of us.

THE RULE OF GIVING

Throughout the ages, mentors (meaning evangelical Christians) through all generations have revealed to us "true revelation knowledge" as revealed to them by wisdom imparted by the Holy Spirit and evidenced, as well as collaborated, by the Bible. We are told to test the spirits. That is why many trusts the Baptist, or Methodist, or the Assemblies of God church as well as the Church of God, including the Seventh-day Adventist church to be preaching the truth of giving. And, as we know, they all need money to function, that is why God addressed the principle of giving in the Bible.

Most evangelical pastors understand the principles of giving and preach the ten percent tithing rule, plus any extra someone may want to give for other causes. To understand the principles of giving as directed by the Bible, and the principles behind that giving, all one must do is listen to John Hagee, Charles Stanley, or Dr. David Jeremiah, as well as most of the Protestant preachers who are preaching for the right reasons, those who stayed on God's line, if you know what I mean.

Many refer to the place where Paul met with Melchizedek, the king of Salem, (meaning peace) to discuss the giving to God. Genesis 14:18. This meeting, demonstrated by the actions and exchange of conversation between Melchizedek and Abraham, that something was to be given to God. Paul addresses the amount in Hebrews 7:4 where it spells out the amount given to Melchizedek and is the guide for giving money. When it comes to tithing, even the Mormons have this one right.

THE CHRISTIAN ISSUE

As surprising as it may sound, it is not necessarily the money issue I want to deal with, as mainline Christians have addressed that issue many times. I would like to address other issues regarding the teachings, as well as the core beliefs of some of the faith preachers. I would like to pose the questions asked earlier: Can they find their church in the Bible? Are the prosperity preachers preaching the gospel of Christ? (For the most part, they are. It is their insatiable desire for money, along with their motive, and core beliefs that are in question.) Does their motivation, along with their core beliefs, place them in the land of cultism? Only you can be the judge of that after studying what the prosperity preachers have professed over the years and brought to us by the many who have studied them.

For example, earlier as we saw, for Kenneth Copeland to say that God is the biggest failure in the Bible is a ridiculous thing to say. For Copeland, Price, and John Avanzini to say that Jesus had a big house and lots of money, and for Copeland to say Jesus wore designer clothes (the connotation being that Jesus had money, and lots of it) are all ridiculous things to say. And for Benny Hinn to say that Adam was a superman capable of flying to the moon or swimming with fishes was ridiculous, as well as absurd. For him to say there are nine members of the Trinity is again absurd—he later changed his stance on this one during a discussion between him and Paul Crouch.

Or for Fred Price, (although not officially a prosperity preacher, yet considered one by many) and Marilyn Hickey to say the Holy Spirit is not interested in anyone whose body is less than perfect is not only foolish but leads one to question the thinking of the person, as well. For Price and some others to mockingly make fun of Job, a person highly esteemed by God and a person greatly admired by Christians, is not only offensive, but also it is unwarranted. See what you think about what has been said. First the observation of the Holy Spirit:

> How can you glorify God in your body when it doesn't function right? How can you glorify God? How can He get glory when your body doesn't even work? What makes you think the Holy Ghost wants to live inside a body where He can't see out through the windows (that eliminates the blind), and he can't hear with the ears (that eliminates the deaf). What makes you think the Holy Spirit wants to live inside of a physical body where the limbs and the organs and the cells do not function right? Wow! I wonder if Marilyn Hickey still feels this way.

And then there was Job, sometimes, the actions of God towards Job are questioned because of what God allowed Satan to put him through just to prove a point, but for him to be jeered as dumb and lacking in understanding as some of the prosperity preachers preach seems to be foolish thinking. Besides, God seemed to have no choice when Satan said that He and Job had a deal. That God would prosper him if he worshipped Him. Then looking God straight in the eye, he said, Therefore God, you are not worthy of worship because you must pay people to worship you. Wow! You will not find those words exactly that way in the Bible, but the implications are there as pointed out by Pastor Jeremiah. Was Job an overcomer? Was he an overcomer because he had a good life? No! He was an overcomer despite everything that happened to him by holding on to faith in God. Not only in the bad times but also in the good times, that is what made him an overcomer. A great lesson.

Fred Price is another one many considered a prosperity preacher. Fred died February 2021 which obligated me, at least I felt it obligated me, to delete what has been said about his millions. And since his death, I hate to mention his name in conjunction with any beliefs. Considering I have no say over his future as that lies in the hands of God, I feel obligated to point out a couple of things he has said as they remain as doctrine in some circles.

Taking that into consideration, I am including a couple of important points of his teaching that need to be addressed. Price brought to our attention that Jesus, as well as the apostle Paul and others (including us), call God a fool every time we ask for his will to be done. That is right: as incredible as that sounds, you heard correctly. We call God a fool every time we pray for His will to be done according to Price. As with all the prosperity preachers, the words are there but the spiritual understanding appears to be missing.

When it comes to praying, Fred Price and others have for some time now said that a prayer including the words "if it is your will" is a prayer of doubt and disbelief. Robert Tilton has been known to say this from time to time, calling it a "mealy-mouthed" prayer." With this logic, Jesus would have been praying a foolish prayer when he was in the Garden of Gethsemane just hours away from dying for humanity when he said, "Father, if it is not possible for this cup to be taken away unless I drink it, may your will be done." (Matt. 26:42 NIV). The apostle Luke 22:42 KJV confirmed this when he said: "Father, if you are willing take this cup from me, yet not my will, but yours be done." In both verses, Jesus was praying, "If it is your will, then let it be fulfilled." Remember, Jesus prayed to his Father, "Not as I will, but as Thou wilt." (Matthew 26:39).

As we have seen many of the prosperity preachers have said some rather foolish things, and Christians should expect better from their clergy. We hear questionable words coming from preachers who claim to be born-again, Spirit-filled Christians who assume the responsibility of leading others to the truth. While the money issue ranks rather high on the deception meter, and questionable words should cause concern, it isn't either I want to address. Again, it is the Christian issue. Are these people teaching the truths of Christian theology as defined by the Bible? Only you can decide that after learning more about them.

For example, would the Christian community consider someone knowledgeable of the essence of the word of God if they said they were a "god" and then suggest by being born-again they could have the ability to redeem humanity—if only they had been given the knowledge that had been given to Christ? It is that "redeeming humanity by someone other than the Son of God" that many have trouble with. Again, would this thinking resonate as truth (or even logical) within the Christian community? Probably not. But that is exactly what Copeland has been known to preach. It appears that it was not Christ dying on the cross and the shedding of His blood that drew men to Him and saved humanity, which is the core of every evangelical Christian's belief, but rather, it was a reborn man spending three days in a prison cell under Satan's control "serving our sentence."

What Copeland believes, or at least what he has been known to preach, is that Christ's "emancipated, poured out, wormy little spirit (his exact words) descended into hell and served our sentence" by sitting in a cell three days where Satan had imprisoned Him. And all the demons were there attending the biggest three-day party during which time they were tormenting Him, and then, as Copeland puts it, God rescued him. You know why God was able to rescue him? It was found, according to Copeland, that Jesus had not sinned and therefore, on a technicality, Satan had to release him. Joyce Myers seems to embrace this type of nonsense as well. She says by going to hell, Jesus paid our debt. No! He paid our debt at the cross.

Some of the faith preachers apparently used Acts Chapter 2, verse 31 from the King James Bible to write a whole set of beliefs. A religion that includes Christ descending into hell where Satan had Him locked in a cell being tortured by demons until God came to rescue Him. They may get this from the time He descended into a place defined in the Bible as a prison and offered salvation to those in prison who were lost in the flood during the time of Noah. (1 Peter 3:19-20).[49] More regarding this subject later.

Another interesting fact put forth by Copeland is the suggestion he could have descended into hell and accomplished the same thing as Jesus—sit in a cell to pay the price for our sins because he, Copeland, was a "reborn man" or "twice born-again man"—(the physical birth of water and the spiritual birth by fire) if only he had been given the knowledge that was given to Christ. Once again, this information is all spelled out on the tapes produced by Hank Hanegraaff titled *Christianity in Crisis* and in Walter Martin's book *Kingdom of the Cults*.

In describing his own ability to do the same as Christ (defeat Satan and redeem humanity), Copeland said, "The Spirit of God spoke to me and He said, 'Son, realize this. Now follow me in this and don't let your tradition trip you up.' He said, 'Think this way—a twice born-again man whooped Satan in his own domain.' And I threw my Bible down...like that. I said, 'what?' He said, 'A born-again man defeated Satan, the firstborn of many brethren defeated him.' He said, 'You are the very image, the very copy of that one.' I said, 'Well now, you don't mean, you couldn't dare mean, that

---

49   This requires knowledge of the theology referred to as a "Sixth day creation." A belief that God created people prior to Adam and Eve and never introduced himself as God, nothing about overcoming or salvation. (That occurred in the first chapter of Geneses). Then God created Adam and Eve through which the "Thread of Redemption" began. That occurred in the second chapter of Genesis.

I could have done the same thing?' He said, 'Oh yeah, if you'd had the knowledge of the word of God that He (Christ) did, you could've done the same thing, cause you're a reborn man too.'"[50] Unbelievable!

The core religious beliefs of many prosperity preachers seem to be derived from bits and pieces of Mormonism, as well as the theology of the Jehovah's Witnesses and the Christian Scientists, with some New Age mentality thrown in, along with Gnosticism and stirred around with Christianity. As Justin Peters says, there is truly little theological reality present when one delves into the core of their teachings. They present a good show with lots of "religious overtones," but deep down, from what Copeland said, some prosperity preachers appear to not believe in the atoning blood, or that the blood of Christ was necessary in the plan of salvation, which makes them a cultic religion.

SOME STRANGE BELIEFS

There are three areas of theology I would like to touch upon. One is the Holy Spirit/Faith issue, the second is the Trinity, and the third is a vile doctrine called "the Serpent Seed Doctrine."

Regarding the Holy Spirit/Faith

When it comes to the subject of the Holy Spirit, the faith/prosperity preachers have their own definitions. They say, "The Holy Spirit is a substance, a power force…a tangible force…a conductive force on the same order as electricity." Invisible but one can feel the effects of it. This is a belief that deviates from those who embrace a "Trinity" concept and a belief shared by most secular scholars, as

---

[50]   *Christianity in Crisis*. Also, 1989 tape #00-0202, side 2 Substitution and Identification.

well as some Church of God members. To an evangelical Christian, as discussed earlier, the Holy Spirit, being part of the Trinity, is one substance performing different functions. It is just that simple. I think maybe they might be overthinking this one.

Then there is faith. *Faith*...what an interesting word. The Bible tells us we are saved by faith in Christ. Sometime back, Dean Hamer, former Chief of Gene Structure at the National Cancer Institute, published a book called *The God Gene: How Faith Is Hardwired into Our Genes*, wherein he wrote that people have been wrestling with the roots of faith since faith itself was first codified into Scripture. (God has) set eternity in the hearts of men, says the book of Ecclesiastes.

Probably the best description of faith I have ever come across simply said, "an openness to things not literally provable." (This is where Penn Jillette of Penn and Teller gets hung up.) Hebrews 11 tells us that faith is the substance (proof) of things hoped for, which one day will be evidenced. Again, the lack of evidence in the "here and now" (or as some might say, the lack of ability to see the here and now for what it really is) is what Penn, along with Bill Maher and many non-Christians get hung up on.

Is the Trinity from Satan?

Regarding the Trinity, would any evangelical Christian believe the Trinity to be a vile doctrine from Satan? While I have not heard Hinn, Copeland, Paul Crouch, and others come right out and denounce the Trinity as being a concept spawned by the devil, they do however seem to support those who openly believe this concept. One example is William Branham, who, though deceased due to an auto accident, still could be considered one of the important people within the United Pentecostal Church, a movement supported by the prosperity preachers and Trinity Broadcasting Network.

His exact words were: "Now my precious brothers don't get excited. Let me say this with Godly love, the hour has approached where I cannot hold still anymore...Trinitarian is of the Devil. I say that, 'thus sayeth the Lord.'" How about that? God told him that a belief in the Father, the Son, and the Holy Spirit, commonly referred to by Christians as the Trinity, is of the devil. This comes from a man that the late Oral Roberts, Copeland, Hinn and many others looked to for inspiration.

The Serpent Seed Doctrine

As amazing as their belief is regarding the Trinity, the following intrigued me even more. Mr. William Branham (along with Arnold Murray, who hailed from Shepherd's Chapel before his death, a church located in Gravette, Arkansas now managed by his son) believed in what is referred to as the "Serpent Seed Doctrine." This is basically a pagan doctrine of the devil that has infiltrated Christianity, a doctrine teaching that Eve was impregnated by Satan, from which Cain was conceived, thus beginning a lineage of half-devil people consisting of the blacks and Jews. This doctrine is held in high esteem by the Aryan Nation groups.

Was Cain conceived by Satan? Not according to the Bible, which says: "Adam lay with his wife Eve, and she became pregnant and gave birth to Cain" (Genesis 4:1, NIV). Either they are wrong, or the Bible is wrong, or they are using the wrong Bible. We can decide for ourselves. Now, Copeland and Hagin supported William Branham (a believer in the Serpent Seed Doctrine and in the Trinity being of the devil) as not only a true man of God but also a great man of God.

The confusion I have is that Copeland and Hinn support the doctrine of the Trinity but then praised William Branham and called him a true man of God, a man who said that the Trinity is of the devil...and had a belief in the Serpent Seed Doctrine. Also, Paul and Jan Crouch of TBN thought William Branham was a lovely person, and he may well have been. Finding the good in people is what made Paul and Jan and TBN extremely popular even though many thought they promoted the theology of the prosperity preachers and embraced the doctrine of the Pentecostal churches by supporting them as much as they did. Many of the prosperity preachers come from the ranks of the Pentecostal churches, especially the Assemblies of God.

The Pentecostal Church

Many of the prosperity preachers support the United Pentecostal Churches, an organization that openly denies the doctrine of the Trinity and a church organization that is considered a "cult" by many Christian families. Hey, that is not my opinion, but that of Hank Hanegraaff, Wayne Martin and others. This is an organization that claims the Trinity, an essential element of the Christian faith, is a pagan doctrine. They also accepted the teachings of A. A. Allen, who died from alcoholism while preaching against it. There are those who would dispute that, but the evidence appears to be overwhelming. Before Allan's demise, his healing powers, and his ability to raise money were equal to Branham's.

It was said that he would pray over shredded pieces of his old tents (he was into tent revival) and sent them to followers as a healing point of contact—in exchange for a monetary gift, of course. At least that is what Arlene Sanchez-Walsh told us on June 28, 2013 on the website usreligion.blogspot.com. Apparently, not much has changed as some still offer miracle water or a cloth of some sort—for a slight donation.

While both Branham and Allen promulgated the Pentecostal movement, it was a lady by the name of Aimee Semple McPherson who is credited as founder of the Foursquare movement (a movement associated with the Holy Rollers, from which some Pentecostal churches evolved). It is said McPherson died from liver failure.

Regarding the term "Holy Rollers" as discuss earlier, during the 60s and 70s, the idea behind the epithet is that believers of certain denominations engaged in bizarre behavior during their worship services, including falling on the floor and rolling around in the aisles. Or as some may say, "a member of an evangelical Christian group that expresses religious fervor by frenzied excitement or trances. The term Holy Roller has always been considered derogatory in the past, but the times have changed.

As for the Pentecostal churches in general, I believe the name "Pentecostal" relates to Spirit filled churches, but some have problems recognizing the true Holy Spirit. I say that after visiting several and finding the same in all. I have even been in Pentecostal churches when they have had evangelist visit where plenty of "amen," "hallelujahs," and "bring it on" fill the air, but nothing like I felt in that United Methodist Church I attended or a few others.

When attending some Assemblies of God churches, I observed a soothing, washing of the Holy Spirit, sometimes accompanied by the raising of hands, and/or maybe a tear or two, the same Spirit as was present in the Methodist Church I attended for a while, a church that overflowed with the Holy Spirit. Sometimes, when attending a church, any church, any denomination, and listening to all that Christ did for us, especially if delivered with the power of the Holy Spirit and received with the same Spirit, it is hard to contain our emotions, and some arrive at an emotionally overflowing place of worship. That is the Spirit most churches strive for.

As we know there are evangelical Christian families, of which I would consider the Assemblies of God, who may have relatively minor doctrinal differences, but those differences have never distorted the core message of the Bible, at least not to my knowledge. Many Christians who have studied the beliefs of the faith preachers come away with an understanding of just how perplexing and distorted some of the ideas and concepts embraced by those preachers really are.

Bottom Line: Search for the Truth

We must each analyze the information put forth here regarding the truthfulness of the message delivered, not only by Joel Osteen and Joyce Meyer but all who preach for money. Test the Spirits. In addition to the information that has been revealed herein, continue expanding upon knowledge to make an intelligent and informed decision regarding the faith/prosperity preachers who have been exposed, as well as who follow in their footsteps, those coming on the scene almost daily. The Bible lets us know deception will increase in the latter days, and I do not believe many Christians would deny that.

As a Christian might say, test the spirits for truth. In other words, you might hear a prosperity preacher say, *"The Holy Spirit laid it upon my heart that God has a blessing for you."* Then they continue: *"Trust the Spirit, go to the phone right now and arrange to send in that $1,000-dollar pledge."* Should you do that or not? Ron White said they apparently had the wrong person in mind when asked to send them money. Anyway, that is a decision only you can make. Just remember, the money you send to most of these charlatans is spent for their pleasure as we discussed. And while you are making that call donating your hard-earned money, keep in mind, both Jessie and Copeland, especially Jessie, still wants another plane so they won't have to encounter "demons" as they say they would on a commercial airline. Even traveling first class.

So, I say, keep the money and spend it on yourself, or your family. Better that than having it going towards some luxury item or vacation for another prosperity preacher. Or perhaps buy someone another $23,000-dollar antique marble-topped commode No matter what one calls it, that's a $23,000-dollar toilet. This spending of the "Rich and Famous" leaves the Christian community questioning their motives, but again, that is between them and God.

It would probably be here that my friends would say, "He said all of that to say this." For anyone wishing to delve into anything that has been discussed regarding the faith preachers, he or she need only to order the tapes *Christianity in Crisis,* produced by Hank Hanegraaff, and a book he edited, *Kingdom of the Cults,* by Walter Martin. You can order a copy of either or both by calling 1-704-887-8200, or writing to Christian Research Institute International, PO Box 8500, Charlotte, NC 28271.

CHAPTER VIII

FATHERS OF EARLY CHRISTIANITY

In addition to the early Fathers of the Catholic Church, there were apostolic Christian theologians who lived in the first and second centuries who are believed to have personally known some of the twelve apostles, or to have been significantly influenced by them. Some of the more influential Fathers would be Clement of Rome, (35-99 A.D.). While being declared a pope from the age of 88 until his death at age 99, he was considered the first apostolic Father of the early church. Others would include Ignatius of Antioch, an early Christian writer and bishop of Antioch. Then there was Polycarp of Smyrna, a Christian who converted many from Gnosticism to Christianity.

Some early Fathers wrote theology that was adopted by both Catholics and Protestants, which is why one will find an overlapping of Catholicism in some of the Protestant churches and in the Greek Orthodox Church, as well. In the first two or three centuries of the Christian church there were scholars writing the theology that many churches adhere to today. Others would include men such as Irenaeus, (130-202 A.D.), who was a Greek bishop noted for his role in combatting heresy and defining Catholic orthodoxy. Of all the earlier scholars, Origen of Alexandria was perhaps the most

Protestant Christian, as well as Tertullian,[51] he was considered a Protestant Christian as well.

And then we have St. Augustine along with others who contributed most to the Christianity we see today in both Catholic as well as Protestant churches. Some, as we saw, received inspiration from philosophers such as Cicero, Plato, Socrates, Aristotle, and so on. It was not until later when the reformers entered the picture, or one might say, reemerged from the dark ages that the hold the Catholic Church had on Christianity was broken and the Protestant belief in salvation by faith, as present in the first century, once again, became the bedrock of one's salvation.

In addition to the Fathers discussed above, in both the Catholic Church and Eastern Orthodox Church, there are four who are called the "Great Church Fathers."[52] There was Ambrose (AD 340-397), Jerome (347-420), Augustine of Hippo (354-430), and Pope Gregory I (540-604). Other church Fathers include Basil of Caesarea (c. 329-379), Athanasius of Alexandra (296-373), Gregory of Nazianzus (329-389), and John Chrysostom (345-407), who was Archbishop of Constantinople. John Chrysostom was the first to label the Jews as Christ killers and began an era of anti-Semitism. You heard that right—he has been quoted in his homilies (lectures) as saying:

> The Jews are the most worthless of all men. They are lecherous, greedy, and rapacious. They are perfidious murderers of Christ. They worship the devil; their religion is a sickness. (I wonder if he will tell us how he really thinks.) The Jews are the odious assassins of Christ, and for killing God there is no expiation possible, no indulgence or pardon. Christians may never cease vengeance, and the Jews must live in

---

[51] It was Tertullian (AD 160-229) who said, "The blood of the martyrs is the seed of the church."

[52] https://en.m.wikipedia.org.

servitude forever. God always hated the Jews. It is
incumbent upon all Christians to hate the Jews.[53]

Wow! That is even more intense than what John MacArthur
said about Hank Hanegraaff joining the Greek Orthodox church,
and about the NAR movement. Even with the knowledge of John
Chrysostom's anti-Semitic remark, George Weigel on page 9 of his
recently published book, *God's Choice* (a book about John Paul II),
acknowledges him as one of the great Fathers of Christianity. Also,
he was called a "saintly patriarch of Constantinople," where he
was known as the "Golden Tongue" because of his eloquence and
mastery of scripture, so says Thomas Bokenkotter on page 66 of his
recently published book, *A Concise History of the Catholic Church.*

How about one more by John Chrysostom? In a series of eight
Sermons Against the Jews, he sought to chasten both Christians
who were still embracing forms of Jewish practices and the Jews
themselves. In one of his homilies he said, "I know that many people
hold a high regard for the Jew and consider their way of life worthy of
respect at the present time. This is why I am hurrying to pull up this
fatal notion by the roots…(A) synagogue is not only a whorehouse…
it is also a den of thieves and a haunt of wild animals."

Wow! Again, Wow! To many a Protestant that is probably
blasphemy in the most royal form. And George Weigel, along with
many current leaders, think of him as one of the great Fathers of
Christianity. Other leaders following the leadership of the Catholic
Church declared synagogues "a place where Christ is denied…a
haunt of infidels, a home of the impious, a hiding place of madmen
under the damnation of God Himself." If many of the early Catholic
Fathers were not so reserved maybe they would tell us what they
really think about the Jewish people. Who would have known
Catholicism, or at least the deep seeded roots of some leaders of

---

53   John Hagee, *Jerusalem Countdown: A Warning to the World* (New York:
FrontLine Publisher, 2006).

Catholicism, could hold such deep resentment against the Jews? This information was brought to our attention by Charles Kimball.[54]

During the early days of the church many scholars, those who possessed the Spirit of God and some who didn't, passed through the halls of Christianity and left their mark. As Richard Marius writes in his book, *Martin Luther—the Christian Between God and Death*, there are those who choose to follow the sentiment of pagan writers who were present throughout the history of the church. Poets and philosophers such as Cicero, Plato, Lucretius, and many others who were noted for their wisdom and eloquence prior to the birth of Christ. Respected scholars who assumed that death was the end of life and that the truest wisdom of all was to live as if death did not matter (antinomian theology). Cicero, following the death of his only daughter made a valiant effort to find some hope of immortality, but his efforts only ended in skepticism.

Of all the Fathers of religion, as you have probably surmised by now, would have to be St. Augustine. He certainly had the most impact upon religion as it is his philosophy that many Christians, especially Catholics, have incorporated into their brand of Christianity. Someone that important might warrant a fleeting moment of our time.

St. Augustine the Man

St. Augustine had the most impact upon the religion that many follow today in both the Protestant as well as the Catholic Church. It was St. Augustine who introduced the doctrine of the Elect. Again, the most controversial issue among Christians today. It was St. Augustine who began to introduce disputed theology into Christianity that many opposed, but then many accepted. Richard Marius tells us in his book, *Martin Luther,* that Augustine was one of the most fanatical, superstitious, and ugly-tempered men in

---

54   Charles Kimball. *When Religion Becomes Evil.*

the history of Christianity. Regarding St. Augustine's disposition, outside of Catholicism it seems that many agree with Marius.

I have studied St. Augustine a bit and he appeared not to have liked himself very much. Something to do with the tormenting guilt of having a baby out of wedlock and living with a woman outside of marriage, and a mother who was constantly reminding him he was living in sin, while he was preaching salvation and creating the Christianity that many follow even now. This is perhaps why the Catholic Church mitigates sin and instructs its priest to not admonish their parishioners. Seems he was not able to do anything about his feelings of guilt outside of having faith in God to forgive and forget and accept His word that he will. But St. Augustine never seemed to find the peace that comes with forgiveness. One might conclude his attitude was like King Saul, another one who did not seem to like himself very much or find peace.

St. Augustine had a great influence upon the Catholic Church, as well as the Protestant Church, especially those churches who broke with the Church of England, which itself broke with the Catholic Church, forming the Anglican Churches.[55] The only noted exception would probably be the Methodist family, which was started by John and Charles Wesley after breaking with the Church of England— but they still carried forth some of the Catholic teachings. For example, Charles Wesley believed in the sinless nature of Mary throughout her lifetime. A belief most Protestants question and I believe the Methodist church has since ignored.

The Emergence of the Bible

In the beginning was the Torah. The first five books of the Bible that were translated into Greek at the request of Ptolemy II

---

[55] Facts: The Episcopal Anglican Church originated when King Henry VIII split from the Roman Catholic Church in 1534, when the pope refused to grant the king an annulment.

Philadelphus (285-247 B.C.) by seventy Jewish scholars. From that the Septuagint Bible, as it was called, originated when the Hebrew Bible, or Old Testament, was translated into Greek. According to most biblical experts, the Greek Septuagint is the first translation ever assembled.

This was accomplished in approximately A.D. 132, when a collection of Hebrew and Aramaic scrolls were translated into Greek. It was from the Greek Septuagint that Jerome in approximately A.D. 400, at the request of the Catholic Church, translated the Greek Septuagint into what became known as the Latin Bible (the Vulgate Bible). This manuscript included all 39 books of the Old Testament and the 27 books of the New Testament in the same language: Latin. It was this Bible that early Catholic Masses were being conducted and the only Bible for centuries authorized by the Catholic Church.

It is from the roots of the Greek Septuagint that evangelical theology is derived. Eventually, this information made its way to the forefront of people's thinking, when laypeople could read for themselves the written word translated directly from the Greek Septuagint. It took a while but, the written word became the voice of many, and, as with those who left the church to spread that word, such as Martin Luther and John Huss, many paid dearly for that voice.

When a mention of the written word, the Bible is interjected into many conversations, the question that seems to come to mind is which Bible? Regarding the Bible, I am referring to the (New) King James Version, the American Standard Version, and the New International Version—Bibles many find trustworthy. Regarding trust Christian's place in the Bible, I found that the trust is justified even when some questions concerning what could be construed as discrepancies might appear to be an area of contention; when, in fact, many believe the information contained in the Bible is correct but can only be ascertained by wisdom—one of the gifts of the Holy Spirit.

The Bible points to God as its author, even though it was penned by human hands. We are told by Ellen G. White, in her book, *The*

Great Controversy…Ended, that the Bible was written throughout different ages by men who differed widely in rank and occupation, and in mental and spiritual endowments. The books of the Bible present a wide contrast in style, as well as a diversity in nature of the subjects unfolded. As several writers present a subject under *varied aspects and relations,* there may appear to the superficial, careless, or prejudiced reader, to be discrepancies or contradictions, where the thoughtful, reverent reader, with clearer insight, discerns the underlying harmony.[56]

After Johannes Gutenberg's work on the printing press began in approximately 1436, the word of God spread quickly. Between 1466 and 1522, there were twenty-two editions of the Bible in print. A translated version reached Italy in 1471, the Netherlands in 1477, and Spain in 1478, and a copy was being distributed in France around 1474. Even Martin Luther participated as one of his major life projects in the translation of the New Testament into German, beginning around 1521. Every one of the translators, if caught, as well as anyone who possessed a Bible, was arrested, and put to death.

For the first time, the church was being held accountable for its teachings and some of those teachings were being challenged. From this time forward, until the time of Martin Luther, one could say Christianity went into the deep freeze. The Fathers of the Catholic Church, as one might expect, did not want to relinquish any hold they had upon Catholicism/Christianity. Until Gutenberg's printing press came along, they had gone unchallenged and were accepted by the masses. Now it was too late to change anything as they were and still are considered by many to be the only "true" Christianity since the days of Constantine.

Now at the fifteen century the Catholic Church was being challenged. And prior to Martin Luther, those who would challenge the church's authority would be considered heretics, religious

---

[56] E. G. White, *The Great Controversy Ended…A Glimpse into Eternity* (Silver Springs, MD: Better Living Publications, 1990/2002).

outcasts worthy of being burned at the stake. And they especially did not like to explain themselves or their doctrine. But they didn't seem to have a problem teaching and promulgating Catholicism. As you have probably guessed, those who did the challenging never came together after the Catholic Church went their separate way embracing doctrine that was questioned by Protestants, but never explained. Considering this, I will still stick with the Apostolic Church as defined in Acts, the Church the apostles and the Holy Spirit established.

Targeted Protestant Groups

Two groups the Catholic Church targeted the most were the Cathars and the Waldensians.[57] Two underground groups that protected the Protestant line of Christianity by sending forth individuals whose main mission was to preserve the flame of the Church of the Way as defined in Acts. The church that was born on the day of Pentecost, the church that Ananias and Sapphira lied to and paid the price for that lie. The Catholic Church came later, and via "tradition," they claim roots to the Christianity that began on the day of Pentecost by appointing Peter as pope.

Those who did not accept Peter as pope, or even the "Christianity" of the Catholic Church were the target of the Church until the time of Martin Luther, who was responsible for bringing light back to the Protestant church by breaking the yoke of Catholicism. But until that time, Christians who remained true to the apostolic faith were hunted down and executed. The main mission of the two groups, the Cathars and the Waldensians, was to preserve what they perceived as truths that had been taught by Christ. Just a point of interest, the

---

[57]   It was the Waldensians that the Seventh-day Adventist took after the most. And according to Ellen G. White, they embraced the Sabbath day as the day of worship. The Waldensians were being severely persecuted by the Catholic Church.

Seventh-day Adventist trace many of their roots to the Waldensians who embraced "Sabbath Day" theology.[58]

Eventually, the persecution had to stop. However, prior to that time, many reformers, as well as the many followers of the reformers, would be martyred rather than rescind one word they had spoken against what they considered false teachings that had infiltrated the church. Teachings that did not seem to line up with the Bible, but rather lined up with the teachings from earlier philosophers and became associated with Christianity by the connection of what many refer to as "traditional" theology. The foundation upon which Catholicism is built. Much of which we will be discussing shortly.

It appeared the teachings of the Catholic leaders had been successfully challenged and exposed by the light from reformers who were willing to be put to death at the stake before compromising one syllable of the written word. Not only would they not compromise their understanding of the Bible, but they were also quite outspoken about how their understanding seemed to be in direct contradiction with the teachings of the Catholic Church. While the teachings of the Catholic Church were successfully challenged by the reformers, nothing changed. And, since the Greek Orthodox church is more Catholic in their formality of worship than most Protestant churches many questioned the move by Hank Hanegraaff when he converted (probably not the correct word) from Protestantism to Greek Orthodoxy.

It appears there is a Greek Orthodox as well as an Eastern Orthodox church. They each seem to suggest, a form of Christianity that resembles Catholicism, except that they have a few twists and turns of their own on the way to salvation. Hank said he had been following them and attending the Greek Orthodox Church for some

---

58   For those interested in this period, Ellen G. White's book The Great Conversation…Ended is an excellent read. Some consider her and the Seventh-day Adventist a cult, but they are not. They just embraced some strange theology after that great day of disappointment that occurred on October 22, 1844.

time and conveyed he felt at home within the church as he related to their form of Christianity including the Sacraments.

The Greek Orthodox Church recognizes seven sacraments, same as the Catholic Church but they are somewhat different. The Sacraments are, baptism, chrismation, Communion, holy orders, penance, anointing of the sick, and marriage. While the Protestant church only recognizes two commandments of God in this area, and that is baptism and Communion. Hank has a book to be released soon that discusses why he switched, and it was not a decision he took lightly.

I am looking forward to the release of his book as I believe it will be a window into the differences between some forms of Christianity from a mind that has pondered this decision for quite some time. I look forward to reading Hank's book, as I know I will learn much from his personal journey and the decisions that he was presented with because of that journey. For now though, I am going to remain Protestant and trust in a church system that is a result of the many who gave their life so that we may have knowledge and perhaps acquire some roots upon which to help build a solid foundation.

Regarding Hanks decision to switch his method of worship, that move is irrelevant as that decision will not remove his name from the book of life as he knows the one who died at the cross. The one who put his name in that book and why. John MacArthur assessed the move from Protestantism to Greek Orthodoxy as a move that was questionable at best, and he let Hank, a born-again follower of Christ, know what he thought. Sometimes it just gets you to wonder.

CHAPTER IX

THE ROMAN CATHOLIC CHURCH

Many may have noticed by now that the Catholic Church has been conspicuously missing from the churches that are currently mining for souls. The Roman Catholic Church has theology that differs somewhat from the Christianity as found in most of the evangelical churches I have visited over the years. We will examine the theology of the Catholic's who recognize Christ, and yet there remain some striking differences in what they accept as theology and are taught, as opposed to the teachings of most mainline evangelical churches—the Protestant churches of today.

As we journey through some of the doctrine of the Catholic Church, I must repeat the words, "This is nothing personal." If anything, it is about the ego of a system that was able to introduce theology that many said tainted the bloodstream of the Apostolic Church. In the beginning the Catholic Church wielded great power in the world of Christianity, especially after Constantine moved the seat of Roman power to the Byzantine empire, upon which the Greek Orthodoxy seem to get their roots. They, would adamantly disagree, affirming that they get their roots through the apostles, especially the apostle Mark, but other than through "tradition" I see no connection. If the truth be known, the only Christian movement that can claim roots to the apostles and even to the cross, without using the word "tradition" is the Apostolic Church of which evangelical Christians belong.

Many ask of the Catholic Church, if doctrine can be proven to be untrue, then why is it believed as truth? Or when doctrine seems to be questionable, how is it possible it can be accepted as gospel? If we think something to be true, does that make it the truth? That is not an easy question to answer. Man's history abounds with examples of people believing error even when the facts prove otherwise. For example, for centuries, people believed the earth was flat. The earth has always been a sphere of course, yet those who knew and proclaimed that as truth were ostracized, persecuted, and even imprisoned. Just as those who disavowed Catholic teachings that swore the sun revolved around the earth and were persecuted, imprisoned, and even executed for those beliefs. Today, both beliefs would seem ridiculous.[59]

There was a time when one did not dispute the teachings of the Catholic Church. It took the reformation to break the hold the Catholic Church had on religion and bring forth the church, the family of God we see today. In the early centuries the Catholic Church began to grow in wealth, power, and prestige, and like secular monarchs, popes seemed to have become obsessed with ceremonial splendor, lavish extravaganzas, and artistically designed cathedrals. The Catholic Church was constantly living beyond its means and was always in need of cash.

Looking at the history of the church many might surmise it is a church system that has been built upon money, power, and prestige, with a lot of ego thrown in rather than the teachings of the apostles and passed down through the Apostolic Church. The church that even to this day, preaches the birth, death, resurrection, and eventual return of Jesus Christ. The church defined in the book of Acts as

---

[59] The Philadelphia Trumpet. March 2006, Vol. 17, No. 3. From an article written by Dennis Leap.

the church that trusts by faith in the words Jesus introduced to us regarding His Father and the salvation that comes with that knowledge—the amazing gift of eternal life.

Constantly in the pursuit of money to meet financial needs, popes extracted payments from bishops—in effect, imposing taxes on ordinary Christians for special services such as hearings in the papal courts that controlled disputes between clergy and laity and dealt with matters such as marriage and wills. It was during this time that "indulgences" (a certificate to ensure entrance into heaven, or to shorten time spent in purgatory) was used in conjunction with other services and became a huge money maker for the church.

There was a time when the Catholic Church was more powerful than any governing body in existence. Even kings and kingdoms quivered at the name of the pope. But instead of accepting this responsibility—the position given them with the humility of Christ—the church instead exhibited its spirituality with pomp and arrogance. A clear distinction of the humility of Christ and the pomp and arrogance of the Catholic Church is illustrated by paintings that began to appear in Prague around the ninth century. One of the two most popular paintings depicted Christ entering the city of Jerusalem sitting upon an ass followed by his disciples in travel-worn garments.[60]

The other painting portrayed a pontifical procession—the pope arrayed in his rich robes and Triple Crown mounted upon a horse magnificently adorned, preceded by trumpeters and followed by cardinals and prelates in dazzling array. Due to this arrogance of power, it was a time of spiritual darkness for a people who looked upon the pope as the representative of God himself, A God to them holding the keys of heaven and hell and possessing the power to invoke temporal as well as spiritual judgments.

It was during this time that some within the Catholic leadership decided that the pope was, in fact, Jesus hidden, (their words) under

---

[60]   E. G. White, *The Great Controversy Ended.*

a veil of flesh. Some serious Catholics today still believe this. It seems that most believe the pope is always appointed by God. Meaning that, they believe it is His Son, who becomes the pope. That is another reason the Catholics believe the pope has authority over spiritual things, including salvation, and with the establishment of the Sacraments, they did not need the salvation from above, they had salvation appointed by the pope and the Sacraments to teach them how to be a "Catholic." The Protestant church teaches what it means to be a Christian and they trust in the power of the Holy Spirit to do the rest, of course with a lot of help from others. It is during the Sacraments that one receives Christ by way of digesting a wafer, whereas a Protestant teaches faith, spiritual faith, as opposed to a pragmatic act.

Through the Sacramental system of the Catholic Church, the leaders devised a way to retain joiners for life, and they partition Mary to intercede for them. I dare you, find Christ, except in name only, in this religion. Now all they needed to do was establish themselves as the "Elect," the Church, the people, God chose as His to carry forth His instructions. It was this thinking that introduced "Replacement theology." More about that later.

It was believed that the gates of heaven were closed against the people of a region if the pope so declared it. As mentioned earlier, it appears, at least to evangelicals, that it was from this base of self-assertion by the leaders of the church that some controversial issues of theology entered the bloodstream of the Apostolic Church and became a part of it. Theology with issues that continue to plague the halls of Christianity today as they have for approximately the past two thousand years.

For example, Catholics believe in works as prescribed by the church, which is the price necessary to atone or pay penitence for sin. The Catholic Church also introduced what is known as "antinomian theology," "purgatory," and "replacement theology." All are unacceptable theology when compared to what is being preached in the non-Catholic churches. Are they wrong? Probably fifty percent of the religious community would say "no" while the other fifty percent would say "yes." We will discuss each of these controversial issues later, as you might find them interesting.

Indulgences once played a large part in their past, but Catholics have done away with this practice. Or so I thought. Then I was watching a morning Mass titled, "The Rosary and St. Joseph with Fr. Donald Calloway MIC," when he said during a sermon promoting his new book, "10 Wonders of the Rosary," "Did you know that each day 150 thousand people die on this planet? If you add that up for one year that's 55 million people a year dying." (I did not check his math.) He continues by asking a question, followed by an answer that might leave you scratching your head: "Are most of those people prepared for death? Probably not. But if we pray the Rosary you can gain an indulgence for them. We could be making a big dent in purgatory if we do this." Wow! Did he just say that? Who would have thought in today's time and age we would hear those words promoting those ideas?

An evangelical Christian would have a problem with that teaching. It is the differences between the way Protestants approach Christ, understand Christ, and even think about Christ, and one might even say worship Christ, and so on, as opposed to the way Catholics approach Him, and those differences beg for understanding. Hopefully, this chapter will reveal an understanding of what the Catholic Church defines as its beliefs and where some of those beliefs originated.

As with the others we have discussed, we will hold a mirror against the Catholic Church and see what is reflected to us as proclaimed truths. Nothing personal as this has nothing to do with a Catholic per se, as all Christians, including Catholic Christians, believe that every individual heart belongs to God and is His, and only His, to evaluate. Believing that, then one might accept that this book has been written to discuss with the Christian community, those who took a different path than those who stayed on the apostolic path.

Having this discussion may bring us all closer together as we understand one another, at least it will give us a better understanding of what Protestants and Catholics embrace as Christianity while at the same time respecting the fact that there will be born again followers of Christ going to heaven from every church that accepts by faith Jesus as the Son of God and confesses that belief with their mouth. Words spoken by the apostle Paul. And, if we study Paul's writings, we find that he did not add any conditions beyond accept and confess as a requirement to be born again. He fought against those who would impose Jewish law upon the gentile converts. And it is upon those words of Paul, and a desire to follow Christ, that one will be born into the family of God.

One will encounter Protestantism defined by Catholicism as a term that generally refers to a departure from, or denial of, the essential core beliefs of the Catholic Church. A Pastor from the Missouri Synod group of Lutheran Christians told me that as a Protestant, I did not understand the Sacraments of baptism and Communion. I thought to myself, that can't be right. Then I thought, just so there is no misunderstanding, that is exactly what a Protestant believes as they depart from or choose to be an evangelical Christian as opposed to accepting Catholicism, but that shouldn't mean we cannot get along when it comes to discussing religion. Afterall, did not Christ tell us to love one another? That would seem to indicate getting along is important to God.

CAN WE ALL LOVE ONE ANOTHER?

I, along with most members of the Protestant family, love the Catholic family, as we know they love us. This is not about who loves the other more, or who worships Jesus more, or who revers Him more, but about the teachings that differ between the two religions, and nothing more. Catholics are considered by many to be in the Christian family and perhaps dying for the cause of Christianity even as we speak. Having said that, let me begin by saying, "Thank you Lord, for the Catholics who look to your Son for salvation."

Remember, this chapter is not directed at individuals within the Catholic family, but more toward defining the theology of the church itself. Now, we are discussing information within the Catholic Church that has been handed down over the centuries and embraced by the leaders of Catholicism. Again, this is not against Catholics who are members of this organization, at least not those who would give up their lives, or have given up their lives, defending their faith in Christ, as many have.

Conflicting feelings accompanied my writing, as I was constantly reminded of St. Paul, where he writes in the 14th chapter of Romans (KJV) concerning the law of love and concludes his position with verse 19, "Let us therefore follow after the things that make for peace, and things wherewith one may edify another." The NIV Bible puts it this way: "Let us therefore make every effort to do what leads to peace and to mutual edification." Probably one could interpret that as "it is good neither to do anything by which your brother stumbles, is offended or is made weak." That seems to be the creed most Christians ascribe to and try to follow.

The information contained in this chapter, as mentioned, is not about the Christianity of a Catholic offered to them through Christ or the "saving grace of God." But it is about their beliefs, nothing more. While pursuing information, some beliefs of the church seem to inspire questions. The more research I did, the more inspired I became to find answers regarding ideas and beliefs embraced by Catholicism. It is the questioning of some of these beliefs that inspired the writing of this chapter.

I concur with John Hagee when he wrote the following letter on May 12th, 2008, to Mr. William Donohue, president of the Catholic League for Civil and Religious Rights:

> In recent decades, Catholics, and Evangelicals of good will have worked together to defeat the evil

of Communism, promote what Pope John Paul II called a "culture of life" that protects every human life from conception to natural death, (we have certainly thrown that one out the window) and honors the institution of marriage and defends the right of the poor…. Both Catholics and evangelicals have been engaged to assert the primacy of faith and values in our increasing secular society.

Signed, John Hagee.

Again, I agree. However, there remain some differences, and it behooves every Christian to understand those differences, as some might be considered extremely questionable. By discussing some differences, perhaps a question or two might materialize in one's mind from a seed that has been planted, and that might be all one can expect. I am not anticipating anything changing, but how some of the differences developed is somewhat interesting. Plus, one might grasp an understanding of how dangerous some of the theology might be.

Regarding important similarities, and there are some, as John Hagee just pointed out, there also are some differences, as we will see. I discovered some information provided by Charles Kimball[61] regarding "A Christian America." He said: "Self-proclaimed Bible-believing Christians became a powerful presence on the political landscape during the final two decades of the twentieth century. The Moral Majority, headed by the (late) Jerry Falwell, and the Christian Coalition, founded by the Reverend Pat Robertson[62] have been the most prominently visible among a number of organizations making up the New Religious Right." A religious right that seems to continue losing its voice with the passing of time.

---

[61] Charles Kimball. *When Religion Becomes Evil.*

[62] Pat Robertson embraces a reconstructionist theological position. This orientation challenges the mechanisms of the state and seeks to bring all of life under God's rule.

Then Charles continues: The groups (self-proclaimed, Bible-believing Christians) vary in focus and structure, yet they tend to converge and cooperate on a variety of issues—abortion, homosexuality, gun control, and support of prayer in school, school vouchers, and capital punishment—often grouped under the rubric of "family values." Values shared by both Catholics and Protestants. Again, all good values and virtues followed and embraced by Christians. As mentioned, the Catholics endorse these virtues as do Protestants, but good values alone do not make one a Christian—a follower, a born-again believer.

So, other than both religions having good virtues, there are undeniably differing beliefs shared by the two Judeo-Christian religious groups, (as opposed to Muslims) and that is what this conversation is about, the differences of two Christian organizations. Perhaps with some understanding we can respect one another's perspective and maybe that will bring us closer together in our thinking as Christians. But first, let us discuss some of the differences and similarities we share.

Outspoken Issues of Catholicism

Catholics have always stood up to be counted when taking positions. Some outspoken positions considered deleterious by Catholics include humanism, anti-Semitism (as you will see later, how they overcome the anti-Semitism of the early church Fathers regarding the Jews, I do not know), apartheid, sexual misconduct, and homosexuality. They contend that the tendency toward homosexuality is not a sin but a psychological disorder that needs treatment and deserves sympathy.

Catholic teaching on homosexuality is laid out in the Catechism of the Catholic Church and a number of magisterial documents. The church teaches that while homosexual acts, like all sexual acts outside of marriage, are sinful, having a homosexual orientation itself is not a sin. The church also teaches that LGBT people, like all people, are to be treated with respect.

Pope Francis, elected in 2013, has repeatedly spoken about the need for the Catholic Church to welcome and love all people regardless of sexual orientation. Speaking about gay people in 2013, he said, "the key is for the church to welcome, not exclude and show mercy, not condemnation."[1][63] He said, "If a person is gay and seeks God and has good will, who am I to judge?" He continued by saying, "We must be brothers." [3][64] Pope Francis also reiterated the Catholic Church's teaching on homosexuality, including its position on marriage

He was outspoken on the need to be compassionate towards LGBT people and was named the Person of the Year by the LGBT magazine, *The Advocate*. In 2019, Pope Francis reiterated that Catholic teaching states that homosexual tendencies "are not a sin."[4][65] Many embrace the thinking that homosexuality is not equated with same-sex attraction in the same way that a married heterosexual person might have some attraction toward a person of the opposite sex with whom he/she is not married. If a person does not take any action on that attraction, it is not a sin. At least not a sin that leads to death, the spiritual death. These are both examples of temptations, not sins. The apostle James in his epistle says the same thing. Unless and until a though, or temptation is acted upon, it is not a sin.

The widespread acceptance of a homosexual style of life is, and probably will be, up to the acceptance of each church family. When it comes to the acceptance of homosexuality within the Christian church, some will say "yes" to the idea, while others will say "no." Regarding those who say "yes," I just heard that the Episcopalian

---

[63] HYPERLINK "https://en.wikipedia.org/wiki/Pope_Francis_and_homo sexuality" \l "cite_note-Davies-2."

[64] Ibid.

[65] Ibid.

Church (the main one) voted in March of 2015 to change the words in their constitution to read "a marriage is between two people," rather than "a marriage is between a man and a woman." I personally know what the Bible says, but any judgmental call from me is above my pay grade. Way above.

I would say the Catholic Church should be the first to point the finger of "guilty" toward themselves when it comes to immorality. Regarding the issue of sexual misconduct that has plagued the Catholic Church for multiple decades, I agree with what Donald Miller had to say in his book, *Searching for God Knows What*. He said, "Yesterday I watched the C-SPAN coverage of the report issued by the independent committee that investigated the Catholic Church, and they have discovered more than ten thousand cases of sexual misconduct by priests against children."

Even though Donald wrote that information several years ago, the number of assaults must have continued as the amount of money to defend the church is staggering. When I Googled just how much has been paid to date, I was shocked to see $3,994,797,060.10 has been paid out as results of the sex abuse scandals. Wow! Anyway, Miller continues: "This is a very sad thing because most of the Catholics I know are quite wonderful people who love one another and care about one another, and who are involved in defending social justice."

I can relate to what Miller just said, as I have wonderful and caring Catholic friends, as well. We just agree to disagree and talk about the weather and how our fantasy sports teams are doing. Again, this has nothing to do with Catholics because they are great people; it is the Catholicism brought forth by some of the earlier Fathers of the church that gets in the way. For example, it was the lack of spirituality that initiated replacement and antinomian theology. And the leaders who allowed that dogma to become a part of Christianity, that is what is being discussed. And the lack of spirituality within the church that would allow such atrocities to occur is a different spirituality than the one found in many of the evangelical churches. Perhaps a religion that has been built upon pragmatism as opposed to the spirituality that the apostolic (reformed) church Fathers were building upon, and in many cases costing them their life.

On Thursday, August 10, 2017, in *USA Today*, we were once again reminded of the shameful atrocities of the church as the headlines read, "Shattered Faith, Guam's Catholic Church Crisis: Horrifying stories of sexual abuse span decades." How many decades? Let's see if we can get a glimpse from the following information beginning from information contained in the article: "If you tell anyone, no one will believe you because I am a priest," from an accuser describing what his alleged tormentor told him in 1975. Going forward from 1975, and perhaps prior until 2017 when the atrocities were brought to light, is a long time and several decades of abuse. And why would Christ, the pope, as the Catholic Fathers have said. concealed under a vale of flesh, allow such atrocities?

Jarring allegations coming from lawsuits that never seem to stop, and the corruption that goes into trying to hide and shield the abominations as they spring up from everywhere in the world, are atrocious. Recently, one of many lawsuits claiming assault from 1985 to 1988 describes rampant child sexual abuse by the priest of Guam, assaults by some of Guam's most revered men. An investigation by the USA Today Network's *Pacific Daily News* unearthed allegations of decades of assault, manipulation and intimidation of children raised on the remote, predominantly Catholic U.S. territory. Sounds a little like a sexual predator's Paradise. On and on the lawsuits go, and on and on the manipulation continues, never seeming to end.

ONE CHRIST, TWO PATHS

I was having breakfast with a friend the other morning when I noticed three people sitting at a table that I had to pass when I left the restaurant. I noticed the fish symbol with a cross through it on the gentleman's shirt as I was passing their table (it looked cool) and mentioned it to him. The gentleman said they were going to church at 11:00 a.m. and invited me to join them. Noticing the emblem on the front of the shirt pointed to Catholic, I said, "I see you're Catholic," which he confirmed. I said, "I would love to attend Mass with you, but I'm a Protestant." They said, "That's okay." I politely offered to attend perhaps at another time while in the back of my mind arose all the differences between the two religions.

Catholicism has evolved from the beliefs written in the early days of Christianity. Beliefs handed down through the ages, upon which both Catholic and Protestant Churches were built. Protestants can trace their roots to the day of Pentecost when the Holy Spirit began to indwell Christian believers. Since the theology and doctrine one might find when attending a Catholic Church is so different compared to the doctrine that one might find when attending a Protestant Church, many might suggest that somewhere along the way, they must have taken different paths.

As we know, the plan of salvation probably began with God before the foundations of the earth were even poured, but the concept of Christianity began with the death and resurrection of Christ. Without the resurrection we would not have Christianity. It was in trying to understand how someone could have died and yet live that Christianity was born. The crux of a Christians belief is that a human being was resurrected from the dead and walked among the people for forty days to fulfill earlier prophecies before ascending into heaven. Many earlier Christians were probably struck with awe during the first couple of centuries just trying to figure everything out. A man died and yet lived. How could that be? And was it true?

The research and diligence that must have occurred to find out everything there was to know about this person must have been overwhelming—who He was, what He taught, and so on—and who did He teach it to? In answering those questions, a couple of different interpretations emerged as a result of "understanding." It appears that two major interpretations of the Bible were declared as gospel. Not the Bible, per se, but interpretations of that book were revered differently.

It was around A.D. 64 at the death of the apostle Peter that a struggle began to emerge involving the church of the apostles, the Apostolic Church, also called the Church of the Way in the book of Acts, and those who would initiate a differing opinion of the Bible. A struggle for influence that intensified for several years continuing even after the apostle John, author of the book of Revelation, died around A.D. 100, and continued until the time of Constantine around A.D. 300. Then after A.D. 313, the Catholic Church became the dominate religion of the west and the Apostolic Church began going underground to survive.

Shortly after his "conversion," Constantine left Rome, moving the Roman Empire to what was then known as the Byzantine Empire. This occurred between 300 and 313, at that time the name was changed to Constantinople and referred to as "the new Rome." Many have said it was during this time that the Greek Orthodox Church took roots, Anyway, this move of the Roman empire by Constantine to Byzantine left the western church practically free from imperial influence to develop its own form of religion, especially since Christianity has now been declared an accepted religion. The Pope, the Bishop of Rome, in the seat of the Caesars, was now the greatest man in the west. You know why Constantine left Rome? For military advantages of course, but I believe it was his biographer who said that Constantine left Rome because it had become too vile and corrupted.

Constantine, while still retaining power as Emperor, was instrumental in overseeing the first Council of Bishops, known as the Edict of Milan, ending the persecution against Christians. Constantine and Licinius the Emperor of the East at that time, entered into an agreement in 313 to end Christian persecution. Then in A.D. 325 the Council of Nicaea conducted a meeting between Roman officials and elders of the "Church" to establish a pathway to knowing, understanding, and receiving Christ, as well as dispelling some heretical theology.

This meeting gave rise to the departure from the original New Testament Church with the introduction of the first set of rules regulating the new religion as adopted by the council and mandated as the religion of the land. During the reign of Constantine, Christianity began to transition from the apostolic faith to the dominant religion of the Roman Empire, an empire that would become known as the Holy Roman Empire going forward and the religion of that empire was known as Catholicism.

East Verses West

Many consider the move by Constantine the genesis of two religious powers, the Catholic Church of the west (old Rome) and the Eastern Orthodox church of Constantinople (new Rome), and it was this way until 1054 when the final split came between the East and the West. They had been at odds over the authority of theology for some time, as each had their own ideas of Christianity that came from the power base each held, and when those ideas did not synchronize, a clash would usually ensue until the final split came.

Do you know one of the reasons why they split, other than not getting along? Michael Cerularius, Patriarch of Constantinople, and Pope St. Leo IX were not friends, and each one mistrusted the other. Cerularius crossed the line when he wrote in a letter that the Latin use of unleavened bread during the Eucharist was Jewish and not Christian. Catholics were using unleavened bread as opposed to the Eastern Church, which was using leavened bread. By so doing, Cerularius was denying the validity of the Holy Eucharist in the Western Church, which Leo countered by saying that the patriarchs had always been puppets of the Byzantine emperors.[66] You probably have noticed there was not much love between the two religious entities.

---

66   https://www.dummies.com.

Another irritation came when Pope Leo III crowned Charlemagne king of the Franks, as Holy Roman Emperor in 800, which he had no right to do. A pope was never given the authority to appoint emperors, and it was as if the church of the East was of no consequence. From this disrespect alone a split was inevitable. The major split that brought finality to the situation came when the earlier Fathers of Christianity decreed that the Holy Spirit is given only by God, which was written in stone at the first Nicene council and agreed upon by all. Now some words were about to be added by the church of the west in what became known as the filioque (more in a second) over the strong objection of the church of the east.

These are just a couple of examples of centuries of disputes and disagreements that eventually culminated in the eleventh century split between the ruling parties of Eastern Orthodox (Constantinople—the New Rome) and Western Orthodox (the Old Rome). For centuries, the relationship between the east and west was estranged but under the Roman Pope Nicolas 1 (858-867) a schism arose over a dispute that involved papal claims of "absolute power."

To emphasize the point, he put in a letter in 865, addressed to the Eastern Orthodox church, which was not received very well by anyone outside of Catholicism, with the following bold statement: "The Pope is endowed with authority over all the earth, that is, over every Church."[67] Wow! Not only did the church of the east reject that statement, but as far as I know, so did the Apostolic Church.

This was the beginning of what would become the final separation that occurred a couple hundred years later, again, known as the great schism. Two major heavyweights in the arena of Christianity, but the other family, the family of apostolic Christians were always present. True Protestantism was never a part of the Catholic Church, although there are Protestant churches who embrace some Catholic theology. The Catholic Church evolved from the Church of the Way.

---

[67]   Timothy Ware. The Orthodox Church. Penguin Publisher: New York, N.Y. 1993.

As late as 1204, even though several attempts were unsuccessful to reunite the two, the church of the west became what many would describe as indelibly separated from the east. New Rome (Constantinople—considered the center of the Byzantium Empire, which is currently Turkey) continued to live in a Patristic[68] atmosphere, using the ideas and language of the Greek Fathers of the fourth centuries. But in the west, (Old Rome) the tradition of the Fathers was replaced by Scholasticism—that great synthesis of philosophy and theology worked out in the twelfth and thirteen centuries.

As we have seen, a separation known as the Great Schism had been coming for some time over the control desired by each that finally culminated with what is called "filioque" (pronounced *fil O quay*). This changed the wording of the Nicene Creed written in 325, which had been introduced as the first uniform Christian doctrine to say that the Holy Spirit proceeded only from the Father, until the church of the west decided to add the words, *and the Son.*

The adding of words to what had already been put in stone (much like adding words to the Ten Commandments) was the final straw, and to this day that is still a contested issue between the two. I just found that interesting information and did not know if I would get a chance to include it later. Eventually, the Byzantine Empire was conquered by the Muslims in A.D. 1453 on their way to capturing Jerusalem. That was what the Crusades (c. 1095-1492) were all about, to reclaim Jerusalem for Christianity. Again, I just found that interesting.

---

[68] Patristic. I had to look that one up myself. It is the study of early Christian writers who are designated Church Fathers and synthesis was the merging or blending of philosophy with theology associated with those early Christian writers.

Was Peter a Pope...

...as Catholicism claims? And does one ingest Christ by consuming a wafer, or is this only a symbolic act? These are probably two of the most frequently asked questions of Catholics by Protestants. First Peter was never a pope and hopefully, this will be substantiated as we proceed, and yes, a Catholic does receive Christ via a wafer. A pragmatic act symbolizing the "receiving of Christ." Since Peter lived prior to Catholicism being integrated into the original church, it might be hard to conceive of him being pope of a system he had never heard of and was non-existence in his time. If one studies the book of Acts, they find it refers to Christianity more in the Protestant vernacular than in the Catholic. Because of this, many might question the claim that he was even a Catholic, much less a pope. As we will see shortly there is a reason for Catholics to include this dogma in their theology.

Prior to the great Protestant movement of 1517 to reclaim the Apostolic Church of the apostles, there were some questionable doctrines being introduced into the blood stream of Christianity and Peter being declared a pope was one of those questionable assertions. And then the body, the literal body of Christ being received via a wafer at Mass was the other questionable assertion that took center stage. When one studies Catholicism they understand how the earlier Fathers applied certain aspects of the Bible to justify their beliefs, as they should. Protestants understand that and use the words of the Bible to do the same, placing considerable value on the meaning of Sola Scriptura for example. It was dubious theology being introduced into Christianity during the early church that would forever change the complexion of what it meant to be a Christian, including salvation, redemption, and even the method of receiving Christ.

So, the question becomes, where and when did all the instructions originate that became necessary to become a Christian? All the rules and regulations, as well as the Sacraments and questionable doctrines, such as purgatory, antinomian theology, and even replacement theology. And this does not even begin to address that for payment of sin one must participate in some form of restitution—preform some functions which allows one to feel worthy enough to once again be in good standing with God and the church.

It is as if our slate of sins, misdeeds, disobedience, and so on, are wiped clean after each confession, and if we die with some unconfessed sins on the books, we go to purgatory to do penance until they are all eradicated and then we move to heaven. If only it were that easy. If only we were given a second chance to enter heaven. As we will see shortly, attending confession to erase our sins might not accomplish what one is led to believe.

Then, as pointed out, there is the issue of Peter being named the leader of a church system that was not even present when he was alive. That's right. Peter was one of the Fathers of the Church of the Way as discussed in the book of Acts. That is important information for a Protestant to understand. Peter was never a Catholic, yet he was *appointed* the first apostolic pope of Rome. That was done so the Catholic Church could claim that they have a connection to the Apostolic Church and claim the title of "first on the block" with lineage that can be traced through Peter to Christ.

That is according to Catholic tradition. *Tradition.* Someone declares it, as in Peter being a pope, or Catholicism being the first religion on the block, and so on, and people believe it because of the authority behind it, and after a while it becomes a tradition. For evangelicals of today to affirm uncritically what evangelicals thought and did in the past is to be trapped by a tradition. It does not matter whether the tradition in question is evangelical or not. The key point is that it is a tradition.[69] Tradition is to be honored where it can be shown to be justified and rejected where it cannot.[70] If it is

---

[69] Fudge, Edward William. *The fire that consumes.* Eugene Orgon: Cascade Books. 2011

[70] Ibid.

based upon tradition established by circumstances or occurrences, or because someone such as a pope said it, it is referred to as a dogma. Many who study the Catholic Church find much of Catholicism has been built upon "traditions."

The Protestant church family connects with the apostles, as our roots go deep into the Christianity of the first church as brought to us by the apostle Paul, who wrote most of the New Testament. Never once did he, or Peter, or any of the other apostles, mention the Catholic Church. Protestants can trace their roots to the first church by reading the Bible, especially the book of Acts. A church that began on the day of Pentecost, a church that was on the verge of being eradicated a couple of times but made a full recovery during the time of the Reformation.

Again, a time that cost many their lives but without that bloodshed, Protestants would not know about their roots. When confronted with the logic of the Apostolic Church being the first movement of Christianity, both the Catholics and Greek Orthodox Church members counter this by saying they are "traditionally" bound to the apostles. They also say their teachings are justified by scripture as we will discuss later.

The Catholic Church claims authority to assert themselves as the true religion of the land because of the conversation between Peter and Jesus when it was revealed to Peter that Jesus was the Messiah, the Christ. Then Jesus called Peter the rock, (Matt. 16:17. NIV) A rock of understanding and stability and said that upon this rock, a rock that many construe to mean the revelation that Christ was the Messiah. It was upon the revelation given to him that the church of believers would be established. And since the Apostolic Church is the church established by the apostles, that would make Peter a leader in the Protestant Church, the Church of the apostles not the Catholic Church.

As mentioned, the Catholic Fathers reached back in time to appoint Peter the first pope as a way of claiming access to the Apostolic Church and proclaim themselves the first on the block, thus the "true" Christianity of Jesus. The Greek Orthodox church reaches back and connects with the apostle Mark, thus claiming they are "the church" God anointed, and Protestants connect with the day of Pentecost claiming they were the first and continue to be the true Christianity Christ established. And Jesus appointed the apostle Paul to teach us what that means.

When Peter gave his first sermon on the day of Pentecost and three thousand people joined the church, they began a movement that later became the church of the Way, the Apostolic Church. Thinking about that for a minute, some of the apostles saw Jesus depart this earth after being resurrected from the dead, and that is the message they carried forward—the resurrection. And according to Christ, all who believe upon that will be saved.

Then of course there was John the Baptist saying to repent and be baptized for the forgiveness of sin. For the most part, that appears to be it. I do not remember reading anywhere in the book of Acts where there were conditions placed upon salvation, or how we must attend Mass to receive Christ, or receive the Holy Spirit by accepting the Sacramental System of Catholicism. Instead, I find that when one goes from being a nonbeliever to a believer in Christ as Savior and Lord, accepting Him as the Son of God, they would be saved and become born again. Learning how to become a follower is fulfilled by the desire to be a follower. That is why when we accept Christ, we are given the Holy Spirit, the Spirit of God. By the acceptance of Christ, we become born again and become indwelled by God's Spirit, the Holy Spirit whose job it is to now teach and lead us in all truths.

In addition to the disagreement about Peter being the first pope, Catholics and Protestants disagree about receiving Christ in a wafer during the Mass, referred to as the Eucharist/Communion. Since this is such a big deal between the two, does that mean one is wrong? To a Protestant, receiving Christ via a wafer appears to be a pragmatic act rather than spiritual (as in faith) and is questionable. They both do the Lord's Supper with reverence and respect, that is not what this is about. In Catholicism, when one receives the bread one might ask, are they really receiving Christ? This is theology that was conceived by Aristotle, a Greek philosopher in ancient Greece during the fourth century. He influenced Judeo-Islamic philosophies during the Middle Ages as well as Christian theology and the scholastic traditions of the Catholic Church.

St. Augustine (355-430 A.D.) was someone who Catholics considered one of the Fathers of the Church. Someone who himself had been influenced by Aristotle, (384-322 B.C.) who was influenced by Socrates (470-399 B.C.) as well as some earlier philosophers. It was their input that began to influence Christianity with new thinking. Remember patristic?[71] Much of that new thinking abounds today and when it manifests itself, it changes the original teachings of the apostles, making Christianity more pragmatic than spiritually driven. Socrates—now, there is an interesting person. When he was an old man, the citizens of Athens condemned him to death, alleging that he denied the reality of the gods, and as we know the Greeks had many of them, so eventually he was found guilty of corrupting the youth of Athens and that he must die. In the end, he calmly drank poison—hemlock—and died a noble death.

From the early days of Catholicism—or more precisely, during the time of St. Augustine, theology was being introduced into the apostolic system by what had now become the "Universal" Christianity of the West. Questionable theology was being introduced into Christianity during the time both Catholicism and the Greek Orthodox Church were still interwoven—between 300 A.D. and 1054 A.D. Perhaps that is why they embrace some of the same theology. It was a lot of this theology (much more from Catholicism than the Orthodox churches of the East) that caused Martin Luther and others to leave the church, bringing forth the Protestant reformation which resulted in the Christianity embraced and enjoyed by Protestants even to this day.

---

[71] Patristic. The study of early Christian writers who are designated Church Fathers. And synthesis was the merging or blending of philosophy with theology associated with those early Christian writers.

CHAPTER X

EVOLUTION OF THE CHURCH'S THEOLOGY

What has been brought to our attention on a couple of occasions is the fact that the apostles established the first Christian church. A Protestant church in the minds of many, even though the origins of the word Protestantism did not officially appear until 1529. That is interesting information when one thinks about it. Martin Luther, the great reformer, was born in 1463 and died in 1546. So, we all became known as Protestants during the time of Martin Luther's rebellion against the Catholic Church which began in 1517.

Up until the time Luther nailed his 95 theses to the door of the chapel in the university town of Wittenberg, which was the catalyst to the reformation, Catholicism had ruled Christianity and was the religion of the land. Brutality was a constant part of Christianity for centuries prior to 1517, but there came a time when truth could no longer be contained, nor was enforcing different beliefs by force any longer an option. Although, as we know, persecuting Christians continued for many more centuries. Christianity has never been free from persecution but now it was a time Protestants of the early Apostolic Church were able to once again, come forward as a force competing for the souls of those they considered to be lost. And that passion among many evangelical Christians is still alive today.

It was during this transformation from the Apostolic Church to the Catholic movement that began around A.D. 64 and later becoming the church age that many consider to be a period leading to the dark ages of Christianity. While Christians have always suffered persecution as Jesus said they would, that persecution became a serious reality around A.D. 538, when the Catholic Church enforced their understanding of "Christianity" upon the world and had a problem with those who passed upon the offer of becoming a Catholic. A very dark period for Christianity ensued, but perhaps without those times we would not have the Christianity we have today, at least we would not have hindsight that allows us to ascertain the truth for ourselves. If not for the blood of martyrs, those who died horrible deaths during those dark ages, we may have never known the truth.

Many might say it was the life of those martyrs to save the original intent of Christianity that the present evangelical movement exists. Earlier Protestants were responsible for bringing back the light of the first Apostolic Church, and it has burned brightly ever since. Regarding the darkness of the past, Tim LaHaye puts it this way in one of his books: "The light that Jesus Christ entrusted to His Church all but flickered out during the Dark Ages and was not rekindled until the days of the Reformation."

Finally, the time had come for the hours of darkness to end, but unfortunately, as just mentioned, this was at the expense of many a Protestant, who shed their blood defending their understanding of Christianity. But it was the shedding of their blood that in many lands appeared as tokens of the coming dawn, a dawn we are privileged to enjoy today. This period is referred to as "the age of enlightenment," an age that undermined the authority of the monarchy and the church and paved the way for the political revolutions of the 18th and 19th centuries.[72]

---

[72]   https://en.m.wikipedia.org

Over the centuries, the supreme authority of the Roman Catholic Church has been questioned by those desirous of a deeper understanding of Christianity. Many early followers of Christ believed the accession of the Catholic Church to power marked the beginning of the dark ages of Christianity. As her power increased, the darkness deepened. Faith was transferred from Christ, the true foundation, to the pope of Rome. Instead of being led to God and trusting in the Son of God for salvation and forgiveness of sins, the people looked to the pope, the priest, and the prelates to whom the pope had delegated authority.[73] They were taught that the pope was their earthly mediator and that none could approach God except through him; *and further, that he stood in the place of God to them and was therefore to be implicitly obeyed.* It appears that this loyalty to the Pope has not changed nor wavered over the centuries.

During the earlier days of Catholicism, the Catholic Church proceeded to establish itself as the only "true religious organization" and the only organization from which "true salvation" could be bestowed. With the establishment of the papacy and the Catholic bishops and priests firmly embedded as spiritual leaders in several major cities, and with Constantinople, Alexandria, and Antioch falling to the east under the influence of the Greek Orthodox Church, the Roman Catholic Church was beginning to become entrenched as the only "true" church of the west.

To grow its base of operations and its membership, the church eventually integrated with paganism. At the time, of Constantine's conversion pagans were worshiping the "sun god" and paying homage to their idols. To entice the pagans to join the church, the leaders of the church sought ways to make the "church" more accommodating to pagans, and therefore the church came under the influence of questionably theology. One of the changes they made was to change the day of worship from Saturday (the Jewish Sabbath) to Sunday, the day the pagans worshiped the Sun God.

---

[73]   Elaine Pagles, *The Gnostic Gospels.* New York: Vintage Books, 1979.

This is one thing that the Adventist harp on and admonish other Christians as they say we "sold out" by joining the Catholic Church and commenced conducting services on Sunday rather than Saturday. Because of this, they think of themselves as the "pure" church family that God will be coming for. The Adventist claim other church families are breaking a commandment by following the Catholic Church and conducing services on Sunday rather than the Jewish Sabbath, and thusly, will be excluded from heaven.

But then, that is the Seventh-day Adventist. For the rest of us we know it was during the early centuries that paganism was being introduced into the blood stream of Christianity and began to corrupt the pure faith of the Apostolic Church and one of those changes was the day of worship. Alexander Hislop, author of the book, *The Two Babylons*, pp.105-106, writes: To conciliate the pagans to nominal Christianity, Rome, pursuing its usual policy, took measures to get the Christian and pagan festivals amalgamated, and, by a completed but skillful adjustment of the calendar, it was found no difficult matter, in general, to get paganism and Christianity—now far sunk in idolatry—in this as in so many other things, to shake hands.

Protestants, especially the Seventh-day Adventist have trouble accepting pagan integration that began early in the life of the church as they saw this integration more to entice pagans to join the church rather than to impart the message of Christ. The religious leaders also, as mentioned, encouraged changing the day of worship from Saturday to Sunday to entice even more pagans into the church. Pagans, who were less sincere and less devoted in their beliefs of an actual virgin birth and physical resurrection, could join the church—mainly Greco Romans who believed Greek mythology and were having a hard time understanding the message of the Bible.

When they joined the church, they clung to their idolatry and pagan ways, only changing the objects of their worship to include images of Jesus, Mary and even the saints. Just a note, there is one difference I found interesting between the Catholic Church and the Greek Orthodox Church regarding how they recognize iconic symbols. The Greek Orthodox Church does not worship them or place them upon pedestals as do the Catholics but uses images and décor to tell the story of the Bible. If one is given the opportunity to visit a Greek Orthodox Church and take a walk with a priest, listening to the stories that are inscribed upon the walls, do it.

The Introduction of Works...

...And the changing of times and laws. During the advancement of Catholicism, many anti-Christian practices of questionable origin were adopted by the church because of pagans who were being allowed to join the church without a Christian conversion, or a spiritual conversion, perhaps more of a pragmatic conversion—but the spiritual one is still in question. As we have seen, the Seventh-day Adventists and the Church of God have a serious problem with both decisions: allowing pagans to join the family of God on their terms and changing the fourth commandment in the catechism regarding the day of worship.

They also have trouble with the Catholic Church omitting the second commandment forbidding idol worship. During the Middle Ages, the papal church compromised the second commandment and introduced graven images into Christendom. Today, Catholic catechisms omit the Bible's second commandment, thus turning people away from the Creator by changing times and laws. Then, according to Pastor Doug Batchelor, they have split the tenth commandment into two parts to still have ten.

During the evolution of the church, the church began to shroud itself in "mystery" and ritualism that had a strong resemblance to Babylonian mysticism. Gradually, these changes became more prominent than the original teachings of Christ as handed down by the apostles. Mysteries of darkness prevailed which were only capable of being unlocked by those who possessed the keys, keys the Catholic Church declared were entrusted to them. Yet there are those who denounced the leaders of the church as heretics, saying, "Although they do not understand (the) mystery…boast that the mystery of truth belongs to them alone."[74]

As the church's power increased, the darkness deepened. We are told by Ellen G. White in her previously mentioned book[75] that faith was transferred from Christ, the true foundation, to the pope of Rome. Every time I read that, it is as if the sky turns black accompanied by dense, black rolling clouds of thunder and lightning. Thick and palpable clouds of darkness that must have prevailed and overshadowed Christianity to the point that men could, and probably did, justify questioning which way they were to go. One Christ, with two teachings, so what is one to do?

To the Apostolic Church the answer came in having a belief in the birth, death, and resurrection of Christ. Protestants have faith in the price Christ paid at the cross as being sufficient payment for salvation, (anything else seems to have man's fingerprints all over it) and that His death on the cross paid our debt in full. Acceptance of that is the cornerstone of an evangelical's belief. They believe that when Christ died at the cross that ended the Leviticus laws of sacrifices. Christ paid our sin debt in full and all He asks from us is that we accept that by faith.

On the other hand, in answering that question, the leaders of Catholicism promoted a religion that came with instructions on how to be a Christian. Instructions that included the Sacraments thus making Christianity easy as it was more pragmatic than spiritual or let us say, rather than being faith based, it was based upon works in conjunction with faith (faith in the works rather than the cross) for the absolution of sin. Giving the Catholic Church complete control over the price to be paid for the various sins, thus eliminating the need in asking for God's forgiveness.

[74]   Ellerbe, Helen. *The Dark Side of Christian History.* New York: Morningstar and Lark, 1993.

[75]   E. G. White, *The Great Controversy… Ended.*

One might find upon entering the Catholic Church that by following a set of instructions they will be just fine. That is what Martin Luther was told. Again, if one thinks the Catholic Church can help in forgiving sin, then pragmaticism may work for you. Catholicism may be the form of Christianity for you, but as the Seventh-day Adventist say, it might be time to think about that decision. That is what Martin Luther found out.

It was at that moment, the moment that absolution of sin by works, and salvation (by the church), as well as the implementation of the Sacraments confirming one a Christian, along with receiving Christ via a wafer, that the power of the seat of Christ was transferred from Christ to the Catholic Church and the pope, that many classify Catholicism as a cult. Of course, everyone knows that is an opinion, just as those who believe it is not. Although, it was, and still is, at the completion of those instructions one becomes a Catholic Christian as opposed to a Protestant Christian who believes by faith that Christ is the Messiah and that He is the way, the truth, and the life.

Faith without works

We have seen where Catholicism introduced many requirements based upon interpretations into Christianity that were disputed by many of the early church Fathers. And that is the belief in faith alone being enough for salvation and the atonement for sin as taught by Protestant churches, or do we, as the Catholic Church says, need both to maintain salvation? In other words, must we include works in addition to faith to show we are followers of Christ and obedient to His word? *Works.* The very connotation of the word "works" seems to arouse some intellectual questions as the Bible does include works in connection with faith.

As we know the Bible says in James, "Faith without works is dead." And every Protestant understands the meaning behind those words. Would anyone, especially a born-again Christian who believes in the Bema judgment, think they could be, or want to be a Christian, and not do good works? Maybe, but that is not what this seems to be about. It appears to be a matter of whether one can be a Christian by faith alone, or do they need both faith and works to be justified (stand righteous) before God.

Does someone find salvation in the Catholic Church and remain saved by their works as assigned at confession, or are they a Christian and remain a Christian independent of their works while at the same time understanding works are important? To the Catholic Church, the two are intertwined as a requirement for salvation, whereas a Protestant separates the two. To a Protestant, works have nothing to do with salvation, or remaining a Christian.

Protestants believe in repenting with a remorseful spirit (as they are truly remorseful for a moment of weakness, and they have the assurance that God is understanding—if not, that would make a liar out of Jesus) and they trust in God by faith for restitution of the soul. The Catholics I have spoken with say just telling God we are sorry for sinning against Him is not enough. But then the Bible seems to convey that it is.

Catholics feel there must be more to it than just telling God we are sorry with a repenting, contrite, remorseful, and apologetic heart. Catholics say restitution must be paid for complete atonement. For example, a young boy breaks a neighbor's window playing baseball. It would be proper to say one is sorry, and truly mean it, but the Catholic Church says that is not enough. They say someone must pay for the window. In the secular world that would be the case, but in the spiritual world Christ already paid for the window by his death at the cross. Catholics contend, we do not get off that easy. A personal sacrifice of self-commitment must be made. Somewhat perhaps evolving from those we see from time to time parading through the streets thrashing themselves into a bloody pulp seeking absolution.

Since this self-mutilation is not a requirement of the Bible nor was it taught by the apostles, one might find that, while the Catholic church does not require self-mutilation, they do prescribe works as a requirement for self-satisfaction, but be assured, "functions" of a pragmatic nature are not required for the "complete" remission of sin, Faith and trusting in the word of God is. The practice of those who mortified their own flesh by whipping it with various instruments began as a fourteen-century movement consisting of radicals in the Catholic Church.

The theology of works has been questioned by Protestants and labeled as wrong when that theology was introduced, and it is still labeled as wrong. Questionable to the point that many perceived the church of Rome (again, dare I say) of becoming a cult. Regarding Catholicism being considered a cult, Justin Peters puts it this way, "they are a cult—not a sociological cult, not a drinking the Kool-Aid Jim Jones kind of cult, but a theological cult as it denies and compromises some of the fundamental doctrines of the Apostolic Church." And compromising the truth is all I have been discussing.

Lord God the Pope?

In her book, *"The Great Controversy Ended,"* Mrs. White (a person who was very instrumental in establishing the Seventh-day Adventist church family) declared that to "secure worldly gains and honors, the church was led to seek the favor and support of the great men of earth; and having thus rejected Christ, she was induced to yield allegiance to the representative of Satan—the bishop of Rome." Also, the popes see themselves as having been given the very titles of Deity, and the pope has been styled *"Lord God the Pope."* and has been declared infallible.

To quote Pope Leo XIII, (1810-1903) Encyclical Letter, *"The Reunion of Christendom"*: "We (the popes) hold upon this earth the place of God Almighty." Another claim as stated in the Catholic National, July 1895, "The pope is not only the representative of Jesus Christ, but he is Jesus Christ, Himself, hidden under the veil of flesh." Now if this was said around the first few centuries, then one could say the motivating factor was the "one-upmanship" that seemed to prevail. But since it was written when it was, then it can probably be assumed it is still a belief of the Catholic Church. Many have a hard time accepting that the pope has appointed himself "God" as declared by the Bull (decree) Unum Sanctum, issued by Pope Boniface VIII, and appearing in Time magazine on May 25, 1981. Again, this was not written during the period of "one-upmanship." Or the time when serious dogma was being introduced into the church system.

The decree reads as follows: "The Roman pontiff judges all men but is judged by no one. We declare, assert, define and pronounce: to be **SUBJECT TO THE ROMAN PONTIFF** is to every human creature altogether **NECESSARY FOR SALVATION**…that which was spoken of Christ 'thou has subdued all things under his feet,' may well seem verified in ME…I have the authority of the King of Kings. I am all in all and above all so that God himself and I, the vicar of God, have but one consistory, and I am able to do all that God can do. **WHAT THEREFORE CAN YOU MAKE OF ME BUT GOD?"** Remember, the Catholic Church claims infallibility, meaning it is incapable of mendaciousness (lying) or making a mistake.

Also, they say God himself is obligated to abide by the judgment of the Catholic Church. Wow! Think about that for a moment. According to the church, God Himself appears to be obligated to allow priests to either pardon (forgive sins) or not, accordingly, they may refuse to give absolution. Think how much power this perception of authority gave the church. And according to Doug Batchelor from his studies of Catholicism: "God subscribes to allowing priest to forgive sins." From a sermon given 10/22/2017 by Doug Batchelor of *Amazing Facts* from one of his end time sermons.

Forgiving sins. Wow! Forgiving sins. The ability to forgive sins might justify what Pope Leo XIII brought to the table when he said, "We hold upon this earth the place of God almighty." Pope Leo XIII was head of the Catholic Church from February 20, 1878, until his death on July 20, 1903. Just to recap, we were just told the pope holds the place of God, then we are told that popes, are considered Christ concealed by a vale of flesh, and now are told that he and those who follow him can forgive sins as well as pass judgment as to who is saved or not. Wow! I find myself speechless. This might be the justification behind the thinking that led Pope John Paul II to say, "All who live a just life will be saved even if they do not believe in Jesus Christ and the Roman Catholic Church."[76]

Someone needs to help me with that one as I find it to be misleading and just between us, quite obnoxious as well as below the intelligence of a Christian. The theology of Pope John Paul II is also embraced by Pope Francis, according to John MacArthur and Jack Van Impe, who bring the following to our attention. Pope Francis has said that you do not really need Christ to go to heaven, as well as saying atheist will even be admitted into heaven, which is very problematic for many Christians. According to Jack, nineteen academics accused Pope Francis of heresy. On May 1, 2019, a group of nineteen Catholics, including some prominent academics, have published an open letter to the bishops of the world, accusing Pope Francis of heresy. And from where many Protestants sit that letter seemed to be justified.

Some say the current pope is so off-the-wall and his statements are so bizarre that many contend he does not even follow basic Catholicism. Many say he steals the honor and authority of the Lord Jesus and attributes them all to himself. He claims to be the Holy Father with supreme and unhindered authority over all people. Nothing new there. Remember, it was Pope Boniface VIII who said to be "**SUBJECT TO THE ROMAN PONTIFF** is to every human creature altogether **NECESSARY FOR SALVATION**...that which

---

[76] As quoted from the New York Times December 9th, 2019 and brought to our attention by John MacArthur preaching on Inclusivism, Catholicism and Billy Graham.

was spoken of Christ 'thou has subdued all things under his feet,' may well seem verified in ME." And that applies to Pope Francis. He condemns those who do not submit to his "infallible" dogma, and he proclaims a false and fatal gospel that leads people to the eternal lake of fire. This is information brought to us by Pastor Mike Gendron,[77] who reveals the false teachings of Pope Francis.

Considering everything that was just brought to our attention by Doug Batchelor, John MacArthur, Mike Gendron and Jack Van Impe, I do not ever remember seeing a deeper case of deceptive theology as what has been uttered by Pope Francis. Remember, the Catholic Church claims infallibility, meaning it is incapable of lying or making a mistake. It was the eleventh pope, Pope Gregory VII, who proclaimed the perfection of the Roman Church. Among the propositions that he put forth was one declaring that the church had never erred, nor would it ever err, according to the scriptures.[78] He also declared that no sentence he pronounced could be reversed by anyone, but that it was his prerogative to reverse the decisions of others.

Regarding that "declared infallible" statement sanctioned by Pope Gregory VII, I discovered some interesting information the other day regarding Galileo and the Catholic Church. Some of you may already know this. In 1632 Galileo had been propagating the idea the earth orbited around the sun, a belief the Catholic Church did not share at the time. The church had decided the idea that the sun moved around the earth was an absolute fact of scripture that could not be disputed, even though scientists had known for centuries that the earth was not the center of the universe.

Eventually Galileo was placed under house arrest for publishing a book contrary to beliefs of the Catholic Church and in 1633 was brought to trial. Church officials found him guilty of heresy for

---

[77]   Mike Gendron was a Catholic for over 38 years. He was taught from an early age to trust and rely on the church, its priests, the Sacraments, and his own good works for salvation. Worldviewweekend.com. (wvwtv.com).

[78]   MacCulloch, *The Reformation*.

asserting the Copernican theory that the earth moved around the sun—again, meaning the earth was not the center of the universe. He was still under arrest at the time of his death on January 8, 1642. The church eventually admitted "fallibility." I just found that interesting.

Once again, I would like to repeat, this is not about those who find solace in any of the churches mentioned. It is about those from which some problematic theology came into Christianity. As far as individual Catholic members, I would have to say: Sometime back two Catholics were killed in the Middle East in the name of Islam defending Christ. Who would say they were not heaven-bound? Just as there are many Protestants headed for heaven, there are also many great Catholics headed there as well, so again, I must repeat, this is not about the Catholics per se, as they are great people who love God and search for understanding just as do those who follow evangelical Christianity. But again, there are undisputable differences, as we have seen that must be acknowledge.

Two churches, two faiths, two paths, varying theology. When the veil split in the Temple of God when Jesus was dying, that was a sign to Christians that individuals did not need to have someone intervening for them, as it had always been. Believing in the Apostolic teachings, Protestants accept the doctrine that the splitting of the veil gave those who now came to Christ, through faith, full access to God, yet, as we just saw, Pope Boniface VIII declared we need him and every pope that proceeded him to stand in our place and be subject to them for salvation—in other words, placing themselves between us and God, even to the place of being authorized to forgive our sins.

Folks these are men just like you and I who have given themselves this authority. People bow on their knees before them, mere mortals who look and act righteous. We think they are holy because they tell us they are holy, but they are mere "men" who do not speak for or represent God in any way. When they say our sins are forgiven that means nothing. Just like Protestants, Catholics need to go directly to God and eliminate the middlemen.

CHAPTER XI

DOGMA AND THE CHURCH

We know it was during the time of 330 to around 336 AD and following subsequent years when paganism and Christianity were merging that Christianity became diluted and compromised. A time many consider to be the mixing of secularism of the Holy Roman Empire (clay) with the teachings of the Apostolic Church (iron) described as the last empire of Nebuchadnezzar's dream. All the other empires fell, and many believe we are at the end of this one. The end of the age of the gentiles. An age that many consider began when much of the questionable dogma[79] began to be introduced into the bloodstream of Christianity by gentiles being allowed to join the Catholic Church without a spiritual conversion.

Tim LaHaye gives us excellent insight into some of the practices that were being introduced. I hope he will not mind if I list them here. Tim says, "Gradually these changes became more prominent than the original teachings of Christianity." Think about what Tim just said: "Gradually these changes became more prominent than the original teachings of Christianity." In other words, as mentioned

---

[79] Dogma. Prescribed doctrine proclaimed as unquestionable true by religious studies or group, Dogma can be true or false, good or bad, and even questionable theology. For our purposes, dogma is used to denote false religious studies.

earlier, dogma, or as many may describe as "questionable theology" presented by philosophers and implemented by the Catholic Church, became more prominent than the teachings of Christ. Following are some of the changes and/or insertions Tim was talking about, along with others I have discovered:

AD 300:   Prayers for the dead.

AD 300:   Making the sign of the cross.

AD 313:   The first Ecumenical Council conducted by Constantine.

AD 325:   Council of Nicaea —Catholic domination began.

AD 375:   Worship of saints and angels. (Turning from the apostolic faith).

AD 394:   First Latin Mass.

AD 431:   Worship of Mary began (More turning from the apostolic faith).

AD 500:   Priests began dressing differently than laypeople.

AD 526:   Extreme unction (last rites).

AD 593:   Doctrine of purgatory introduced. You would think this would be somewhere in the Bible and not introduced by the Catholic Fathers in 593.

AD 600:   Prayers directed to Mary (Many say the completion of turning away from the apostolic faith).

AD 606:   The first official pope— "God on earth."

AD 1000:   Transubstantiation doctrine.

AD 1015:   Celibacy of Priest mandated.

AD 1054:   The year of the great schism with the Greek Orthodox Church. How about a couple more?

AD 1192:   Indulgences introduced.

AD 1311:   Sprinkling replaced immersion for baptism.

AD 1517:   The Reformation began.

As we have seen upon studying Catholicism, one finds a lot of man-made insertions passed down by Roman pagans who were being allowed to join the church and contributed to the writing of its constitution, its understanding, and its beliefs. For example, in addition to the above, as we have seen, they were instrumental in changing the day of worship from Saturday to Sunday. Saturday has always been acknowledged in Scripture as the Sabbath, and it was on this day Christ worshipped as was the Jewish custom. Does it make any difference as to which day one worships Christ?

A born-again Christian is a Christian, is a Christian, and as a born-again Christian many prefer to worship on Sunday, but Saturday works just as well. When it comes to the dogma, questionable dogma as presented by the literature of the church, several points are debatable such as the Assumption of Mary, along with the sinless nature of Mary and the assertion that Mary did not have any other children. Let us take a walk through a few of these assertions, beginning with the Assumption of Mary.

The Assumption of Mary

The Catholic Church teaches as dogma that the Virgin Mary "having completed the course of her earthly life, was assumed body and soul into heavenly glory."[80] This doctrine was dogmatically defined by Pope Pius XII, who served as head of the Catholic Church from March 1939 until his death in 1958. On November 1 of 1950, as documented in the apostolic constitution Munificentissimus Deus by exercising papal infallibility,[81] he declared that Mary was delivered from death and taken directly to heaven, as were Elijah and Enoch.

While the belief that Mary's body was preserved from corruption and taken to heaven and reunited with her soul is not scriptural, it

---

[80]   https://en.m.wikipedia.org.
[81]   https://en.m.wikipedia.org.

also is not dangerous to our salvation. Catholics contend that Mary entered heaven with a body that had not experienced the normal pains of death. Again, the Bible seems to convey that Mary lived a normal life after the birth of Jesus, even having more children. I know this is sacred ground to a Catholic, but the Bible describes Mary and Joseph living a normal life after the birth of Jesus. A changed life, a destined life, but a normal "married" life, bringing forth four named sons and at least two daughters.

The Catholic Church, after centuries of pressure from Catholics, finally succumbed to the desires of their parishioners by adopting the theory of Mary's Assumption into heaven in 1950 and declared this belief a truism. However, the Bible goes to great lengths to emphasize that Mary, just as we all do, needed an understanding of the mission of Christ. Jesus emphasizes this when he responded to the woman who shouted, "Blessed *is* the woman who gave you birth and nursed you," with "Blessed *rather* are those who hear the word of God and obey it." (Italics for emphasis).

Paul Tillich asked fellow Protestant theologian Reinhold Niebuhr in March of 1950, about eight months before the decree was promulgated if he expected the pope to make the declaration about Mary's Assumption. Niebuhr replied: "I don't think so; he is too clever for that; it would be a slap in the face of the whole modern world (I'm going to take that as being an insult to the intelligence of the Christian community), and it would be dangerous for the Roman Church to do that today."[82] Many believe it was questionable theology in 1950 as they do today, yet most Catholics believe it to be true. That is an excellent example of false Catholic dogma—questionable theology being conceived as truth only because it has been declared as truth. To most the Assumption of Mary is dogma, it is not as dangerous a dogma as other forms of dogma embraced by the Catholic Church, but it is dogma, nevertheless.

---

[82] Ibid.

Richard Bennett

The Sinless Nature of Mary

In 2013, Fr. Timothy Pavlatos wrote, "In most, if not all, Christian circles outside of the Orthodox, to say that Mary was sinless would be an objectionable statement. Holy Scripture is noticeably clear regarding sinlessness, 'for *all* have sinned and fall short of the glory of God' (Rom. 3:23 NIV). With Scripture being so clear, how then are we to understand the teaching of the Orthodox Church that the Mother of God was sinless?" Again, Catholics as well as the Greek Orthodox Church embrace the sinless nature of Mary.[83]

While some including Greek Orthodox may disagree on the Assumption of Mary, they do agree she remained sinless throughout her lifetime, thus never consummating the marriage. To equate virginity with being sinless is beyond strange, especially since God commanded Adam and Eve to be fruitful and multiply. He was not talking about fruit, he was talking about creating children, as a result of sex. Protestants, on the other hand, believe Mary consummated the marriage and had other children.

Is this a salvation breaker? Of course not, simply different understandings of the Bible. Matthew 1:25 KJV seems to confirm she had relations when it says, "He (Joseph) knew her not *till* she brought forth her first born son: and he called his name JESUS. The NIV puts it this way, "But he did not consummate their marriage until she gave birth to a son. And he gave him the name Jesus." I know the Catholics, and the Orthodox churches pretend she remained a virgin throughout her life but that is not what the Bible conveys.

While the Greek Orthodox consider Mary special, they do not pray to her. They do, however, regard her as free of any sin. How is that possible? For a sinless nature to be a truism, Mary would have been either immaculately conceived, or the sinful nature was instantly removed at birth. The theory of Mary's sinless nature sparked fierce debate during the fifteenth century, despite the

---

[83] www.Stjohngoc.org.

254

insistence of Pope Sixtus IV, who embraced the theory of Mary, the mother of Christ, being born sinless and remaining sinless during her lifetime. They say, "Mary was preserved exempt from all stain of original sin at the first moment of her life, and sanctifying grace was given to her before sin could have taken effect in her soul…The formal active essence of original sin was not removed from her soul, as it is removed from others by baptism; it was excluded, because it was never in her soul."[84]

It appears Mary had been conceived without sin (immaculately conceived) and was, immediately, upon her birth, granted the grace to avoid committing sin. It appears that the Catholic Church contends both are true. However, Protestants turning to the Bible and being unable to find evidence of this theory, have rejected it as false theology. Yet, the Catholics include it in their religion as a reality because a man, a mere man, Pope Pius IX in 1854 declared that "Mary, from the moment of her conception in her mother's womb—the mother of Jesus Christ—was preserved free from original sin." When asked to explain how this is possible, they say it is a convoluted issue. There is just no other way to describe this belief other than as convoluted.

According to Diarmaid MacCulloch, as he conveys in his book, *The Reformation: A History*, the beginning of the deification of Mary began when laypeople crowded in on their clergy demanding to know as much as possible about their Savior and His mother. From this opportunity, the church seized the moment and did their best to revere her as the "mother" of the church, interweaving that idea into the tapestry of the church. This was sanctioned by Pope Paul VI and it was from this premise that a fundamental belief of the church was adopted—more tradition. When one thinks about the reverence and praise heaped upon Mary, including the sinless nature, the ascension as well as the fact Catholics pray to her, one could almost perceive her to be equal with Christ.

---

84   Catholic Encyclopedia. Ibid). *The Reformation: A History*.

Praying to Mary

Catholics embrace the theology that Mary is the greatest of all the saints, with the distinct honor of being sanctioned "mother of the church." It was from this declaration and the fact that all the "faith" in the universe was somehow now manifested in and through her (more on this in a minute), that Catholics felt the desire to pray to God through Mary, believing her to be a powerful intercessor. A substitution or transferring of worship from Christ to Mary, a type of deification. The church contents that with the death of Christ, when he was hanging on the cross, seemingly abandoned by everyone the whole of remaining faith of humanity (all the faith left in the world) was concentrated in Mary's unwavering faith alone.[85] Thus, they perceive her as being the mediator intervening as the appointed one to hear our prayers.

This is another reason for the rift between the Eastern Orthodox and Roman Catholic Churches. The Orthodox Church believes that the mother of God was sinless of her own free will, and that she remained ever virgin, ever sinless, but they do not pray to her instead of to God. Now see if this does not sound like semantics: they say that we seek her intercession before her Son, asking her to pray on our behalf, but we do not pray to her. Sounds much like the same thing, perhaps without the divine reverence part.

Most Protestants consider this devotion to Mary by the Catholic Church deification and point to Ephesians 3:12 in the NIV, wherein it conveys the authority to approach God with freedom and confidence. To establish this relationship was the primary mission of Christ. Again, that is why the veil in the Temple separating the Holy of Holies (the place where God resided with his people) was ripped from top to bottom at the death of Christ.

This deification of Mary came about as the result of paganism and Christianity becoming united. When the church realized the

---

[85]   Diarmaid MacCulloch, *The Reformation: A History.*

power in Mary as a virgin, and remaining a virgin, as well as the mother of Jesus, they began to include the reverence of her in their theology; although, it was the early pagans joining the church who placed Mary upon a pedestal (metaphorically speaking) as they did with their other gods and began idolizing her. This is a ritual that has become a mainstay of Catholicism and handed down through each generation of Catholics.

Mary's Other Children

Another issue that stands out as questionable theology is the issue of Mary not giving birth to more children. Catholic, Assyrian, Greek Orthodox, Eastern Orthodox and Oriental Orthodox believe in the perpetual virginity of Mary, as did some of the Protestant leaders. For example, Martin Luther, Zwingli, John Wesley, and their respective movements, which could possibly include the Methodists (as they are a result of John and Charles Wesley separating from the church of England), but I have never met a Methodist who believes in the sinless nature of Mary, even though John Wesley did, Charles Wesley, not so much.

Catholicism contends that the mention of Jesus' brethren in the scriptures is to be interpreted as more generic than specific (as in "everyone is my brother"), or that the children were Joseph's before Mary, or that they were adopted, teaching that Mary gave birth to no other children. Regarding other children, it sounds straightforward when the apostle Mark writes that the people who knew Jesus—who had watched him grow up—were amazed at His teachings, which prompted them to ask, "Isn't this the carpenter? Isn't this Mary's son and the brother of James, Joseph, Judas, and Simon? Aren't his sisters here with us?" (Mark 6:3, NIV) Again, this sounds straightforward; there is nothing ambiguous about this doctrine. Mark 6:3 and Matthew 13:55-56 both state that James, Joses (Joseph), Jude and Simon were the brothers of Jesus. This should not even be a discussion as the Bible conveys this information very clearly.

Since they had different fathers, they were only half brothers and sisters, but apart from Jesus, James, Joses, Judas, Simon, and at least two sisters, they were the actual children of Joseph and Mary—at least that is how most Protestants understand the issue regarding Joseph and Mary having more children. They were not Joseph's children from a prior marriage, as some teach, or a misquotation of the Bible as taught by others, but they were the actual children of Joseph and Mary, just as the Bible indicates. I believe most Protestants would go with the Bible on this one.

Regarding Mary remaining childless after Jesus, especially throughout her lifetime, Bill O'Reilly (a devout Catholic) in his book, *Killing Jesus: A History,* confirms that the gospel clearly states that Jesus had four brothers and a sister or two. No biggie—I just found that interesting. The contention that Mary went childless after Jesus throughout the remainder of her life is just a different understanding of the Bible between Protestants and Catholics.

Much of the Catholic Church is built upon bringing their theology to the party rather than accepting the written word as gospel. Gospel they introduce when people could not see for themselves. Beliefs, embellish until they eventually become tradition, including the Assumption of Mary, the sinless nature of Mary, praying to Mary, and Mary not having other children. Nothing dangerous about these understandings of the life of Mary, except for praying to her and revering her as they do.

These are all accepted as reality by the church because a council of men approved them to be an accurate representation of the churches understanding of the scriptures. In other words, theology that many considered unverified dogma when it was introduced just as it is today. Catholics incorporate their understanding of the Bible into Christianity, and by way of the many council meetings and synods, attended mainly by the early Fathers of the Catholic Church, we have a religion presenting biblical words and phrases, and even an understanding of many things that warrants a constant search for the truths by both Catholics and Protestants alike. Again, the Catholics beliefs regarding Mary are not considered dangerous, except for the reverence paid to her.

One will not find complexities within Protestant Christianity as they will in Catholicism. Especially, nothing convoluted as embracing theology that says, Mary, the mother of Jesus being born sinless and remaining sinless throughout her lifetime gives us freedom to relish upon her reverence to the point of asking her to intercede for us with her son. They acknowledge this as fact because it fits into their "mode of operandi." Born again Christians embrace theology that gives them full authority to approach God with confidence. Unfortunately, that theology does not fit into the Catholic system. And I know this is hard to accept, but again, Catholicism excludes Christ except in name only.

CHAPTER XII

PAGANISM AND THE CHURCH

A moment ago, I mentioned that the believed deification of Mary was the result of paganism meeting up with Christianity and becoming united. This is a union that has constantly come under fire for what many consider bringing forth a distortion of the word of God through misinterpretation. Also mentioned earlier, pagans, who were less sincere and less devoted in their beliefs of an actual virgin birth and physical resurrection (the principal mainstays of a Protestant's belief), could join one of two churches and be considered Christians.

They could join the Church of the apostles that was meeting and expanding underground, clinging to the teachings and essence of what Christ taught. Or the other choice was a church that was visibly changing times and laws by implementing a religious system that was so unique, so inclusive, it seems to have excluded Christ from the necessity of redemption and remaining redeemed through him, as that authority now came from the Catholic Church, the proclaimed new Israel, the apple of God's eye, because of "replacement theology" (more shortly). And it is only through them the mysteries and truths of the Bible can be learned and understood. Mysteries that they alone claim to understand.

As we know, those mysteries are explained in the literature of the church and become defining of the church. When one understands the differences between the two religions, the differences of understandings embraced by each, then one will understand what separates the two. Choosing one religious system as opposed to the other is up to us as everyone can decide for themselves which road appears to be more spiritual, fulfilling, and satisfying. One path seemingly follows Christ while the other seemingly follows a religion that excludes the heavenly Christ while crafting a system that includes an earthly Christ.

The popes as confirmed by their own literature is, "Christ concealed under a veil of flesh." Or, declaring as popes have, "what God can do we can do also," **"WHAT THEREFORE CAN YOU MAKE OF ME BUT GOD?"** One more just in case one is still questioning the deity of the Pope. Let me quote from an article by F. Lucii Ferraris as recorded in a book that was printed at Rome and is sanctioned by the Catholic encyclopedia. Listen to these claims: "The Pope is of so great dignity, and so exalted, that he is not a mere man, but as it were God and the Vicar of God. The Pope is, as it were, God on earth, chief king of kings, having plenitude of power."[86] And what has been said has never been rebutted.

In the early days of the church many who were imparting this understanding, as well as the people to whom it was being introduced, were mostly raised with roots that were deeply imbedded into Greek mythology with many individuals retaining their Greek heritage even after the conquest of Greece by Rome in 146 A.D. Thus, establishing roots imbedded into Greek philosophy that did not end with Roman occupation. An occupation that brought paganism (total secularism) into the equation with their conquest of Greece.

Now we have the paganism of Rome mixed with the mythology of the Greeks all the while being stirred around with a lot of secularism. The conquering Romans largely adapted Greek mythology, believing that gods and goddesses had power not only over agriculture and

---

[86] An excerpt from Prompta Bibliotheca Canonica Juridica Moralis Theologica, (Volume VI, pp. 2529) by F. Lucii Ferraris.as reproduced by Joe Crews in the pamphlet "The Beast, the Dragon, and the Woman." Amazing Facts, Inc. California. 2013.

weather, but also over all aspects of life. They worshiped Ceres as the goddess of the harvest, Vesta as the goddess of the hearth and home, and Jupiter, (who later became their supreme god and protector) while Juno was the queen of the gods and Apollo was the god of the sun, but the ultimate Greek god was Zeus—the supreme god who was believed to rule from his court on Mount Olympus, and was a symbol for power, rule, and law.

After the death of Christ, that was the mixture of pagan beliefs that came together to form a church dedicated and devoted to an organization, a system from which the Catholic Church germinated. And for the most part, the religion of Catholicism was developing from ideas and understanding by those joining the church who were themselves into the paganism and mythology of the day, as well as those who were pontificating philosophy that had been passed down by earlier philosophers, many of whom were instrumental in writing and implementing their interpretation of the Bible and codifying those understandings into the constitution of Catholicism.

Christianity is a spiritual connection that is impossible to understand without being born again, or as many say, having a "spiritual awakening." Many new converts who were joining the Catholic Church lacked an understanding of the born-again experience as that experience is only accessible by faith. A concept many of the new "Christians" joining the Catholic Church were having a hard time understanding just as some do today. Without faith—faith that many might say is induced by the Spirit of God, it is an impossibility to comprehend the message of the Bible, or at least the essence of the message.

The Appointing of a Pope

Without the Holy Spirit—the Spirit that is imparted from above, as John MacArthur says—accepting Christ and the completion of redemption, which to many is a hard concept to grasp, the Catholic

Church introduced pragmatic acts as a substitution for redemption and faith. Protestants, as we are told, once again, in the book of Acts germinated from the awareness of the Holy Spirit beginning on the day of Pentecost and continues today just as it will until the coming of Christ.

On the other hand, in the continuing of the building of the Catholic Church, there was needed a way to offer salvation and redemption without two things that prevailed in the Apostolic Church: One, faith in Scripture alone (Solo Scriptura) and, two, a leader, a Father, someone the Christians of the world could look up to with everlasting respect. Someone who would become known as a Pope.

Remember, in the beginning of the Catholic Church we are mostly discussing converted idol worshipers who could join the church without a conversion, or even perhaps an epiphany moment, but joined seemingly to avoid the torments of hell, a new concept brought about by Christianity. Another reason for purgatory and indulgences. Gentile pagan Greco-Romans from the Roman Empire who accepted the message of salvation as presented by the Catholic Church and continued to be Catholicized by the teachings that were built upon pragmaticism and introduced by man rather than on spiritual faith. A Christianity built upon the intellect of man rather than the spirituality of the Holy Spirit.

The Catholic Church addressed the dilemma of accepting Christ without faith as was being taught by the Apostolic Church. They did this by introducing methods that did not require faith for receiving Christ and retaining salvation. Methods that have become known as Sacraments, developed instructions to Christianize joiners, and a leader who has the authority to represent God on earth to validate them as sacred and a place in which to perform what many consider rituals in the way of "The Mass," designated as a place to receive Christ at the hands of a priest.

And they did this by appointing a pope, a leader, an authority figure, a Father above all Fathers and proclaim him as someone who stood in the place of Christ on earth, someone from whom all truths flowed. Someone who had ties to Christ that would give creditability to the church. A leader that Catholics could place their faith in and follow as head of the church that Christ came to establish. Someone who might add creditability to the claim of being the chosen and approved church that Christ died to give birth to. Someone who had roots in and was a part of the Apostolic Church. Ties that could give creditability to the claim as the "first church on the block."

As we know they installed Peter and subsequent popes to establish what they call "apostolic succession." However nowhere in Scripture did Jesus, the apostles, or any other New Testament writer set forth this idea. What is mentioned in Scripture is the idea that the Word of God was to be the guide that the church was to follow (Acts 20:32). It is Scripture that was to be the infallible measuring stick for teaching and practice (2 Timothy 3:16-17). It is the Scriptures that teachings are to be compared to (Acts17:10-12). Apostolic authority was passed on through the writings of the apostles, and not through someone appointed through "apostolic succession" just so they could claim that they were the first on the block.

The apostle Peter was appointed pope sometime after his death in 64 A.D. Peter taught and preached in Rome, according to Clement of Alexandria. If so, he would be preaching Christ and not how to be a Catholic. Anyway, history shows the first church was founded in the fourth century. A.D. 350 I believe. A church Catholics contend they founded and dedicated to Mary. Since the Catholic Church did not begin its rise in earnest until the fourth century, how could Peter be a Catholic pope?

That decision was made for many reasons of which the most obvious was to have a connection to the Apostolic Church. The fact that Jesus spoke directly to Peter regarding the revelation that He was the Messiah, did not hurt. In fact, that made him perhaps the first to recognize Christ as the Messiah. Besides, if we go down that lane, then the truth is, Peter was one of the founders of the church described in the book of Acts and that is not the Catholic

Church. Nor was a church built upon the person of Peter but upon the revelation of Christ being the Son of God.

It was, and is, by faith in the revelation that Jesus Christ, as the Son of God, came to redeem humanity and gave us the authority to approach God and ask Him to save us from the second death. Protestants consider the "Son of God" to be Jesus the cornerstone, the very foundation, upon which their faith and the evangelical Church was built. Without that essential revelation and the faith to believe, one could never be born again, at least not the way Christ intended when he was discussing the issue with Nicodemus.

It appeared to be this element of faith, spiritual faith, that was missing from the Catholic Church. But then the question becomes, "How can one receive Christ without faith? Spiritual faith that establishes a relationship with Him?" Simple, the Church Fathers rectified that situation by appointing a man to stand in place of God and introduced the concept of the Mass as a way to receive Christ. I am not sure the Fathers of Catholicism ever grasped an understanding of the inspirational Spirit, the Spirit that leads to a relationship with God as, once again, Catholicism is built upon pragmatism.

A personal relationship that Protestants seek with Christ and the Catholic Church says is not possible. That is why Protestants are so grateful for Martin Luther. Catholics despise him and cannot demonize him enough and probably to them justifiably so, but it was Luther that God used to return Christianity to the Apostolic Church. They brought back the light of Christ to the world that had been darkened far too long. The light that rejuvenated souls was being reignited and brough forth, but not before the blood of many a reformer was spilled.

During the time when secularism was being introduced into Christianity by changing times and laws with the major changes being illustrated by way of appointing a person to stand in the place of Christ, then substituting works for faith and accepting Christ via a wafer and changing the day of worship from the Sabbath to Sunday. Just to name a few of the changes that initiated a very dark time for the Protestant community, especially when one adds receiving forgiveness of sin and salvation from a man, who himself needs forgiveness of sins and salvation.

I know Catholics believe the pope is appointed by God, but according to them, he is God, rather they say Christ hidden under a vale of flesh. And yet, he is a human being with no special anointing, no special calling from God, but man who proclaims to have this honor. This dogma brought about disapproval from the Apostolic Church, disapproval the church did not want to hear. It wasn't but a couple of centuries later that Christianity entered a very dark period in Christian history. A time many are proclaiming to have led to the last kingdom in Nebuchadnezzar's dream. A prophetic dream that establishes a timeline of the last kingdom before the return of Christ.

Nebuchadnezzar's Dream

As found in the book of Daniel centuries before the dream come to fruition. When thinking how close we may be to the end times and thinking about the history that is conveyed to us by the Bible one can only stand in "awe." To many that was when the age of the gentiles began—when the secularism of Catholicism began becoming a part of Christianity. When thinking about the merging of secular ideas, hypothesis, and interpretations becoming a part of Christianity, even going so far as to change intents and times and meanings as defined by Christ, taught to the apostles, and carried forth by the earlier apologist, I am reminded of the statute in Nebuchadnezzar's dream and the mixing of iron and clay.

A giant stature of five empires, the Chaldean (Babylon), Medo-Persia (the era of Cyrus), Greek (the time of Alexander the Great) and Rome, (the time of the mighty Cesar's) followed by the last empire consisting of feet made from iron and clay. Iron and clay used in the Christian vernacular could only mean two dominant religions, one true and one false, or perhaps two dominant societies diabolically opposed to each other in the last days. One vying for the minds of humanity while the other is vying for souls.

Let us imagine for the moment as that is all we can do, that the mixture of iron and clay represents an empire of religion comprised of two strong Christian entities. That is how some see the meaning of iron and clay. And considering how the lines in the sand are becoming more pronounced within politics and religion with each passing day they may be right. Many Christians might see the clay as representative of Catholicism, (humanistic) and Protestantism (spiritualistic) being the iron, the solid and everlasting teachings as passed down by the Apostolic Church. A pure church teaching the birth, death, and resurrection of Christ. A stream of pure blood, if you will, that had not been infected or tainted with ideas or opinions outside of the Bible and the teachings of Christ.

That is not until early pagans who were being allowed to join the church without a confession of faith or a born-again experience, and having limited knowledge, were in positions to introduce secularism into the blood stream of the Apostolic Church. Or those who leaned towards the pragmatic side of the brain and missed the Holy Spirit. Many find a voidness of the Spirit within Catholicism. Catholicism began germinating around 64 A.D. and for a while Catholics and Protestants were pretty much on the same page, but then came the year 313 when the Emperor Constantine moved out of Rome giving the Catholic free reign to introduce ideas and opinions throughout the fourth century through councils and synods.

One could say the making of Catholicism begin in earnest in 325 A.D. shortly after Emperor Constantine moved the Roman Empire to the Byzantine Empire with the first of many gatherings (meetings, Synods, councils, etc.), to determine what Christianity was and how to understand the implications of what it meant to be a Christian. We are told that from such council meetings evolved a mixture of Christianity that many equate to the pragmatism of clay (dogma) with the spirituality of iron (faith) sprinkled in. And it is the contention of many that this mixture, would not, will not, and cannot, be united. I believe we can say history bears that out, (Daniel 2:41-43).

Since many might feel we are approaching the end of the current era like a freight train on steroids, they may think the feet represents the last and final empire before the coming of Christ. When one thinks about it, they can almost visualize the closeness the world could be to the end of the current era and the last empire before the coming of Christ becomes a reality. A time when apathy will reign, a time the Bible refers to as the last church age, the last pope age, the last vestige of Christianity, or as John Hagee say's "the terminal generation embracing apathy."

Apathy, a condition, a falling away, a time the Bible keeps referring to as being widespread prior to the return of Christ. Many are expressing their concern that the secular world is just too divided, and with many walking away from God only confirms that end time signs are everywhere, but an understanding of Daniel's dream has far greater implications than just what one sees in the secular world.

Tainted Blood of Christianity

For many, as we have seen, the beginning of the last empire was brought about when pagans joining the Catholic Church could join and yet retained some of their idolatry ways and ideas. Ways, ideas, and understandings that included secular dogmatic paganism and secular perception that mainly came from earlier philosophers living in the pre-Christian era and introduced into Christianity by, once again, St. Augustine who many consider the Father of the Catholic Church, and yet, we find some of what he introduced into Christianity in some of the Protestant churches.

Probably more so with the churches who broke with the Church of England than those who have more direct roots with the reformers. Churches such as the church of England, or Anglican Church, and many of the ecclesiastic churches such as the Episcopal churches, who consider themselves to be part of the one holy Catholic as well as the Apostolic Church, and to be both Catholic and reformed. They uphold many of the customs of Roman Catholicism, while embracing fundamental ideas adopted during the Protestant Reformation. Much could be said of the Lutherans as well.

Into the Catholic Church came dogma that eventually became incorporated into the blood stream of Christianity, thus Christianity as taught and brought forward from the apostolic Christians was becoming tainted. Because of this, many apostolic Christians believed early leaders of Catholicism were responsible for changing times and places, even times and laws by changing the intent of the Bible to accommodate the pagans who were being allowed to join the church without a rejuvenated, regenerated (born again) experience. An experience transforming one from death to life that occurs in our souls as witnessed by our mind and conscience and confirmed by the Holy Spirit when we come to accept Christ and begin a relationship with God. A spiritual relationship.

Many who were joining the church merely changed the objects of their worship from the idols associated with Greek mythology and the Roman gods they had been worshiping to represent the deities brought to them by Catholicism, such as the holiness of Mary, priesthood of Peter, and sainthood of martyrs who were perceived as saints. A whole set of counterfeit doctrines was added so that the papacy could gain prestige with the pagans of the age. Pagan idols and relics, such as those representing the worship of the sun god were left at the door, but idols of Peter, Mary, and the saints took their place.

It was during this period, during the early centuries that many Protestants gave their life defending the apostolic Christianity from the autocracies that were emerging, many we have discussed. The history books are full of stories of martyrs who paid the ultimate price so that we could know the truth about how Christianity was being changed from secularism thinking that was infiltrating the Apostolic Church.

And to this day, Protestants can only say...Thanks. Thanks for taking a stand against the uncertain, and problematic theology that was becoming a part of the "true church of believers" and a stand that cost many their life. Convinced in their faith and their understanding of the message of Christ, early believers were willing to burn at the stake or be mauled by ferocious beast rather than denounce Christ. Or during Nero's time when they were set on fire to light the streets of Rome as well as light up Nero's gardens at night. During parties Nero had Christians wrapped in oil cloth and then set on fire so that their bodies, once dead, would continue burning, serving as lamps for his parties. Talk about someone who belongs in any Hall of Fame, it would be those early Christians.

Much of Catholicism seems to originate from the pragmatic side of the brain and because of this some ambiguous theology entered Christianity, as we have been witnessing. A theology that does not get talked about much is antinomian theology. As you will see it probably should be among the most rejected by perhaps... everyone. Maybe except for those who are aware this theology exists within the deeper parts of Catholicism. That place where one might find "replacement theology" and "purgatory" hidden, along with indulgences that apparently can still be found.

ANTINOMIAN THEOLOGY
AND CATHOLICISM

The definition of antinomian theology teaches that someone receives salvation under the gospel of dispensation by being elected to salvation. And because of theology that propagates the belief that the elect cannot fall from favor as they have eternal security, leads many to believe they have been permanently sealed by God prior to the pouring of the foundations of the earth. A Catholic concept that has been carried over to the Protestant church. Because of antinomian theology residing deep within the Catholic Church many abuses have been recorded and have gone unheeded, as we witness from the abuse that emanating from the Church itself by those who are called antinomians.

Because of this assurance of salvation that began with the Catholic Church, this bred some very strange doctrinal theories among early Catholics and continues to remain within their beliefs even today as can be witnessed from time to time. Modern day Christians who have retained this theology have acknowledged a caveat that goes with the doctrine of the "elect." A caveat that was discussed earlier to bring us closer as a family of unified Christians. A belief that puts most of us on the same page and that is the meeting at the cross. Once we get there, we proceed forward as one family of believers Those who practice antinomian theology seem to forget, bypass, or ignore the cross entirely. Apparently with Antinomian Libertines at the front of the line.

Antinomian theology is followed by those who reject a socially established morality as well as religious, or social norms— antinomian libertines. True antinomianism is a centuries-old heresy whose basic tenet held that Christians are not bound by traditional or moral law, particularly that of the Old Testament; and especially the Commandments, at least the ones they did not agree with, instead, man could be guided by an inner light that would reveal the proper forms of conduct. Perhaps more of a humanist or New Age sentiment, and to a degree, the Christian Science organization as well, rather than Christianity.

While all the components for the theology of the elect were in place during the forming of the early church, the origin of the word "antinomian" dates from the reformation itself. In fact, it was Luther who coined the word in a book published in 1539 titled, *Against the Antinomians.* Earlier pagans joining the Catholic Church around the fourth and fifth centuries A.D. professed to accept Jesus as the Son of God and to believe the written word as much as their conviction would allow, which in some cases was quite limited, especially when it came to sin or understanding disobedience.

For example, when it came to sin, now remember, we are talking about newly converted Greco Romans who just days before were probably worshiping the sun god, or descendants of those who were. Pagans who had no conviction and felt no need of repentance or a change of heart were joining the early Catholic Church where the concept of sin and the guilt attached to sin was foreign to them. Never had they been introduced to guilt as guilt was not something that was associated with paganism and idol worship. This was a new concept they were now facing with Christianity. How to handle this situation was where the thought of antinomian theology germinated.

Accommodating Pagans

To accommodate the pagans who were joining the church, the church adopted the theory of the "elect," which allowed pagans to join and believe that they possessed eternal salvation, whether or not they accepted "all" of the Bible. More importance was placed upon completing the church's requirements for membership, which usually meant how to become a Catholic, which usually meant learning and embracing the Sacraments.

And to accomplish this task the church implemented instructions that, if followed, almost guaranteed the converts assurance that they did not have to worry about eternal salvation if they remained Catholic, attended Mass, confessed their sins to elevate any guilt, and fulfill the prescribed penance. That would assure them a ticket to either purgatory or heaven. Many Protestants never subscribed to this thinking as they view it as removing the totality of relying on faith for salvation. And again, where is Christ? When Martin Luther questioned his salvation based upon the teachings of the church, he was told "not to worry about it, he would know if he made heaven soon enough." To answer the concerns Luther, as well as many others were experiencing, God introduced faith into their life.

Confession, works, antinomianism and even purgatory grew out of a need for the removal of guilt that seemed to accompany this new religion sweeping the land. Guilt that now was being placed upon Greco-Roman pagans and pagan philosophers and advisers to the church, who were being allowed to join even though they lacked the spiritual awakening of a new birth. The Catholic Church fulfilled their needs by sitting aside the spirituality, along with the necessary faith, one will find in most Protestant churches and introduced pragmatism into the blood stream of the Apostolic Church. The time when secularism entered Christianity was the day when Satan infiltrated the Apostolic Church and changed the message of Christ—as the Bible says changing time and laws.

And because of this lack of spirituality, pagans joining the early church felt immune to personal guilt because of sin, or at least the connotation of sin. Remember, we are discussing pagans who were mainly of Greek and Roman heritage, many of whom were raised worshiping the sun god. To them the ability to recognize sin as disobedience towards God was a foreign concept as that belief infers guilt, and guilt implies the threat of judgment, and some religious organizations (remember the Christian Scientist) do not believe in this judgment. This is the premise from which the Catholic Fathers operated to improve membership and grow the base of influence the Catholic Church strived to achieve.

Protestants on the other hand, believe judgment from the recognition of sin is the very basis of God's law. To a Christian, the very act of disobedience toward God, as defined by our conscience, implemented by God with the fall of Adam and Eve, implies judgment. It seems to be the guilt associated with this judgment that God relies on to keep us focused on what is important. Many believe antinomian theology works in conjunction with a pragmatic mind much better than a spiritual one. It was from this pragmatic frame of mind towards sin, and the guilt associated with sin, that antinomian theology was introduced into the world.

I found what John Calvin, a sixteenth-century reformer had to say about unbelievers can also be applied to those following antinomian theology. He wrote in *The Institutes of Christian Religion:*

> Being alienated from the Father of Light, they are so swamped in darkness as to think there is no life after death. However, the light is not so completely extinguished that all sense of immorality is lost. Conscience, which can distinguish between good and evil, responds to judgment of God and so is proof positive of an immortal spirit...the body cannot be touched by fear of spiritual punishment. This can only affect the soul, which again proves its existence.

It appears from the teachings of those embracing antinomian theology that while the conscience can distinguish between good and evil, they are not touched by guilt—sinful guilt that requires a personal relationship with Christ to not only overcome, but also to understand. There is no recognition of sin as brought to our awareness by the Holy Spirit for those who follow true antinomian theology. Otherwise, we would not be witnessing the atrocities we see, hear, and read about from time to time perpetrated by some within the Catholic Church, as well as some Protestant churches. The Catholic church is not the only church that is involved in scandalous behavior from time to time.

The crux of antinomian theology that was being embraced by the early Catholic Fathers came from the introduction of Christianity into the world. Christianity, a religion, perhaps even a movement, whatever it was, it bought guilt with it. Sure it did. Is not a degree of guilt associated with disobedience towards God? A guilt that was not present prior to Christianity as there is no guilt associated with idol worship. But the good news is they give instructions on how to overcome the guilt. Now we see the need for confession.

Probably because of this thinking, it was the contention of the church that wicked actions are not sinful acts, nor are they to be considered as instances of their violation of the divine law, and because of that, they have no occasion either to confess their sins or to break them off by repentance. [87] That was until guilt was introduced which begat the confessional booth where one knells to a man to get "right" with God. If that is what they say then, okay, I guess. I don't know any Protestants who would do that. To this day the discussion of guilt associated with sin is somewhat an elusive topic for the Catholic Church.

Antinomian theology ranks right up there with the best of dogma and would probably top any deception meter as it breeds antinomian libertines. As Richard Marius states in his previous book, "If I feel certain that I will be redeemed, I may eat, drink, and be merry and live like the devil. This is the sin of presumption." Again, this is antinomian theology. That could also apply to those who embrace "once saved, always saved" theology, but by listening to Charles Stanley, one finds he preaches against the sin of presumption. And of course, we know Christians of the Protestant faith run from antinomian theology like it was the plaque and adopt more of a dedicated desire to be true to the commands of God.

Antinomian Libertines

Those who follow "true" antinomian theology (sometimes referred to as "antinomian libertines"), are purveyors and perpetrators of licentiousness (wicked, shameful, and lewd living). We have read about some of the priest over the years who possess characteristics of antinomianism. Priest that are still associated with the church. This crowd lives for the complete gratification of every fleshly lust in existence and condones such lifestyles under the guise of Christian

---

[87] McClintock and Strong, "Antinomians," *Cyclopedia.*

liberty.[88] In fact, this was another reason for purgatory. Those early converts needed a place other than hell to go. Hell implied no chance of heaven, and before 1215 the burning punishment of a fire consuming flesh but never eliminating it was the preaching of the day.

It must have been this mindset that established purgatory. Robert A. Morey accuses antinomians of "holding a weak view of Scripture and claims that they are trying to 'justify their wicked lives' and to 'defend their evil ways.'" Purgatory also allowed sinful man to have an escape from the fires of hell as well as the fear that hell seemed to impose. The hell and the fear of the hell that was being preached to the laymen at the time was frightening.

And to mitigate that fear was the beginning of "once saved always saved." (Nothing personal to my Calvinist friends as we are on the same page because of what happened at the cross). That is why indulgences were such a big hit as a way of escaping hell, and just one of the reasons why Martin Luther rebelled. But then God had a hand in that. When Luther heard God's voice telling him the just shall live by faith it instantly changed his life. It was then that Luther bolted and never looked back upon his decision to leave the church.

The theological system of Catholicism seemed to placate the natives (pagans) and today the Catholic Church is still allowing antinomian to exist within their ranks, and they embrace pragmaticism as opposed to the spirituality one feels when attending an evangelical Church. But remember, antinomian thinking along with Catholicism is mostly theology from the minds of those who were themselves trying to understand. Even though during this same time many were living a life of promiscuity. Sure they were. A life that antinomian Christians could justify living without worry, especially with all the safety nets they had implemented.

---

[88]   Jack Van Impe, *Sabotaging the World Church* (New York: Jack Van Impe Ministries, 1991).

St. Augustine was a prime example of what I am talking about. Unfortunately for the Christian community, many of the earlier church Fathers made Christianity, and an understanding of Christ and His mission, much harder, much more difficult, much more complex than it must be. One finds buildings full of Catholic literature explaining everything one would need to be a Catholic whereas a Protestant takes one book and say's; "Believe upon the Lord Jesus Christ as the Son of God and you will be saved." The Holy Spirit will be very instrumental after that commitment to assure heaven and eternal life. Simple and to the point. Nothing convoluted.

CHAPTER XIII

CATHOLICISM AS DEFINED BY COUNCIL

Being an early follower of Catholicism seemed to require a commitment to be a Christian just as it does now—at least that was how the early church Fathers seemed to view the issue of joining their church. Protestants still believe that way today. But the Catholic Church developed a religious system that was appealing to pagans, those who were into paganism and bowing before idols. Many, of those who joined the church lacked a spiritual understanding of the commitment needed to be a follower of Christ—a follower of the Church…yes, but a follower of Christ…questionable as the essential "born again" experience appears to be missing. In Catholicism the born-again experience and the Holy Spirit is only received through the Sacraments.

This redefining of Christianity began with the Nicene council in 325, called by Constantine to put in writing some of the requirements defining a Christian, and to deal with heretics, such as Arius who began the heresy known as Arianism. He did not accept the concept of the Trinity, and said that Christ was a created being, somewhat on the same order as the Jehovah Witnesses. The Nicene council was the first time anyone had established a gathering to discuss being a follower of Christ and what that meant.

It was also the beginning of establishing a power base of religion that has never been duplicated. Remember, Emperor Constantine moved the base of the Roman Empire to the East locating in the Byzantine empire just a few years earlier where the beginning of the Greek Orthodox Church began to get roots. That move gave the Catholic Fathers free reign to assimilate and promote a Christianity that eventually became the all-inclusive Roman Catholic Church of the West.

Many believe it was about here, between 313 when Constantine moved the Roman Empire and 325 that the wheels were beginning to come off the apostolic teachings and wheels were being put in motion to write a religion that deviated from what many considered to be the "true" religion as was passed down through the apostles.

The next Ecumenical council meeting followed in 381 and was convened by Emperor Theodosius who wanted to unify the entire empire behind the orthodox (Catholic) position and decided to convene a church council to resolve matters of faith and discipline. A council that became known as the First Council of Constantinople and was attended by 150 bishops to denounce Arius and his followers once again as heretics and to seek consensus confirming the Nicene Creed and expanding the doctrine to deal with many sundry other matters. More honing of Catholicism that was destined to becoming the Catholic Church, the church that for some time, dominated Christianity.

Later came the Sacraments that many Protestants believe completed the transfer of the true Christianity from the Apostolic Church to the Catholic Church. A move that began with St Augustine and has continued through all who sit atop this all-inclusive institution. This transfer came with a full set of instructions that completely omitted Christ except in name only. As we have seen, instructions that many ascribe to early church Fathers who wrote much of the current day Catholic theology that sets them apart from main line Christianity.

It appears that the dark clouds of cultism have begun to accumulate around the Catholic Church as now they are in the process of truncating all semblance of the first church, the church of the Way, as established by the apostles and wrote about in the book of Acts. The transfer of Christianity from the Apostolic Church to the Catholic Church began sometime prior to 64 A.D. the year when Peter died, but real transformation began around 100 A.D. and found solid ground around 300 A.D. According to Catholicism the apostolic see of Rome was established in the first century by Saint Peter and Saint Paul, but it was not until the fourth century that the transfer of Christianity as handed down to the apostles by Christ was completely owned by the Catholic Church. Again, the reason for the reformers.

The ability to become a Christian—without repentance or a change of heart from which the born-again experience is derived—had now been implemented by the Catholic Church through the Sacramental system. A "learn how to become and stay a follower of Christ" system had now become a vessel that will transport one to heaven. Again, I ask, where is Christ in this? A total system of pragmatism that pagans joining the church found accommodating. More of a pragmatic religion rather than a spiritual one based upon faith as followed by evangelical Christians. I know that comment might be upsetting to some but am I wrong? Where do you see Christ in their religion? Just think about it. Such blind allegiance to a man-made system subverts the purpose of theology by making humankind, not God, its ultimate authority.[89]

Everything about Catholicism is doing something, even to the point of receiving Christ by an action or completing some "penance" (works) for the "fulfillment" of atonement for disobedience. And much of their connection to Christ and the Apostolic Church is accomplished by "tradition" even to the point of appointing Peter

---

[89]   Fudge, Edward William. *The fire that consumes.* Eugene Orgon: Cascade Books. 2011.

280

as pope of a church that was nonexistence in his time. A complete church with accommodating theology that they themselves wrote. Accommodating theology that brought forth dogma that resembled Christianity.

Martin Luther during the time he was associated with the church, was a prime example of someone who had problems with the accommodating Catholic replica of Christianity that haunted him most of his early life. When he had fears about his salvation, always questioning whether he was saved, he would spend 12 hours per day confessing his sins, deadly afraid that he might forget one of them and go to hell. Once he discovered the doctrine of saving grace through faith alone as presented in the book of Romans, he began questioning those above him seeking answers. But no matter how many times he broached the subject of faith verses works he never received resolution as to how works could justify the removal of sin and insure salvation.

The Catholic Church teaches that Peter was the pope (Holy See) of Rome where the first church began. When reading what Nicola Denzey had to say on March 6, 2021, as found on biblicalarchaeology. gov, they find the earliest testimony to the apostle Peter's presence in Rome is a letter from a Christian deacon named Gaius around 170 or 180 A.D. where it discusses Peter's time in Rome where he established a church—in fact, *the Church*, the Roman Catholic Church at the site where St. Peter's Basilica is today. That same informational site also said that there is no biblical prove that Peter was ever in Rome—thank you. Again, we have "church tradition" that brings us the assumption that Peter and Paul taught together in Rome and founded Christianity in that city.

Luther, Huss, and Pragmatism

To Luther works without faith equated to denying the complete absolution of sin as described in the Bible along with his understanding of justification. Does not the Bible say we are justified (brought into righteousness) by our faith, therefore obedience to works, with a limited understanding of faith was a constant conflict within his mind? And that conflict never seemed to abate by being faithful to the Catholic Church. As well as attending Mass to receive Jesus, praying the rosary, attending confession every time the confessional booth was open, even though the requirement was only once a year, and then he would do the required penance (works of a pragmatic nature) to assure his continued salvation.

Luther had the opportunity to experience firsthand that the Mass, as initiated and implemented by Catholic Fathers to receive Christ, did not fulfil the longing he desired to have a relationship with Jesus, to feel forgiven, to feel closer than he was feeling. Especially when receiving Christ via a wafer, which gives a Catholic the right to claim, "they have received Christ" but a pragmatic move that seemed to replace faith and always seemed to leave him feeling empty. And confession that led to repentance for the absolution of disobedience towards God never satisfied that longing Luther felt—thus the 12 hours of atoning.

That desire to know God on a more personal level always felt missing. Always felt elusive and that haunted him most of his earlier life. What Luther seemed to be missing during his time with the Catholic Church was the "spiritual" indwelling of the Holy Spirit. Both him and John Huss had conflicting feelings about disobeying a church that they had been taught to be the truth, and the only truth, and the only way by which salvation was obtained but it never seemed to witness to their soul.

Speaking of John Huss, a bit of information you might find interesting regarding Martin Luther and John Huss was the fact that they were warring mentally against the church—against many of the principles of the church, as well as against the abuse of authority by the church. This brought on a terrible conflict between their understanding of Catholicism and the claims of their conscience which precipitated an interesting question: "If the authority was "just and infallible" as they believed it to be, why did they feel compelled to disobey it?" Why, indeed? "To obey was in direct conflict with their conscience, but why should obedience to an infallible church be such an issue?" Why, indeed? This was a problem they could never seem to resolve and continues to remain a question by modern day Christians as they search for that answer.

When Luther looked to the Church for answers regarding whether he was saved, he was always told to stay loyal to the commands of the church as they apply to the Sacraments, pray for guidance, pray the rosary and he would know when he got there if he made it or not. That answer for the modern-day layman who may be seeking answers would probably not be satisfying as it seems to exclude the fact that we, as born-again Christians, can know we are saved with a ticket to heaven. When many of the Catholic Fathers, those Luther considered knowledgeable clergy, were unable to answer such a basic question as to whether they were saved had to plant doubt in both Luther's mind as well as John Huss.

John Huss was just one of the many reformers questioning the teachings of the Catholic Church who were preaching "justification by works" rather than "justification by faith." In other words, John Huss taught that we are brought into righteousness by our faith rather than by our works. And for this "teaching" he was burned at the stake.

Luther Meets Faith

After years of doubt, agony, and anguish God gave Luther what he had been seeking to bring peace to his soul. As Luther was ascending the stairs in Rome on his knees as many were doing to receive an indulgence, and find favor with the pope, the same stairs by the way that Christ descended in Jerusalem on the way to his execution that somehow miraculously was now in Rome, Luther heard a booming voice that plainly said, "The just shall live by faith."

Upon hearing that voice, Luther instantly bolted from those stairs, as well as Catholicism, and never once seemed to question his decision. The discernment Luther had on that day while ascending those stairs in Rome is what Protestants rely on every day to give them the ticket into eternity without the fabricated theology of purgatory.

As a matter of fact, it was his discernment regarding the theology of the Catholic Church that when writing about them incited the leaders of Catholicism with so much rage they wanted him dead. And to this day he is considered a heretic, a deceiving lying devil that does not deserve to live. All because he challenged them for the "real" truths, and they could not deliver. It appears they got defensive then, and to a degree, seem to remain defensive even unto this day when challenged to explain some of their theology. By their own admission, it would be impossible to change even if they agreed they were wrong.

Protestants following the doctrine of faith find faith to be enough to forge a personal and lasting relationship with Christ. That's it. *Faith.* The Bible tells us that "the just shall live by faith" and "it takes faith to please God." But then the Catholics continue by saying, "faith without works is dead" and they would not be wrong as that is what the Bible says. But again, to believe in, and follow the theology of works for the absolution of anything, would make any religion more of a pragmatic religion than a spiritual one. And choosing pragmatism that includes works is a lot easier to commit to than one requiring faith.

Sure it is. One can live the life he or she wants, go to confession, and do the penance, (reparation, self-punishment, amends and so on) required for the redemption of sin, stay true to the Catholic Church, and they, with the assurance of the pope, get a ticket to heaven, or at the very least purgatory. And if a Catholic still feels unsure, they can always buy an indulgence. Wow! Quite a system of intricacies to become a follower of Christ but intricacies according to the Catholic Church with an almost guarantee into heaven.

Faith Without Works

Intricacies such as works rather than faith was being assigned by priest for the completion of atonement. Works that were necessary to complete the reparation process began by Christ on the cross. It was works in addition to confession that kept members in good standing with God and the church. Works is justified by saying, as the Catholics do, "Faith without works is dead." Works done for the right reason, the right motivation, will stand during the Bema judgment, Christians knowing this, perform works that glorify God, not for additional atonement that to many indicate Christ dying on the cross was not entirely sufficient to warrant complete atonement.

Remember, as mentioned earlier, how some Christians, mainly Catholics, did not feel total absolution from sin by just telling God they are sorry for messing up and asking for His forgiveness? And as we all do, promising him we will not continue repeating the same offence. And when we do, we, once again, repent and ask forgiveness. It is reassuring to know that Jesus tells us he will forgive us seven times seventy if we ask him. (And he will not take away our salvation for messing up). I thought about that seven times seventy and decided that anyone needing forgiveness that many times may have more problems than just disobedience.

Asking to be forgiven for, letting Christ down, and asking him to once again, plant our feet, on higher ground. Meaning putting anything between us and God in the review mirror. That was and will always be the purpose of why Christ came. But in Catholicism Christ dying on the cross and shedding His blood does not complete the atoning process. The death of Christ does not seem to be sufficient to accomplish complete absolution from sin. Although, adding anything to the sacrifice made by Christ would seem to indicate that the sacrifice He made on the cross was insufficient to accomplish the job of achieving "total and complete" atonement for sin, and that seems to be in direct contradiction to the teachings from the Bible.

Because of this thinking, theology has been passed down by the Catholic Church requiring additional atonement (ascribed works) prescribed by a priest during confession to remove the stain of the sin from our conscience, leaving us with a feeling of completion. And just as importantly, we are assured by the Catholic Church that our sins are expunged from our record in heaven, which allows one to stand before Christ forgiven of all confessed sins. At least, that is hopefully what happens, but when one confesses their sins to the church and the church forgives those sins, (men acting in place of God) then maybe that is saying the church stands in place of God. That is exactly what they say.

To many evangelical Christians, this would rank high on the false theology meter. Martin Luther expressed his opinion regarding the issue of Christianity and salvation by works when he said, "Without the law (as has been written upon our conscience since Christ) human pride turns to the notion that good deeds make the good man when these good deeds done for such a motive are, in fact, sins." And according to Pastor Jeremiah, "Religious works do not make the worker religious."

Most Protestants seem to agree that physical works as a replacement for spiritual faith, or misguided faith as in antinomian theology, purgatory, and replacement theology, is misplaced faith taught by Catholicism, and is not biblical. And if one wants to get technical, it is false theology, as it is pragmatism, as opposed to true spirituality. Some concepts of Catholicism change the intent of the Bible, such as replacement theology, a discussion that will be coming up, but let us first discuss the origin of the Sacraments and see what part they play in Catholicism.

When this journey began, there were three areas of interest to discuss in Catholicism, as they represented a great part of the Catholic Church's beliefs. They were antinomian theology, which we just covered, and purgatory, (including indulgences), which we will discuss in depth later along with replacement theology. We will cover the remaining two shortly, but first let us discuss the Sacraments, as they are the foundation upon which Catholicism is built.

CHAPTER XIV

THE BIRTH OF SACRAMENTS

To understand the importance of the Sacraments, one must "understand the importance of the Sacraments." Let us read a paragraph in its entirety from the "Sacrament Guide," referred to as a *study guide to understand the Sacraments*:

> Christ passed on His healing power to the 12 apostles and those other chosen disciples referred to as "the group of 72" (Luke 9:1–2, 10:8–9). Through their successors, Christians today continue to have Sacraments as a means of salvific (the power of the Lord leading to salvation) healing. Jesus established His Church, itself a Sacrament, to further the mission of salvation. He instituted the saving grace of the Sacraments so that His work to make mankind whole, to reunite humanity with God, would be continued by His people. In fact, the Sacraments constitute the only and necessary gateway to the Lord.

That last line, "The Sacraments constitute the only and necessary gateway to the Lord," reveals just how questionable Catholicism is, as, once again, it writes Christ out of the picture almost entirely.

Sacraments mean that one can maintain a relationship with Christ through acts of pragmatism put in place by the early church Fathers. How about that, we have just been told the Sacraments constitute "the only and necessary gateway to the Lord." Really, the Sacraments represent the only and necessary gateway to Christ? That is what they say which once again, is beginning to border on cultism as the dark clouds are getting darker and darker.

Just to recap: Catholics believe that it is altogether necessary to be a Catholic for salvation (the only church from which salvation comes), and that we are absolved from sin by performing certain church-assigned functions (works instead of faith, but then some might argue faith is in doing the works as atonement for the sin). And they pray to Mary, asking her to intercede for them with the Father and for her to ask Him to forgive them of their sins, which, once again, seems to exclude Christ from everything, except in name only. Considering what has been discussed so far, probably all any evangelical Christian attending a Protestant church can say is, "Wow!" And we are just getting started.

Evangelical Christians put Christ between God and them, whereas Catholics seem to put the Sacraments, the pope, the priest, and even Mary between themselves and God which excludes them from having a personal relationship with Jesus. While many might consider this skeptical theology, with some even considering it dangerous, but would these sentiments make Catholics, those who follow a pragmatic religion, "unchristian?" That would fall under the category of the question asked earlier by Neale Donald Walsch, when he asked if we will not be accepted into heaven for practicing the wrong religion. Most Christians are probably thankful that this is not their call, as they prefer to leave the answer to that question up to God.

What is being discussed by way of the Sacraments is a series of instructions and deeds for being a follower of Christ placed upon Christians, unnecessary conditions that Protestants have rejected ever since the Reformation. And Protestants do not need "tradition" to connect them with the Apostolic Church, since they believe that they are the Apostolic Church. Since the Catholic Church places so much importance upon the Sacraments, even going so far as to say they are necessary for salvation, we might as well try to grasp an understanding of just what they offer to us.

THE SACRAMENTS OF THE CHURCH...

...Or as some may say, the "Sacramental System to Salvation." Richard Marius tells us in his book, *Martin Luther: The Christian between God and Death*, that, "The Sacramental system developed slowly. Only with Peter the Lombard in the twelfth century did the church come to a consensus that there were seven Sacraments—the traditionally sacred number—baptism, confirmation, the Eucharist, penance, ordination, marriage, and extreme unction." (They were affirmed in 1439.) Richard Marius continues: "These were considered vehicles of divine grace to help the Christian pilgrim, the viator, make the journey from earth to heaven."

According to Marius, "Each Sacrament shared the nature of Christ, for each was an incarnation of sorts, an invisible spirit or power, clothed and communicated in physical form, just as Christ had been divinely clothed in flesh."[90] That is according to Pope Leo I, who reigned as pope from 440-461. But again, who does the Catholic Church say was the first pope? As we know, they say the apostle Peter. But, as we saw earlier, he was appointed to this position sometime after his death as he had no connection with a "Christianity" that did not exist. I believe that popes were first elected from the twelfth century forward. However, the first bishop of Rome to be contemporaneously referred to as "pope" would be Damasus I, (366-384).[91]

---

[90] Richard Marius, *Martin Luther: The Christian between God and Death* (Cambridge: Belknap Press of Harvard University, 1999).

[91] https://en.m.wikipedia.org.

Pope Leo I wrote, "What was visible in Christ has passed over into the Sacraments of the church."[92] Think about what was just said. They claim that they now have the authority of Christ, and what was possible through Christ is now possible through the authority of the pope and the Sacraments of the church. The authority to act in place of God, as written into Catholicism by the early writers of the church's constitution, was now in place and has been embraced by the Fathers of the church ever since, beginning from the first council of Nicaea called by Constantine in 325. And as we have seen there was also another council meeting in 381 to continue defining Christianity.

Two large council meetings that had been arranged to define the requirements of being a Christian, with the assertion that the information from these meetings was to be regarded as being established, accepted, and self-evidently true. Many refer to this as an axiom, probably on the same order as dogma. It was not long after this that Christianity entered what many consider the dark ages for the Apostolic Church for not agreeing with the Catholic Fathers and their incredulous theology. And again, these differences boiled to the surface when Martin Luther nailed his 95 theses to the chapel door in Wittenberg, Germany.

It was Pope Leo X (1475-1521) who declared Luther a heretic and excommunicated him after Luther refused to retract his statement at the Diet of Worms in 1521 where Luther said, "Unless I am convinced by the testimony of the Scriptures or by clear reason…I am bound by the Scriptures. I have quoted and my conscience is captive to the Word of God."[93] It was shortly thereafter that Emperor Charles V (1500-1558) declared Luther to be an outlaw and authorized his death.

Luther as well as many of the reformers, John Calvin (1509-1564), John Knox (1513-1572), Huldryeh Zwingli (1484-1531),

---

[92]   Richard Maris *Martin Luther: The Christian between God and Death.*

[93]   David L. Hudson, Jr. *The Handy History Answer Book.* Canton, MI. Visible Ink Press. 2013.

Conrad Grebel (1498-1526), and later notable reformers such as John Wesley (1703-1791) and Charles Wesley (1707-1788), who were instrumental in forming the Methodist church, were all persuaded that the leaders of the Catholic Church had abandoned the faith and that the elitist Roman Catholics wrote Christ out of the picture in trying to accommodate the pagans who were joining the church without an understanding of the necessity of a spiritual conversion. By so doing they were fulfilling a goal of establishing the "Church" as the universal religion of the land, and as the—once again—*only true means of salvation* and the pope as the "Christ," or as Pope Boniface VIII said, head of the "only true Church."

These are not my words, or the words of Richard Marius, Diarmaid MacCulloch, Ellen G. White, Doug Batchelor or the words of thousands of others who have written about the information imparted by those early philosophers, such as St. Augustine, Aristotle, and others who contributed to the understanding many church members have of Christianity even today.

What has been passed along by many are words that have been "written by the church" and conveyed as truths, forming the theology that has been embraced by the church and has become known as Catholicism. The writers are only repeating what the church conveys and how it differs from the beliefs of other Christians—nothing more. The important thing to remember regarding the Sacraments, is that the Catholic Church teaches everything that was possible with Christ is now possible through the pope and the Sacraments—including the assurance of salvation. Thus, again, eliminating Christ except in name only.

Think about the implications of what was just said for a minute. We have just placed Christ on the back burner, implying that He is not needed for salvation, but rather relying on the Sacraments and the pope for our salvation. While at the same time writing a religion around Christ to accomplish their goals, which appears to be the largest and richest religious movement the world has ever seen. The religion of all religions, making everyone who joins them a family of like thinkers. A melting pot of Christianity if you will.

Even if that means compromising some principles, as Pope John Paul II did, when he said that "all who live a just life will be saved even if they do not believe in Jesus Christ and the Roman Catholic Church."[94] That would include atheists, such as Bill Maher or Richard Dawkins, who have no business in heaven without a change of heart. That would make a mockery of what happened at the cross by implying that there are no requirements to be a Christian, such as believing on the cross for salvation. Or Pope Francis saying as he did earlier that one does not really need Christ to go to heaven. Wow! An evangelical would have nightmares from that theology. An understanding of Catholicism must give many the shivers.

Once again, those dark black clouds with lightning and thunder rumbling and billowing around us could give one the illusion that Catholicism is a church that has been built upon false theology, or at least a religion considered questionable at best. Especially since one is told that after salvation is bestowed by the pope via our membership into the church along with the forgiveness of sin and following the requirements of the church, we are a Christian. A Catholic Christian, but a Christian, nevertheless. We have learned that the church stands in place of God, and now our obedience to the Sacraments developed by the church leads to the fulfilling of requirements to be a good Christian, beginning with the Sacrament of penance.

The Sacrament of Penance

Confession and penance, penance, and confession…they seem to go together. There are those within the Christian community who

---

[94]   As quoted from the New York Times December 9th, 2019 and brought to our attention by John MacArthur, preaching on Inclusivism, Catholicism and Billy Graham.

consider the Catholic Church responsible for replacing the Bible's definition of repentance as defined by the Protestant church with the Sacrament of "penance" as defined by the Catholic Church. The Sacrament of penance and reconciliation (or confession) is one of the seven Sacraments of the church (called sacred mysteries in eastern Catholic Churches). A hypothesis in which the faithful, who obtain absolution for the sins committed against God and neighbor, are reconciled with the community of the church and God. By this Sacrament Catholics believe they are freed (absolved) from sins committed after baptism.[95]

The application of this Sacrament is designed to forgive sins committed after conversion to Catholicism through confession to a Catholic priest, and then absolution by the priest upon doing penance for the sin as assigned by the priest. The fulfillment of this Sacrament is supposed to place one in good standing with God and the church. Again, where's Christ? Also, once again, the question becomes, is forgiveness of sin by a priest a valid forgiveness? That is an interesting question.

It is especially interesting, since writers who support such a belief such as Origen (241), Cyprian (251), and Aphraates (337) are clear in saying "confession is to be made to a priest." An evangelical Christian would say confession is to be made directly to God. If one wants to talk to a pastor or counselor, they have that option, but they would not expect to hear the pastor say that your sins are forgiven my son. All that is asked of you is to do some acts of penance as they would from a priest at confession. Then you will be right with God. If one confesses transgressions against God to a man and man tells one what to do, then where is God in this equation. They get their authority from the pope who is Christ concealed by a vale of flesh.

It was Pope Leo I who said absolution can be obtained only through the prayers of the priests. In other words, priests and the church are put between God and us, with instructions for us to

---

[95]   https://en.m.wikipedia.org.

ask them for forgiveness. Again, where is Christ? I am with Pastor David Jeremiah on this one, as he says there is only one person in the universe who can forgive our sins, and that's God almighty. Your priest cannot, and your pastor cannot, only God Himself can forgive sins and restore our joy. But this is strictly a Protestant belief. As was pointed out earlier, the Catholic Church believes they have this authority, as now they think they are the apple of God's eye by way of replacement theology as we will see later.

Each pope, including the current one, Pope Francis, being a Father of the Catholic Church through a line of succession, must believe priests have access to the authority to erase sins from God's book. The one mentioned in Exodus 33:33. He must believe this theology to be true, as it is the theology of the earlier writers of the constitution of the church. Protestants, on the other hand, believe that any confession for disobedience towards God must be done through Christ, whose death gave us access to God. This means that we need not put any man, church, or organization between God and us. Since God tells us that repeatedly, there must be some merit in what He says.

One man forgiving another man's sins? Come on. Common sense must prevail in this situation. Question: Who is going to remove the sin from God's book, the book that keeps a record of our sin? Some refer to that book as the book of deeds. The Bible mentions "Books" to be open at the Great Judgment and a book titled "the book of deeds" seems to fit. Anyway, only God and those to whom he gives authority can forgive sin, and as of today, that was only God, Jesus, and the apostles. Again, another reason for the Catholic Church to initiate Replacement Theology.

Now this could possibly be important. Regardless of what the Catholic Church says, there is a very good chance that the sins confessed through confession to a priest remains unforgiven, since the only one who can forgive those sins and blot them from God's memory, or as the Bible says, His book, and not hold them against us is God. No priest or anyone outside of God has that authority. Regarding the sin being forgiven by merely confessing the sin to a man and performing some actions as assigned by a man, may be considered by some as false, as well as dangerous, theology.

I had never heard anyone express an opinion regarding this issue until the other day when I heard Dr. Charles Stanley convey almost the same understanding. I nearly fell off my chair. In other words, it becomes questionable theology to expect sin to be removed by the loyalty displayed to a confessional belief. It is simply great to have someone of Dr. Stanley's stature preaching the consequences of false theology.

To my knowledge (and apparently to Dr. Stanley's), the ability to forgive sin has never been passed on to anyone. Thus, the potential of the sin remaining on the books is a good bet, and to expect otherwise is considered by many to be dangerous theology. Whereas, if I go straight to God then I know He will forgive me as he tells me he will, and by faith, I believe that. Only time will tell, but until that time I am putting my eggs in the basket with other evangelical Christians and walking by faith in the words of Christ that God will forgive me of my transgressions when I stand before Him.

The Catholic Church seems to have adopted the theology that they have the authority to forgive sins from John 21:23, where Jesus says; "Peace be with you! As the Father has sent me, I am sending you!" And with that He breathed on them and said, "Receive the Holy Spirit. If you forgive anyone his sins, they are forgiven. If you do not forgive them, they are not forgiven." (John 21:23 NIV). What one makes of those words is up to them, but remember, when Jesus said those words to Peter, Peter was destined to be one of the founding Fathers of the church of the Way, the Apostolic Church of yesteryear that many equate to the Protestant church of today. Many believe this was exclusively given to the apostles and since those days, no man is capable of forgiving anyone's sins.

One man forgiving another man's sins? Come on. Common sense must prevail in this situation. Anyway, only God and those to whom he gives authority can forgive sin, and as of today, that was only God, Jesus, and the apostles. Again, another reason for the Catholic Church to initiate Replacement Theology.

As we found out, through the Sacrament of confession and penance, the absolution for sin is granted by a priest, a representative of God assigned by the Catholic Church. I disagree with Tertullian saying, "Satisfaction is determined by confession, penance is born of confession, and by penance God is appeased." Information from saintjamesrcc.org. Wow! "And by 'penance' God is appeased?" Really? And this is from one who many consider to be an early apostolic Father.

Sometimes it gets hard to keep the players straight, as the theology of many seem to bleed into every fiber of Christianity. God has repeated that it is by faith we are justified (brought into righteousness), and it is by faith we will remain justified. I believe it safe to say this difference of opinion regarding absolution for sin creates a major split between theology embraced by Catholics and theology embraced by Protestants.[96]

Catholicism teaches the absolution of the confessed sin is the result of the penance required and that depends upon the sin. For example, a priest may say to someone confessing a lie, "Say five Hail Marys and repeat the rosary each day for ten days." Or someone may confess to stealing and he or she is told, "Say ten Hail Marys and attend Mass five times, and your sins will be forgiven." I have no idea what the penance for adultery might be—community service for a month? This equates to forgiveness by works, as initiated into the church by St. Augustine for the reparation of sin. This is different theology than one might find in a Protestant Church. Protestants boldly approach God through the blood of Jesus with complete authority as they feel that is scriptural.

The Sacrament of Baptism...

...and the "born-again" experience. I found a bit of interesting information contained in the "*Sacraments: A Catholic Study Guide*,"

---

[96] Tertullian. C. 155-c. 240 A.D. was a prolific early Christian author.

published by Twin Circle Publishing Company. The writer said, "If I were to ask the average parents presenting their child for baptism why they do so, I can safely say that 95 percent would suggest the removal of original sin as their reason." To remove original sin... while that is impossible to do, this is correct doctrine for Catholics.

The Catholic Church, along with the Lutherans and a couple of others, baptize adults to deal with the original sin issue, as well as being considered "born again." This Sacrament seems to go together with the Sacrament of confirmation, where one is believed to receive the Holy Spirit. Both Catholics and Protestants agree that to be saved, we must be born again. Jesus said that unless a man is born of water and of the Spirit, he cannot enter the kingdom of heaven. Christ also in a discussion with Nicodemus in the book of John describes the necessity of being born again. (By the way, this is the same Nicodemus that assisted Joseph of Arimathea with the burial of Jesus Christ.)

The baptism of water is as if passing through the blood of Christ for the cleansing of all prior sins and the removal of those sins. Many seem to feel there is a regeneration associated with the new birth, both from the baptism of water and being born of the Spirit (receiving the Spirit of God upon the decision to follow Him), so there is probably no argument regarding this theology. Some might say one exchanges their filthy robe of stain and shame for a clean white one, thus receiving a brand-new slate on which to write the future. Just a benefit of following Christ.

Baptism among Protestants would probably be explained this way. Baptism symbolically removes past sins and repentance removes any future sins. Since I am told that I will be judged for every word that I speak, repentance is particularly important to a Christian. Considering this, the question becomes, how am I going to know that every word I speak is always on the plus side of forgiveness, instead of the negative side of condemnation? We do not, but God does. And according to his word, all sin must be purged prior to entering heaven. This is where the Catholics insert purgatory.

The one sin even Catholics acknowledge that will guarantee spiritual death is not believing and confessing Christ as savior and Lord. Several churches preach this as the "unpardonable sin." Christians understand this and are constantly seeking God to maintain a relationship with him. This is where repentance verses penance comes into play, as it conveys a much deeper meaning. If we were not going to sin, do something wrong after baptism, the word repentance probably would not be in the Bible. Most Christians agree that sins after salvation will not affect their actual salvation but will affect their fellowship with God. I am sure most would agree with that. That is the message I hear when I go to church.

While not a Sacrament, born again theology seems to go along with our acceptance of Christ and baptism. A question I found quite interesting when studying Catholic thinking was, "How does the Catholic Church perceive the doctrine of evangelical thinking when it comes to 'born again' theology?" Interesting question After discussing the evangelical understanding of "born again" theology we will discuss the Catholics response to it. Protestants accept as fact that, "If we believe in the Lord Jesus Christ and believe he died for our sins, we, for all practical purposes, are born again." Born from death into life.

That is what being born again is all about, going from being a nonbeliever to a believer. And how is that accomplished? For an evangelical Christian the journey to becoming a "born-again" Christian started somewhere, usually with an invitation to attend a place where Christ was being preached and they felt something that told them "this was right." Somewhere that seed was planted in the heart of an evangelical Christian to follow Christ and according to the Catholic Churches, when explaining a Protestants accepting that invitation often occurs as follows:

A person goes to a crusade or a revival, or perhaps into a church and listens to a sermon like the one a minister such as the late Billy Graham used to deliver, or the message that his son Franklin Graham delivers now, or perhaps Charles Stanley or Dr. David

Jeremiah telling him or her of his or her need to receive Christ and be "born again." So, the person makes a conscious decision for Christ and decides during the alter call to go forward, or remain where they are, to be led in the "sinner's prayer," pledging to repent of their sins and become a believer in the death and resurrection of Jesus.

It is the belief of an evangelical that when we cross the threshold of unbelief into belief we have been born into the family of God, thus avoiding the second death, the spiritual death the death that eternally separates us from God. Regeneration (being born again) is the transformation from death to life that occurs in our souls as witnessed by our mind and conscience as revealed by the Holy Spirit when we come to God with a repenting heart, and it is then we are justified—brought into righteousness. That is a promise of God and by faith, evangelical Christians believe that promise.

Upon going forward at a crusade to commit to Christ, or as you may hear ministers say, that if you said the sinner's prayer from anywhere in this auditorium and meant it, you have been born again. But are the ministers right, the Catholic Church asks? Followed by the answer, "Not according to the Bible."[97] When I read that I only had one thought: Who can say whether a person is saved or not? Only God knows their true intention, as He is the only one who can fully understand the heart of an individual. According to many Protestant pastors, when we confess our sins to Jesus and accept him as our Savior and agree to follow Him—to obey Him, to become like Him, to understand Him, then we are saved. I believe many would agree that to say otherwise is beyond the spiritual pay grade of anyone.

Most evangelicals would probably say that being "born again" or "getting saved" consists of a personal conversion experience, a personal commitment, maybe even an epiphany moment. A moment in time when one repents of his or her sins and turns to Jesus Christ for salvation and they believe by faith that they are saved into eternal life.

---

[97]   https://www.catholic.com.

Catholics say that is too easy and have established a way to complicate this thinking or simplify it—depending upon one's thinking, with instructions necessary to become and remain a Catholic Christian by way of the Sacraments. As has been mentioned a couple of times, the Catholics have initiated a pragmatical sacrificial system that almost eliminates faith as well as Christ, except in name only.

A future evangelical Christian becomes a Christian by saying "the sinner's prayer," which is very simply, "Lord Jesus, I'm sorry for my sins and I want to accept your gift of forgiveness and salvation. Come into my life and make me your disciple forever."[98] Catholics say if this is all there is to it, then every Catholic is a "born-again" Christian. And I say, okay. One gets no argument from me if Catholicism does not get in the way. It is not until instructions from interpretations as handed down from some of the earlier philosophers that evangelicals began, and continue, to question certain theology. Perhaps with infant baptism being right up there as being considered theology that many seem to question. Once one understands why infants are baptized, they may understand why many feel it is an unnecessary act.

Infant Baptism and Original Sin

Infant baptism. When it comes to questionable theology, one of the most contentious disagreements between Catholicism and much of Protestantism is infant baptism. The Catholic Church baptizes infants to remove original sin. That is an interesting doctrine, as that takes one back to the time of Adam and Eve and the very first act of disobedience, which is considered the "original sin." Now think about that. That act of disobedience is indelibly imprinted upon the mind of every born-again Christian, and to remove it would probably require a lobotomy.

---

[98] m.ncregister.com as posted by Fr. Dwight Longenecker, April 2018.

There is no such thing as "removing original sin," as there is no sin to remove with which we are born. Sin was introduced into the world with Adam and Eve and will remain with us until the end. So, how is the first act of disobedience towards God removed by baptizing an infant? Baptism is to remove the stain of sin and to give us a clean slate—that is true, but infants do not have sin, that is literal sin in their lives. They were born with the capacity to commit sin, that is the definition of "original sin" which gives us the capability to understand right from wrong.

Sin, or the knowledge of sin, was established in the Garden of Eden when Adam and Eve disobeyed God and partook of the tree that was designated as the tree containing the knowledge of good and evil, and when they did their eyes were opened to disobedience for the very first time. Now they would surely die, both physically and maybe even spiritually (the second death). But, as Christians know, all of this plays an especially important role in God's plan of salvation, because the spiritual death, the second death, is overcome with the acceptance of Christ by faith.

It was upon the act of disobedience towards God that death entered the world, so Satan as a serpent was lying when he said, "You will not surely die." "For God knows that when you eat of it your eyes will be opened (and they were) and you will be like God, knowing good and evil." (Genesis 3:4). Thus, evil, recognizable by our conscience, entered the world and God's plan for salvation was implemented. Once someone knows the difference between good and evil, they have choices to make and one of those choices is to be baptized. But not before understanding the importance of baptism. This is where Protestants and Catholics take a different road. The act of baptism is just that—an act, a pragmatic act, and the "act" prior to understanding is just that--an act, a motion without a foundation of knowledge. In baptism it is the knowledge of the act that is as important, if not more important, than the act itself.

Now back to Adam and Eve, their fall from grace and how that ties in with infant baptism. It was the very first act of disobedience towards God that allowed Satan entry into the world, as now he had access to our conscience and our mind, and even our emotions. It was a time when Satan and all his buddies entered the world as our conscience was now opened to understanding evil, where before we only had access to good. All of this is God's plan for man to have an opportunity to live forever. If we had stayed as Adam and Eve before the fall, with no opportunity to obey God or not, we would have been marionettes, and as we know, that is not what God wanted.

Some Protestants believe the sins of the individual are removed at baptism, while others believe sins are removed at the time one receives salvation—when they receive Christ as Savior. Let us take a moment and look at these viewpoints. I believe that we can unequivocally state that there is no salvation in baptism, yet it appears that baptism serves two functions: one, it removes the stain of sin. Baptism is a symbolic act, but many believe that this act erases sin from God's ledger. As for us, there is no man that has that kind of ability, but God does as He conveys to us through the apostle Peter.

It was Peter who said, "Repent and be baptized every one of you in the name of Jesus Christ for the forgiveness of your sins, and you will receive the gift of the Holy Spirit." (Acts 2:38 NIV). I would say adding, as he did, "receiving the gift of the Holy Spirit after water baptism part" appears to clarify that water baptism is not the same as the baptism of the Holy Spirit. The apostle Paul wrote that John the Baptist's baptism was one of repentance. Receiving the gift of the Holy Spirit will be discussed in more detail later.

As we have seen, all Christians affirm that baptism is important, and some even believe it is necessary to enter heaven. After we receive salvation in Christ by acknowledging that we have sinned against Him, we desire to be cleansed and purged of our sins, as we are told by our pastor. A frequently asked question is whether we are saved between the time we accept Christ and the time we are baptized. In other words, is baptism necessary to enter heaven? Some say yes, probably more say no, each with the same amount of conviction as the other. The thief on the cross who believed in Christ never was baptized, and yet went into eternity with Jesus.

Baptism shows the world that we have accepted Christ and have asked Him to come into our life as our Savior, and now we are asking Him to remove our sins and place our name in the book of life. (Although the name adding part was done the moment we accepted Christ as our Savior). Most of the Christians I have spoken with say baptism symbolizes the death, burial, and resurrection into a new, life. Just as Jesus died, was buried, and then rose again, we symbolically died to the flesh, was, buried and emerged victoriously from the water to begin a new life.

It is upon this action that our old life passed away and that our new life began—with a clean slate—as many might say, a new person, a Christian. Baptism is not, as the Catholics contend, to remove "original sin" but rather "all" sin except for the original sin that allowed our eyes to be opened, our spiritual eyes, and made salvation possible. At what age does one receive baptism in a Protestant church? When they ask to be baptized. That is like asking when is a person saved? When they ask to be saved.

Regarding the age of accountable as explained in the Jewish Bible. In Judaism, a child becomes an adult at the age of thirteen. But of course, as we know, one could be any age when they acquire an understanding of the message of Christ and feel a desire to be saved and then baptized. Protestants believe that prior to the age of accountability nobody has the mental capacity to commit any sins; they have the sinful nature, but only when they have the capability to understand sin and the consequences of sin will they be judged for sin; therefore, they get a pass until they reach the age of accountability. Again, this is evangelical thinking.

According to the Catholic Church, an infant child's baptism is intended to seal the child into the kingdom of God and the Catholic Church. Without this baptism to remove the original stain of sin as introduced into the world by God through the actions of Adam and Eve, the child upon an early death would have to go to purgatory and do penance to remove the stain of the original sin. Why is that? Catholics say one cannot enter heaven without the stain of the original sin being removed; therefore, excluding the baptism by the church, the child, as well as the adult, must do time in purgatory.

Protestants skip the infant baptism part and go right into the "age of accountability" part. That is when a Protestant minister would baptize someone. Again, when they are old enough to understand baptism and request it. Now, they may dedicate a child to God, but that is entirely different than trying to remove any stain of sin from the infant's life. Especially from his or her life who is without literal sin, as in lying, stealing, cheating, and so on.

Question: If one is without knowledge of sin, as would be an infant, or maybe even someone in the deepest part of Africa a hundred years ago, who had never heard of Christ, or sin, or salvation and so on, how can they be held accountable? How can anyone transgress again God without knowing what constitutes transgression? The Catholics' answer for this dilemma is purgatory as they say, "everyone has transgressed against God and must do penitence, including infants." But that answer depends on whether there is a purgatory.

Speaking of sin without knowledge, here is a question for you: Why did Christ descend into a place the Bible refers to as a prison to offer salvation to those who lost their lives during the time of Noah, those who died prior to the knowledge of sin being a part of this world? Those who had no knowledge of the consequences for being disobedient, or how judgment relates to sin. Probably a good example of this would be a child being unaware he or she is being disobedient. One cannot be disobedient until he or she is educated about what constitutes disobedience. The wickedness of those who were lost in the flood we are told by God was only equaled by Sodom and Gomorrah, every thought they had was vile, but they did not know that as nobody told them their thoughts and actions were wrong. Not until the creation of the Garden of Eden as found in the second chapter of Genesis.

One finds the information regarding those lost in the flood in I Peter 3:19, where it says Jesus went to a prison and offered salvation to those who were lost in the days of Noah. As we have been discussing, it appears that from the moment of our conversion, our acceptance of Christ, we will only be accountable to God for our disobedience towards the knowledge of sin.[99] It would be unjust of God to hold us accountable for something we had no knowledge of as in coveting our neighbor's wife, or car, or house, or money, or, or, or….. You know what I am saying.

The apostle Paul seems to shine some light on this issue by giving us the answer. He seems to concur with the age of knowledge and the accountability theory when he mentions in Romans 7:7, that he would not have known what sin was if he had not been told; therefore, he says one is not accountable for sin without the knowledge of sin. He said that he would not have known what it was to covet if he had not been told. Also, Dennis Prager of Prager University has a video series, in which he explains so plainly in one of his videos about the Ten Commandments that "you may think murder is wrong, but without God you cannot know that murder is wrong."

It is true that most Christians declare baptism an essential element of the Christian faith, they do not necessarily agree that it is "salvation" within itself or meant to impart salvation. Some churches place so much importance on baptism that they say baptism by anyone other than them may not be a valid baptism. They also say that one cannot enter heaven without being baptized, I am assuming that they mean being baptized by them, as does the Catholic Church. Regarding baptism, most would probably agree with the Presbyterian Church on this one. As Leo Rosen points out in *Religions of America,* "While baptism is urgently recommended in the Presbyterian Church, and while its omission is regarded as

---

[99] Tomorrow's World publication. Gerald E. Weston. November-December 2017. (Volume 19, Issue 6).

a grave fault, it is not held to be necessary for salvation." Again, most Protestant family members would probably agree with that assessment.

One more thing I found interesting as quoted in the *Sacraments: A Catholic Study Guide* publication mentioned earlier: "Although all Christians acknowledge the critical importance of baptism, not all interpret its effects in the same way. Some fundamentalists (evangelical Christians) would see this ritual as the culmination of the conversion experience, while on the other hand, Catholics see it as only the beginning." Catholicism may not realize it, or even give it much thought, but Protestants look at baptism as a new beginning, as well. Evangelical Christians embrace this moment (conversion and baptism) as "only the beginning" …the beginning of a new life that will continue unfolding daily, weekly, monthly, and yearly revealing exciting times, interesting times, and challenging times.

Christianity is a world of its own. A world of new awakenings that eventually will permeate the soul and bring joy, true joy to our life, the joy that will cause great relationships to develop. Joy in addition to happiness, but happiness comes and goes with varying circumstance, whereas pure joy stays to become a part of our life. It is the time of awaking new beginnings in our life. A time of being born anew, a time where hopes and dreams are renewed. Those born of the Spirit will sail to new heights as their world continues to expand. Wisdom will prevail and guide their way, and eternal life will be assured.

Wow! How great it is being a Christian, a born again, baptized Christian. Can I get an amen, somebody? Since we do not see the world running to get baptized, one could probably assume for us who desire to receive baptism God has touched our heart in some way, and that we are the recipients of His grace. And for those who understand the story brought to us by the Bible there are not enough "amens" or "thank-you(s)" in the world to compensate for what Christ did for us.

The Sacrament of Confirmation

In Catholicism, the Sacrament of confirmation encompasses the Holy Spirit, along with the Sacrament of completion, the Sacrament of maturity, and the Sacrament of Christian witness. Baptism, the Eucharist, and the Sacrament of confirmation together constitute the "Sacraments of Christian initiation" into the Catholic Church. It must be explained to the faithful that the reception of the Sacrament of confirmation is necessary for the completion of baptismal grace. For by the Sacrament of confirmation, along with baptism and the Eucharist, we are more perfectly bound to the Catholic Church and are enriched with a special strength of the Holy Spirit. Hence, Catholics are, as true witnesses of Christ, more strictly obliged to spread and defend the faith by word and deed."[100]

As mentioned, confirmation perfects baptismal grace; it is the Sacrament from which the Holy Spirit is given and received in order to root Catholics more deeply in the divine filiation, incorporating them more firmly into Christ, strengthening their bond with the Catholic Church, associating them more closely with her mission, and helping Catholics bear witness to the Christian faith in words accompanied by deeds.[101] In combination, these attributes attempt to capture the essence of the Sacrament of confirmation.

One could say confirmation (validation, approval, and ratification) is the vehicle used by the Catholic Church to impart the Holy Spirit. "God our Father has marked you with His sign; Christ the Lord has confirmed you, and has placed His pledge, the Spirit, in your heart."[102] An understanding of confirmation gives the Catholic permanent and full status in the family of the church, and from everything I can ascertain eternal salvation is assured. It should

---

[100] (www.vatican.va. Section two, The Sacraments of Christian Initiation. Article 2).

[101] Ibid.

[102] https://en.m.wikipedia.org

be as they believe in the theology of the elect, (a Catholic) always being saved and going to heaven; it may be by way of purgatory, but it is almost assured.

Regarding the family of the church, the Anglican theologian William Temple said he observed that "the church exists for those who are not yet members of her."[103] Interestingly, this is true. He was speaking of the Catholic Church family, but the evangelical church family exists for people to join, as well. They both will present their version, their understanding of Christianity, and based upon that information the question becomes, what do I personally want to believe?

A candidate for confirmation who has attained the age of reason must profess the faith, be in a state of grace, have the intention of receiving the Sacrament and be prepared to assume the role of disciple and witness to Christ, both within the ecclesiastical community and in temporal affairs. The essential rite of confirmation is anointing the forehead of the baptized with sacred chrism (consecrated oils), together with the laying on of the minister's hand and the words: "Accipe signaculum doni Spiritus Sancti," meaning "be sealed with the gift of the Holy Spirit."[104]

The essence of this Sacrament seems to be: While Jesus was present on earth, the Spirit of God in human form dwelled amongst men. He was the bodily presence of the spiritual God who came to earth as Jesus, conceived by the Holy Spirit to lead us to the Father God. How else can one explain what happened? That also seems to be what Protestant ministers preach. Remember the Godhead: Father, Son and Holy Spirit work together to assure that we make it to heaven. Now the theology embraced by the Catholic Church is that they think because they are filled with the Holy Spirit of God,

---

[103]   *Sacraments: A Catholic Study Guide* (New York: Twin Circle Publishing Company, 1984).

[104]   (www.vatican.va. Section two, The Sacraments of Christian Initiation. Article 2).

from this pragmatic understanding, or as some might say "ritual," and they are now the earthly body of Christ. Every evangelical Christian would probably agree with what was just said about the church if the church mentioned was the actual body of Christ being referenced, and not only the Catholic Church.

It would probably be safe to say that Catholics, as well as other Christians in the family of God, are fulfilling God's purpose by being the light unto the world. When this light (the Holy Spirit) is taken away (and it will be), the world will be thrown into total spiritual darkness. Remember, the body of Christ—whether that be the Catholic Church or the Protestant Church or a combination of both—that light of Christianity is the only means by which God's presence is currently made visible to the world, and while Protestants and Catholics have differing views, they both agree that Christ existed to bring salvation to the world.

One thing I found interesting about this Sacrament is that in the early church, prior to the Sacrament of confirmation being written into the theology of the Catholic Church, the Eucharist was open to anyone who wanted to participate. The Sacrament of confirmation stopped this. The reason behind eliminating this practice was this: it seemed strange to allow the recipient access to the Eucharist (remember it is during the Eucharist that one receives Christ) before one was a "full-fledged member of the Catholic Church."[105] Have you ever attended a Catholic Church where you have not felt invited to receive Communion, which, of course is the Catholic Eucharist? Now you know why.

Protestants, on the other hand, welcome everyone to participate, and all that is requested is that a person understands what it means to be a follower of Christ. Beyond that could be considered judging or setting inappropriate rules to commune with God. Besides, denying anyone the opportunity to receive communion is taking away a moment to remember all that Jesus went through leading up to

---

[105] Ibid.

the crucifixion. The Catholic Church practices closed communion, with only baptized members of the Catholic Church in a state of grace being permitted to receive the Eucharist. But then, again, as we know, this is the time a Catholic receives Christ, over, and over, and over.

After learning about being baptized "into the Catholic Church" and "confirmation by the Catholic Church," one then participates in the Catholic Church's fullness of salvation by attending Mass and taking part in the Eucharist. All of these biblical interpretations, "Sacramental interpretations" that seem to encompass the views and understanding of many of the early philosophers, were embraced by many and backed by the succession of popes and administered by the priests. Remember, Catholicism, as has been mentioned a time or two, is an "all" inclusive religion. Pope Leo I conveyed that bit of information when he wrote, "What was visible in Christ has passed over into the Sacraments of the (Catholic) church."[106]

Combine that with what we heard Pope Boniface VIII (1230-1301 A.D.) say earlier: To be **SUBJECT TO THE ROMAN PONTIFF** is to every human creature altogether **NECESSARY FOR SALVATION**…that which was spoken of Christ 'thou has subdued all things under his feet,' may well seem verified in ME…I have the authority of the King of Kings. (God gave him the authority to be God). I am all in all and above all so that God himself and I, the vicar of God, have but one consistory, and I am able to do all that God can do. (Again, the authority of God has now been passed to the pope and his successors). **WHAT THEREFORE CAN YOU MAKE OF ME BUT GOD?"** There it is, he just out right said "I AM GOD."

Except in name only, I ask again, where is Christ in all of this, and the message that was passed to us by the apostles? And that seems to be addressed by saying, as Pope Boniface VIII just did, that all things which were spoken of through Christ are now possible

---

[106] Richard Maris, *Martin Luther: The Christian between God and Death.*

through me. They have been subdued under my feet now and have been verified (substantiated, corroborated and confirmed); in other words, what was possible with Christ is now possible through me as presider over the Catholic Church, what therefore can one make of the me but that I am God, or as some say, Christ concealed by a vale of flesh. Information that was floating around during the early age of Catholicism when philosophers and many early church leaders were trying to be more impressive and more knowledgeable than the next one and the age of one-upmanship seemed to prevail.

I did however learn one small point of interest when talking with a couple of rabbis and priests. While listening to them defending the "first on the block" theology, I found that most of their theology is tied to Catholic Church tradition, whereas the Protestant church has been built upon the actual words of Christ. Narrowing that down a bit further: believe on the Lord Jesus Christ and you will be saved, confessing Him as the Son of God. As far as the rest goes, that is perhaps learning how to have a relationship with him. According to the book of Acts as written by Luke, the apostles carried forth that message in what has been referred to as the apostolic age, and that message was to believe in Christ, in His birth, death and resurrection. That's it. Then man came along and started adding conditions.

Confirmation appears to be the Sacrament from which the Holy Spirit is imparted after one has been properly prepared. Another deviation from Protestant beliefs. There is no preparation necessary when listening to Protestant preachers. They say the Holy Spirit is automatically sent to us by God when we become a believer, a follower, a converted gentile. It is the Holy Spirit who is defined in the Bible as One who comes into our life and is always present, guiding us correctly in acquiring a life described as a life of overflowing joy. It is that Spirit that some deny, such as the Church of Christ, or as others are taught, they receive the Holy Spirit by basically joining the Catholic Church and preparing through a series of instructions how to receive the Spirit. Protestants say all that is required is for one to be aware of the Holy Spirit and ask Him into our heart. Now, in Catholicism once the Holy Spirit is imparted by way of confirmation, one is prepared to receive Christ at the Eucharist, which is performed while attending Mass.

The Sacrament of the Eucharist

In short, during the Mass, this Sacramental theology is when a Catholic receives Jesus by digesting him through a wafer, a consecrated wafer as brought forth by St. Augustine, as documented in his understandings that became a part of Catholic theology—with the help of Socrates and other philosophers, who were instrumental in formulating how the bread is now the body of Christ. This Sacrament was implemented to answer the question as to how the believer receives Christ, followed by the answer: by attending the ceremonial Mass, indulging in the Eucharist, and receiving the body of Christ through a wafer.

Asked the same question as to how one receives Christ, a Protestant would probably say they receive Christ when they agree to follow him; in other words, when they become a believer and receive the Holy Spirit, a believer as opposed to a nonbeliever. Catholics believe they receive Christ during the Mass by consuming a wafer that has been miraculously transformed into the actual body of Christ. The Catholic may say what they want about consuming the actual body of Christ through receiving a wafer, but since many consider that physically and logically impossible, I must assume they are speaking symbolically, as otherwise this would be impossible literally. Many might say this Sacrament is an action and as such is a substitution for faith, unless one is saying faith is in the thought of the wafer containing the body of Christ. Of course, that is entirely a possibility.

If that is the belief, then the question becomes, how did the body of Christ become transformed into a wafer? Thus, enters the term "transubstantiation." *Transubstantiation*. MacCulloch tells us in his previously mentioned book that Thomas Aquinas, a thirteenth-century Dominican genius, was determined, along with some other geniuses, to show that human reason was a gift from God, designed to give human beings as much knowledge as necessary to understand the miracle of transubstantiation. No offense to Mr. Aquinas, but I am sure I am not the only one who still does not get it.

Richard Marius presents an interesting question when he writes in his book, *Martin Luther:* "Exactly how is Christ present in the theory of transubstantiation?" An interesting question to ponder. Marius also addresses the confirmation of transubstantiation when he says, "The fourth Lateran Council of 1215 confirmed transubstantiation, the doctrine that the substance of the bread and the wine changed by miracle during the Mass. No longer is it bread and wine; it is the actual body and blood of Jesus." Have you ever been to a Mass where you saw this miracle take place? Can we trace an eyewitness of this account in the Bible? Did anyone after Christ confirm this miracle or is it just someone's word that a miracle occurred?

We learn from studying religion that the Greek Orthodox Church embraces theology regarding this miracle. Just prior to the priest offering the bread as the body of Christ, the priest sanctifies the bread by praying over it, asking the Holy Spirit to come and bless the bread and wine so that they will become the "body and blood of Christ." Both the Catholic Church and the Greek Orthodox Church believe in this miracle. If I am not mistaken, so does the Lutheran church, but I'm not sure, as I have a hard time with their linguistics as they say: "Lutherans explicitly reject transubstantiation, believing that the bread and wine remain fully bread and fully wine, while at the same time being truly the body and blood of Jesus Christ."[107]

Personally, I have not seen a miracle transforming the bread into the body of Christ, nor do I know anyone who has. I have only heard, according to the Catholic Fathers, that a miracle takes place. No offense to the Catholic Fathers who implemented this

---

[107]   https://en.m.wikipedia.org.

theology, but in the Bible, I find Christ emphasized faith in Him as a requirement rather than faith in the teachings of men. It is by faith that we become Christians indwelled with the body (Spirit) of Christ from the moment we believe--the moment our eyes are opened. Most evangelical Christians will trust their salvation to the doctrine of, as Christ seemed to emphasize, that it is by faith one is justified (brought into righteousness) and it is by faith in Christ that He imparts His Spirit to us to lead us into truth and reveal deception. A common bond all Christians shares.

The question regarding the conversion of the bread into the actual body of Christ is an interesting question, and the answer lies, as we have seen, in what is referred to as transubstantiation. The question is how in the Mass the bread lying on the paten and the wine in the chalice turned into the body and blood of Christ, making the body of Christ as corporeally (bodily) present as He had been in Jerusalem. Probably the better question might be, where did this thinking originate, and is it biblical? That is another couple of question evangelical Christian's wrestle with from time to time in grasping the understand behind reconciling the idea of receiving Christ in a wafer as opposed to receiving him by faith. But then, it takes a lot of faith to believe one is receiving Christ by digesting a wafer.

Do This in Remembrance

Many are familiar with the verses in the Bible that say, "Take and eat; this is my body." Matthew 26:26 NIV. Also, in Mark 14:22 (KJV) those words are repeated: "Take eat; this is my body." While they were eating, Jesus took bread, gave thanks, and broke it, and gave it to his disciples, saying to take the bread and eat it, as this is My body. If this were all there was to it, one might not have such a hard time justifying Christ being digested into our body through the Mass. It is through this action that Catholics say they "have received Christ" and mean that through this pragmatic act *they have received Christ.*

The Catholics also borrow from John, chapter 6, where Jesus said, "I am the living bread that came down from heaven. If anyone eats of this bread, he will live forever. This bread is my flesh, which I give for the life of the world" John 6:51 (NIV). Jesus continues with verse 54: "Whoever eats my flesh and drinks my blood has eternal life and I will raise him up at the last day." Then in John 5:58: "Your forefathers ate manna and died, but he who feeds on this bread will live forever." Upon saying those words many of his followers turned away saying, "This is a hard teaching, who can accept it?" (verse 59). It is hard teaching if one takes it literally, as did the early Romans, who said that the Christians were into cannibalism, which created even more reason to hate them and want to persecute them.

We know it is impossible to literally digest Christ through a wafer, which, as we know, is a substitute for receiving Christ through faith. Being Protestants, we know it is by faith we receive Christ we must hope for the sake of the Catholic Church they are right regarding this point of pragmaticism" Just how is Christ possibly digested via a wafer? It took applying some intelligence to a very complicated subject, but the earlier fathers figured out a way to do just that.

The Eucharist is where one finds the miracle of a transformation that took place and that transforming of the bread into the body of Christ was called, transubstantiation. A doctrine put forth by early Catholic Fathers (based upon Socrates who theorized this transformation) and that theorizing remains even to this day. This is a doctrine that many do not accept, thus becoming another stumbling block between Catholics and Protestants. Evangelical thinking regarding communion is found by turning to Luke 22:19, where Christ took bread, gave thanks, and broke it. Then he gave it to his disciples saying, "This is my body given for you. Do this in remembrance of me." (Luke 22:19 NIV). Protestants partake of communion, not to receive Christ as do Catholics, but they receive communion in remembrance of the price Christ paid just hours prior to his crucifixion. A very sacred time for a Christian.

The Sacrament of Ordination

The Sacrament of ordination is ordaining someone with power, authority and/or position who is in a lesser position than yourself. In other words, a promotion. The Catholic Church ordains priests and deacons and says: "Let everyone revere the deacons as Jesus Christ, the bishops as the image of the Father, and the presbyters as the senate of God and the assembly of the apostles. For without them one cannot speak of the Catholic Church."

This Sacrament is usually associated with the priesthood. A Catholic priest is considered a servant of Jesus Christ and is asked to sacrifice or dedicate his own life, even unto death, to serve God. The priest's concern for the church must be total, so that his individual attention and love are centered on his ministry.[108] This Sacrament involves three ministries within Catholicism: the diaconate (the office of deacon), priesthood, and episcopate (governing of the church by bishops). All three contain approved members of the Catholic Church. For membership into the priesthood, the call must come from God, which is then validated by the church.

The liturgy of the church and the Sacrament of Ordination sees in Catholicism the priesthood of Aaron, the brother of Moses. Aaron, the chief priest of the tribe of Levi, a son of Jacob, was called of God to carry forth the instructions as laid out by God to Moses on Mt. Sinai and be the liaison between the Israelites and God. Catholicism embraces the Old Testament and has developed theology from that era that substitutes the pope for Aaron and the Levites as the priest, bishops, and cardinals of the church, and they are all dedicated by the Sacrament of ordination.

This Sacrament is the holy orders of the church. In all three (the diaconate, priesthood, and episcopate), men are commissioned by a bishop with the laying on of hands, which enables them to serve

---

[108] *Sacraments: A Catholic Study Guide* (New York: Twin Circle Publishing Company, 1984).

the church. Then comes the training. The Sacrament of ordination begins the introduction to the training that is known as Catholicism. Your advancement through this religious organization is based upon how smart you are and how well you learn. For anyone interested in joining the priesthood, he would probably begin the journey with this Sacrament. Most Protestant ministers go through some form of training for ordination as well called seminary where they are trained to carry the word of a risen Lord to the world, whereas Catholicism is more prone to train, through ordination, how to carry forth the Christianity of the Catholic Church.

The Sacrament of Marriage

Regarding marriage, I found the following in the guidebook, *Sacrament: A Catholic Study Guide.* "It is often heard from people I don't agree with the church's position on divorce and marriage." To such people, committed Christian couples will say: "Please do not say, 'I disagree with the church.' Better to say, 'I disagree with Christ's position.'" To discuss this Sacrament with any kind of wisdom is way beyond my pay grade. To establish boundaries might be construed as a form of legalism. For the most part, Protestants go along with the sanctity of marriage, as do Catholics.

Protestants, as well as Christians everywhere, have always been appreciative of the outspoken stance the Catholic Church has taken regarding morality. Most evangelical Christians feel the world would be a lot more liberal toward the vileness that exists if not for Catholics. They, like Protestants, have been very outspoken on such controversial issues as abortion, homosexuality, and same-sex marriage. The latter is an extremely hot issue right now, but as liberalism becomes more acceptable, the abominations against God will become more widespread. Eventually same-sex marriage will prevail in our culture, as well as the acceptance of homosexuality, and with this acceptance, Christians who stand against these moral issues will have their voices increasingly silenced.

While stating that both homosexuality and same-sex marriage seems to be a problem to some churches, God, He loves homosexuals, but abhors the—oh, God, let me say it—the homosexual lifestyle. However, to disburse judgment—not to discuss it, but to pass judgment upon those who accept such a lifestyle—is way above my pay grade. It probably should be above the pay grade of most Christians, although there are some pastors who have no problem broaching the subject.

It appears, Protestants as well as Catholics, are outspoken regarding the sanctity of marriage. They have outlined conditions for marriage, as well as for living a married life, along with positions on divorces, annulments, and remarriages. Are they right? I do not know, but what the Christian community teaches sounds right. When problems arise, and they will, take everything before God and ask Him what you should do. Listen to God. He will intervene with guidance through the Holy Spirit. I do not have any statistics, but I would say a Christian family has a better chance of staying together than a secular one. Just thinking out loud.

When it comes to marriage, all I can add is, "patience." To say what anyone should do during his or her own personal journey and whom he or she should do it with (including marrying, not marrying, who to marry, or staying married) is, once again, way above my pay grade.

The Sacrament of Extreme Unction

This Sacrament is also referred to as the "last anointing" or the "anointing of the sick" or "Sacrament of the sick." This Sacrament has even taken on the parlance of "last rites." This ritual, performed by a priest, is implemented to give assurance to the sick or dying, as well as to their family, that the dying person would be redeemed and purified/purged from any unconfessed sins, which would allow the dying member to be secure in the knowledge he would at least escape the fires of hell, even if it might be by the way of purgatory. This Sacrament is the epitome of the Catholic's Church fulfillment of acting in place of God.

It is commonly admitted within the ranks of Catholicism that Sacramental absolution was granted by the earlier Fathers at the time of confession to those who were in danger of death. The Catholic Church, in fact, did not, in her universal practice, refuse absolution at the last moment, even in the case of those who had committed grievous sin. (Again, standing in place of God). Or at least, that is how it was supposed to work but widespread corruption was present. Priest were withholding communion from some or requiring a sum of money from others. This issue was addressed by St. Leo writing in A.D. 442 to Theodore, Bishop of Frejus, saying: "Neither satisfaction is to be forbidden nor reconciliation denied to those who in time of need and imminent danger implore the aid of penance and then of reconciliation." And do not forget, Catholics believe in purgatory, so at the least this last rite would give the hope of that. Again, information from saintjamesrcc.org.

If you wanted to have a shot for at least purgatory, then do not get caught without a priest to administer last rites. St. Celestine, in A.D. 428, was considered by some to be the first "official" pope, as the previous popes had been appointed to establish the line of succession to Christ. It was St. Celestine who expressed his horror at learning that penance was refused to the dying, and that the desire of those not granted penance and absolution (let's not forget that absolution means being forgiven, pardoned, released, or liberated from our sins), in the hour of death sought this remedy for their soul. Refusing one this Sacrament, he says, "is adding death to death and killing with cruelty the soul that is not absolved." Same informational source.

After this Sacrament is administered, the person will either go to heaven or stop by purgatory on the way to heaven. Again, if this can be proven, sign me up, put me on the list, and call me Catholic. I would join the Catholic Church any time, if for no other reason than this safety net—as I am sure every Christian would. If Christianity consisted of going to confession, doing some tasks to remove any sins I might have committed—any at least that are unresolved since last confession, and then when this life is over, I may go to either heaven or purgatory—but eventually, I will get to heaven and eternal life. If this safety net were in the Bible, it would be available to all Christians, not just Catholics but to everyone.

Regarding the ritual of "last rites," I found interesting what an ex-Catholic friend had to say regarding this Sacrament. In the early days of gangsters, when they went to "wax" someone, they took a priest with them just in case they got "waxed" themselves. The priest was there to administer the last rites, so the person was assured a place in heaven, or at the worst, "purgatory." Purgatory—a stopping off place for enlightenment. As we know, purgatory seems to be a vital part of Catholicism. Why? Where did the notion of purgatory come from since it is not in the Bible? I found purgatory, as well as replacement theology, so interesting they were both afforded their own chapter in this book.

CHAPTER XV

CATHOLICISM'S PURGATORY: A PLACE OF ENLIGHTENMENT

Purgatory! A place embraced by every Christian, every pastor, every evangelical, every Catholic, a place embraced by everybody who would like for there to be an alternative to what the Bible describes as the "lake of burning sulfur," which is a place of total separation from Christ, with no chance of eternal life. If purgatory were real, everyone would probably believe in it. What a safety net this would be! Unfortunately, there is no such place. I found the theory of a purgatory interesting. It is dogma, but it is interesting dogma. And to most non-Catholics, it is extremely dangerous dogma. It is dangerous because it is unscriptural, and to rely or depend upon something "unscriptural" (especially when it involves our eternal soul) begs the question, what if there is no purgatory? I believe most would consider that a fair question. Catholics say they have answered that question, but if there are questions that persist, then perhaps it has not been addressed enough.

It appears to most evangelical Christians that the whole concept behind the theology of purgatory in the first place was a way for the church to raise money from the selling of indulgences, which were certificates designed to assure a person a ticket into heaven. Certificates that were distributed beginning around AD 1190. This was a "get out of hell" free card. Originally, purgatory was implemented as a safety net for those who embraced antinomian theology, but when the concept of indulgences came along, the church could not resist the money-making potential. Over time, indulgences proved illogical and impossible for the church to defend, and therefore were eliminated. Although, some Catholic priests still endorse them. On the other hand, purgatory, a concept that began to germinate around AD 593, eventually became a part of Catholicism. Even though the church does not acknowledge indulgences anymore (or so I thought), the concept is quite interesting (more on indulgences in a minute).

Just how does "purgatory" play out within the Catholic organization? As mentioned earlier, within the Catholic structure are rules and traditions that convey the message that our sins are forgiven by our works, as assigned by the church. If we have some unresolved issues to address when we die, issues for which we haven't confessed and done penitence to have absolved, and being a nice person, a likeable person, then by the very act of being a Catholic, we go to a place between heaven and hell to complete our penitence.

To believe in a purgatory, one must believe in a place of torment, in which the souls of such who have not merited eternal damnation are to suffer punishment for their sins, and from which, when freed from impurity, they are admitted to heaven.[109] Purgatory is also a place where the departed who contain some possibility of goodness within are prepared for the full enjoyment of God's blessings by such cleansing and purifying as may be required. Not a consuming fire, not the fire of hell, but a cleansing fire. A place where believers who have put their faith in Christ but have not satisfied the demands of God's justice by repentance and deeds of repentance (works) and therefore must go to this place in ordered to be prepared over years, sometimes hundreds of years, to be fit for heaven.[110]

---

[109]   MacCulloch, *The Reformation.*

[110]   Archpriest Father Josiah Trentham at Saint Barnabas Orthodox Church in Costa Mesa California. Published Jul 28, 2018).

When it comes to penance how about this one? In the early church, many Catholic priests were living with women, and their bishops knew about it. Upon confession, they were instructed to simply pay a bishop a sum of money, referred to as a woman's tax as the price for repentance.[111] If priest or others, after paying any required sum for what may be considered a sin tax, have any unresolved issue remaining, there is always purgatory. Again, what a safety net. Many would like to believe in a place between heaven and the total separation from God, as in hell, but one is hard pressed to find it.

The Origin of Purgatory

Just where did the concept of a purgatory originate? Probably more than anything, it came from the minds of individuals who had an insatiable desire to understand the future and where the eternal soul fits into that future. Regarding the hereafter, it would probably be safe to say that most, if not all, of us have a curiosity regarding any afterlife. Diarmaid MacCulloch in his book *The Reformation: A History,* said that as early as the twelfth century Christians began to speculate about life and death, heaven, and hell, and if there was an in-between. According to MacCulloch:

> It was natural therefore for creative Christian thinkers to speculate about some middle state, in which those whom God loved would have a chance to perfect the hard slog towards holiness that they had begun so imperfectly in their brief earthly life. Although the first thoughts along these lines came from eastern Greek-speakers in Alexandria, the idea blossomed in the West, and this place of purging in wise fire, with its promise of an eventual entrance to heaven, was by the twelve-century given a name—purgatory.

---

[111]   Ibid).

This was a concept that existed from AD 593 onward, but when the concept of indulgences came along in the twelfth century, a place known as purgatory became incorporated into Catholic theology and was quickly embraced by the Catholic Fathers as gospel and remains so to this day. Purgatory was understood as an intermediary place where souls spent an undetermined amount of time after death before moving on to a higher level of existence.

Many Christians point to, the theology of purgatory as dangerous theology. It is dangerous because the very concept of a purgatory is misleading, the results of which could be devastating as the following will illustrate. If the Catholic Church has ever thought about serious dogma, they really need to examine the reality of a purgatory and the harm the concept of a purgatory brings within the realm of Christianity. But as I mentioned earlier, nothing will change which brings me to one of the main reasons I wanted to write this book. For anyone who has left the Catholic Church and is having withdrawal pains, the information contained within this book should help ease the thought of returning.

I was watching EWTN (a Catholic TV station) the other day, and I cringed when I heard a woman repeat what her son had said to her that morning when she was leaving for work. He said he was glad there was a purgatory. Of course, he was speaking of the concept of a purgatory. What he was saying was that he had been taught a doctrine that was conceived by the mind of man, rather than from the mind of God, and it was this doctrine that was going to be his safety net as he journeyed through this world (thus, the cringing). To most Christians, the concept of a purgatory indicates that forgiveness of disobedience was not fully completed at the cross. While that is an issue the bigger issue is the reliance on a safety net that does not exist. One might find those fighting words, but if one does, then take it up with God as he is the one who spoke them when He said, "It was finished." (John 19:30). Jesus said them, the Bible delivered them, and I just wrote them.

Purgatory and the Bema Judgment

The idea of purgatory has roots that date back into antiquity. A sort of prototype of purgatory called the "celestial Hades" appears in the writings of Plato and Heraclides Ponticus, and in the writings of many other pagan writers. The celestial Hades was understood as an intermediary place where as mentioned, souls spent an undetermined amount of time after death before either moving on to a higher level of existence or being reincarnated back on earth. I looked that one up, and the Catholic Church does not believe in reincarnation which it regards as being incompatible with death.

As we know, the concept behind the dogma of purgatory was a safety net for those who embraced antinomian theology. To a populace that looked upon the pope as Christ Himself, he had only to speak and it became truth. If the pope (Christ concealed by a vale of flesh) said there was a purgatory, then by gosh, there must be a purgatory. But, my friend, Christ did not say there was a purgatory; the pope and some cardinals did, and if this is like other theology, then it is probably traditional more than biblical. So, the question becomes, do we follow the teachings of the pope and theology put forth by early philosophers and the Catholic Church, or the teachings of Christ and the apostles? Just a couple of questions to ponder.

According to Catholics, the justification for purgatory comes from 1 Cor. 3:10-15. Since Protestants do not exactly interpret those verses as Catholics do, that might lead one to believe those verses are subject to interpretation. It does not say in the Bible that we enter a place known as purgatory, but rather that our virtues are illuminated as gold going through fire. Catholics seem to consider this Bema judgement to mean purgatory for the removal of sin, while Protestants, who have already been forgiven by accepting the coming of Jesus, the price He paid, and the blood He shed for total absolution, find no need for purgatory. With that in mind, Protestants will take a pass on purgatory theology.

But that does not exempt them from the Bema judgment, Bema seat, or Bema—translated as court or tribunal to determine rewards based upon motives, perhaps even intentions, but motives for sure, of each deed done in the name of Christ. The apostle Paul says that all things will become clear at this judgment. This judgment or tribunal is only for Christians, —born again, committed followers of Christ. I am almost ready to say, "for evangelical Christians"—born again, evangelical Protestant Christians, Those the reformers gave their lives for (as in the days of Nero) so that we would know the truth, but that might be too limiting. The unsaved will not be included in this judgment as their destiny is already determined by their rejection of Christ and no rewards will be handed out where they are going.

As born-again Christians entering the heavenly realm immediately upon death, we pass through the Bema judgment with the assurance that we are saved. The unsaved are still in the grave, although, as we will see later, only their physical body will be there and will be for some time. Remember the unsaved will be raised to stand in judgment after the 1,000-year reign of Christ. As followers of Christ, we will stand before the Bema tribunal, overseen by Christ himself, and with the angels he has at his disposal, time will not be an issue. This appears to be a great time of discussing our good deeds, those done for the right reasons, those that bring us closer to Christ resulting in rewards, or lost rewards as this is a judgment of motivation—a judgment of ulterior motives.

Protestants, believe they will eventually be tried as going through a fire during the Bema judgment for the purging of any last-minute iniquity, while believing all the while that their iniquity was removed with our acceptance of Christ, and spending time on our knees asking forgiveness and trusting in God to be faithful to his word. Catholics, on the other hand, accept purgatory theology to complete the journey of salvation. The works, (the good deeds) of an individual will be revealed with fire, as described in 1 Cor. 3:10-15 and the fire will test the quality of each person's works, just as the Bible says.

All deeds that survive this judgment (a judgment of motivation as well as intent), will receive rewards. Remember, when Christ comes for his bride at the time of the Rapture, he comes with rewards in hand for those saints who have died, gone through the Bema judgment, and are waiting in Paradise where they will be taken to heaven to receive those rewards. There does not seem to be any room for the logic of a purgatory. This gathering will also include those Christians who are alive on earth and are awaiting His coming.

The key to receiving rewards seems to be those done in the name of compassion, caring, and love, all emotions close to God's heart. I do not believe, along with Charles Stanley, the works assigned by a priest, approved by a pope, and backed by a Cardinal for absolution of sin will survive. Perhaps, as the Catholics say, they themselves will be saved, but then as Protestants say, the works done for the absolution of sin will not survive the Bema judgment. When we pass through the Bema judgment only the works motived by the mind of Christ as guided by the dependence upon the power of the Holy Spirit will be recognized, everything else will burn up because of this judgment, but they themselves will be saved. The fire alluded to as purgatory by Catholics in 1 Cor. 3:10-15 is the fire of the Bema judgment according to Protestants.

Catholics seem to think they must go to a place of burning flames where they will be purged of sins that were not purged at the cross by Christ. His mission was not completed at the cross and as a Catholic they will complete the redemption process that began with Christ by fulfilling the Catholic Churches requirements. Then and only then will they enter heaven. Of course, Protestants reject that theology. I ask, does that sound right? Or does the theology of the Bema judgment make more sense? Many questing the logic of purgatory ask, does the theology of purgatory line up with the Bible? Just a couple of questions to think about. Just because a religious organization says there is a purgatory, then there must be a purgatory, but purgatory does not line up with the Bible, just as receiving Christ through a wafer does not line up. When logic is applied both beliefs become very questionable, and at best they both seem to be missing some logic that would make them plausible.

Anyone who believes in purgatory and says, as does MacCulloch, of the judgment at the end of time—at the end of time, what does that mean anyway? Maybe after the one-thousand-year reign of Christ when all will be brought before Christ? MacCulloch continues, "Some were marching into heaven, newly released from purging their sins in the trials of purgatory to enjoy eternal bliss." MacCulloch may say that, but that just does not appear to be accurate. Nowhere in the Bible have I found that information.

The Bible conveys to us there will be some leaving the Great White Throne Judgment seat of Christ and going to eternal bliss, while others will be eternally separated from Christ, and that is true, but nowhere in the Bible does it say any will be coming before the judgment seat of Christ from "purgatory." Hell maybe, Hades maybe, Shoals perhaps, defined as the grave, but nobody will be coming from a place called "purgatory." As the Catholic Church is the only church to teach purgatory as a reality, it must be assumed that those who believe in the concept of purgatory have a Catholic background (although MacCulloch was an Episcopalian the last I heard).

CHAPTER XVI

THE PURGATORY INDUSTRY AND INDULGENCES

Purgatory, indulgences; indulgences, purgatory. At one time it was hard to separate the two. A combination that created an industry, and what an industry it was! While both purgatory and indulgences were a part of Catholic theology, as we saw earlier, over time indulgences proved illogical and impossible to defend, and went by the wayside. And yet, one can still hear a priest or two embracing indulgences to as a way to save your soul. Perhaps because of indulgences being illogical, there was not any way for indulgences to remain viable, so the concept of indulgences was eventually dropped, while the concept of purgatory remained. Once again, this disproves the infallibility of the Catholic Church as proclaimed by Pope Gregory VII.

It was from the sale of indulgences that money poured into Rome, as everyone knew someone who might not be a candidate for heaven, but also was not sinful enough to spend eternity in hell. The hell back then was equivalent to Dante's Inferno, as a matter of fact, Dante's Inferno was about purgatory. The Catholic Church got rich from the sale of indulgences. Both the concept of purgatory and the selling of indulgences were great hits among the laity, even being responsible for the building of saint peters basilica.

And why not, when Christ, by way of the pope concealed under a vale of flesh, said the purchase of an indulgence could be used to almost guarantee one entrance into heaven, even if it was by way of purgatory, why would anyone refuse to spend money? An indulgence could also be used to shorten the purchaser's time in purgatory. Or perhaps even shorten the time an infant child might have to spent in purgatory as a requirement of Catholicism to remove the stain of the original sin. Or an indulgence could be purchased to pray someone out of purgatory, as well as perhaps reducing the time they are to serve in purgatory.

It was during the late fifteenth and early sixteenth centuries that "indulgences," combined with "works," were used to shorten the time souls would have to spend in purgatory. For example, parishioners were told upon the purchase of indulgences that if they would repeat the Lord's Prayer along with fifteen Hail Marys per day for one year, they could reduce the time spent in purgatory by 5,475 years (15 x 365 = 5,475).[112]

If purgatory was going to be too much trouble for the wealthy, they could—for a "very" large donation to the church—obtain a *plenary* indulgence that excluded purgatory altogether. If you had the money, you could arrange to be shot straight into heaven upon death, thus skipping purgatory regardless of the number of confessions one missed or sins they have committed. Wow! The only requirement then as well as now was to be Catholic. Wow! That is all I can say. Again, would a question of whether purgatory really exists be out of line? I heard a priest the other day discussing plenary indulgences and how important they were in the life of a Catholic. Unbelievable.

The Catholic Church preached hell, the place of burning sulfur that burns flesh but never consumes it, a place one did not want to go. That is one of the reasons why purgatory was introduced into Christianity. Purgatory gave the people hope of a place other than hell. It was also from the fear of eternal torment that indulgences

---

[112]   Ibid.

were so popular, as they almost guaranteed a ticket into heaven, even if it was by way of purgatory. That is unless you had enough money to buy a plenary indulgence.

Perhaps that is why the times were referred to as "the dark ages." It appears that logic and common sense was missing in some theology embraced by the Catholic Fathers. But again, they were men and still are "men" who found themselves responsible for implementing an ingenious plan on earth that seemingly duplicated the one in heaven by implementing the same salvation as offered by God, Christ, and the Holy Spirit. Martin Luther said he used to pray up to twelve hours a day just to make sure he did not miss anything during his confessional time. Paid whatever the penance was for his confessions, studied hard, questioned everyone all the time to the point of perhaps becoming a pest, but he was seeking the meaning of life and how Christianity played a role in that life. He eventually found it, but this is not about Luther, at least not at this time.

For those living, as well as those already deceased, to continue raising money for the church from the sale of indulgences the pope appointed a Dominican friar by the name of Johann Tetzel. He preached that someone could purchase an indulgence, and, upon that purchase, he, Tetzel, would ring a bell and the soul for whom the indulgence was purchased would then be released from purgatory into heaven. Come on! Does that sound right to you? Question that theology question the Catholic Church! The only thing that has changed is prayer and lighting candles instead of a bell. Logic would dictate that this theology should be questioned.

Johann Tetzel was quite a salesman as he turned a flair for preaching about indulgences into a catchy commercial to attract new buyers: "Won't you part with even a farthing to buy this letter? It won't bring you money, but rather a divine and immortal soul, whole and secure in the Kingdom of Heaven."[113] Don't forget, Tetzel got his orders from the pope, who was looked upon as Christ himself.

---

[113] MacCulloch, *The Reformation*.

So, the parishioners had no reason to question the validity of either indulgences or purgatory, same as today.

Considering the path, we, as Protestants, might have taken because of Catholicism, perhaps never knowing about a personal relationship with Christ based upon faith we owe a lot to the earlier "Protestants" who stood tall when the times demanded. I guess I am saying, we should be ever so grateful to Martin Luther and the other reformers who listened to God and who paid a tremendous price so we could know the truth. "And the truth shall set us free." Think of the bondage we could have been under if not for the intervening of God and a vessel with the courage of Martin Luther. I know Catholics consider Martin Luther the greatest heretic the world has ever known, but they just do not understand.

Anyway, it was in Germany, where a heavy concentration of Catholics resided, that the church saw a phenomenal surge in the sale of indulgences, with no sign of letting up. Beginning around 1450, money poured into Rome from the concept of purgatory and the sale of indulgences—that is, until the system imploded in 1520 under the impact of Martin Luther's theses, which among other issues, triggered the Reformation. We are told by many history books that Martin Luther was infuriated by the sale of indulgences, as every assumption behind the indulgence system brought on by the theory of a purgatory conflicted with his understanding of the Bible (although he didn't seem to have a problem with purgatory, although, many say he later found the concept of purgatory an unacceptable theology).

Speaking of Luther, that reminds me of the Lutheran church and their take on purgatory. They, like other Protestants, do not believe in it. They believe in justification (brought into righteousness by grace through faith) and say that the key doctrine, or material principle, of Lutheranism is the doctrine of justification. Lutherans believe that humans are saved from sins by God's grace alone (Sola Gratia), through faith alone (Sola Fide), based on Scripture alone (known as Sola Scriptura). It is upon this basis, especially the "faith" alone part, that many of the Protestant leaders have questioned

Hank Hanegraaff's decision to embrace the religion of Greek Orthodoxy...while still retaining the ability to embrace the beliefs of Protestantism.

If you will notice I did not discuss remaining a Christian, as there are Christians in every church, and by Hank switching families, as he did, he has made it perfectly clear that he is not denouncing his relationship with Christ, as he believes in the resurrection, the cross, Jesus as the Son of God, and God Himself. All commonalities of Christendom, whether Protestant or Greek Orthodox. However, the Greek Orthodox Church, as with the Catholic Church embraces the Sacraments, receiving Christ through a wafer, and atonement through works, and therein lies some of the major problems Protestant leaders have with this move by Hank. Not to mention a hundred smaller nuances and innuendos that come with the Sacraments that are rejected by Protestants.

Anyway, as discussed, it was the selling of indulgences (and the issue of "faith" versus "works") that pushed Martin Luther to finally rebel against the authority of the papacy and set-in motion the Reformation. Luther and Calvin both rejected the Roman Catholic doctrine of purgatory, not because they made a thorough study of scriptural eschatology and found it missing, but because purgatory clearly contradicted the doctrine of justification (brought into righteousness by faith) that they had discovered in the Bible.[114] The Catholic Church's position regarding the issuance of indulgences was, "Since the Pope is the Vicar substitute of Christ on earth, it would be criminal meanness on his part not to dispense such a treasure to anxious Christians on earth. The treasure of merit can then be granted to the faithful for an absolute guarantee." Did you get that? "An absolute guarantee"— "into heaven or to shorten the time spent doing penance in purgatory."[115]

---

[114] Fudge, Edward William. *The fire that consumes.* Eugene Orgon: Cascade Books. 2011

[115] MacCulloch, *The Reformation.*

The church also received money through wills for the release of souls from purgatory. Within the purgatory industry, it became big business to receive money through wills and from the estates of the beloved deceased. Some priests, upon receiving sizable donations from family members, were conducting Masses for the wealthy dead, which, once again, were designed to reduce time spent in purgatory. As pointed out earlier, the Catholic Church is the only religious organization that claims this privilege, and, as we saw, they do so through the Sacrament of penance. As for most other churches, they point to the Bible, where it says: "I, *even* I, (God) *am* He that blotted out thy transgressions for mine own sake and will not remember thy sins" (Isaiah 43:25, NKJV). Again, Protestants have never accepted the dogma of the Catholic Church, including the theory of a purgatory.

As a matter of fact, two reformists, Nicholas Ridley, and John Bradford, around 1550 were last seen in prison awaiting cremation at the stake for crying out against the distortion of the Mass, purgatory, and in their opinion, the false teachings of the Catholic Church. The same arguments of Martin Luther. Basically, the same teachings exist today as they did in 1550; there just is not anyone being burned at the stake, at least not lately.

Forgoing the erroneous dogma of the Catholic Church that has already been mentioned, the dogma discussed in the following section is a part of Catholicism that many consider to be the most dangerous, and considering purgatory, that is saying a lot, but it changes the intent of the Bible. Can you believe that? While the concept of purgatory may be considered dangerous theology, it does not change the intend of the Bible. There is theological dogma that literally changes the intent of the Bible. Just as there is nothing in the scriptures to justify a purgatory, there is likewise nothing in the scriptures to justify the doctrine embraced by the Catholic Church, known as replacement theology.

CHAPTER XVII

CATHOLICISM AND REPLACEMENT THEOLOGY

Supersessionism, also called replacement theology or fulfillment theology, is a Christian doctrine which asserts that the New Covenant through Jesus Christ supersedes the Old Covenant, which was made exclusively with the Jewish people and solidified on Mt. Sinai, known as the Mosaic Law. Supersessionism is a theological view on the status of the Catholic Church in relation to the Jewish people and Judaism. It holds that the Christian Church has succeeded the Israelites as the definitive people of God or that the New Covenant has replaced or superseded the Mosaic covenant.[116] As one might suspect, Judaism rejects supersessionism.

As someone once wrote: We Catholics are the new Israel. Christ's Church fulfills all the prophecies and makes the continuation of the old Israel historically out of date. The church is the kingdom of God. Jews are the most tragic people in the world in that they "missed the time of their visitation."[117] Thus, the main tenet of replacement theology is that the Jews were formerly God's chosen people during the time of the Old Testament, that is until the coming of Christ, but because they did not accept Jesus as Messiah of Israel, God

---

[116] https://en.m.wikipedia.org
[117] https://www.hebrewcatholic.net

then rejected them and formed a new people instead —the Catholic Church.[118]

This "theological dogma" has roots originating with St. Augustine in the fourth century. One man. A single man had a hand in changing the intent of the Bible with dogma. This theology teaches that the covenants (promises) God made with Abraham were cancelled by Israel's rejection of the Messiah, and that Israel has no future in God's plan as a distinct people and nation. One does not get this from the Bible, as the entire Torah explains the calling of a specific group of people and how those people, the nation of Israel, was going to be the nation Christ will be coming to protect in the end times at the battle of Armageddon.

The Bible from beginning to end is about the Jewish people, and the coming of Christ to redeem them as His chosen people. As to the coming of Christ, there are over three hundred prophesies in the Old Testament of His first coming. And, as foretold, He came as was predicted. Then we have twice that many prophesies of his Second Coming in the New Testament. Just something to think about.

At the end of the Church age, the age of the gentiles, the Second Coming, it will not be the Catholic Church that Jesus will be coming to save at the battle of Armageddon, it will be the nation of Israel and God's "true" chosen. His very elect. And all because of the faith of Abraham and the convection of Isaac and Jacob. One cannot take that calling away from them, although, according to Jack Van Impe, there are those who try. When he was addressing this issue, he said there were seventeen Protestant churches that are preaching replacement theology, saying that God is through with the Jews forever. Jack says that is a lie from the pits of hell. He says, "my Bible says that God has chosen the people of Israel FOREVER." (Jack Van Impe Presents April 20, 2019).

The Roman and Greek elitist (Greco-Romans and philosophers) wrote dogma that teaches the Catholic Church inherited all the

---

[118]   Ibid

covenants and promises made to Abraham when Israel rejected Christ. After all, they were the ones responsible for killing Jesus, and by so doing they forfeited being the chosen of God—and now that honor has been transferred to the Catholic Church. The promise of, "I will make you very fruitful; I will make nations of you, and kings will come from you, I will establish my covenant as an everlasting covenant, (an everlasting promise) between me and you and your descendants after you for the generations to come, to be your God and the God of your descendants after you" (Genesis 17:6–7, NIV) now belongs to the Catholic Church. Also, Genesis 17 tells us that Abram will no longer be called Abram but will be called Abraham "for I have made you a father of many nations" (Gen. 17:5, NIV) and nowhere does one find that promise taken from Abraham or his descendants.

It seems to be that in the fourth century St. Augustine, along with John Chrysostom and others, were responsible for introducing theology into the mainstream of Christianity that is questioned even today by many. Including, but not limited to, replacement theology. Theology that continues to remain questionable. Since Augustine and Chrysostom are considered among the Fathers of the Roman Catholic Church, this theology continues to be embraced even to this very day. After laying the groundwork of establishing the Jews as the most licentiousness of all people, and the ones who killed Christ, and the ones to be hated, it was only a small step away from implementing replacement theology.

The implication by the Catholic Church that the promise for Israel to become the father of a great nation no longer belongs to the Jews (the descendants of Abraham, Isaac, and Jacob) but to the Catholic Church. Another promise to Israel from God is that "I will bless you and make you famous, and all peoples on earth will be blessed through you." The thinking of replacement theology totally negates the first five books of the Bible, as God called Abraham, followed by Isaac and Jacob, from which to establish a "thread of redemption" leading to Christ. The first five books explain the "why" of this calling, as well as establishing the strength of that calling— a calling and a belief that Jews continue to observe even to this day and will until the last of days. If this were not a truism, if one cannot see the hand of God over Israel now and in the past, then they have missed something somewhere along the way. Kingdoms have come and gone, but tiny Israel endures.

Believing in replacement theology begs the question of whether God means what he says. For example, when it comes to the promises God gave to Abraham, such as, "For all the land that you see I will give to you and your off springs forever" (Genesis 13:14–17, NIV) does He mean it? The Bible says God gave the land of Israel to the nation of Israel, land they still occupy and according to the Bible, will until He comes to establish his kingdom on David's throne in Jerusalem. To deny this is to question the word of God and question if God means forever or not? Everything sounds straightforward, nothing convoluted about what God said to Abraham. But if we listen to the Catholic Church then the question becomes: Does God mean what He has said about Israel or not? So far it looks as if He does. So, the question seems to be, who do we believe?

It's interesting to read about the promise that was given to Abraham being confirmed to Jacob, Abraham's grandson in Genesis 35:10–12 NIV: "God said to him, your name is Jacob, but you will no longer be called Jacob; your name will be Israel. So, he named him Israel." Then God said to him, "I am God Almighty; be fruitful and increase in number. A nation and a community of nations will come from you, and kings will come from your body. The land I gave to Abraham and Isaac I also give you, and I will give this land to your descendants after you." (Gen. 35:11-12 NIV).

These promises, known as the "Abrahamic Covenant" are also spelled out in Genesis 12:1 NIV, "The Lord had said to Abram, 'leave your country, your people, and your father's household and go to the land I will show you.'" For Abraham's faith, God was going to bless him and make him the Father of a great nation. God backed this covenant with a "blood oath" assuring Abraham that

His promise would be with him forever. Also, in Psalms 89:28–34, (NKJV), God reaffirms his oath to David that he swore to Abraham, when He said:

> My mercy will I keep for him for evermore, and My covenant shall stand fast with him. His seed also will I make to endure forever, and his throne as the days of heaven. If his children forsake my law and walk not in my judgments, then I will visit their transgression with the rod, and their iniquity with stripes."

The Old Testament testifies to that. Time and time again they were punished for disobedience. Some people have a problem with the brutality as witnessed in the Bible, but God gave instruction by saying, if you do this then I will do that, nevertheless, "My loving kindness will I not utterly take from him, nor suffer My faithfulness to fail. My covenant will I not break, nor alter the thing that is gone out of My lips."

God may punish their transgressions, but He will never take His promises from them. To put the importance of the Abrahamic Covenant in perspective, the focus of the Bible message from Genesis 12 to Acts 2 is the recipients of its promises: Abraham and his descendants.[119] Not the Catholic Church or the religion of Islam, or even the descendants of Ishmael or Esau. There will never be anyone taking the place of Israel, to understand that is to understand the message God brought to us through Christ.

Although the Catholic Church has convinced their family of believer's they are the only true family, as appointed by God, to bring Christ and his teachings to the world by way of their Christianity, which includes a Sacramental system as opposed to the "go to God

---

[119] Hal Lindsey, *The Everlasting Hatred: The Roots of Jihad* (New York: Oracle House Publisher, 2011).

Richard Bennett

by faith" system embraced by Protestant Christianity. And they have done this throughout history with the mentality of replacing God with the pope and writing a religion around that premise. The premise that the Pope can do all that God can do, therefore, what can anyone think of him but God. And that is where replacement theology comes into play as it is from this authority the Catholic Church operates.

Replacing God's Promise

Although, accepting the religion of Catholicism, especially replacement Catholicism, is to deny the very words, intent, and understanding of the Bible. The Bible says that the Jews are the chosen people of God, regardless of what John Chrysostom has to say. It was to them he made a blood oath to stand by forever, an oath that he promises will never be taken from them. Since both, the Catholic Church and the Jews lay claim to one covenant, someone must be wrong.

The Bible tells us that the Catholic Church is wrong. And because of this erroneous theology, many have been misled. For what? Power? Money? Prestige? Not to mention, fostering a breeding ground for anti-Semitism. (For an interesting and informative read, refer to John Hagee's book, *Jerusalem Countdown: A Warning to the World,* and turn to the chapter "Centuries of Mistreatment.") When it comes to anti-Semitism, it pains me greatly to say that Martin Luther was a bit of an anti-Semite.

Replacement theology is frightening theological dogma, especially with the end times being as close as many biblical experts are predicting. And folks, by looking around at the condition of the world and looking at the Bible, they just might not be wrong. Think of the ramification's replacement theology brings to the table, especially combined with the "Concordat of Collaboration" (an agreement, which, if invoked, would subordinate all cultural and

340

educational activities of the Catholic Church to the ideology of the Jews being the killers of Christ).

And in the last of days many believe the Catholic Church will play a vital role in organizing religion (Christianity) into the power church defined in Revelation as they seem to be flexible when danger is at the door. It was Pope Pius XII who is called by historians "Hitler's Pope," as he joined Hitler in the infamous "Concordat of Collaboration," which turned the youth of Germany over to Nazism and opened the door for the persecution of the Jews.

Most people would be shocked to learn that history links Adolf Hitler and the Roman Catholic Church in a conspiracy to exterminate the Jews.[120] All under the guise of replacement theology...a theology that originated with the early church Fathers and has been accepted and totally embraced by the Catholic Fathers of the Church as a truism ever since. Those times of affliction in the name of Christ were some turbulent times, not only for the Jews, but also for apostolic Christians as well. It has been a wild ride from the beginning of the dark ages of Christianity, which were about to come to an end, under the impact of Martin Luther's 95 theses. The Catholic Church has wielded much power in its time and introducing erroneous theology was just more theology that initiated brutality from the base of power the Catholic Church was enjoying.

It appears that much brutality has been released upon the world as a result of replacement theology, and I would like to discuss some, but first, let me, once again, mention the thinking of a "new covenant" as the promises given to Israel now belong to the Catholic Church I know the Church of Christ believes in a new covenant since the coming of Christ, which means they embrace the New Testament and somewhat disregard the Old, but would that constitute the need for a new covenant? A covenant that almost justifies the "Jesus Only" cult, a cult that omits most of the Old Testament.

---

[120]   John Hagee, *Jerusalem Countdown: A Warning to the World* (New York: Front Line Publisher, 2006).

Has there been a new promise between God and the Catholic Church, or for that matter, the Church of Christ as well, that others do not know about? Hal Lindsey puts it this way in his book, *The Everlasting Hatred: The Roots of Jihad:* "They (meaning the Catholic Church) believe that the Catholic Church has now become 'Israel' in place of the literal, physical descendants to whom the promises were exclusively made." I believe you will find the logistics of accomplishing that transfer interesting. And of course, that is what this chapter is about.

Hal continues by discussing the power the church had at that time, the time of St Augustine, (354-430 A.D.) A renowned theologian and prolific writer who embraced and promoted replacement theology and was instrumental in inserting it as a reality from his understanding of the Bible, along with the assertion of several early church Fathers who initiated the idea. The teachings of St. Augustine have constantly been questioned by Protestants, and when the church, and several of the beliefs of the church, came under scrutiny, (which eventually led to the reformation) the writers of Catholicism got very defensive as they now claimed ownership of the promises God gave to Abraham, thus considering themselves the heavenly church on earth, as declared by, wrote about, and initiated by those early church Fathers. And this was all done by the transfer of the Christianity of the Apostolic Church—lock, stock, and barrel, to the authority of the Catholic Church, and the teachings they promoted.

And during this journey to complete the transfer of the Apostolic Church and the transfer of the Christianity established by the Holy Spirit to the Catholic Church, they needed an authority figure, someone on earth who would garnish respect, someone the people could look up to as an earthly Father. In other words, someone who could stand in the place of God with the ability to accomplish all that God could accomplish, including imparting salvation, as well as the authority to anoint the church with the ability to forgive sin. And most importantly, someone acceptable to the people. Thus,

Peter was appointed as this figure, an everlasting Father who can do all that Christ can do.

Peter had nothing to do with the theology that makes the Catholic Church tick, and yet the heart of the Catholic Church begins with him. It was the theology that followed, beginning in earnest around 300 A.D., that defined the Church and began distorting the Christianity of the Apostolic Church. The Catholic Church was evolving prior to this moment, but during the fourth century it took the opportunity to define Christianity, and how to view the Church, and how to receive salvation as well as retain salvation by defined works described as penance. Then when you include the Sacraments, you really do not need anything outside of the Catholic Church to go to heaven or purgatory. Either way, Catholics listening to the "Fathers" or Catholicism think, they have all the answers.

It was Martin Luther who exposed the deception of the church when God showed him that it was faith rather than his obedience to the Catholic Church that would get him to heaven. Upon that epiphany moment, he ran from the Catholic Church and never looked back. Of course, when God exposed the deception of the Catholic Church through Martin Luther, and he was willing to die rather than recant one word, they considered him the greatest heretic that ever lived. I guess we can see why, but to Protestants they know it was God rekindling the Christianity of the first century church.

When they appointed Peter as pope, they completed the transfer of the Mosaic law and all the promises of God that went with the covenant of blood between Israel and God. Those promises now belonged to the Catholic Church because of replacement theology. Replacement theology is man-made doctrine that many non-Catholics think is more dangerous than believing in another man-made doctrine...purgatory.

If Catholicism was the true theology as put forth by the church, then the book of Acts would be written quite differently. But by ignoring the book of Acts, the church has established itself as the "true" church from which Jesus is received and salvation is achieved. To challenge that was considered being a heretic and that usually resulted in one's demise, therefore, they were not to be challenged or questioned. The death of many Protestants who dared question them are prove of that.

It was this power and authoritarian narcissism that justified the rationale for the Catholic Church to expand by any means possible as expansion brought more power, more prestige and fame, and eventually brought finality to the Catholic Church being the "only" true church of the land, and that expansion did not exclude barbarism. Everything was in place for the church to grow, and in the process of this growth, Christianity was led through some very dark times, especially during the Crusades that began in 1095 (and ended in 1492) with an urgent plea from the Byzantine Emperor Alexius I (1084-1118) for aid in fighting back the fierce Muslims who were a threat to Christianity, the pope agreed to help.

To many scholars the Crusades (nine total) were the beginning of the dark ages of Christianity and the expansion by the Catholic Church. That expansion sort of came to an end in 1517, but, not before the 397 years of Catholic persecution between 1095 and 1492. A period that brought some of the darkest moments for the Jews and Christians, and the Apostolic Church in general, with some of the darkest times coming during the Crusades.

The Crusades...

Many say that replacement theology somewhat led to the Crusades. David L Hudson, Jr. tells us in his book, *The Handy History Answer Book* that the Crusades were a series of Christian military expeditions that took place during the end of the eleventh century and throughout the twelfth and thirteen centuries. The stated goal of the Crusades was to recover from the Muslims the Holy Land of Palestine. Also, Pope Urban II (1035-1099) viewed the Crusades as a way of unifying western Europe: He believed a foreign war would unite western and eastern (Byzantine) Europe behind one goal. If successful, the expeditions would expand the pope's authority across a greater region.

Perhaps that invincibility of narcissism and the appetite for power precipitated a desire to dominate Christianity by any means possible and a new-found power that came from replacement theology helped the Catholic Church dominate much of western Europe. It was this proliferation of Catholic philosophy at any cost that set up the Holy Roman Empire over many parts of the world. A religion of rules and regulations that consisted of secularism mingled with Christianity. The dark ages were some dark times indeed, an appalling vision enveloped in a black cloud, drunk with the blood of the Apostolic Church was ravaging through the body of Christ as well as through the heart of Judaism on the way to liberate Jerusalem from Islamic domination by removing the religion of Islam and replacing it with Catholicism.

While many, probably all the infidels of the world, may agree that the Crusades might have been a setback to Islam, there are many who do not consider that a bad thing. When the Muslims invaded the Holy Land, as we saw, they killed thousands of men and enslaved thousands of women and children. They burned the Churches and shrines and deprived the inhabitants of decent dignity, treating them more like dogs than people.

Again, it was not necessarily a bad thing to eliminate Muslim domination over the Holy Land but many question the intent. Perhaps the true intent of the Catholic Church, since it has been estimated the death toll at the hands of the Crusaders were approximately one million men, women, and children, was the intent to promote Catholicism or punish all who were not Catholic. Since the world had around four million people at the time, that would equate today to about six million inhabitants of this planet being eliminated by the Catholic Church. The knights of Europe, under the orders of the pope, slaughtered tens of thousands of Muslims, along with similar numbers of Jews and Christians on their way to liberate Jerusalem from Muslim control. It was this ruthless arrogance that began the push to remove Muslims from the Holy land, reclaim Jerusalem for Christianity and establish once and for all their dominance over religion.

The Crusades were formed for the task of rescuing the surviving Jews from the brutal conditions the Muslims were imposing upon them, those who were barely surviving under Muslim domination. But in the process of eliminating Muslims, they also almost eliminated Judaism while handing Islam a defeat. Most would probably say the Catholic Church had good intentions, but considering the brutality of the Crusaders, Christianity has been under a dark cloud ever since and do not think the Muslims have forgotten this brutality. They have not. And have promised retaliation by removing every Jew, thus taking the Holy Land back and returning it to Allah, the rightful owner, and the rightful God. It was Allah who was ruling over Jerusalem at the time of Muslim control, and it was to remove him and those who worshipped him and to liberate the Holy Land from the oppression from him, that Pope Urban 11 put in motion the Crusades in 1095.

Before the conquering and pillaging to reclaim Jerusalem began, the pope blessed the crusaders, even going so far as to promise each an indulgence (a plenary indulgence) to forgive the atrocities they were about to commit at the request of the Catholic Church. Atrocities committed with the assurance of the pope that the perpetrators would not have to spend any time in purgatory but would go straight into heaven. Considering the blessing of the church, they must have thought they would be doing right by paving the way into heaven for many by eliminating Muslims and non-Catholic infidels. Religious domination. Something both Catholicism and Islam have desired to accomplish for centuries.

John Hagee tells us in his book, *Jerusalem Countdown,* "The Crusaders are often presented as holy men on the road from Europe to Jerusalem and back pursuing a righteous cause with the blessing of the pope (All for the noble cause of liberating Jerusalem from Muslim control). Nothing could be further from the truth." Hagee continues to relay to us the brutal truth surrounding the Crusades that implies they were military campaigns of the Roman Catholic Church to gain control of Jerusalem from the Muslims and to punish the Jews as the alleged Christ killers. That's right. On the road to and from Jerusalem, the slaughter of the Jews was justified because of the teachings of the Catholic Church that portrayed the Jews as the killers of Christ and who are lecherous, greedy, and rapacious people.

We are told in various books that the Crusaders were a motley mob of thieves, rapists, robbers, and murderers. Some of those who took up arms did it not for Christianity but for their own personal gain such as acquiring more land, expanding trade, or recovering religious relics, but perhaps the biggest reward was a pardon from the Catholic Church forgiving any bad deeds committed during the Crusades. Karen Armstrong puts it this way in her book, *A History of God:* "During the eleventh and twelfth centuries, the Crusaders justified their holy wars against Jews and Muslims by calling themselves the new Chosen People, who had taken up the vocation that the Jews had lost," Of course, we are speaking of "replacement theology." We will discuss replacement theology later. But for now, whether the Jews "lost" the promises given to them by God or not, promises that were sealed with a blood oath, has been a topic of discussion for some time.

Perhaps it was this mindset that allowed for the most unfortunate example of brutality in the name of Christianity, even looking back through history until modern times. During the time of the Crusades, one notable instance of cruelty brought to us by John Hagee in the name of Christianity was perpetrated by the Catholic Church, or should we say those ordained by the church. Upon entering the city of Jerusalem in 1099, the crusaders trapped more than nine hundred Jewish women and children in their synagogue and burned them alive, while singing "Christ, We Adore Thee."

I would not have believed that as a fact unless I read it from a reliable source. Such an absence of the awakening of the Spirit of God that comes with a born-again spiritual awakening seems evident. Hagee says this kind of action to impose a belief upon anyone is no different from a member of the Taliban who straps himself with a bomb and murders Jews (or anyone) who refuse to believe in Islam. I believe it was in one of John Hagee's books that I read where he alludes to replacement theology this way: "Those who teach that God has broken covenant with the Jewish people teach a false doctrine based on scripture ignorance and a narcissistic attitude." I believe most Protestants would go along with John. The Jews may have resisted heaven's grace, abused their privileges, and slighted their opportunities, but the Bible tells us they are still God's chosen people.

The Crusades were a result of replacement theology as was introduced into the Catholic Church by early Catholic Fathers such as St. Augustine and many early philosophers who have been embraced as Fathers of the Church, and from the theology of replacement theology the Catholic Church justified some horrendous atrocities in the name of Christianity. Another example of horrendous behavior by the Catholic Church was during the Inquisition that lasted over 600 years and as many as 50 million Bible-believing Christians were tortured and put to death to stop the spread of the gospel outside of the Catholic Church.

While the Inquisition brought its own misery to the party so did the crusades in a more concentrated effort to punish anyone who was not conforming to Catholicism, especially, Muslims and Jews. Although, according to some books, Augustine was not counted among those who would do harm to the Jews, it was more Basil, Jerome, and Chrysostom who introduced into Catholicism the anti-Semitic notion of the Jews being the killers of Christ, and therefore should be hated. However, Augustine seized the opportunity to transfer the promises God made with Abraham to the Catholic Church with minimal opposition, as the Jews had now been labeled "Christ killers" by early church Fathers and stripped of their inheritance.

Most Christian families consider the Catholics to be Christians, however, as we know, there are others who believe Catholicism to be a cult for many of the reasons we have discussed. But then, one might be hard-pressed to say that Catholics who die as martyrs defending the name of Christ would not be heaven bound. The eternal destination of anyone is beyond my pay grade, as is understanding those who consider the Catholic Church the "Mystery Babylon," a rich and wealthy church full of abominations and fornications. Many refer to the Catholic Church as the "Mother of Harlots," a church system described as a fallen woman—an apostate church, as identified in Revelation 17.

Many will argue that being a Protestant rather than a Catholic, I have views so opposed to Catholicism that I will burn in hell along with Martin Luther and the many others who dared challenge the institute of Catholicism. Catholics believe that unless we are one of them our chances of finding hell are extremely good. Again, unless someone is a Catholic, they have not found salvation as the pope only bestows salvation upon Catholics. Once again, excluding Jesus.

And they contend that Protestants have no conception of the understanding of the Eucharist (Communion) and baptism. They say Protestants violate the sanctity of both as they are being administered outside of the Catholic Church, which to them is the only church authorized to perform them. I found the same thinking in the Lutheran (Missouri Synod) church when they said that Protestants don't have the authorization to perform either Communion or baptism. I found the Evangelical Lutheran church to be a church I enjoyed, where the Missouri Synod made me feel unwelcome. Not to step on more toes, but if not for the reformers bringing to our attention the dogma that was being allowed to permeate the Apostolic Church, we would ourselves, be engulfed by the dark clouds of Catholicism.

CHAPTER XVIII

THE BLACK CLOUDS
OF CATHOLICISM

After transferring the authority given the Jews to the Catholic Church by way of replacement theology, such atrocities as burning people at the stake were justified as the results of the church's acceptance of this theology. While persecution came at different periods of time from both the Roman Emperors and the Catholic Church, they came from different mind sets as well.

The persecution by the Catholic Church was an attack against Christianity itself, against the "true" church, the church of the apostles with the introduction of theology that changed times and laws as well as adding to and taking from the Christianity that had been accepted by first century Christians who knew the apostles. From 33 A.D. until 64 A.D. the Christianity of the day was the message that did not include anything to do with Catholicism, and everything to do with the book of Acts where the apostles recorded what they saw, what they heard, and what they did, and there is no mention of the Catholic Church but there are about three mentions of the Church of the Way.

Perhaps this is just me. Someday when you have a few minutes, read the book of Acts, and see if you can find some shred of evidence that would lead anyone to think the apostles had anything to do with Catholicism or anything to do with the Catholic Church in general. And yet, they seem to think the apostles belong to them and that they, the apostles, especially Peter, condoned, even started, the Catholic Church.

As we know, there was persecution being applied by the Roman Emperors during their time, followed by persecution from the church during their time. The different mind-set behind the motivation when it came to persecution by the Romans who were feeding Christians to the lions, and the motivation behind the Catholic Church who were burning people at the stake were for different reasons.

The persecution by the Romans was against Christians who would not bow before their authority, their power. While the persecution by Catholics was to dominate Christianity and have no completion. That was another reason they detested Luther. He challenged their authority and they got upset. Then when he posted his 95 theses, they threw him out of the church. We can only be thankful they did, otherwise we might all be receiving Christ in a wafer, praying to Mary, reciting the Rosary, and asking a priest to forgive us of our transgressions. But since people could read the written and think for themselves, we will always have Luther's spirit. Peter as pope

The black clouds with lightning and thunder that had billowed and swirled around the Catholic Church with the intent of bringing change had been hanging over Christianity since the rise of the Catholic Church to unmitigated power, and they were about to get even darker because of the changes that were being introduced into religion. To most evangelical Christians as well as most clergy, if you ask them, they will say much of the theology introduced by the Catholic Church was bad theology then and it is bad now. Apparently, it is, otherwise we would not be discussing it as we are. Besides, as we have seen, much of Catholicism is more from the mind of man rather than from the mind of Christ and therefore needs to be discussed as we are doing.

The darkest times for Christians initiated by the black clouds of change that hung over the teaching and theology of the Apostolic Church, those same black clouds that began appearing at the beginning of Catholic domination were intensifying with but one goal, and that goal was to enforce the religion of Catholicism. Not the Christianity one might find in an evangelical Church, not the Christianity one might hear preached at a Franklin Graham crusade or preached in David Jeremiah's church but the Christianity one might find in a Catholic Church.

Changes being implemented that cut a very wide swath between the two religions, Catholicism and Protestantism, creating almost impossible conditions for conversation to exist causing Protestants to have concern for their Catholic brothers and sisters. But then the feeling is probably mutual. However, it was not the Protestant church that brought those dark clouds of change into the very heart of Christianity.

To be exact, the black clouds, the dark black clouds that transferred salvation from God to the Catholic Church and established a Sacramental system that excludes God except in name only has been deemed dangerous theology to bring to an unsuspecting world. Then the introduction of Confession with instructions to confess your sins to a priest instead of Christ and follow the instructions of the priest. On the other hand, Christianity would say, take it too the Lord in prayer. Doing otherwise is changing the intent of the message of Christ and is quite questionable as even being safe theology.

Then the acceptance of works initiated by man for the absolution of sin rather than going directly to God, even though that is what the Bible instructs, as we have discussed, is dangerous in so many ways. Combine the changes discussed so far and then add how Christ is received through a Sacrament rather than a born-again experience and those dark clouds get even darker. For many of the reasons being discussed, some have accused the Catholic Church of being compared to a, should I say a cult. Are they? Answering that question is by far way above my pay grade.

Catholicism, while considering the popes as Christ concealed by a vail of flesh, many say he is appointed by God. But when I hear of popes who abuse their position it is hard to take them seriously as appointees of God. For example, while pope Pius XII seemed to "sell out" to the Germans, he was not the worst in the history of popes. That honor was held by pope Alexander VI considered the "Devil Pope." He would become to some, the black sheep of the papacy, a pope whose lust for wealth and power knew no bounds. That lust also extended to women of which there were many, from which came four illegitimate children. He and his family, the Borgias, whose influence spread across Europe would be accused of many, many crimes on his way to becoming pope and continuing throughout his papacy. When historians speak of the Borgias, they speak of events that include murder, adultery, theft, nepotism, and rampant corruption. Their sins were plentiful to say the least.

In 1468 he was ordained into the priesthood, but that did not change his ways. He wanted wealth and power and he wanted to seduce those he was attracted to. Antinomian in its truest form. His rise to the papacy came in 1492 at the death of Pope Innocent VIII for which he paid dearly to assure his ascension was successful. And considering the church was steeped deep in politics, and with a reputation of having a crooked nature there was enough quid pro quo to go around. To this day Alexander VI is symbolic with the corruption of the Catholic Church and he paved the way for Protestantism that would happen not long after he died in 1503.

Knowing he was on his way out, he made a confession to a Bishop surrounded by cardinals that the last rites were administered, to at least assure he would eventually reach heaven. I wonder how that is working out? As much damage as he did, he did that much good, but the Catholic Church remained mired in controversy. And 14 years after Alexander died a German reformer named Martin Luther would famously walk up to a church and nail his 95 theses to a door outlining the corruptions of the Catholic Church. Luther's words defining the corruption of the church spread around Europe as fast as a plaque and Luther's words in modern parlance "went viral." And the world of Christianity was forever changed. And as members of the Protestant family of born-again believers, we can only be exceedingly thankful for the calling upon Luther' life to stand in the gap, even when his own life was being threatened.

Final Thoughts

As we have discovered the world of Catholicism is a Christianity full of mysteries. Mysteries that when revealed by holding a mirror up to them, the truth of the church is reflected. And as with other Christian families we have a choice and included in that choice is Catholicism. I can unequivocally say that if Catholicism made sense when logic is applied, like it does in the evangelical Christianity of Protestantism, I would be a Catholic in a second. Mainly because of purgatory. Who wouldn't? But as with others, if I accepted Catholicism, I might be able to look forward to purgatory, hoping it is real, but when purgatory is based upon the understanding of 1 Cor. 3:10-15 and is the fire of the Bema judgment, my understanding of the Bible prevents me from accepting purgatory. Knowing this, I must question the entirety of the Catholic Church and when I do, I find problematic theology throughout. Unacceptable disputed theology that Protestants would have to accept, and they cannot do that.

And because they cannot, they may burn in hell according to the Catholics along with thousands of others who have decline the offer of becoming a Catholic Christian. I have tried, really tried, to be fair and not present ideas and understanding of a church system that is so different, so all-inclusive, there is no need for Christ, but I found that was impossible to do. Especially with the black clouds obstructing the sanctity of Christianity that are so apparent. If not for the reformers bringing to our attention the dogma that was being allowed to permeate the Apostolic Church, we would ourselves be engulfed by those clouds of darkness.

These past few sections have been discussing the differences between evangelical churches, as opposed to the Catholic Church. Again, the differences of primary importance seem to be purgatory, antinomian theology, works as a continuation of atonement as opposed to faith, and considering the pope to be God from which salvation comes. All of this, including replacement theology, is questionable theology. Theology that seems to question the validity of the Bible. When considering everything, it might bring up enough concern to warrant the question: Should I be or not be a Catholic?

Most Protestants feel that the world would be a lot more liberal toward the vileness that exists if not for Catholics. Catholics, like Protestants, have been very outspoken on such issues as abortion, homosexuality, and so on. Regarding abortion, Catholics support the stance that every decision to abort, no matter how early in pregnancy the decision is made, is a decision to kill an individual, unique human baby. I believe most Protestants would agree with that.

We see almost daily disagreements regarding abortion, same-sex marriage, and the acceptance of the gay lifestyle. These are contentious issues and will probably be contentious issues for some time to come—maybe until either secularist squelch the voice of Christians or Christians squelch the voice of the liberals. That is, unless we turn to God, which many believe is a time that has passed us by. One might hear that message expounded upon by various pastors, but most seem to say we are living in a "Post-Christian Era." The days of "Onward Christian Solder" are words that only live in the memory of days gone by.

The current Christian era is an era that will continue witnessing moral deterioration, as well as a time when brother will turn against brother, and a society that will continue calling evil good and good evil as we seem to witness every day. As Gary Gibbs of the

Seventh-day Adventist says in one of his pamphlets, "For lack of moral fiber, the United States is unraveling at the seams." "… The Bible states this as the inevitable result of exalting man's reasoning above God's truth." All signs indicating the closeness to the return of Christ.

Before moving on to the next section, the Seventh-day Adventists section, I would like to address one last thing. Karl Keeting wrote a book for Catholics titled, *Catholicism and Fundamentalism*, wherein he expressed his opinion of a Fundamentalist, he wrote: "One might as well subscribe to an obscure Eastern cult (as to becoming a Fundamentalist/Evangelical Christian) …to most Catholics that would be just as sensible." Then he continued, "To embrace it (Fundamentalism) is to reject Catholicism outright." Good choice of words. That is probably true. One would probably have to reject "Catholicism" with a move toward Fundamentalism, but that is entirely different than a rejection of Christ. Entirely different.

Just what is the description of Fundamentalist Christianity that Mr. Keeting compared to that of an "obscure Eastern cult"? The *Oxford American Dictionary* defines a fundamentalist as someone who maintains strict traditional orthodox (accepted, approved, and established) religious beliefs, such as the literal truth of the Bible. So, I say to Karl:

If a Fundamentalist is a born-again Christian (as defined by Christ to Nicodemus in the book of John) who believes in the Bible and salvation through faith in Jesus Christ and Him only (the just shall live by faith), then include the millions of born-again Christians in that camp of evangelical Christians. Where, on the other hand, an Eastern cult would probably reject Christ as their Lord and Savior. Sorry, Karl, but I must disagree with your assessment of a born-again, evangelical Protestant Christian. A Christian who will be enjoying the life as presented in the chapter Life After Death following the chapter discussing the various views the families have pertaining to their understanding of the thousand years we will be spending with Jesus.

CHAPTER XIX

MILLENNIUM THEOLOGY

As we are about to see, there are three beliefs embraced by the various denominations that you might find interesting. There are three theories that are worthy of discussing as they are very divisive and have an overall impact on our thinking. The Bible seems to be clear as to the eternity all Christians will have, yet many harbor different views. It appears there is one of the following three theories that follows scripture a bit closer than the other two. Maybe that is just me, see what you think.

As we continue following Christ to our permanent home, I guess the question becomes how and where it will be in relation to where Christ will eventually be reigning. As we have seen, there appears to be some discussion surrounding that question. It has been discussed in many places throughout this book, that Jesus will establish an earthly kingdom and that fact is now confirmed by the Moody Bible Institute, as they say: "Before He establishes His kingdom on earth, He will come for His Church, an event commonly referred to as the Rapture." Sounds good to me. There are those who harbor different views of the coming end time events and the Rapture, as we are about to see.

Three Views of Millennialism

Will the 1,000-year reign of Christ be on earth, as some preach, considered to be the view of the premillennialist? Or perhaps the views will be what is referred to as postmillennialism or amillennialism. It might be interesting to discuss the three views that Christians harbor regarding our permanent home and what some believe will be the journey many of us will be taking to eventually arrive at the place where we will spend eternity. Keep in mind that each millennialist belief is an interpretation of chapter 20 of the Book of Revelation. When will Jesus reign? How will He reign? And where will He reign?

How the various families present their understanding regarding that chapter gives one a view of how the Bible is interpreted or understood when explaining the thousand-year reign of Christ. We must recognize that there are significant differences between these views. These differences affect how we understand almost every key event of the end times. Each of these theories has a very different understanding of what will happen both before and after Jesus returns to earth.

Mark Hitchcock[121] tells us that "Broadly speaking within evangelical circles there are three main theories of the end times— amillennialism, premillennialism, and postmillennialism." Mark continues, "As you can see, the main word in each of these terms is the word *millennial*. This is because the crucial element that each of these views interprets differently is the timing of the thousand-year reign of Christ on earth, a period called the Millennium, and its relationship to the Second Coming of Christ."

In a nutshell, premillennialism says the Second Coming will occur *before* the millennium begins. Postmillennialism says the Second Coming will occur *after* the millennium ends, even though they say it began with the resurrection of Christ. I'm I the

---

[121]   Mark Hitchcock. 101 Answers to the most asked questions about the End Times. Multnomah Publishers, Inc. 2001.

only one who sees some irony to that? And amillennialism say we are in the millennium now and it will conclude with the Second Coming. Each of the three views are held in high regard by some respectable members of the Christian community. For example, John MacArthur embraces Premillennialism, while R. C. Sproul, a Presbyterian and founder of Ligonier ministries, seems to embrace Postmillennialism. And yet the organization that he helped build seems to embrace Amillennialism.

Premillennialism

Premillennialism is the oldest of the three views. The actual establishment of an earthly kingdom rule of one thousand years by Christ following the Great Tribulation when Christ comes to put an end to the woes of the world. That's it. Nothing complicated. A kingdom that will be established at His Second Coming. Premillennialism was the view of the early church but began to wane and was replaced by amillennialism as the prevailing view. Some modern-day premillennialists are Charles Ryrie, Hal Lindsey, John Walvoord, John MacArthur, Tim LaHay, and Charles Swindoll. But before them came those who held such views. Early church Fathers such as Clement of Rome, Barnabas, Ignatius, Polycarp, and Justin Martyr. All the noted second and third century Christian scholars promulgated the tradition of a literal, earthly millennium. Some would be Irenaus, Apollinarius, Tertullian, along with others. The second century scholar Justin Martyr stated:

But I and every other completely orthodox Christian feel certain that there will be a resurrection of the flesh, followed by one thousand years in the rebuilt, embellished, and enlarged city of Jerusalem, as was announced by the prophets Ezekiel, Isaiah, and others.

Premillennialists believe that the newly established kingdom in Old Jerusalem will be the earthly location where all true believers will spend eternity with Christ. They teach that the Second Coming of Christ will occur before the millennial reign of Christ begins. In other words, He will return at the end of a literal seven-year period of terrible tribulation to establish His earthly kingdom. To many, that seems to be biblical. But as we have seen, not everyone believes that. Perhaps the information I came across the other day explains why. I was listening to a podcast produced by a representative of the Adventists and heard—now this is hard to believe—but I heard: "They (premillennialists) are forced to conclude that everything in the book (Bible) is literal." And that is wrong because...?

Would any Christian be willing to concede that they are not to take the Bible literally? I must have missed that class. I thought we were supposed to take the Bible as the literal word of God. That is what Solo Scriptura is all about. I find nowhere in the Bible to justify their thinking that we are not to take the Bible literally. To think otherwise is to make the Bible conform to our thinking rather than our thinking conforming to the Bible.

Having said that, all three of these views believe that Jesus Christ is King of kings and Lord of lords and that He rules or will rule over a glorious kingdom. And all three of these views hold that Jesus Christ will one day return to this world literally, physical, visible, and gloriously as the judge of all the earth.[122] But there are differences in the overall views of the three beliefs and according to Mark Hitchcock and others, the premillennial position is the only position that consistently interprets Bible prophecy literally, and yet there are differences in beliefs as we are finding out.

Postmillennialism

Postmillennialism is the view of eschatology teaching that the current age is the millennium, which is not necessarily a thousand years. Postmillennialists believe that the kingdom of Jesus Christ

---

[122] Ibid

will gradually be extended through the preaching of the gospel. A progressive growth of righteousness, prosperity, and development in every sphere of life as this growing majority of Christians struggle to subdue the world for Christ. Only after Christianity has dominated the world for a time will Jesus Christ then return. Postmillennialism differs from premillennialism and amillennialism in that postmillennialist are optimistic that this victory will be realized without the need for a spectacular return of Christ to impose righteousness. Instead, they believe that it will result from the faithful application of the present process.[123]

Postmillennialism also teaches that the forces of Satan will gradually be defeated by the expansion of the kingdom of God on this earth, after which Christ will return, His Second Coming. The belief that good will gradually triumph over evil has led proponents of postmillennialism to label themselves as "optimillennialists" in contrast to pessimillennialist. (en.m.wujuoedua.org).

Postmillennialism is very similar to amillennialism in that both theories maintain that the millennium is the period between the first and the Second Coming of Christ and is not a literal one thousand years. Both postmillennialist and amillennialist contend that the binding of Satan in Revelation 20:1-3 occurred at the first coming of Christ and that Satan is bound right now during the present age. Notice how specific Revelation 20:1-3 is in its description of Satan's binding. It says Satan is "laid hold of," bound" and thrown "into the abyss" But only when Jesus comes to establish His kingdom, referred to as His Second Coming. The abyss is then "shut" and "sealed over him" where he will remain for the duration of Christ's earthly reign. Nothing like this happened at the first coming of Christ. But it will happen when Christ returns. Not during the Rapture but at His Second Coming.

The primary difference between these views is in the nature and scope of the kingdom in this present age. Postmillennialists believe

---

[123] What is Postmillennialism. Timothy J. Demy and Thomas Ice. Crosswalk.com.

that the church will "Christianize" the world during this present age, thus paving the way for the return of Christ. A belief that Jesus Christ establishes His kingdom on earth through spreading the word which will complete His redemptive work that began in the first century. Then he equips postmillennialist with the gospel, empowers them by the spirit, and charges them with the First Commission, which is to go forth (Matt 28:19) and disciple all nations. Many who embrace postmillennialism thinking expect that eventually most people living will be saved, and then Christ will return. Increasing gospel success will gradually produce a time in history prior to Christ's return in which faith, righteousness, peace, and prosperity will prevail in the affairs of men and of nations. I gotta tell ya, I don't see it happening.

A certain group of Christians who embrace postmillennialism believe that Jesus Christ will not come back to earth until after the 1,000 years of kingdom living has occurred. Here is what that means: The Church, meaning all Christians who embrace postmillennialism, are considered to be the Church that will bring about the return of Christ through the preaching of the gospel. According to their views, more and more people upon the globe will be converted and the world will gradually be conquered for Christ. God's justice will prevail across the earth and Jesus will at last return to a utopian world to take up the throne, the earthly throne, that was won for Him by His church. No Rapture. When someone disagrees with Rapture theology, they may be a postmillennialist.

The golden age of spiritual prosperity will arrive by degrees as the gospel spreads throughout the earth until the whole world is eventually Christianized. Jesus' reign will grow on earth as believers in Christ exercise more and more influence over the affairs of this earth. Ultimately, the gospel that Jesus preached will prevail, and the earth will become a better place, after which Christ will appear to usher in eternity.

When asked about the beginning of the 1,000 years of kingdom living, the time when inhabitants of the earth are supposed to prepare the earth for the return of Christ, I was told the clock to begin the countdown to the purification of the earth began with His resurrection around 32 or 33 AD. The only response I received was that the 1,000 years is only symbolic. a response when I brought to their attention that it has been more than 1,000 years since the resurrection occurred. Regardless, if we listen to the Bible, we are told how terrible the world will become just before Jesus returns, with no indication it will be getting better anytime soon.

This view flourished until World War I, when people began to doubt if this teaching was credible, as the world was not getting any better. By the time of World War II, postmillennialism thinking primarily died for lack of logic. To a degree it is somewhat making a comeback but will probably never have the influence it did at one time. This is the observation of Dr. Jeremiah. In other words, postmillennialists seem to embrace an evolution towards a peaceful world.

After an extensive era of such conditions, Jesus Christ will return, visible, bodily, and gloriously, to end history with the general resurrection of the sheep on the right and the goats on the left at the final judgment after which the eternal order follows.[124] So they believe that Jesus Christ will establish his kingdom on earth. Someday. After the world has become "Christianized" enough and "pure" enough so that Christ will return—His Second Coming. Remember, we saw earlier where the Seventh-day Adventist say, "When the character of Christ shall be perfectly reproduced in His people, then He will come and claim them as His own."

When thinking of their dedication to their beliefs in this area, I imagine them continuing to convince people to get into the ark (their church) as the conditions of the world are worsening. And the only way to improve the conditions is for Christ to come and establish His kingdom, but for that to happen, a degree of purification must come first. Would that not create a paradox? Great people and a

---

[124]   Ibid

great church family, but I must ask: as impractical as this theology seems to be, does it have anything to do with one's salvation or their relationship with Christ? I say no. But I have fun thinking about those who believe this way and how surprised they may be when the Rapture occurs. Since being a born-again follower of Christ is a prerequisite of being included in the Rapture, postmillennialists can be members of God's family if they embrace born-again theology and as such, they will find themselves included in the Rapture. Surprise, surprise.

Outside of this difference in beliefs, postmillennialists are great people, and like the Seventh-day Adventists, they have some degrees of thinking that differs from some other families, but they are solid members of the international family of born-again, Spirit-filled followers of Christ by accepting Him as their Lord and Savior. By that alone, we are part of the international family of believers. You know, the Bible tells us that many cannot say Christ is the Son of God, and the Bible refers to them as having an antichrist mentality.

But those who can, they will be with every one of their relatives who found that golden ring just as they did and held on for dear life. They found the field that contained golden nuggets and sold everything they had and bought that field. Meaning that emotionally, they left the temporal world of illusion and embraced the permanent world of forever, as exposed to them by the word of God. Each bit of wisdom revealed to them is as a golden nugget of knowledge. And it never seems to end.

When it comes to these theories one must consider what Dr. Jeremiah points out as an exceptionally good point, a point many might find interesting as well as absolutely true. Not only regarding this issue, but many others as well. David says, "how a family presents their understanding about this issue perhaps gives one a view of how other issues of the Bible might be interpreted." That makes a lot of sense.

Before leaving the postmillennialism thinking and moving on to the amillennialist views, I came across information posted by Wayne

Jackson[125] discussing another issue, but he was discussing it from a postmillennialist view. I found he described the views so clearly and precisely that I wanted to borrow them. He said: The context of Revelation 20:1-6 describes a period of 1,000 years during which Satan is bound. Wayne says that the 1,000 years symbolizes an era of full victory for Christian people.

Wayne says the thousand years does not refer to a literal millennium with Christ reigning on the earth from Jerusalem, as the premillennialists believe. Well, that is quite interesting, since the Bible does seem to indicate Christ will be reigning from his earthly kingdom for the thousand years. While postmillennialist have problems with that theology, the premillennialists accept it as solid gospel, and they also have trouble accepting the fact that Satan is currently bound and not involved in the affairs of the world. Again, nothing to do with salvation, just a different way of interpreting and understanding the Bible.

Amillennialism

Pronounced ahhhhmillennialism. Anytime you put an "a" before millennialism it negates the value of the word," so amillennium means "no millennium." A belief held in high esteem by the Catholic Church. Mark Hitchcock tells us that the amillennial position is the dominant view of modern Christendom. In addition to the Roman Catholic Church, it is the view generally accepted by the Anglicanism, Lutheranism as well as some Protestants. The genesis of this view is usually traced back to St. Augustine (A.D. 354-430). This was the view of reformers John Calvin and Martin Luther.

A view that Christ currently reigns in Heaven with the departed saints; such an interpretation views the symbolism of Revelation as referring to a spiritual conflict between heaven and hell rather

---

125

than a physical conflict on earth. It sounds as if they do not accept a battle referred to as the battle of Armageddon as do many Christians. Amillennialist do not view the millennium mentioned in Revelation as pertaining to a literal thousand years, but rather as symbolic, somewhat similarly to the postmillennialist, and they see the kingdom of Christ as already present in the church beginning with the day of Pentecost in the book of Acts.[126]

They appear to interpret the meaning of the 1,000 years mentioned in the Bible as symbolic and believe that the Christian church inherited all the blessings given to Israel. (Catholicism calls this "Replacement Theology"). According to amillennialists, we are currently in the millennium. What is happening now is considered the millennium reign of Christ even though it is going on 2,000 years. Amillennialist believe the church is currently reigning with Christ, so we are in the millennium and have been since the resurrection.

Amillennialists. Those who hold to the theory that there will be no millennial reign of the righteous on earth. As mentioned, amillennialists interpret the thousand years symbolically. Again, somewhat on the same order as the postmillennialists. They regard the "thousand years" mentioned in Revelation 20 as a symbolic number, not as a literal description; amillennialists hold that the millennium has already begun and is identically in synch with the current church age. Eventually Christ will return in final judgment and establish a permanent reign in the new heaven and the new earth. It appears obvious that the amillennialist do not share the same view as the premillennialist who hold that Jesus Christ will physically reign on earth for exactly 1,000 years.

As mentioned, there are some, as with the amillenialists and the Seventh-day Adventists, who do not accept a literal 1,000-year reign of Christ on the earth as do the premillennialists. They believe

---

126 En.m.wikipedia.org. An article about Premillennialism in Christian eschatology.

in a reign that began upon the resurrection of Christ and will end when He comes sometime in the future. Whether or not we believe that the thousand-year reign is in heaven or on earth, whether we are currently living in, or will in the future be living in, the period referred to in Revelation as the thousand-year reign, it doesn't really matter. We will be with Christ somewhere, and many say that somewhere will be on earth.

As we continue following Christ to our permanent home, I guess the question becomes how and where it will be in relation to where Christ will eventually be reigning. As we have seen, there appears to be some discussion surrounding that question. That question is discussed in many places throughout this book and seems to establish the fact that Jesus will establish an earthly kingdom and as we saw, that is now confirmed by the Moody Bible Institute,

The Bible tells us that God has always ruled, and that He will rule from heaven during the time Christ will be reigning from earth, and again, we will be right there with him. That is the final phase, and it is encouraging that in the kingdom period, the time of Christ, all that was lost in the fall is restored. That is why it is called the times of restitution or the regeneration. When Jesus establishes His final kingdom either before the 1,000-year reign as in premillennialism, or sometime in the future as in post and amillennialism thinking, it is going to be Paradise regained. The Garden of Eden was considered a Paradise, a place that sounded rather good by anyone's standard. A place I believe we could all hang for a while. And Jesus will be our Lord and King.

CHAPTER XX

LIFE AFTER DEATH

Those who favor a spiritual separation, as does Dr. Jeremiah, explain their understanding of life after death this way: in the Greek there is a word "Koimeterion" used by earlier Christians, which meant hotel or motel, such as Holiday Inn, or Ramada Inn, or perhaps the Hilton, but it also meant cemetery. It sounds like what is being said is, when you bury your loved ones in the cemetery, just think of it as checking them into a motel, expecting them to wake up the next day and be in heavenly Paradise.

While Catholics, when passing from this world to the next, may rely on a place called purgatory, a safety net if you will, to improve their chances of making heaven, it appears for the rest of humanity, they will find themselves in a place the Bible refers to as either heaven or hell. Heaven or hell, those seem to be our choices. Although, as we know, hell, the abyss and death will eventually be thrown into a pit of burning sulfur. We know as Christians that we want to avoid that place at all cost.

We will discuss the roads traveled by those who find their way to heaven, as well as those who might find themselves where Satan and his buddies will eventually end up. Where they will be engulfed by fires, the fires that constantly burn without consuming the flesh, whereas others might end up in a place called heaven. But what does that mean? What does the connotation of the words, "heaven" and "hell" and even Paradise suggest when thinking about them? They mean what we have come to believe they mean, Hell is bad, heaven is good, and Paradise is somewhere in the middle. At least that is what I grew up with. But as we know, there is more to know about the afterlife than simply good and devastatingly bad, at least that is what the Bible as well as some pastors seems to be telling us.

We are going to discuss all three with the hopes of acquiring a more personal understanding of each, perhaps even acquiring a deeper respect for each. We will also discuss, on a more innermost level as we acquire knowledge, those the Bible seems to indicate who will find their way to one or the other. The Bible is noticeably clear as to who will go where. It would probably be safe to say that most, if not all Christians know as well. For example, we know that atheists, those who reject Christ as the Son of God, (described in the Bible as a form of antichrist) are destined for an unpleasant location upon their demise while a born-again believer, an acceptor of Christ, will find their way to heaven, or a heavenly home. But again, what does that mean? And what does the trip entail?

There are myriads of teachings available discussing the here and now and the afterlife, and some who have expressed their own personal opinions, such as an actor claiming to be Buddhist who said, "I don't think necessarily heaven and hell happen in some other life. I think it's right now."[127] Beliefs along the same line as the Christian Science. Then there was a well-know "Christian" minister, who claims to be speaking from the Bible, who describes heaven as "a place where you can eat all that you want and not get fat."[128] A description of heaven that many would love to believe and a description that denies heaven.

During this journey of discussing life after death, a journey for most that seems to elicit questions that hopefully will be answered,

---

[127] The Philadelphia Trumpet. March 2006, Vol. 17, No. 3. From an article written by Dennis Leap.

[128] Ibid.

keeping in mind, a lot about the hereafter is conjecture, opinions, and hypotheses. All we can do is study several of the well-versed pastors—David Jeremiah is the one I quote the most, as he is the one I find the most descriptive when discussing the Bible. But there are many good pastors who put their faith on the line almost daily by carrying forth the word of God. Many have been discussed throughout this book.

Most pastors preach the Bible, but David explains many things deeper than others regarding some topic. I am going to say that most, if not all, of the information in this chapter is in lockstep with his understanding and what he preaches. And that includes answering questions such as, how soon after death will it be before the Spirit leaves the body? Where does it go, heaven or Paradise? And when is the consciousness of mind reunited with Christ? Most say immediately, as the Bible tells us that to be absent from the body is to be present with the Lord.

To be present with the Lord is a given after we die, but when? Some say right away while others say not so fast, remember the Seventh-day Adventist? Does Christ personally welcome everyone immediately upon their death? And where does the Bema judgment fit into the picture? Still some mysteries to be understood. What is exciting for Christians is knowing that all the answers will one day be revealed to us. We can speculate but one day we will see for ourselves. And to that truism, ever Christian might say, Amen, it took long enough, but we made it. Praise God.

As I sit here typing, I am thinking about how blind some people are, specifically thinking of Bill Mahar and Richard Dawkins—considered the most influential living atheist, and yet they think they are the smart ones. I think, while it does not make sense, it is not even smart, to brush the message of salvation aside. Especially, since there is so much to gain or lose without at least listening for a minute or two, especially while thinking about what is being said.

By not even considering biblical truth, or outright rejecting them one is exchanging an eternity of sunsets for one sunset. An eternity of sunrises for one sunrise. An eternity of love for one moment of love. A moment in time, a day, a single day of life one could say, in exchange for an eternity, an eternity that has been described as beyond comprehension. So, at the most, one would be exchanging eternity for a life span of maybe 80-100 years tops, while eternity awaits and is forever, and the invitation is at hand. To pass on that invitation begs the question; just who is the one that is blind?

So unbelievable is the alternative to heaven that it prompts the question as to who would not at least listen to what the invitation put forth by Christians is all about? Especially when the word of God has been put to the test and found to be true to those who have faith enough to believe. Unless one believes that, then they may not make the best witnesses. We know the outcome that awaits those who pass on their invitation; in other words, they do not want it, or refuse it, or just outright reject it and continue in the world of illusion, a world of discontent perceived as contentment, a world that is being dragged away from Christ, a world that is becoming colder by the day—a world becoming more and more controlled by Satan.

But then Satan is only allowed to act within the framework of a "pre-written" script. A script that allows him to complete God's plan as initiated in the Garden of Eden when the knowledge of good and evil—what is right verses what is wrong—was awakened within our Spirit, but more importantly, the knowledge of right verses wrong was imbedded into our consciousness, our psychic, our very soul, thus, making salvation possible.

If one thinks about it, without Satan the concept of salvation which introduces a hell might not exist. Without the entry of Satan upon the scene, as he is the one who initiated the need for a hell, then logic would probably dictate that we would not have need for a place of burning sulfur. A place where many will proceed after standing before Christ at the last judgment, the MAIN judgment, the Great White Throne Judgment that is to occur at the end of the thousand-year reign of Christ. A final judgment where the saved and lost souls will appear, some will be standing on the right and some will be standing on the left awaiting their fate at that final judgment.

I believe it was pastor Jeremiah who said only the unsaved will be there, so we might be there or not. Personally, maybe even as with you, I do not care to be there. If we are there, we will be welcomed with the words, "enter thou good and faithful servant." If that be the situation, then the saved would be wasting time only to hear Christ tell those on the left to "depart from me, I never knew you." Wow! Who would want to hear those words? Unfortunately, many will, at least that is what the Bible tells us. Is that God's fault? Again, I think of Kenneth Copeland who decided to depart from the denominational line of preaching Christianity when he decided the money was not right—"on God's line."

Many believe the Bible is telling us that we are coming down to the end of times. Christians know it and secularists can feel it. Knowing this, it might not hurt to make sure the unsaved have one more chance to hear how near the end really is. After that, their fate and their eternity is between God and them. On the other hand, according to Dr. David Jeremiah, and most of the pastors I discussed this topic with, for a Christian it is a different story—an entirely different story. An exciting story compared to an unbeliever's story of gloom and doom. A Christian's story begins to unfold from the moment of death when they arise to go to Paradise. Dr. Jeremiah unwinds an interesting hypothesis between death and our eventual arrival time in heaven, or Paradise. We will unfold each hypothesis as we continue.

THE CHRISTIAN PARADISE

There seems to be a difference of opinion as to whether, upon death, a Christian goes to Paradise, or directly to heaven. Some say Paradise was emptied at the time of the ascension and now at the demise of a loved one he or she goes directly to heaven. We will look at a couple of theories shortly, but for now, let us assume Paradise is still a viable option for the interim heaven, just as Sheol appears to be an interim hell where the unsaved will be awaiting the great judgment. And that interim hell appears to be a place of torment by burning flames. A place where the rich man in the story of Lazarus went upon death. A place prepared for those who are perishing. They perish because they refused to love the truth and thus be saved. (Luke 16:19-31 NIV). The Bible tells us that when Lazarus the beggar died angels carried him to Abraham's side or bosom. (Referred to as Paradise).

The place many say Christians will go immediately upon death. Not necessarily heaven per se, as that time comes later, as we will see, but Paradise, a place where our Spirit goes, that part of our consciousness that follows us into heaven while our physical body "remains in the grave," returning to dust. Sometime in the future our physical body will reconnect with our spiritual bodies, and according to many, that reuniting of body and Spirit occurs at the time of the Rapture. The time when we who are awaiting in Paradise will be ushered from Paradise into heaven, but not before those Christians on earth rise to join us.

Paradise, Our Interim Home

Paradise. A heavenly abode many define as a place where born-again Christians will spend time between their earthly death and the time Christ comes for His family at the Rapture. The time many have experienced when they narrated to us how they die and was sent back to reveal to us there is a hereafter. They seemingly float over their bodies then see a tunnel with a bright light at the end which many refer to as a light reflecting the Glory of God, considered by many to be the Bema judgment. Upon going through the light, they enter Paradise to be welcomed by those loved ones who went earlier.

Remember, the Bema judgment determines our rewards based upon motivation of efforts done in the name of Christ. In other words, deeds done with the right intention. Not the works done for any atonement. Anyway, Jesus said he will be bringing our rewards with him at the Rapture. A time all Christians are waiting for with great expectations. Again, we can only hope the pretribers are right about when Christ will be coming.

What a great time we will have being among friends receiving rewards. Rewards that will be awarded when we arrive in heaven to attend the great banquet, some refer to it as the Marriage Supper of the Bride or Lamb that will last for seven years. I'm getting excited just talking about life after death. And we haven't even discussed our heavenly home as well as our earthly home.

At the time of the Rapture, we, as a complete society of Christians, including those who will still be alive on the earth, and will be joining us, will be ushered into heaven with new glorified bodies. Physical bodies as Benjamin Franklin once said, are in a "new and more eloquent condition, revised and corrected by the author," glorified, incorruptible, purified, and immortal. Some say like the body of Jesus after His resurrection since He is referred to as "the first fruits of the dead." We will be pure, perfect, and free of sorrow, sickness, sin, and death. And again, if one uses their imagination, they may think that we will have bodies like those given to Adam and Eve in the beginning, only with the glorified incorruptible mind of Christ.

When thinking about that information we find it to be the only time the entire body of Christ will be together as a complete unit and it will be this family unit who will be transported to heaven. This is the First Resurrection; the second death will have no power over us. Since the earth, after the Rapture, will be void of any born-again followers of Christ, the only ones to enter after the Rapture will be those who become believers and die as martyrs for their testimony.

Dr. Jeremiah continues describing his perception of understanding the hereafter when he says that at the time a believer dies his or her body goes into the grave, but not the Spirit. His or her Spirit departs this world and is ushered into heaven, but not before being given an intermediate body so that he or she is not unclothed when they enter heaven. Many say we receive our new bodies when we go through the Bema judgment prior to entering Paradise. Either way we are clothed in white garments with gold embroidering.

Until the coming of Christ at the Rapture, we are in Paradise, enjoying the beginning of eternity from the instant we pass away.[129] Think of it this way: when we die, our physical bodies are buried, remaining in the ground to return to dust. But our spiritual bodies, (our psyche, our consciousness) will, as with Lazarus who ate crumbs from the table of the rich man and went to Paradise, we apparently will go to Paradise as well. It is there that we will be spending time with others who chose the same path as we did.

What interesting stories we will share while enjoying the great banquet (feast) when we arrive in heaven from Paradise as we will be with others who are of like mind where we are all receiving our rewards. The only ones who will be missing are those who will be coming out of the Great Tribulation that is raging on earth, those who are being martyred for their testimony and who will be joining us as they are being martyred.

Dr Jeremiah refers to them as Tribulation Saints, those referred to in Revelation 6:9. According to Dr. Jeremiah, the souls that were clothed in white robes under the alter that John saw were those who had come out of the Great Tribulation and were begging God to end the carnage and avenge their blood. Others say the souls under the alter are those who have been martyred for Christ throughout history. Many might say it sounds like a combination of both. Either way, God responded by telling them to have patience until all their brethren had been saved.

---

129   The Bema judgment then paradise. The reason many place the Bema judgment between death and paradise is the thought of entering paradise before any purifying. Others place the Bema judgment after the Great White Throne judgment.

As martyrs are coming out of the Great Tribulation and arriving in heaven, I assume they will each have a spot reserved for them at the head table with Christ. Or, they will be invited to the Captain's table, as if on a cruise as we are told they will rule and reign with Christ during His thousand-year earthly reign (Rev. 29:1-4). The Bible also indicates that all will reign with Him and to that I ask, who would they be reigning over if everyone is reigning.

Regardless, what a horrendous time it will be after the Rapture. Perhaps this is some sort of a reward for those who found God and endured. Some perhaps with the same intensity as when Nero wrapped Christians in tarp dipped them alive in oil, and then covered them with straw before they set them on fire to light the streets of Rome as well as Nero's gardens at night. Many believe the times that are coming are going to be, once again, horrendous.

But on the flip side of that what a joyous seven years that is going to be for the complete family of Christians. Those who passed the test and overcame adversity finding themselves worthy of being included in God's family and worthy of being called a Christian, and worthy of being included in the Rapture. For the very first time since the creation of the earth the Christian family will be together as one special assembly with one common bond—we are going to live forever with Christ, and we will have access to God when we visit heaven. You will see what I am talking about in a minute. How awesome is that going to be? What started in the Garden of Eden finished with us in heaven looking forward to eternal life. Again, how awesome is that? There may be myriads of Christians as there are angles, but Christ said the path is narrow and few find it.

And with the love Christ will bring to the great bridle festival and the essence of God being witnessed everywhere which only adds to the wonder and excitement that fills the air as only the Holy Spirit can provide, one can only imagine the time that will be had. A small example of the feeling I am describing would have to be provided by the Holy Spirit. If anyone has felt the Holy Spirit, the anointing of the Holy Spirit, or a touch from God, then they know what I am talking about. A euphoria feeling of the Spirit that Christians search different churches to find. A feeling that Charles Stanley says is like no other.

The Evacuation of Paradise

It was mentioned earlier that there are two theories of when Paradise may be emptied, and its residents taken to heaven. I believe most would agree that any understanding of when the event to empty Paradise and take its occupants to heaven is speculation at best. Dr. Jeremiah and I both have encountered a couple of different understandings. Neither is wrong, just a different understanding of the timing of the event that empties Paradise. Dr. Jeremiah says Paradise is currently empty while others say it isn't. Dr. Jeremiah is the real deal, which makes him the favorite of millions, so when one discusses a difference, especially on a subject such as this, people take notice. Especially a subject that many are curious about.

The difference of understanding is regarding the time Christ empties Paradise. Dr. Jeremiah believes this was done at the time of the ascension of Jesus to heaven. The time during the resurrection when Jesus ascended into the clouds with a few of the apostles watching. Some say it was on his way to heaven that He stopped to pick up the occupants of Paradise to take them with Him, thus having the effect of leaving Paradise empty. He did stop by a place described as a prison and offered salvation to those lost in the flood, and, as we will see, He took those who accepted His invitation with Him to heaven.

There is a group, perhaps a forgotten group that Jesus did take to heaven at His ascension, and as just mentioned, that would be those who were washed away in the flood during Noah's day who had no knowledge of God and were being retained in a place described as a "prison." Why a prison? That makes sense if one thinks about it. They had lived without a chance to know God, those who God said every moment of their thought was vile and depraved, therefore they could not go to Paradise or heaven, or even hell, as they were not guilty of any transgressions against God, so they were held in a place referred to as a prison. We find in 1 Peter that Christ went to offer them salvation, indicating that they had not heard about salvation previously. And we are told everyone will be offered salvation. To accept or not is one's choice.

As I was typing that I was asking myself, why would anyone refuse? Then I remembered the words of my editor when he said that "there are many who are so rebellious against God that they don't want to be saved, they don't want anything to do with God." Unbelievable as that may sound, the Bible confirms it to be true. To escape hell, they may be agreeable to accepting salvation and their words may be right as with the prosperity preachers, but their heart reveals otherwise.

It appears that either way, now or later, we end up in heaven, or as some would refer to heaven—our glorious permanent eternal home. A home that will exclude those who do not want to be there, such as Bill Maher, and Richard Dawkins and the many others who consider us slightly off our medication and therefore slightly crazy. But again, I must ask, who is the loser? I have heard many pastors say that after this journey is over, what we have hoped for, dreamed for, and prayed for, will be fulfilled, and we will be rewarded with the fulfillment of the realization that everything we had faith to believe is now a reality. And we know that day is coming because Christ conveyed that information to us before He left, and the Holy Spirit confirms it as truth. And nothing will put Christians on the same page better than knowing that.

OUR PERMANENT HOME

Some question the thinking of an earthly kingdom from where Christ will reign, but the Bible tells us that it will be from David's earthly throne located in Jerusalem that Christ will be coming to occupy. And we are told His throne will be established amongst His people, of which we are now, by way of the cross, included as part of that family. Revelation 20 tells us that after seizing Satan and binding him for a thousand years, Christ establishes His kingdom on earth. Then Revelation chapter 21 tells us of the heavenly home of God—heaven itself—descending for God to take His place among His people for all eternity. And He will, from heaven, His eternal home, while at the same time we will be residing on earth with Christ with an open invitation to visit heaven whenever we please and even live in a place Christ said He personally was going to prepare for us.

The Bible seems to allude to perhaps each of us having two residences, one in heaven and one on this earth. If that be the situation, then that would tend to make everyone happy, those who say we will spend eternity in a place defined as heaven while agreeing with others who support the earthly kingdom version. Either way we are in heaven. But that logic would require a belief in two residences. Now before you pronounce judgment, hear me out.

The first is a place prepared for us where we will spend the seven years following the Rapture attending the great feast and receiving our rewards. Remember Christ himself said that in my Father's house are many mansions and I go to prepare a place for you. The place where God resides, the place of all knowledge, all wisdom, all knowing. A place of forever learning. We may want to play golf or tennis or "eat and never gain weight" and you will have as many angels as necessary to make life as great as possible, the place where our earthly home is located, but heaven is where the answers to the mysteries of the universe are contained. The place where we will encounter mighty thinkers who have the answers to questions that have stumped mankind throughout eternity.

Each gifted lecturer is assigned by God to impart interesting information that satisfies the longing for learning. To get involved, all one must do is join a group discussion being held under the enormous tree of life, or one of the other heavenly locations that one will find throughout heaven. As most would probably agree, our life after this one is not going to be boring. But then, that is what every Christion is counting on.

Some adamantly deny the establishment of an earthly kingdom, for a thousand-year reign, but as we will see later that just seems illogical. That sounds more like postmillennialism or perhaps even amillennialism thinking as opposed to those who follow premillennialism. A believe that Jesus will establish His kingdom and reign for a thousand years from the throne of David in "Old" Jerusalem. The Bible seems to indicate that we will have a home there as well as heaven. Let us not limit God or our imagination.

A Hypothesis of Heaven

For the moment, let us visit heaven, the heavenly place where God resides, but first it might be interesting to discuss a hypothesis using the words from Paul when he said he had the privilege of going to the third level of heaven. Some define this as "other dimensions," others describe it as atmospheres, (Stratosphere, Mesosphere and Thermosphere) while others just say they don't believe in different layers of heaven. Some Christians define a distinct separation of the earthly kingdom where we will play and the heavenly kingdom where we will learn and be amongst the greatest of the great. Those who make heaven the place it is.

The heavenly heaven, or kingdom, consists of three levels as Paul brought to our attention. The first level is where one will find the giant tree of life spreading over a river of beautiful clear water flowing from the throne room of heaven—the New Jerusalem, the third level. What would be considered the second level is a level that is much the same as the first, but the learning is much more advanced. It is from this level that we will have the opportunity to proceed to acquire knowledge leading to the third level, the level where God resides and where all the glory and knowledge of God exists. We begin our journey at the first level where learning is not as advanced as the second level, and definitely not as advanced as the third. Perhaps this is the level the Mormons say Joseph Smith Jr., attained and from there God sent him to earth to be the God of this world, this planet.

The third level, the home of the very throne of God, the New Jerusalem, the level that Paul could not describe is where the heavenly host reside, the place of all wisdom, and we will have eternity to visit the throne room and perhaps have the opportunity to talk with God. A place where hosts upon host of angles reside, as well as those who have acquired enough knowledge to warrant being there in a capacity other than a tourist.

There are no borders separating the three levels of heaven, except for the throne room of God which some say is as big as a hundred cities (Enormous). It is elevated with a high wall surrounding the city having twelve doors guarded by twelve angels and is exactly as John and the Bible describe it. Other than the throne room of God we will have free access to the third level and be able to witness sights that we have been told are indescribable and where the mysteries of the ages will be unveiled.

Once we advance through learning to be in the third level, other than as a tourist, we will have the answers of the universe at our disposal. Eventually maybe we will have the opportunity of getting a diploma of recognition from God Himself. It is here we meet the holy of holies, the patriarchs, the elders who are constantly around the throne, as well as the myriads of others who God has chosen, those whose names are in God's book. Others might even include the apostles, and I am even going to speculate we will have a chance to talk with them as well as with God. Maybe more than once. If we don't get a chance to talk with them in the first billion years, then perhaps a visit can be arranged in the next billion.

Also, it is from this level that God can use us to be his servants just like others who visited earth in human form. This is where some say there are other parallels, other dimensions, other universes and who knows what could be there. Remember, we are discussing God the mighty creator of everything. He has no limits. As mentioned, it must have been from this level that the spirit of Joseph Smith, Jr., had the opportunity to meet with God, and then was sent to earth and infused into the body of Adam. That is why they say Adam is their God. Remember, as man is, God once was; as God is, man may become. Apparently, Adam had reached godhead status.

Unfortunately, Mormons will not have the opportunity of going to the same heaven as we will as they have their own heaven and their own god to lead them there. It will be in Paradise we will begin uniting with close personal family members who accepted Christ from the dawn of creation. People with whom we can go boating, cycling, jogging, hiking, bowling, whatever we enjoy. Whatever we enjoy now will be available in our earthly home. Just think of Ground Hog day, only without the drama. Remember, earth is where we enjoy the physical aspect of life and heaven is where we learn the mysteries of the universe. And, as has been pointed out, we can visit there any time we want with a group of friends.

The New Jerusalem

John describes the heaven that was descending as the New Jerusalem, a city prepared as a bride for her groom as described in Revelation 21. "…and I heard a loud voice from the throne saying, 'Look! God's dwelling place is now among the people, and He will dwell with them.' The old order of things has passed away. He who sits on the throne said, 'I am making everything new!'" And everything will be new, but there is a question of when.

Then we are told by John that the New as well as the Old Jerusalem will be incredible. We are told that there will be an unbelievable bright light from the New Jerusalem, a heavenly light so bright that the Bible tells us the earth does not need the sun or the moon to shine on it, for the glory of God gives it light. The nations will walk by its light, just as we currently do by the light of the sun, only this place from where the heavenly light is being generated will be accessible to all. The glorious heaven that was before creation will always have a welcome mat out for those whose names are written in the Lamb's book of life. A book that will always be on display as proof of being an overcomer. A time we will be in the essence of God's presence and He will be among His people. We are told, and can see for ourselves, that there will be so many who do not make it.

And yet, here we are, in the most beautiful setting in creation, the Holy city—the New Jerusalem, the capital city of heaven, seeing our name on display and remembering all the times Satan tried to lure us away. Some of those battles were not easy, but Christ never let any of us down no matter how tough the going was. Now, here we are in heaven, thinking about the times God reached down and helped us when Satan appeared to be winning. And now here we are in heaven. The fulfillment of our ultimate desire while on earth.

And as every Christian knows, it took faith to hang on. Remember earlier when Steve Hill told us in his book titled, *Spiritual Avalanche* about conditions that cause some to remove themselves from the family of God. Some that just cannot stay the course, and according to the parable of the sower, they fall by the wayside. And now here we are, together for eternity. Now folks, it truly does not get any better than that. We do not know what we will be doing for the second billion years, but we will have the opportunity to pursue anything we want. And after that, we will have untold billions more years to pursue something else. Remember the movie Groundhog Day? We will become good at whatever we enjoy and have fun doing it.

While John was visiting heaven, prior to being invited to the throne room of God, he took the opportunity to give us a tour. He begins by describing the place as indescribable, but he tried. He said, we will witness streets of gold, spun as clear as glass emanating from the very throne of God. The Bible tells us that the city, every part of it, was decorated with every kind of precious stone imaginable. In the center of it all, will be God's book—the Book of Life, and that book will forever be on display for review.

Surrounding the inter city where the very throne of God is located, John said he witnessed a great high wall with twelve gates each gate made of pearl with the names of the twelve tribes of Israel chiseled into each one of them. There will be one angel stationed at each of the gates for a total of twelve. The wall of the city was made of jasper, and the city of pure gold, as pure as glass with the wall having twelve foundations, and in them were the names of the twelve apostles of the Lamb.

The Throne Room of God

After describing the outer heaven, John tells us he was eventually invited to the throne room of God Himself. Revelation 4:2-3, describes it this way: "I was in the Spirit, and there before me was a throne in heaven with someone sitting on it." John continues, "And the one who sat there had the appearance of jasper and carnelian. A rainbow, resembling an emerald, encircled the throne." Around the throne were twenty-four thrones, and seated on the thrones were twenty-four elders, clothed in white garments, with golden crowns on their heads.[130] From the throne came flashes of lightening, and rumblings and peals of thunder, and before the throne were burning seven torches of fire, which are seven spirits of God.

We find these spirits in the churches described as the seven churches of Revelation. It was to this setting that John was summoned to receive instructions necessary to write the book of Revelation. We find a description of this assembly in 1 Kings 22:22 when the assembly met to discuss the question of what to do with Ahab, the King and husband of Jezebel, who herself was a Baal worshipper

---

[130] Also referred to as patriarchs, or the host of heaven. Those who were in on the decision to send a lying spirit to convince Ahab to go to war where he would be killed as had been predicted. (1 Kings Chapter 22:20-23).

and pagan princess. The same God who was in the Garden of Eden is now relating to John what must happen to bring everything to a close. And a close to a Christian means realizing we will spend eternity enjoying a place John is describing to us "as indescribable."

As he was taking the tour an angel showed him the river of the water of life, bright as crystal, flowing from the throne of God and of the Lamb. Even though Christ will be reigning from David's throne in Old Jerusalem, he will always have a throne next to His Father. I think of Christ mentally projecting himself to the throne room of God, or anywhere in heaven He wants whenever He wants. We probably have the same ability, but I always imagine taking an escalator for some reason with several friends from the earthly home to the heavenly home and back.

The crystal-clear water appears to be constantly flowing from the throne through the streets and parks of heaven, as well as the streets and parks of earth. In heaven stands the giant tree of life that bears twelve fruits, a different one for each month representing the twelve fruits of the Holy Spirit: Charity, Joy, Peace, Patience, Kindness, Goodness, Generosity, Gentleness, Fidelity, Modesty, Self-control, and Chastity. The streets of earth will be lined with trees bearing fruit as well.

Wherever the water flows to make an earthly Paradise, the water of life will forever flow. In the middle of the street with roots on each side of the river was the "tree of life." An enormous tree with outflowing branches creating beautiful park-like settings as far as the eye can see for all to enjoy. In the beginning Adam and Eve were prohibited from partaking of this tree, but we will have full access to its fruits.

The Earthly Kingdom

Orchards will bloom with beautiful colors everywhere, fields of gold, and so on. The inhabitants of the earthly kingdom will be surrounded with beauty—peaceful, tranquil, beauty. And on each side of the rivers, streams, and creeks, are trees lining the waterways producing a different fruit each month just as in heaven from which everyone will be invited to enjoy.

We will have eternity to meet with people who have been nice to us, who have smiled when a smile was needed, people who offered a kind, encouraging word when needed, people who will become our friends in Paradise as well as when we get to heaven. People with whom we can go boating, cycling, jogging, hiking, whatever we like. I'm looking forward to improving my golf game. Although, it might take eternity to accomplish that. But then I will have eternity.

As has been pointed out, we can visit heaven any time we want with a group of friends to listen to the Masters explain the mysteries of, well, of everything. Maybe have angels prepare a delightful picnic lunch for us to enjoy while we relish in the fact that we are in heaven. Eat and enjoy what you want as everything is free and prepared by servant angels. Same as when were at home at our earthly kingdom. *Heaven*, God said if we accept His Son as our Lord and Savior we can expect to be in heaven, and I take him at His word.

Whatever we enjoy now will be available in our earthly home. What pleasures we enjoy now will follow us into heaven. Again, it is not going to be boring. I am not sure the Bible explains everything exactly that way, as what you have been reading was pieced together by information supplied by many including, Dr. Jeremiah as well as many pastors over many years, perhaps your own pastor has discussed heaven a few times as well.

The Alternative to Heaven

Those who will not be joining us throughout eternity are those who could not leave the temporal pleasures of this world. We know them, we see them everywhere. We can watch Bill Maher joking about how misled Christians are and we can read Richard Dawkins books whenever we want. They will not be joining us while we are enjoying the pleasures of eternity with unbelievable benefits with those who also found the key that unlocked the door to the mysteries of the universe enjoying the greatest life imaginable.

Before we can take occupancy of our earthly home, there will be a purging for the reign of Christ and for us as well. While no one knows when that purging will take place, many speculate it will be at the time of the Second Coming, others say it will be after the thousand-year reign of Christ. Regardless of when a purging takes place there will be a final assault against the earthly kingdom from where Christ will be reigning.

Satan is just being humiliated by God at this juncture. He can't win but he will go down fighting. The last assault is described as the final purging of sin from the earth after which time Satan is thrown into the lake of fire along with everyone who has rejected their offer of salvation. After the thousand years has passed comes the last assault against the earthly kingdom by Satan followed by the Great White Throne Judgment.[131] Remember, it was different at the time of His Second Coming.

The people against him then were devoured by the word that preceded from his mouth (2 Thess. 8). And verses 9-12. Now they are being consumed by fire, those who have been raised to come against the earthly kingdom of Christ once again, those who have been deceived and will be perishing. The devil who deceived them will be thrown into the lake of burning sulfur at that time where the beast and the false prophet had been thrown earlier. There sentence

---

[131]   The Seventh-day Adventist church embraces theology that says everyone throughout time from dawn until the very end will be raised to join Satan to come against the earthly kingdom of Christ. Perhaps that is why Satan is working overtime in these last days. The more recruits the better the odds. Upon defeat they will go straight to the Great White Throne Judgement never to be seen again. It is at that time God will remove everyone and everything that has not recognized his Lordship. Some say that is the final purging before we occupy our new home.

had already been pronounced, no trial needed to be conducted. A life sentence in torment day and night for ever and ever. Rev. 20 verse 10.

Also, Verses 9-11 of Chapter 14 tells us that those who take the mark of the beast will be tormented with burning sulfur in the presence of the holy angels and of the Lamb as well. And the smoke of their torment rises *for ever and ever.* Wow! Their agony will be available for at least the angels and Christ to witness. Some debate whether we will have the same access. Can you imagine a separate place where we can visit whenever we want to view those who rejected God? A place that could have been our fate.

A place perhaps of rather hot, extremely hot, flames like the place the rich man went while Lazarus was escorted to Paradise. They were able to discuss the predicament the rich man was enduring, but Lazarus was unable to do anything about helping the man as his situation was decided by God's judgment for the way he lived his life. But he will not be the only one. As for the rest of humanity, those who rejected their invitation as we have seen, their consciousness, their awareness, their spirit, from the moment of death, will wait in the tormenting fires of Sheol until they are called forth to stand before Christ.

But wait, does not the Bible say in Ecclesiastes 9:5 that the dead know nothing? Yes, and everyone who died prior to Christ are dead and will remain "dead" until after His thousand-year reign, then they will be raised where they will be escorted to stand before the Great White Throne to be judged by Christ when the time is right. They squandered their reward while on earth pursuing pleasures of the flesh. After they are judged they will be remembered no more. Wow! Would not want to be at that judgment, especially standing on the left. Their life is over while ours is just beginning.

Well, that's about it for me. All I can think of is being on the right looking forward to a time of joy and excitement. Looking forward to an eternity of fun that is overflowing with the ecstasy of jubilation. Looking forward to realizing the times I had hoped for are now a reality. And, I am going to believe every Christian would say "it just doesn't get any better than that." Again, that's about it for me. The next chapter is the conclusion, and for those who believe in a pretribulation Rapture, looking around, we might be out of here before you finish the chapter.

CHAPTER XXI

CONCLUSION

Sometime back I came across a book titled, *Finding God in the Questions*, written by Dr. Timothy Johnson describing the various church families. I can't remember his exact words, but better words describing the family of God I have not heard: "A church is a place of refuge, a sanctuary, a place to process our spiritual search and to share it, to find both challenge and encouragement. A lifelong group of people with whom to travel through this earthly journey in some common commitment to God and to one another."

In the process of searching for that perfect family, I came across many great Christian families preaching a message of hope and well-being, and along the way learned many things, beginning with why Christ lived and who He was, followed by His death, resurrection, and ascension into heaven, with the promise that He will come back one day for His family of believers, at which time the substance of what has been hoped for will be revealed. Even with all its quirks, twist, and turns, and even with many idiosyncrasies, Christianity as conveyed by those who call themselves evangelical Christians, "born-again" evangelical Christians, and their message of hope, continues to reverberate across the land. While it might be getting louder in some arenas (amongst Christians) and silenced in others (amongst the world), it is still and always will be heard.

Everything that has been written has been what I learned from Protestant Ministers, research, and listening to other Christians. I found the message of Christ to be very consistent in all the Baptist, Methodist, and Assemblies of God churches that I visited, along with most of the nondenominational churches as well, and all the rest, including those families who can trace their roots to the Church of England, such as the Episcopalian's. Many preach that same overall message, regardless of the name of the denomination. The message one will hear preached is the message of saving grace that comes with an understanding of the birth, death, resurrection, and eventual return of Christ as verified by the Holy Spirit, while fulfilling the great commission of Christ.

I hope you have enjoyed reading this book as much as I have enjoyed writing it. I especially found interesting many things about the Catholic Church that I never knew, and like many, I had a curiosity regarding Catholicism. Many mysteries swirl around that religion, and it was interesting to explore some of them and find out why so many differences exist. Also, it was interesting to visit with Hank Hanegraaff, during which I had the opportunity to ask him personally why he joined the Greek Orthodox Church.

That visit led to the opportunity to explore the early history of the Church. I found the Greek Orthodox Churches embrace a beautiful form of Christianity. Again, Hank has a book coming out that may shed more light on the Christianity that would help bring a more complete understanding of the Eastern and Western churches. He might be the only one who is capable of this accomplishment.

Before concluding, I found one area of the evangelical family disturbing as any Christian should. I would just like to reiterate once more how there is only one way to Christ. With that in mind, it seems impossible to believe that approximately 56 percent of evangelical Christians could possibly accept that there are ways to the God of Abraham, Isaac, and Jacob, other than through His Son Jesus Christ. To embrace that thinking is to miss the message of salvation. That is not what the Bible conveys when it says that Jesus is the only way to life—here and later. If one does not believe that, then they may have a problem with the essence of the Bible. And yet, we are talking about many who claim to be Christians.

We are told in Deuteronomy to choose life over death (the second death), and we do that by not being deceived. The Bible tells us there is only one God and only one way to Him. The one who can give the gift of eternal life, and the one who brought us that message was His Son, Jesus Christ. To say otherwise, as 56 percent of evangelical Christians do, questions the level of knowledge being preached in our churches.

When I walk into a large popular denominational church, during a weekly Wednesday night dinner, and ask those I am sitting with what they thought of the conversation Jesus had with Nicodemus, many look like a deer in headlights. Basically, I am asking for a discussion regarding "born-again" theology. Sometimes you get it and sometimes you don't. That night I did not get it. We're talking theology that Jesus said was a must to enter heaven and yet many don't even know what that means.

Is that an indictment of our churches? Of our leaders? The Bible warned it would be this way in the waning days before He comes to redeem His Family. Here is another survey that Christians cannot take pride in. From the last survey I read, there are approximately 75–80 percent of Americans professing to be Christians who believe—now get this— that the Bible, the Quran, and the Book of Mormon all contain the same message of faith. Of the 75–80 percent professing Christians, approximately 56 percent believe there are ways to heaven other than through the Bible.[132]

I just cannot believe that Christians would believe the information within each of the non-biblical books mentioned delivers the same message of truth to its followers. I'm sorry, but it just staggers the

---

[132] The Information regarding the survey was brought to us by Jack Van Impe and Roxelle Impe. Two people I have watched probably for 40 years and their message has never wavered: "Jesus is the only way."

mind to think some Christians believe the information that can be found in the Quran and the Book of Mormon has anything to do with the Christianity that is found in the Bible. Many accuse the Mormons of plagiarizing from the Bible to write the Book of Mormon, which to them is an extension of the Bible. Upon comparing the beliefs presented in each of the books one finds that they are so vastly different. Again, we are told in Deuteronomy to choose life over death, and we do that by not being deceived.

While this is somewhat distressing information for Christians to hear, the secularist, humanist, and agnostics would probably say, "Who cares?" Those who believe in and follow New Age thinking have made known their position regarding Christianity. The New Agers state their position very well when they say it is time to do away with "the rotting corpse of Christianity, together with all its adjacent evils and misery and embrace the new faith of humanism." Wow! Rough words.

As interesting and surprising as I found the number of people claiming to be Christians who believe that there are alternate routes to God, I was just as amazed to find that many evangelical Christians believe that the Bible, the Quran, and the Book of Mormon could have anything in common. But then we are told by Jack Van Impe, as well as David Jeremiah, that some Christians believe this. I am reminded of a quote I heard many years ago. I have not actually pursued the author of the quote to prove that it is authentic, but I believe it was the late Billy Graham who said, "Christianity is 5,000 miles wide and 3 (maybe 4 or 5, I can't remember) inches deep." How unfortunate, considering the Bible tells us to steady to show ourselves worthy.

That was another reason I wrote this book, to impart information that I found interesting and valuable and thought others might as well. These are peerless times in which we live and as we saw they are going to get worse because of the times in which we live and because of the times that are coming. That is not what Christians think, that is what they know.

This book started out by just trying to understand why so many variances and nuances exist within the walls of Christianity and what road of the many would give me access to eternal life. I believe I found that road and it is within the walls of those who preach the life, death, resurrection, and eventual return of Jesus. And they accept that by faith.

Anyway, it has been an exhilarating journey that has been informative, as well as interesting. I feel as if I am the major winner as the journey has been fun as well as exciting to travel, and even more fun to write about. I found the evangelical Christian family to be a great family of like-minded people when it comes to the message of salvation. It's awesome that we can still visit the various families from time to time. As most Christians know, our time may be short as liberalism and a rejection of God by the majority will do whatever is necessary to shut us down. Sometimes I go to a Seventh-day Adventist morning service or night service to begin removing some of the world from my mind, and then I go to a different church on Sunday morning.

Sometimes, it's as if I enjoy starting my week with Christ in my mind, rather than the world, but that is probably just what works for me. All I must remember is that the world is temporal, and Christ is permanent, and of the two which is important? I have found, as with most Christians, that the more time I spend with Jesus, the easier my life seems to be. While that did not come overnight and did not come without overcoming many obstacles, it did come. Besides, Christ brings balance in a very unbalanced world, always reminding us of what is important as we travel through this life on our way to the next.

Considering each individual path taken is different, I bet the day will come when it will not matter and we will care less about anything but spending eternity with Christ, thus making suffering worthwhile. We are only one of the many born-again, Spirit-filled Christians, who grabbed that golden ring when we had the chance and accepted the invitation to become a part of God's family. How amazing is that? And, that invitation goes to all, including the "elect," as they must also accept the way of the cross to have access to Christ. Or at least that is what I hear while listening to Charles Stanley. Well, that is it for me. Since I cannot think of anything else to say, it might be time to bring this book to a close and let everyone enjoy the rest of the day or evening. And to that everyone might say…Amen.

BIBLIOGRAPHY

Amazing Facts, Inc. *Amazing Facts Study Guide #7.* Roseville, California, 1994.

Armstrong, Karen. *A History of God—The 4,000-year Quest of Judaism, Christianity, and Islam.* New York: Ballantine Books, 1993.

Bernskoetter, Thomas. *A Concise History of the Catholic Church.* New York: Doubleday, 1990.

Church of Christ Tract: *This is the church of Christ.* Author unknown. Pasadena, Texas: Haun Publishing Company, Date Unknown.

Ellerbe, Helen. *The Dark Side of Christian History.* New York: Morningstar and Lark, 1993.

Fudge, Edward William. *The fire that consumes: A Biblical and Historical Study of the Doctrine of Final Punishment* Eugene Orgon: Cascade Books. 2011.

Hanegraaff, Hank. *Christianity in Crisis.* Christian Research Institute Publisher: Rancho Santa Margarita California, 1993.

Hislop, Alexander. The Two Babylons.

Hoekema, Anthony. *The Four Major Cults*. Grand Rapids Michigan: Eerdmans Publishing, 1963.

Hudson Jr., David L. *The Handy History Answer Book*. Canton, MI. Visible Ink press LLC, 2013.

Impe, Jack Van. *Sabotaging the World Church*. Jack Van Impe Ministries, 1991.

Keating, Karl. *Catholicism and Fundamentalism--The Attack on "Romanism" By "Bible Christians."* San Francisco, Ca. Ignatius Press, 1988.

Kimball, Charles. *When Religion Becomes Evil*. New York: Harper Collins Publishers, 2008.

Leloup, Jean-Yves. *The Gospel of Thomas: The Gnostic Wisdom of Jesus*. Rochester, Vermont: Inner Traditions, 2005.

Lewis, Gordon R. *Confronting the Cults*. Grand Rapids, Michigan: Baker Book House, 1966.

The Bible, the Christian, and Jehovah's Witnesses. New Jersey: Presbyterian & Reformed Publishing, 1966.

MacCulloch, Diarmaid. *The Reformation: A History*. New York: Penguin Publishers, 2003.

Marius, Richard. *Martin Luther: The Christian between God and Death*. Cambridge, Mass: Belknap Press, 1999.

Martin, Walter. *Kingdom of the Cults*. Minneapolis: Bethany House, 1997.

Miller, Donald. *Searching for God Knows What*. New York: Thomas Nelson, 2004.

National Enquirer. (Writer unknown). February 23, 2015.

Novak, Michael. *No One Sees God*. New York: Doubleday, 2008

Pagles, Elaine. *The Gnostic Gospels*. New York: Vintage Books, 1979.

Robinson, James M. "Tripartite Tractale" (1,5579.21–32). New York: Harper & Row, 1977.

Rosen, Leo. *Religions of America*. New York: Simon & Schuster, 1955.

Sacraments: *A Catholic Study Guide*. New York: Twin Circle Publishing, 1984.

Hill, Steve. Spiritual Avalanche. Lake Mary, Fl. Chrism House 2013.

Soros, George. *The Age of Fallibility—Consequences of the War on Terror*. New York: Public Affairs Publishers, 2006.

Strauss, Leman, Dr. *The Book of Revelation*. BMH Books, 2008.

Young, Brigham. *Journal of Discourses*. Salt Lake City: Church of Jesus Christ of Latter-day Saints, 1901.

Walsch, Neale Donald. *Conversations with God: Book 2*. Charlottesville, VA. Hampton Roads Publishing, 2012.

Weigel, George. *God's Choice: Pope Benedict XVI and the Future of the Catholic Church*. New York: HarperCollins, 2005.

White, E. G. *The Great Controversy Ended...A Glimpse into Eternity.* Silver Springs, MD. Better Living Publications, 1990.

Winter, Caroline. *How the Mormon Church Makes Its Billions.* Inside the Mormon Empire. Bloomberg Businessweek, 2012.

Wohlberg, Steve. *The Left Behind Deception*: Coldwater, Mi. Remnant Publications, 2001.